Infant Communication:
Cry and Early Speech

Infant Communication:
Cry and Early Speech

Thomas Murry

*Speech Pathologist, Veterans Administration
Medical Center; and Adjunct Assistant
Professor of Surgery, University of California,
San Diego, California*

and

Joan Murry

University of San Diego

College-Hill Press • Houston, Texas

College-Hill Press
P.O. Box 35728
Houston, Texas 77035

Library of Congress Cataloging in Publication Data
Infant communication: cry and early speech
     Bibliography.
     Includes index.
     1. Infant psychology. 2. Interpersonal communica-
tion. 3. Crying. 4. Children - Language. I. Murry,
Thomas, II. Murry, Joan,
(DNLM: 1. Communication - In infancy and childhood. 2.
Crying- In infancy and childhood. 3. Speech - In
infancy and childhood. 4. Language development.
WS105.5.C8 I43)
BF720.C65I53   155.4'22   80-19354

ISBN 0-933014-62-7

Contents

Contributing Authors

Ronald J. Baken, Ph.D.
Associate Professor of Speech Science, Department of
Speech Pathology and Audiology, Teachers College,
Columbia University, New York, New York.

R.H. Colton, Ph.D.
Associate Professor, Department of Otolaryngology and
Communication Sciences, SUNY Upstate Medical Center,
Syracuse, New York.

Thomas Gardosik
Graduate Assistant, Speech and Hearing Institute, The
University of Texas Health Science Center at Houston,
Houston, Texas.

Harry Hollien, Ph.D.
Director of the Institute for Advanced Study of the
Communication Processes and Professor of Linguistics,
Speech, and Criminal Justice, University of Florida,
Gainesville, Florida.

Ronald S. Illingworth, M.D., Hon. DSc., FRCP, DPH, DCH,
Emeritus Professor of Child Health, The University of
Sheffield, Sheffield, England.

Patricia A. Keating, Ph.D.
Post-Doctoral Fellow, Research Laboratory of
Electronics, Massachusetts Institute of Technology,
Cambridge, Massachusetts.

Maila Koivisto, M.D.
Chief, Unit of Neonatology, Department of Pediatrics,
University of Oulu, Oulu, Finland.

Aimee Langlois, Ed.D.
Assistant Professor of Speech Pathology, Humboldt State
University, Arcata, California.

Marsha Zlatin Laufer, Ph.D.
Research Associate Professor of Health Sciences, School
of Allied Health Professions, State University of
New York at Stony Brook, New York.

Katarina Michelsson, M.D., Ph.D.
Assistant Professor, II Department of Pediatrics; and
Administrative Medical Chief, Children's Hospital,
University of Helsinki, Helsinki, Finland.

Thomas Murry, Ph.D.
Speech Pathologist, Veterans Administration Medical
Center; and Adjunct Assistant Professor of Surgery,
University of California, San Diego, California.

Sie Nakazima, Ph.D.
Professor, Department of Psychology, Kyoto University,
Kyoto, Japan.

Robin Prescott, Ph.D.
Associate Professor, Department of Communication
Sciences, The University of the District of Columbia,
Washington, D.C.

Patti Jayne Ross, M.D.
Assistant Professor, Department of Obstetrics and
Gynecology, Medical School, The University of Texas
Health Science Center at Houston, Houston, Texas.

Sadanand Singh, Ph.D.
Professor of Hearing and Speech and Professor of
Neurology, The University of Texas Health Science
Center at Houston, Houston, Texas

Alfred Steinschneider, M.D., Ph.D.
Professor of Pediatrics and Director, SIDS Institute,
University of Maryland, School of Medicine, Baltimore,
Maryland.

Dr. Carl-Johan Thodén, M.D.
Research Fellow in Pediatric Neurology, Children's
Hospital, University of Helsinki, Helsinki, Finland.

Ole Wasz-Höckert, M.D., Ph.D.
Professor and Chairman, II Department of Pediatrics,
Children's Hospital, University of Helsinki, Helsinki,
Finland.

Carol N. Wilder, Ph.D.
Associate Professor, Department of Speech Pathology and
Audiology, Teachers College, Columbia University, New
York, New York.

Preface

The impetus for compiling the information integrated in this volume was a recognized need to unify relevant past and current research of infant cry and early vocalization. Important findings are reported in regard to normal and abnormal cry patterns, the diagnostic significance of cry, the need to standardize terminology and methodology, and the relevance of cry to early speech.

In this volume, an attempt is made to link an infant's cry with early language and to reveal the many communicative components of cry that make it an integral part of the total human communications process. Although language acquisition has been studied in depth, there remain unsolved questions. The normal child acquires language with impressive skill. With no direct instruction, the child analyzes, integrates, and produces the meaningful sounds of his language early in life. Both crying and language share a creative aspect. The studies incorporated in this volume represent diverse aspects of the value of cry as a communicative act. Whatever can be learned from or about an infant's cry may be instrumental in bridging the gap between an infant's crying and his acquisition of language.

We hope the reader welcomes the opportunity to study the variety of approaches presented by the participating authors. In this volume, the reader may appreciate the philosophies and methodologies of those centers conducting research into cry and early speech.

The editors wish to thank the many persons who have assisted in the preparation of this volume. In particular, we are grateful to the individual authors for their contributions and to the publisher whose encouragement helped change an idea into a reality.

Introduction

Thomas Murry

The cries of infants have stimulated curiosity among physicians, parents, and scientists long before sound spectrography or even acoustic recording devices were known. Early scientists, such as Gardiner and Charles Darwin, working in the nineteenth century believed that the first sounds of infants, especially the cry sounds, contained information about the child, his physical and emotional well-being, and about the cry-provoking situation. In 1832, Gardiner described the infant cry with reference to its location on a piano keyboard and as having an up-down melodic pattern. Although his studies consisted primarily of clinical observations, this up-down or rising-falling pitch pattern has been verified using modern acoustical analysis procedures. Charles Darwin hinted at the notion that cry contains meaningful information when he showed a series of photographs depicting various grimaces in the expressions of crying infants.

The twentieth century ushered in the first acoustic investigations of infant cry. Shortly after 1900, Flatau and Gutzmann investigated infant cry sounds using Edison wax cylinders. In the course of their recordings, they noted that one child with an extremely high pitch also had difficulty in breathing. Early studies of abnormal cries relied on subjective evaluations by pediatricians, mothers, and maternity nurses who reported unusual auditory experiences which often led to the identification of a disease or neurologic abnormality. Since those early studies, numerous investigators have examined the cries of normal and abnormal infants, looking for distinguishing acoustic attributes which might provide clues about the health of the infant that could not be communicated in any other way.

Using more sophisticated techniques, more recent investigators found that the vocalizations of infants provide a wealth of information, as well as a number of questions, about the relationship of cry to emotional state, neurological condition, language acquisition, and environmental influences. From 1960, when Truby and Karelitz and their respective colleagues presented landmark data on both normal and abnormal infant cries, there has been an explosion of scientific information and philosophical conjecture as well as a refinement in the definitions, methodologies, and instrumentation employed in the study of early infant communication.

This volume unifies the clinical, philosophical, and scientific trends of the study of infant voice and speech during the last twenty years. It brings together internationally known scientists who have and are currently conducting research with normal and abnormal infants. Each chapter presents the latest information contained in the cries, coos, and babblings of infants. All who have an interest in the sounds of infancy will appreciate the details in the methodology and findings which are contained in each chapter. Thus, this book provides the most comprehensive collection of early infant vocalization that has been gathered to date.

The first four chapters present a rationale for the study of infant crying and the terminology needed to achieve an understanding of the current status of the discipline. It is not surprising that two of the chapters are from the study group at the Children's Hospital in Helsinki, Finland. The work of these authors, which has been so notably supported by the Sigrid Jusélius Foundation, has provided the stimulation for many of the current investigations of cry and early infant speech production.

Chapter 5 is a comprehensive analysis of the first cries of infants. It contains acoustic information about the fundamental frequency and formant structures obtained from Fourier analysis of newborn infants. Questions about the relationship of the vocal tract to the laryngeal structures are addressed using a large data base obtained in controlled delivery room conditions. Chapters 6 and 7 present acoustic analyses procedures developed and improved at the Children's Hospital in Helsinki, Finland. Both chapters utilize methodologies designed to identify the relevant acoustic information in various cry types. In the eighth chapter, the cries related to sudden infant death syndrome (SIDS) are examined, including the cries of children considered to be at risk for SIDS.

Chapters 9 and 10 focus on the fundamental frequency information contained in the cry sound Included are observations on the relationships between normal children's speech and a model for the acquisition of the prosodic features of language.

In the eleventh chapter, acoustic and perceptual relationships in three types of cries --- pain, hunger, and startle --- are investigated. Some notions about the information contained in the cry sound are presented which contribute to an understanding of those features which listeners use to identify cry types and the sex of the infants.

The final two chapters examine speech activities in infancy. Questions regarding the development of babbling are addressed in Chapter 12. The syllable structure and its importance in language acquisition are discussed in Chapter 13.

The final portion of the book is a comprehensive bibliography of infant vocalization. It contains references from the fields of biology, psychology, medicine, neurology, speech pathology, physiology, and linguistics. Included are references to infant voice, speech and language from journals published in the United States, England, Europe, Japan, and South America.

CHAPTER 1

The Development of Communication
in the First Year and the
Factors Which Affect It

Ronald S. Illingworth

INTRODUCTION

Although there have been many textbooks and other publications on the normal development of speech in infants, there is not a wealth of information on other aspects of communication, especially cry and non-verbal communication. Moreover, it is difficult to find research concerning the variations in the development of communication and the basis for the variations. This chapter deals briefly with the development of speech and concentrates on other aspects of communication and the variations which occur.

PRINCIPLES OF INFANT DEVELOPMENT

In all aspects of infant and child development, whether intellectual, physical or emotional, it is essential to understand the normal, the normal variations, and especially the reasons for those variations before one can hope to diagnose the abnormal. The sequence of development is the same in all children; for instance, all children learn to sit before they learn to walk. However, the rate of development varies from child to child, and it is commonly different in various aspects of development. Speech development does not necessarily parallel development in other maturational areas, such as posture control and ambulation.

Development is profoundly affected by environmental, intellectual, psychological, or physical factors. For example, almost all aspects of development, particularly communication, are greatly affected by the mother's attitudes and by mother-infant interaction; they are greatly affected by the child's level of intelligence, by his personality, or by physical defects, such as deafness or cerebral palsy.

Bonding

It has long been recognized that contact between mother and child at the moment of birth may be of great importance for the establishment of the normal firm bond between the two. Throughout the animal kingdom there are innumerable examples of the mother's instinctive need to lick and inspect her young at the moment of their birth. If the fulfillment of this instinctive desire is prevented, the mother will reject her young. For instance, if the kid is removed from the goat before the goat has licked it, the goat will kick the kid to death when it is returned to the mother a few hours later. Animals inspect their young for abnormalities, and in many species an abnormal animal will be rejected and eaten by the mother. Many mothers feel the urge to put the newborn baby to their naked breast at the moment of birth; mothers who do this are more likely than others to breast-feed their babies. This immediate skin contact is felt by many to be important for the development of normal mother-child interaction, and therefore for mother-child communication.

Non-Verbal Communication

Infants communicate with their mothers by crying, watching her, smiling, laughing, playing, showing affection, clinging to her, kissing her, vigorous welcoming movements, frowning, pushing her away, and by vocalizations leading to speech (Sheridan 1964). Social play is often accompanied by rapid respirations and by generalized mass movements involving all limbs.

By five months, long before he can ask for them, the baby can reach out and grasp objects that he wants. Soon he pulls the mother's sleeve or coughs to attract attention. He holds his arms out to his mother to pull him up to a sitting position. At about 10 months, he characteristically points to objects with his index finger; he waves bye-bye and plays clap-hands on request after learning to imitate her movements.

Non-verbal communication is greatly affected by the mother's responsiveness, her love for the child, her tone of voice, the expression on her face, the time which she devotes to talking to him and playing with him. It is greatly affected by the baby's intelligence. All aspects of communication are delayed in the mentally subnormal infant and are often accelerated in the mentally superior infant. The baby has to learn what effect the sound he makes has on others. The more intelligent he is and the more responsive he is to the mother, the sooner he learns.

NEWBORN DEVELOPMENT

Until recently many had regarded the newborn baby and the infant as a mere reflexive being who just cried for his needs, wet his nappy, sucked milk, smiled, and only much later showed the development of understanding. Recent psychological studies have shown that the baby, even in the first month or two, shows far more understanding than many had realized. When the baby is born, he is equipped with the basic requirements for interpersonal communication. By two weeks of age the baby can distinguish his mother's face from that of a stranger (Carpenter 1974). By three weeks of age he reacts differently to persons and objects (Trevarthen 1974). Eimas et al. (1971) studied speech perception by means of conditioning and habituation responses and showed that in the first two or three weeks speech perception was well developed. Mills and Melhuish (1974) showed that babies recognized their mother's voice in the first week or two. By six to ten days of age, babies distinguished their mother's smell from that of strangers. They reacted more to the mother's face when she was talking than when she was expressionless. They turned to sound in the first week.

Trevarthen also found that even in the second month babies would imitate mouth movement or tongue protrusion. He found that when the moher was speaking to her baby she used a special type of speech that was slower and more gentle than her normal speech. The child responded by watching her, opening and closing his mouth, breathing rapidly, and moving his limbs.

These responses appear to be related to the child's maturity at birth and also in part to his 'intelligence' (if one can apply that term to the young infant). A child with superior potential is likely to achieve perceptual skills (such as those described by

6

Trevarthen) early. A mentally subnormal infant, such as a mongol, will be much later in achieving such skills. A mentally subnormal child is late in all aspects of development, except occasionally such gross motor development as sitting and walking. He is later than average in responding to his mother's overtures, in smiling, vocalizing, and responding to sound and to moving objects. Hence, the mother's responses to the baby are considerably affected.

The infant's responses are considerably affected by his mother's attitudes. The baby may be unwanted or rejected because he is not of the desired sex or he has a distressing abnormality such as a hare lip or cleft palate. Some babies, for other reasons-- including their own personalities -- are naturally less responsive. Consequently, the mother responds less to them. Mothers confidently, and probably correctly, remark that in the first two or three days their second or third child is very different in personality and behavior than their previous child.

Displeasure: The Cry

Adler (1946) declared that the first cry "represents an overwhelming sense of inferiority at thus suddenly being confronted by reality without ever having had to deal with its problems." To the pediatrician and obstetrician, the cry at birth is a welcome sign that the infant is breathing normally. Delay in the establishment of respiration may signify serious brain damage, or at least the risk of it, from deprivation of oxygen. Animals do not cry at birth. On rare occasions babies cry *in utero* and such a cry can be heard if the membranes have ruptured (Illingworth 1955).

It is not known why babies cry at birth, but thereafter the cry becomes the first signal to the mother, the earliest vehicle of communication between infant and mother. We cannot always know the reason for a baby's cry. Some cry for no apparent reason and some cry much more than others, perhaps indicating something about their future personalities. Babies cry because they are hungry, perhaps because hunger makes them feel uncomfortable. When the cry of hunger is soon heeded, they begin to connect food with the relief of discomfort. The cry, initially a reflex, becomes purposeful as memory and understanding develop. When babies are fed by the self-demand method, crying for

7

hunger is short lived. When a rigid feeding method is used, crying may be prolonged and persistent. Crying may result from wind, a sudden noise, or an unpleasant smell or taste. Some babies in the first three months of life have evening colic, which consists of rhythmical screaming attacks with a typical circadian rhythm and occurs especially between 1800 and 2200 hours (Illingworth 1954). Some babies cry when the light is put out; some cry when it is put on.

Many (if not most) babies cry when the head or limbs are firmly held or even when a tape measure tightly surrounds the head. Many cry when the mother suddenly changes the baby's posture. Some cry when too hot or too cold or when the nappy is wet. Some babies in the newborn period cry when put to the breast and are awkward about suckling. Commonly, when a baby cries he becomes quiet as soon as he is picked up. Although contact with his mother seems to soothe him, the baby who is crying because of hunger, colic, or other discomfort will not stop crying at least for more than a few minutes. This is yet another important signal that helps the mother interpret his needs. In fact, when normal bonding has occurred, some mothers rapidly learn to interpret the reason for the baby's call. The sooner the mother acts in response to the cry, the sooner the crying stops.

In the case of the older baby (three to six months), if the mother promptly responds to cries, the crying normally will stop rapidly. The longer the baby is left to scream (particularly if the crying is from fear), the longer the crying continues when he is picked up. Such crying is often followed by sobbing, sudden inspirations becoming less and less frequent over a period of several minutes. Research has shown that when the mother responds promptly to the baby's signals in the early days, he is much less demanding and much more secure when he is older. By the time he is nine months or soon thereafter, he will demand less contact with the mother. Young babies cry most when alone and least when in the arms of their mothers.

The older baby cries less but with increased vigor. He cries when he is too hot, too cold, or has an irritating rash. He cries when he is thirsty, has a wet nappy, or when he is passing urine or a stool. He may cry when a stranger approaches (particularly when that stranger towers over him as he is lying or playing on the floor). Around six months of age some babies awaken at night with a sudden shriek, usually

8

resultling from a nightmare. Some cry when placed in a strange bed or bedroom. Most babies cry from a few weeks old when the nose is cleaned, and many cry when the face is washed. At a few weeks of age the baby cries when his mother leaves the room or even when she returns. From nine months or so, if his parents have a few day's break from him, he may scream when they return and seem to reject them.

Also, from about nine months, he may object strongly to being put to bed at night and left there and cry and scream until someone comes back. His crying now has become an important weapon for controlling his environment.

When the child is old enough to feed himself, he cries if prevented from doing so or when his mother forces him to take food which he does not want. Crying occurs now when any pleasurable experience is brought to an end. He cries from jealousy or when toys are taken from him.

Many mothers in obstetrics hospitals have indicated that they were awakened only by their own baby's cries. Studies of the infant's cry have tested the validity of these assertions (Formby 1967). Tape recordings were made of the crying of 31 newborn infants. Mothers of 23 of the children were asked to listen to the tapes and pick out the crying of their own baby. Prior to 48 hours after delivery, only 12 mothers recognized the crying of their own babies. After 48 hours, all of the mothers were able to recognize the cries of their own infant. In addition, in wards having six beds, mothers were studied to determine how many were awakened only by their own baby. After the third night, 22 of the 23 mothers were awakened only by their own child. It is the experience of many parents that although various noises do not disturb them at night, their child's first whimper immediately awakens them.

Many parents rapidly become sensitive and receptive to their children's needs. Persistent crying can result when a parent is not sensitive and receptive to the child's cry. Such crying can, and often does, lead to child abuse.

Mothers can become exhausted by constant crying, lose their temper, and injure the child. Likewise, children raised in institutions often suffer emotional harm when there is a lack of sensitivity and concern for their needs. If such emotional deprivation continues for three years or so, the child may eventually be unable to give or receive affection. The amount of crying, then, depends on a combination of the mother's responsiveness and such intrinsic characteristics as personality traits, individual needs for love and proximity to the mother, tolerance for boredom, jealousy, and various physical factors, including hunger, pain, and fatigue.

The quality of the cry has been under intensive scrutiny in recent years. The cry of the very young infant is short, staccato, and repetitive (Karelitz, Karelitz, and Rosenfeld 1960). It builds up into a crescendo when the stimulus is applied and diminishes as the stimulus abates. As the infant matures, the cry lengthens and becomes more plaintive, with more variation in pitch.

A hoarse, guttural cry is characteristic of thyroid deficiency. A child with a brain defect, such as kernicterus (due to severe jaundice in the newborn) or a more severe type of brain damage, may have a characteristic high-pitched cry. An infant with meningitis may have a piercing staccato cry, whereas a child with Tay Sach's disease (a lipid storage disease) may have a weak, whining cry. A small preterm baby or a child with the Werdnig-Hoffman syndrome (amyotonia congenita) has a small feeble cry. In the chromosomal defect where there is deletion of the distal portion of the short arm, the child has a cry like that of a cat (the cri du chat syndrome).

Sonographic, spectrographic, and auditory analyses of infants' cries have led to a more accurae understanding of the infant's early communication (Karelitz, Karelitz, and Rosenfeld 1960; Karelitz and Fisichelli 1962; Wasz-Höckert 1967; Wasz-Höckert et al. 1963, 1968; Ostwald, Phibbs, and Fox 1968; Lind et al. 1965). Wasz-Höckert and his colleagues recorded the attributes of the cry signal. They found that by spectrogaphic analyses, the cries of the mongol, the cries of the brain defect, of hunger, pain, pleasure, or of hydrocephalus were of diagnostic value. Babies with diffuse brain damage needed more stimulation to cry than did normal infants. There was a longer interval between the stimulus and the cry, and the cry was not as well sustained. Defective children cried more, not less, as they got older. Michelsson's (1971) study of 310 newborn infants found that the cry of underweight newborns closely resembled the cry of the normal birth weight full term baby. The cry of the anoxic baby, however, differed significantly from that of the normal in the duration of phonation, the maximum

10

pitch of fundamental frequency, and the occurrence of biphonation. Lester (1976) compared the cry of 12 normal with 12 malnourished infants; the malnourished infants had a cry wth a longer initial sound, higher pitch, lower amplitude, more arrhythmia and longer latency between cries. These findings are similar to those of children with brain defects.

Pleasure

All children cry before they smile and all children learn to say "no" before they learn to say "yes." The average full term baby begins to smile at his mother in response to social overtures at four to six weeks of age. Long before that he watched his mother intently as she talked to him and learned to mimick her mouth movements. Gradually, he begins to vocalize as well with a single cooing noise. At eight or nine weeks he begins to smile on hearing his mother's voice even before he sees her face. A week or two later he smiles and vocalizes on hearing her approach. In a few weeks he not only smiles but laughs aloud, along with generalized mass activity.

As the child matures, this generalized mass activity diminishes and disappears (although even adults jump or dance with joy).

Although initially the smile is in response to the mother's overtures, soon smiling will occur at a drawing of a face. The child responds more when his mother talks to him than if she merely stares at him with an immobile face.

Though there have been several studies of the nature of a baby's cry, there have been few studies of the causes of the cry and the reasons for the variations. There also have been some psychological studies of the very early smile, but very few studies of the causes of smiling, laughing, and other expressions of pleasure in the older child.

Infants older than six months smile or laugh at the incongruous. Babies laugh at the antics of their siblings. They enjoy games ("this little piggie went to market") and games with their toys.

Important factors cause variations in the communication of pleasure. As in all aspects of development, allowance has to be made for preterm delivery. If an infant is born eight weeks early, he has missed eight weeks development *in utero* and will be correspondingly later than the full term baby in all aspects of development. Instead of beginning to smile at his mother at four to six weeks, he will begin to smile at her anywhere from four to eight weeks.

Mentally subnormal children are late in smiling and all other aspects of development (except sometimes sitting and walking). A mentally superior infant responds earlier and more to the mother than an average one. The child with autism will not respond at all to the mother's overtures.

Speech Acquisition

MacNamara (1972) discussed the way in which a child learns to speak and recognize the significance of speech. First, he has to learn language by determining the meaning which the speaker tries to convey to him. Next, he distinguishes the relationship between the meaning and the sound. MacNamara suggested that the infant uses meaning as a clue to language, rather than language as a clue to meaning. When the child begins to learn language, his thought is far more developed than his language. For instance, he can show that he wants a toy by his actions long before he can say what he wants. He understands the meaning of innumerable words before he can articulate them.

"The infant is able to relate sound and meaning before he is able to tell what the speaker is speaking about, independent of the speaker's language," states MacNamara. Other important studies of the development of speech in infancy are those of Irwin (1947), McCarthy (1954), who includes 700 references, Lillywhite (1958), Sheridan (1964, 1969) and Morley (1972).

In the development of speech, children pass through essential stages including the following. A week or two after the first smile (which is usually at four to six weeks of age if the baby is a normal, fullterm baby), the infant vocalizes with single syllables. The range of sounds rapidly increases as the infant discovers the pleasure of making sounds. He develops 'babble vocal play', with a constant repetition of sounds. Children of all nationalities go through the same stages of vocalization.

Somewhere between six and ten months of age, the factor of imitation enters, and the child begins to include parts of words which he has heard. By the end of the first year the average child can say two or three words with meaning, but understands the meaning of many more words long before he can articulate them.

Subsequently, at 21- to 24-months he spontaneously joins two or three words together to make primitive sentences. The infants' first sounds are vowels: /a/,/u/,/e/. In three to four weeks these are followed by the addition of front consonants, /m/,/p/,/b/ when is expressing displeasure, and the back consonants, /g/,/k/ for comfort. The infant sighs and grunts as well as cries. According to Irwin (1947), velars and glottals contribute about 98 percent of the sounds in the first month or two, with /k/,/g/, and /h/ being the most frequently used consonants. The early consonants are velars, glottals, and aspirates; later come labials, dentals, and post-dentals (Ausubel 1958). Plosives and fricatives are prominent in early infancy, to be displaced later by semi-vowels and nasal glides.

At two to three months, the pitch of crying is higher and the sound of "gaga" begins. The child coos and gurgles in response to his mother. By three months, he readily turns his head to sound on a level with his ear and now shows a massive response involving all four limbs when he hears his mother's voice He now holds a long 'conversation' with variations of pitch and voice quality when he is in a good mood and his mother talks to him.

At four months, the infant squeals with delight and laughs aloud and says "ah-goo" and begins to babble and engage in vocal play. He enjoys hearing a type of buzzing of the lips or tongue and enjoys the kinaesthetic sense of its vibrations. He begins to use the consonants /m/,/k/,/g/,/p/,/b/ and most vowels.

In the next three months he adds many syllables-- <u>ma</u>, <u>da</u>, <u>ka</u>, <u>der</u>, <u>erleh</u>, etc., and soon) at about seven months) combines syllables to say mumum, dadada,much to the delight of the parents, who incorrectly think that he is referring to them. By six months he vocalizes to himself, his mother, or his toys with many tones of high and low pitch. About half of his vocalizations now include consonants. He responds selectively to loving or angry tones and, by his vocalizations, shows recognition.

At approximately seven or eigh months of age, the child coughs or otherwise vocalizes to attract attention. He combines babbling with gesture; he imitates clap hands (patacake) and 'bye-bye'. At nine months he uses more back vowels with greater variation of pitch. Over half of his consonants are velars and glottals.

Although by ten months he may use one word correctly, it is difficult to define the first correct use of a word. For instance, when the baby sees a dog, or a picture of a dog, he may say /g/,/og/, or imitate a bark. He now reponds to 'no' and to simple requests. Postdental and labial consonants now become prominent, and he imitates a variety of words. He enjoys nursery rhymes and will act out some of them or correct a deliberate mistake in a rhyme by showing displeasure.

At 11 to 12 months he says a few words with meaning. He imitates dogs, cows, clocks and other sounds. He responds to his own name. About three-quarters of vowel sounds and one-third of consonant sounds are recognizable in his speech. Jargon (long rambling vocalizations) begins in which occasional intelligible words are interspersed.

In Newcastle upon Tyne, Neligan and Prudham (1969) carried out a meticulously careful analysis of four early milestones of development, one of which was the age of the first use of single words with meaning, controlling sex, social class, and place in family. Their findings, which are shown in Table 1, indicate that 50 percent of all children used their first meaningful word by approximately one year of age.

Table 1. Percentile and age in months for children to utter their first meaningful word.

	Number of Children	Percentiles for single first word						
		3	10	25	50	75	90	97
		Age in Months						
Male	1824	8.7	10.0	11.6	12.4	15.0	18.0	21.9
Female	1747	8.6	9.8	11.5	12.3	14.6	17.3	20.1

Factors Affecting the Development of Speech

The information describing the average age at which advances in the development of speech occur may vary widely. It is essential to note that all children differ in speech development due to environmental and other factors. The most significant factors that influence speech development will be described. However, it is not the purpose of this chapter to dwell on abnormal development.

Intelligence. The infant's level of intelligence has a profound effect on the development of speech. For mentally subnormal children, speech is retarded relatively more than are other aspects of development. There is delay in passing through all stages of speech development (Karlin and Strazzula 1952). The retarded child takes less notice of what is said, is less responsive to his mother, concentrates less, and is late in all aspects of expression and comprehension.

Mentally superior infants may or may not be advanced in speech development, but they are usually more advanced than average infants in speech comprehension. Some mentally superior children like Einstein or Volta, were later than usual in speech production. It is well known that this caused anxiety to their parents.

The experienced doctor, when assessing the development of babies, notes, among many other things, the quality of the infant's vocalizations.

Prematurity. It is important to allow for prematurity when assessing speech development. There is nothing to suggest that preterm babies are later in speaking than comparable fullterm babies, once correction has been made for the shorter duration of gestation.

Familial factors. Delayed speech development is sometimes a common trait within certain families regardless of other factors. One might question whether or not this is genetic or due to a lack of stimulation.

Delayed maturation. Occasionally, a child is a "slow starter," that is, backward in all or most fields of development including speech. Unexpectedly, he catches up to the average or exceeds it. No one can make a child speak until he is developmentally ready for it.

Sex. Speech usually develops earlier in girls.

Order of birth. The first born is likely to speak earlier than subsequent children, partly because the mother has more time to talk to him and read to him.

Multiple pregnancy. Twins are commonly later than singletons in learning to talk, for reasons that are not clear. It may be that the mother of twins has less time to read and talk to them than she has for a singleton. Morley (1972) showed that a speech defect

15

is rarely the same in both twins. There may be delay in one but not in the other. Retardation is greater in twins in middle classes than in twins in the lower social classes. Rutter and Martin (1972) thought that some of the delay is due to the twins developing a language of their own which no one else can understand or due to the fact that twins use more gestures than singletons. If the co-twin dies in early infancy, the difference from the average is only trivial, indicating the importance of environmental factors.

The environment. Emotional deprivation, such as that resulting from institutional care, profoundly delays speech. In addition, the responsiveness of the mother affects speech development. Some mothers talk very little to their child and do not seem to know what to say. Speech is often delayed in families where the parents both work and spend only a little time with their child.

Lulls in development. When a baby is developing one skill, such as manipulation or walking, the development of speech often ceases for a time but, eventually, the child catches up lost ground.

Deafness. Until the time when the factor of imitation develops, infant vocalizations are the same in the deaf child as in the hearing child (Collins 1954). As imitation develops, the vocalizations of the deaf child may decrease. Without hearing aids and/or other methods of communication, the development of speech is retarded or prevented.

If the deafness is only slight, the child can say the consonants /b/, /f/, /w/ which he can see produced. Usually he substitutes for the consonants /g/, /l/, /r/. If the deafness is only for high tones he will be late in talking and omit high tone sounds, like /s/ and /f/. He tends to omit final consonants, but responds to low frequency whispers. Delayed auditory maturation is a rare condition in which the child of normal intelligence is late in developing signs of hearing and is, therefore, late in developing speech, even though the early vocalizations are normal.

Lenneberg, Rebelsky, and Nichols (1965) studied the development of vocalizations in the first three months of infants born to deaf parents. No differences were found when compared to the vocalizations of normal infants. However, in the latter half of the first year, when the factor of imitation entered, the child's speech suffered.

Cleft palate. Since a cleft palate results in the inability to impound air adequately, the consonants /p/, /b/, /t/, /d/, /k/, and /g/ are distorted or omitted. Thus, some prelanguage activity is lost. Dental malformations and faulty tongue placement may cause other articulation problems. As in the case of all other major congenital abnormalities, a child with a cleft palate is more likely than others to have a lower than average intelligence (Illingworth and Birch 1956; Illingworth 1980) and so his speech is affected.

Cerebral palsy. For children born with cerebral palsy, speech is usually delayed or abnormal for several reasons. Children with cerebral palsy are likely to have a low level of intelligence; deafness is frequent (especially in athetoids); there is a cortical defect; there are mechanical problems related to spasticity and problems of muscle coordination; and the children may lack early sensory stimulation.

Other causes. Such things as tongue tie, handedness, emotional problems, and psychoses may, if severe, have an effect on the normal development of speech and language.

It is apparent from this review that a multitude of factors contribute to the development of infant speech. Observations of general developmental traits, such as sitting, walking, and motor refinement, lead to the use and selective application of the voice and speech mechanisms. Speech may be thought to be the pinnacle of development in the child and as such it is important to observe from birth, beginning with the cry. In the ensuing chapters, the neonatal development with respect to speech will be refined and the methods used to study the sounds of infancy will be presented.

REFERENCES

Adler, A. 1946. The Psychology of Early Childhood, C.W. Valentine. London: Methuen.

Ausubel, D.P. 1958. Theory and Problems of Child Development. New York: Grune and Stratton.

Carpenter, G. 1974. Mother's face and the newborn. New Scientist 61:742.

Collins, V.L. 1954. The early recognition of deafness in childhood. Med. J. Australia. 2:4.

Eimas, P.D., Siqueland, E.R., Jusczyk, P., and Vigorito, J. 1971. Speech perception in infants. Science 171:303.

Formby, D. 1967. Maternal recognition of infant's cry. Dev. Med. and Child Neurol. 9:293.

Illingworth, R.S. 1954. Three months colic. Archives of Disease in Childhood 29:165.

Illingworth, R.S. 1955. Crying in infants and children. Brit. Med. J. 1:75.

Illingworth, R.S. 1980. Development of the Infant and Young Child, Normal and Abnormal. 7th Edition. Edinburgh: Churchill-Livingstone.

Illingworth, R.S. and Birch, L.B. 1956. The intelligence of children with cleft palate. Archives of Disease in Childhood 31:300.

Irwin, O.C. 1947. Infant speech: consonantal sounds according to place of articulation J Speech Hear. Dis. 12:397-402.

Karelitz, S., Karelitz, R.F., and Rosenfeld, L.S. 1960. Infants' vocalizations and their significance. In Mental Retardation, ed. P.W. Bowman and H.V. Mautner. New York: Grune and Stratton

Karelitz, S. and Fisichelli, V.R. 1962. The cry thresholds of normal infants and those with brain damage. J. of Pediat. 61:679.

Karlin I.W. and Strazzulla, M. 1952. Speech and language problems of mentally defective children. J. Speech Hear. Dis. 17:286.

Lenneberg, E.H., Rebelsky, F.B., and Nichols, I.A. 1965. The vocalizations of infants born to deaf and to hearing parents. Hum. Dev. 8:23.

Lester, B.M. 1976. Spectrum analysis of the cry sounds of well nourished and malnourished infants. Child Dev. 47:237.

Lillywhite, H. 1958. Doctor's manual of speech disorders. J. of the Amer Med-, Ass'n. 167:850.

Lind, J., Wasz-Höckert, O. Vuorenkoski, V., and Vallane, E. 1965. The vocalization of a newborn brain damaged child. Ann. Paediatr. Fenn. 11:32-37.

MacNamara, J. 1972. Cognitive basis of language learning in infants. Psychol. Rev. 79:1-13.

McCarthy, D. 1954. Language development in children. In Child Psychology, ed. L. Carmichael. New York: Wiley.

Michelsson, K. 1971. Cry analyses of symptomless low birth weight neonates and of asphyxiated newborn infants. Acta Paediatr. Scand. Suppl. 216.

Mills, M. and Melhuish, E. 1974. Recognition of mother's voice in early infancy. Nature 252:123.

Morley, M.E. 1972. The Development and Disorders of Speech in Childhood. Edinburgh: Livingstone.

Neligan, G. and Prudham, D. 1969. Normals for four standard developmental milestone by sex, social class, and place in family. Dev. Med. and Child Neurol. 11:413.

Ostwald, P.F., Phibbs, H., and Fox, S. 1968. Diagnostic use of infant cry. Biology of the Neonate 13:68-82.

Rutter, M. and Martin, J.A. 1972. The child with delayed speech. Clinics in Developmental Medicine No. 43. Lavenham, Suffolk: Spastics International Medical Publications.

Sheridan, M.D. 1964. Disorders of communication in young children. Monthly Bulletin of the Ministry of Health and the Public Health Laboratory Services 23:20.

Sheridan, M.D. 1969. The development of vision, hearing, and communication in babies and young children. Proc. of the Royal Society of Medicine 62:999.

Trevarthen, C. 1974. Coversations with a two month old. New Scientist 62:230.

Wasz-Höckert, O. 1967. Studies of the cries of newborn and young infants. Acta Paediatr. Scand. 56:323.

Wasz-Höckert, O., Valanne, E., Vuorenkoski, B., Michelsson, K., and Sovigärvi, A. 1963. Analysis of some types of vocalization in the newborn and early infancy. Ann. Paediatr. Fenn. 9:1.

Wasz-Höckert, O., Lind, J., Vuorenkoski, V., Partanen, T., and Valanne, E. 1968. The Infant Cry. A Spectrographic and Auditory Analysis. Clinics in Developmental Medicine No. 29. Lavenham, Suffolk: Spastics International Medical Publications.

CHAPTER 2

Developmental Aspects of
Neonatal Vocalizations

Harry Hollien

INTRODUCTION

The focus on this chapter is upon the vocalizations produced by neonates and very young infants. Of course, if the term "neonatal" was used in its strictest sense -- i.e., a "new birth" -- about the only vocalization that could be discussed would be the birth cry. Fortunately, this term has been redefined somewhat to include both newborns plus infants through the first few weeks of life (a more specific definition is provided below) and this period will provide the basis for the discussions to follow. Moreover, some reference will be made to older infants and children. Quite obviously, it is difficult to discuss the nature of a population, or a series of events, without a reasonable set of referents. Since there is some controversy as to whether or not prenatal vocalizations exist at all (Illingworth 1955; Ostwald and Peltzman 1974), the reasonable reference is to older children. Hence, attempts will be made to correlate the neonatal behaviors to be reviewed with those of older populations.

A PROBLEM OF CLASSIFICATION

As is well known, a large number of professionals are interested in neonatal vocalizations -- and for a number of reasons. However, it should be stated that it is not just the differences in orientation among these professionals that has led to the large variety of classification schemes proposed, it is more often

20

due to the variability of the populations being studied. For example, the differential effects of such parameters as the infant's health, intelligence, nutrition, security in the home, language, approaches to language training and so on, can create substantial differences in the vocal product of those individuals comprising the total population under investigation. It is hardly surprising, then, that presently there does not appear to be a comprehensive classification system for infant vocalizations. Nor are there sufficient baseline data for virtually any of the speech/language characteristics that have been studied. Rather, what is available are bits and pieces only and, while it may be possible to organize them into a reasonable model of neonate vocalizations, no one has done so as of this writing.

In order that the scope of this organizational problem may be appreciated, Table 1 lists a number of factors that may affect the developmental nature and/or extent of infant vocalizations -- at least, in some manner, and to some degree. It should be noted that this set of relationships is illustrative rather than exhaustive. Even so, it is an impressive list and it appears that there are dozens of factors/events that can differentially affect infant vocalizations. Small wonder, then, that it has proved difficult to develop good organization in this area of study.

APPROACHES TO THE PROBLEM

It appears that, first, it will be necessary to define a neonate. In this regard, the definitions suggested by Crystal (1973) appear to provide a useful model. He specified that infancy includes the period of from birth up to (and including) the 104th week of life; a definition which will be adopted for this paper also. On the other hand, his specification of neonates appears to be a little too restrictive. Hence, for the purposes of the discussions to follow, a neonate will be defined as an infant between birth and eight weeks of age.

Neonates exhibit a number of behaviors that result in an acoustic signal. Included among them are such entities as crying, whimpering, grunting, sneezing, sucking, yawning, sighing, coughing, cooing and babbling. Cairns (1975) also includes chuckles, laughs, out-cries, struggle grunts, splutters, snorts,

Table 1*. A list of some of the factors that can differentially effect the magnitude and nature of infant vocalization.

Factor	Reference
Auditory perception	Eilers/Minifie (1975)
Birth position	Weir (1962, 1966)
Brain damage/CNS problems	Fisichelli/Karelitz (1963); Illingworth (1955); Karelitz et al. (1962); Lind et al. (1966); Truby/Lind (1965); Wolff (1969)
Cleft palate/oral-facial anomalies	Massengill (1968)
Colic/health states	Brazelton (1962)
Different languages	Weir (1966); Olney et al (1975)
Discomfort/pain	Illingworth (1955)
Drugs	Ostwald (1972)
Hearing loss (child or parents)	Cairns (1975); Lenneberg et al. (1965); Prescott (1975)
Nourishment (child or mother)	Lester (1975); Zeskind/Stein (1975)
Nursing schedule	Aldrich et al. (1945)
Posture/motor function	Bosma/Smith (1961)
Premature birth	Tenold et al. (1974)
Sex of child	Rūke-Dravain (1976); Bakeman/ Brown (1977)
Vocalizations/activity of mother	Anderson et al. (1977); Bake- man/Brown (1977)
Vocal tract usage	Mattingly (1973)

*Please note that, in some cases, data are reinterpreted relative to the question at hand; in doing so, there was no intent to do violence to the main thrust of the research.

smacks, gasps, and hiccoughs; Ostwald (1972) would add rasp and scream; McCarthy (1952) singing; Irwin and Curry (1941) vowels; Wolff (1969) lalling and gurgling -- and so on. Indeed, when the literature is reviewed, it is found that investigators have listed or defined dozens of vocalizations which they attribute to neonates and other infants.

It is possible that all neonate vocalizations can be divided into no more than two categories; those

Table 2. Neonate vocalizations.
All defined vocalizations are divided into two categories: crying and vegetative.

Communicative	Vegetative
Set A	Set C
crying	cooing
screams	babbling
Set B	chuckles
rasps	laughs
out-cries	gurgling
struggle grunts	lalling
"sobbing"	"phoneme" production
whining	Set D
whimpering	grunts
	sucking
	sighs
	splutters
	snorts
	smacks
	gasps
	Set E
	sneezes
	yawns
	coughs
	hiccoughs

proposed are cry and vegetative sounds. Note that in the neonate, few if any language-specific or even speech-specific sounds are produced primarily because, during this period, the infant is capable of few (if any) volitional communicative acts. Rather, the neonate communicates with his world on a reflexive basis with the crying act his primary mechanism for doing so. Thus, for purposes of this paper, all nenonate vocalizations will be divided into the two categories specified. They are listed in Table 2. Within this scheme, crying (and related activities) are thought to be highly communicative and vegetative vocalizations of relatively low communicative value.

Thus, it may be seen that those activities that directly link the child to his or her environment usually relate in some manner to crying and, hence, to signals that clue other individuals that he is in distress and/or needs aid/comfort of one type or another. All other vocalizations, then, can be placed in the vegetative category. However, it should be noted that the communicative value of vocalizations within each of the two categories vary somewhat, and an attempt was made to order them. For example, the vocalizations listed in Set C of the table would appear to be of greater communicative impact than would the purely life support reflexes of coughing, sneezing, yawning, and hiccoughing found in Set E.

Moreover, since most, if not all, of the listed vocalizations are reflexive in nature, one should not assume that any of them contain cognitive elements. Indeed, even in the most robust case -- when the neonate is crying due to hunger or pain -- the act is not particularly volitional in nature. Hence, it can be said that this model of infant vocalization is based on a reflexive-communicative concept, but one where all such entities are prelinguistic in nature.

Finally, in each of the discussions to follow, the data/materials for neonates will be provided first and will be followed by attempts at perspective. That is, data for infants, and sometimes for older children, will be included so that, where useful, the levels and characteristics of the neonates may be considered on a longitudinal basis.

PRENATAL VOCALIZATIONS

Before considering the type and nature of sounds produced by the neonate, it would appear necessary to consider the possibility that prenatal vocalizations exist. Since the fetus is submerged in the womb fluid, and is not breathing, it would appear physically impossible for it to create sounds within its vocal tract. Nevertheless, several authors (see, for example, Illingworth 1955; Ostwald 1972; Ostwald and Peltzman 1974) have discussed this possibility. Illingworth cites a number of reports that list *in utero* cries, but nearly all of these reports are anecdotal in nature. He further suggests that these sounds could result from some activity by the mother or the attending physician, i.e., by means of "some manipulative procedure, or merely from uterine contractions." Ostwald reports that neither he nor his associates actually have heard a prenatal vocalization but that others may have heard them. However, he also indicates that these prenatal sounds are probably very rare (if they exist at all) and result from the set of conditions suggested by Blair (1965). Blair indicates the process may be as follows: a) the placental sac ruptures prematurely, b) air enters the uterus, c) asphyxia or some operative manipulation stimulates the infant to breathe and, d) "prenatal" crying results. Basically, there appears to be little justification in carrying out any serious discussion about prenatal vocalizations. Indeed, it appears that: 1) they are extremely rare, if they occur at all, 2) they occur only at about the time of birth and, hence, probably are "neonatal" in nature, 3) they probably result from some operative procedure or maternal movement, and 4) they have not been recorded in a form that permits analysis.

THE NEONATAL CRY

The causes of the neonatal cry appear obvious -- hunger or some type of pain or discomfort. Moreover, it would appear that the basic reason for such behavior is life-support in nature. The organism needs or desires attention; hence, it signals this need in a manner most likely to attract attention. It should be remembered also that neonatal crying has few, if any, cognitive dimensions, but rather is a functionally automatic process. That such behavior sometimes is ignored, or occasionally leads to abuse rather than comfort, is immaterial. Moreover, cohesive neuro-physiological models, ones that could explain the operation of this system, are beyond the scope of this paper. What will be considered are the interpretations/perceptions of the cry by others, its acoustic dimensions and, to a limited extent, its physiology.

Perceiving the Neonatal Cry

Conventional thought suggests a number of relationships between the cries produced by the neonate and the way they are perceptually interpreted by individuals who hear them. Among these conventions are the following: 1) mothers, and others experienced with infants, can identify the reason for the cry by perceptual "analysis" of the acoustic signal alone, 2) mothers can identify their infants solely by listening to their crying even when competing cries exist in the same environment, 3) mothers, and other experienced personnel, can determine the sex of a child from perceptual "analysis" of the cry signal, 4) health states can be determined by analysis of an infant's cries and 5) prelinguistic elements can be perceptually identified within the neonate cry.

Perceptual Identification of Cry Types

The first important investigations carried out on cry types were those reported in 1927 by Sherman. In the more relevant of the two experiments, she studied, live, crying by two infants who were three to seven days old. These infants were induced to produce four types of vocalizations as follows: 1) hunger: they were observed 15 mintues after their usual feeding time (but had not been fed); 2) dropping (fear?): the infants were dropped suddenly "for a distance of from two to three feet towards the table"; 3) restraint (anger, rage?): the infant's head and face were held down on the table "with fairly firm pressure" and 4) "sticking with a needle"(pain?): in this case, the infants "were given six successive stimuli in the cheek with a needle." Finally, the procedures were repeated a number of times during the experimental day so as to obviate any procedural contamination. Three groups of observers were utilized: 1) graduate students in psychology, 2) third-year medical students and 3) student nurses. The observers attempted to identify the four conditions by specifying the "emotion" they believed they heard. This procedure resulted in the listing of 12 different "emotions" and "very little relationship was noted between the judgments and the qualitative nature of the stimuli." Sherman's work has been criticized because she presented her stimuli live and because she did not use mothers, and/or other individuals who were experienced with baby cries, as her observers.

A number of subsequent studies, focused on the perceptual recognition of "cry types," have not yielded definitive information either. For example, Aldrich et al. (1945) report an opinion on this issue. However, their research in this area was embedded in a major study on the temporal aspects of neonatal crying. They did indicate that they could not form a conclusion, however, because their results were so variable. More relevant is the study reported by Wasz-Höckert and his associates (1964). They attempted to correlate infant vocalizations with cry evoking stimuli. In this case, "cries" from 24 infants, equally divided into four groups, were recorded for four situations: 1) at birth, 2) prior to noon feeding (hunger?), 3) when the infant was vaccinated (pain?) and 4) "pleasure" cries recorded after a meal. This fourth class of vocalizations does not appear to be crying at all but rather a sound which probably is "vegetative" in nature, at least on the basis of the definitions provided by this paper. Moreover, the ages of the Wasz-Höckert et al. subjects varied substantially, some were neonates, some were not. The ages: 1) birth cry: neonatal, 2) hunger cry: one week to eight months, 3) pain cry: two weeks to eight months, and 4) pleasure vocalizations: four to eight months. Eight nurses (aged 23-37 years) listened to the random presentations of the 24 cries (sample length varied from 5.0-17.7 sec) and correctly identified the cry type 67% of the time (in all cases $P < 0.02$). In a followup study (Wasz-Höckert et al. 1964), these same investigators used parallel experimental procedures and reported that listeners who were experienced with very young children generally scored higher on the task than did listeners who were not experienced; a finding that agrees well with other relevant research. In short, the Wasz-Höckert group claimed that specific cries can be associated with specific stimulus situations and that recognizable perceptual differences exist between and among these cries. However, their studies cannot be generalized to statements about the efficiency of the cry signal as a communicative link between the mother and infant because they: 1) included birth cries and "pleasure" vocalizations in the study and to do so was inappropriate, 2) pre-selected experimental samples which seemed "typical" of the cry-evoking situation -- a procedure that may have biased the perceptual task, and 3) did not control for the possible effects of sample duration and infant age.

Muller et al. (1974) also report aural-perceptual data on mothers' ability to differentiate among several types of cries. Since the infants used in this research were three to five months of age, it is obvious that they cannot be classed as neonates. However, this study does enjoy the feature that the mothers involved had a longer period of time to become familiar with the vocalizations of their children than did the subjects in the previously reported investigations. Moreover, the experiment is fundamentally related to the topic under discussion and provides this area with an important perspective. Hence, it will be included.

Basically, eight mothers responded to the cries of their eight normal, healthy infants (four males, four females), their own plus seven others. Three types of cries were elicited as followed: 1) *pain* was induced by snapping an elastic band (roughly controlled) against the infant's left foot; 2) *startle* resulted from the single loud clap of two wooden blocks slammed together two feet behind the infant at an SPL level of approximately 95 dB and 3) *hunger cries* were evoked by not permitting the infant to continue feeding at the usual time. In one of the experiments, the mothers responded to the cries of their own infant; in another, to those produced by the other seven infants (with whom they basically were unfamiliar). The results of this investigation suggest that mothers cannot be expected to successfully match cry samples with typical cry-evoking conditions. Further, no differential advantage was found when mothers judged samples produced by their own infant.

Based upon a compilaton of all the results reported in this section, it would appear that the cries of normal infants carry too little perceptual information to permit auditors to identify the condition that evoked them. Therefore, it might be hypothesized that, within the normal home situation, the cry generally acts simply to alert the mother and most (if not all) of her suppositions concerning the situation that evoked the crying behavior must be based on additional environmental cues.

Mothers' Identification of Their Own Infants

The second group of studies in this general area considers the ability of mothers to identify their own children solely from perceived vocalizatons. Conventional thought on this issue is that mothers can do so. For example, Illingworth (1955) reports that mothers in a maternity hospital claim they were awakened whenever their own infant cried but did not respond to the crying of other babies. Formby (1967) attempted to test this notion by means of a two-part investigation. He recorded the induced crying of 31 newborns 14-144 hours after birth and played these tapes to the mothers in sets of five samples (her child plus four foils). He also recorded wakings by mothers in response to the crying of their own babies. In the first substudy, Formby observed that the mothers were only able to recognize their own child about half of the time prior to the infant's third day of life (i.e., up to 48 hours) but scored 100% thereafter. In the second study, mothers were found to be waking for their own infant about 60% of the time during the first period (nights 1-3) but that this relationship increased to over 95% after the fourth night.

Murry et al. (1975) also studied this phenomenon; they used the same populations and samples previously described (see Muller et al. 1974). These investigators report that their eight mothers were correct 91% of the time when asked to indicate which of the 96 randomized cries were produced by their infant. However, for only nine (1.2%) of the total of 768 responses did the mothers indicate that their child was not their own. Hence, 87% of the time mothers were in error, they were guilty only of a false identification. Thus, it can be said that the eight mothers used in this study had little difficulty recognizing their own infant solely from the perception of its cries. It further can be argued that research on this issue demonstrates rather well the belief that mothers are capable of recognizing their child from his or her vocalizations under most circumstances.

Identification of Neonate Sex

The literature on sex identification from perceived vocalizationas is a rather substantial one. Unfortunately, however, it is confined almost exclusively to adults. Even in those instances where children are studied, infants are not usually included. One of the few studies where the investigators attempted to determine if an infant's sex could be determined by auditory cues was the aforementioned experiment by Murry et al. (1975). Again, the infant popuplation in this study was aged three to five months and, hence, was somewhat older than neonates as defined. Nevertheless, these infants were young enough to permit some rough interpolation of the data. Basically, mothers were asked to identify the sex of infants other than their own on the basis of three types of crying. It was reported that the auditors scored at about chance levels and, hence, were unable to auditorily identify an infant's sex by means of cry stimuli. There are two questions of some importance to consider in the interpretation of these findings: 1) do male and female infants actually cry differently? and 2) on what percept -- or percepts -- do mothers base their sex judgments? With regard to the first question, there appears currently to be no experimental determinations as to whether a systematic physical difference does or does not exist between cries produced by male and female infants. In contrast, acoustic differences between adult male and female voices have been reasonably well documented (i.e., fundamental frequency level, frequencies of vowel formants, etc.); these acoustic differences serve as common perceptual cues. It is quite possible that the mothers in this study attempted to use these same (adult) cues when judging the cry samples of infants, even though these relationships may not hold for the younger population. For example, Hollien and Hollien (1976) suggest that, for children, females may exhibit lower speaking fundamental frequencies than do males. Thus, the results of the research on sex judgments may be interpreted in at least two ways: 1) the perceptual characteristics that are utilized in sex judgments of adult's voices are not adequate for distinguishing the sex of infants or, more probably, 2) there is no systematic physical difference between the cries of male and female infants and, therefore, no differences to perceive.

Perception of Health States

Some authors have claimed that an infant's health can be estimated by perception of his or her cries. Truby and Lind (1965) indicate that the perceptual analyses of cry stimuli are used by clinicians "as supplementary criteria for the evaluation of neurological function in general and specifically of respiratory function." However, they go on to state that purely perceptual approaches are not valid because the descriptions in use "have been and must necessarily be non-specific, ambiguous and subjective on the part of the auditor." Ostwald (1972) agrees and goes on to indicate that perceptual cues probably are misused in this regard. That is, to expect "one single behavioral manifestation, such as a cry pattern, to point reliably toward only one specific clinical syndrome seems too much to ask of the art and science of medicine." The rejection of perceptual specification of health states from the birth cry or neonate cries by these, and other writers, is probably accurate. Unfortunately, few, if any, experiments have been carried out in this area. Moreover, even though some clinicians argue that perception of such entities as "cri du chat" aids in diagnosis (Ostwald suggests that this diagnosis can be made without ever hearing the cry), there is little systematic evidence to suggest that it is possible to do so -- at least in an organized and structured manner. Hence, it must be concluded that the health of the neonate probably cannot be deduced from perceptual analysis of his or her cries.

Prelinguistic Vocalizations

There is some evidence that phonemes or, at least, speech-related sounds, can be identified perceptually as occurring in the cries of neonatal infants. While it can be argued from logic alone that vocalizations by neonates constitute a specific prelude to the development of the speaking act, the assignment of language structure to such activity appears to be unwarranted. Moreover, it would be expected that prelinguistic vocalizations would be more commonly found in the vegetative productions by the child, and they probably are. Nevertheless, some investigators have catalogued a number of the speech-like sounds that can be found in the cries of neonates. By-and-large, this area can be illustrated by three investigations. Irwin and Curry (1941) report that they independently transcribed the crying sounds of 40 infants, varying from one to ten days in age; their interjudge reliability was 85%. These investigators indicate that they were able to determine that only the vowels /æ, ɛ, ʌ, ɪ/ are used by newborns with any degree of frequency. They also indicate that: 1) front vowels were the most common, 2) back vowels were almost entirely absent, 3) there were no sex related differences among subjects, and 4) patterns of neonate vowel usage were strikingly different from those observed in adults. In a complex reliability study carried out the same year, Irwin and Chen essentially confirm the Irwin/Curry patterns. Finally Stark et al. 1975, studied a smaller group of infants (two females only) during the period one to eight weeks. These investigators sorted all of the vocalizations they observed into three categories: cry, discomfort, and vegetative. They then selected five examples of each sound for each infant at each of three age levels (N=90 samples) and analyzed them for existing speech features. Stark and her associates report that the classes of sounds assigned to each of the three categories differed from each other in several important respects. Vegetative sounds were characterized by "non-sonorant, consonant- like elements - stops, friction, and clicks ... (they were) brief ... (lacked) voicing or (exhibited) voicing accompanied by breathiness." It also was suggested that cry and discomfort vocalizations closely resembled each other with respect to segmental features and both were quite different from vegetative productions in this respect, i.e., they contained fewer consonant-like sounds and those observed resembled glides and nasals. Finally, discomfort and vegetative sounds resembled one another most closely with respect to suprasegmental features. Both "were found in short series, i.e, of one to five segments, and were of shorter duration than cry segments." In sum, Stark et al. also found what might be considered a prelude to language and speech in the vocalizations they observed. Again, however, it is necessary to restrict interpretations of data such as these. There probably are no cognitive components with respect to such activity. Rather, as Jakobson (1941) suggests, the infant probably is simply developing the system by means of random production of the possible sounds at a below-conscious level.

Acoustics of the Neonatal Cry

The acoustic and temporal patterning of neonate and infant crying has been the subject of considerable investigation. Of course, more research has been carried out on the infant than on the neonate. Further, some attempts have been made to correlate acoustic/temporal information with infant health states. These and related issues will be discussed primarily as a function of the individual acoustic and/or temporal parameter.

Fundamental Frequency

This parameter, the physical correlate of perceived pitch, perhaps has been studied more than has any other. Moreover, the focus of investigations of this nature has been more on crying than on vegetative vocalizations. It is recognized that it is much easier to record neonate cries than it is to record vegetative vocalizations. Perhaps this situation is an unfortunate one since it also is obvious that vegetative productions are more closely related to speech than are cry states. Nevertheless, the bulk of the available data relates to crying and, hence, f_O must be considered within that rubric. It should be noted also that most of the data to be reported will be primarily focused on f_O central tendencies. The reason for this is that frequency variability data are not always reported and, even when they are, few if any useful patterns can be observed.

The classic study in this area is that by Fairbanks (1942). He tracked f_O for the experimentally induced "hunger wails" of his own son during the period of one to nine months. He reported the mean f_O for the first month to be 373 Hz; that this feature systematically increased to a mean of 814 Hz at five months and then fell off somewhat to a mean of 640 Hz at nine months. Variability roughly paralleled this pattern; that is, it rose after an initial fall off. The Fairbanks data are plotted on Figure 1. As may be seen, they transcend both the neonatal period and early infancy.

Another study that provides data for both periods is one reported by Sheppard and Lane (1968). In this instance, f_O for two infants (a male and a female) was tracked during their first 141 days of life. The investigators summated their data for 12 approximately equal intervals during the experimental period; they may be seen plotted in the figure. For the male baby, the overall mean f_O for crying was 443 Hz with a range of 404-481 Hz; for the female, these same values were 414, 384, and 440 Hz respectively. As can be seen, the Sheppard and Lane data are more consistent than are those reported by Fairbanks even though the patterns they report are somewhat reminiscent of his (i.e., a drop in f_O followed by a rise -- in this case very slight, however). Moreover, as may be seen, the Sheppard and Lane results are substantially more consistent with those of the other investigators cited.

Ostwald (1972) indicates that the fundamental frequency of a newborn infant's cry will vary between 400 and 600 Hz, but the figure he provides as an illustration suggests a mean which is closer to 450 Hz than to 500 Hz. An investigation that provided more quantitative data about neonates is that by Ringel and Kluppel (1964). These authors selected ten infants (four males and six females) from a newborn nursery and recorded their cries; the age range of these infants was 4-40 hours. The overall mean for all cry samples was 413 Hz with a range of 290-508 Hz. Other data on the f_O of neonate cries are provided by Tenold et al. (1974), who report a general mean of 518 Hz for five 48-hour-old neonates, and by Michel (1961), who lists a mean f_O of 289 Hz for a ten-day-old male and that of 352 Hz for a 13-day-old female.

The Prescott (1965) study provides a great deal of f_O information about both neonates and infants. She studied four babies, first during the period 1-10 days

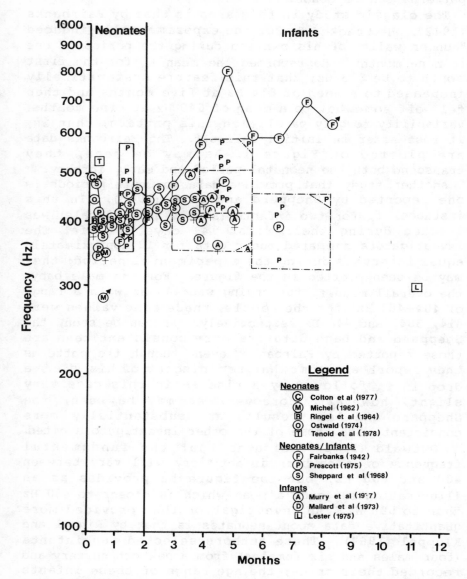

Figure 1. Fundamental frequency levels of neonatal and infant cries plotted as a function of age.

(neonates) and then, later, when they were aged 6-9 months (infants). She also provides data on ten additional children, aged 4-6 weeks, and still ten others, 6-8 months. As may be seen from the figure, the Prescott data are in substantial agreement with those reported by most other authors. They are as follows: the 1-10 day group (N=4): mean 384 Hz, range 354-425 Hz, 2) the 4-6 week group (N=10): mean 453 Hz, range 360-578 Hz; 3) the 6-8 month group (N=10) mean 496 Hz, range 438-596 Hz, and 4) the repeat of the first group at 6-9 months of age (N=4): mean 415 Hz and range 348-451 Hz.

The neonate and neonate/infant data cited above may be "anchored" by four experiments of the f_o levels of crying infants. These include the Murry et al. 1977, who reported data for eight 3-6 month old infants (four males and four females). The f_o levels for these children were: mean for males 457; for females 441, with ranges of 404-532 Hz and 361-466 Hz respectively.[1] The relationships among prepubescent children suggested by P. A Hollien (1976) should be noted again; i.e., f_o/SFF levels of females are lower than those for males. Also plotted are f_o data for the 12 month-old normals reported in 1975 by Lester (mean 308 Hz). Finally, Mallard and Daniloff (1973) provide data on a single child approximately five months old. In this case, f_o is estimated for a variety of vocalizations, one of which is presumed crying. The data are interpreted to provide at least six instances of cry behavior (out of 24 total observations) and the mean fundamental frequency for these six vocalizations is 379 Hz, with a range of 316-441 Hz.

As stated, Figure 1 provides a graphic display of the fundamental frequency levels reported for crying neonates and infants. As may be seen, the main body of the data cluster between 400 and 450 Hz, with the range of 350-500 Hz encompassing nearly all of the values reported. It is noteworthy to observe also that there is a slight trend for crying f_o to be slightly higher for infants than for neonates. However, a reversal of this trend occurs prior to the termination of infancy (two years-of-age).

Fundamental Frequency of Vegetative Vocalizations

Practically all of the research that has been carried out on the fundamental frequencies produced by neonatal

[1]No f_o differences were found among the cry "types" (hunger, pain, startle).

infants has utilized the cry (or distress) signal for analysis. Only two sets of authors report data with respect to how this parameter relates to vegetative vocalizations. Delack (1975) indicates that f_o for both neonates and infants stabilizes at about 355 Hz; he studied 19 infants up to the age of one year. Laufer and Horii (1977) report f_o data on four neonates (two male and two female) during the first eight weeks of life. The mean level they found was 328 Hz, with a range of 318-338 Hz.

Older infants have been studied to a greater extent than have the neonates. For one thing, they are able to provide better responses to experimental stimuli than can neonates. Moreover, children are " infants" eleven times longer than they are "neonates." Mallard and Daniloff (1973) provide f_o information on a child who is four months and three weeks in age. Among the vocalizations analysed are those rated as "euphoric" by the child's mother and six college-age wives of graduate students. The mean f_o for these five vocali- zations was 325 Hz, with a range of 303-352 Hz. Laufer and Horii (1977) report similar data as they continued to study the four neonates cited above until they were 24 weeks old. These investigators found f_o to range from 317 to 342 Hz, with a mean of 335 Hz.

Keating and Buhr (1978) studied a group of six infants from 33-169 weeks of age. While they do not report means for the two infants whose babbling they analysed at the age of 33 weeks, their f_o ranges from the modal register (see Hollien 1974) were 175-490 Hz for one infant and 200-500 for the other, with primary frequency concentrations at 300-399 Hz and secondary concentrations at 400-499 Hz. Thus, the data they report are in reasonable agreement with the previously cited authors and with Carney (1961), who reports a mean of 334 Hz for two 18 month-old males, and with McGlone, who indicates that the mean for his six 13-23 month-old subjects (three each, males and females) was 443 Hz.

Examination of fundamental frequency data for all reported utterances will reveal that this vocal parameter appears to rise slightly as a function of age-- at least until infants are about a year old. This observation is somewhat puzzling especially when laryngeal anatomy is taken into consideration. For example, it is well established that vocal fold size (especially length) increases by about 80% between birth and the child's first birthday. Hence, it would be expected that f_o would be systematically lowered during this period. Yet, based on the best evidence available, f_o values for infants appear to be somewhat higher than do those for neonates; this relationship holds whether the vocalization produced is that of crying or is vegetative in nature. On the other hand, perhaps other physiological considerations and/or the infant's generalized response to his environment are the controlling factors in this case and can account for the cited relationship. After all, it is well established also that an infant's cry vocalizations are accompanied by higher fundamental frequency levels than are his vegetative utterances. Of course, the higher frequency level for the cry can be explained on the basis of increased arousal and related increases in subglottic pressures. Perhaps mechanisms of this type are operative also in the case of the age/frequency relationship.

Spectral Analyses

The effects of vocal tract size and configuration upon infant vocalizations are both extensive and complex. Moreover, they are somewhat difficult to measure. Most often investigators have utilized time-by-frequency-by-amplitude (t-f-a) sound spectrometry for this purpose. Unfortunately, the output of devices of this type is primarily graphic rather than quantitative. Hence, the student of infant vocalizations has to rely on his or her subjective impressions and/or pattern matching abilities-- or those of others -- when attempting to obtain information about the composition of the complex waveforms produced by neonates and infants when they vocalize. However, since spectral information constitutes a major area of interest in this review, its more salient features will be considered.

Five investigations should serve to illustrate relationships in this area. First, Wasz-Höckert and his associates (1963) attempted to classify the birth cries, hunger cries, pain cries, and babbling of 25 newborn children and 55 infants by means of t-f-a spectrograms. They describe the rising and falling patterns of the birth cries but only quantify f_o (300-450 Hz) and cry burst durations (0.55 sec.). Their evaluations of the other three types of vocalizations also are descriptive in nature. However, they suggest that spectral patterns are different among the four types of vocalization. Seláčková (1964) also studied birth cries (N=30) by the sound spectrographic method. She indicated that birth cries are accompanied by high formants with frequencies in the 1400-3000 Hz region. She also classified cry sounds as a function of their resemblance to the vowels /a, ê/.

Truby and Lind (1965) provide a great deal of material about 30 infants (21 males, nine females) 1-12 days in age, as well as for a number of infants 33-43 weeks and others 8-10 months in age. These authors describe three types of cries which they classify as 1) basic, 2) turbulent, and 3) shift. While it is indicated that they result from 1) simple sources, 2) complex sources, or 3) constrained sources (respectively), it is also suggested that they are created from combinations of source energy, resonance (of several types), and frication. Truby and Lind provide a number of illustrative t-f-a spectrograms to portray these cry types However, they do not attempt to quantify their materials and, in some cases, it is quite difficult to generalize them to the act of infant crying.

Lieberman et al.(1971) analysed the crying of 20 normal newborns, 0-4 days in age. They utilized t-f-a type spectrograms also. From their analyses, they indicate that the cries of newborns are similar to those of infant primates but that they do not resemble sounds typical of adults. Indeed, they argue that "this inability appears to reflect, in part, limitations imposed by the neonatal vocal apparatus, which, like the non-human primate vocal tract, appears to be inherently incapable of producing the full range of human speech." The data/opinions reported by Lieberman and his associates do not appear to square with those of Jakobson who suggests that infants produce all sounds of all languages before beginning to learn the "mother tongue." Whether or not it can be demonstrated that Jakobson's postulates are totally accurate is of minimal consequence as he was clearly able to demonstrate that the infant can produce a variety of speech-like sounds.

But what of the neonate? Is it possible that the newborn and other neonates can produce speech sounds, even though they do not do so volitionally? The spectrographic data provided by Ringel and Kluppel appear germain to this issue. They demonstrated that some of the cries produced by their ten neonates (4-40 hours in age) were quite similar in nature to the vowels /æ/ and /ʌ/. In turn, the Ringel and Kluppel data prove to be in good agreement with the perceptual reports by Irwin and Curry, who indicate that they observed the vowels /æ, ε, ʌ/ in the crying of their 40 infants, all of whom were under the age of ten days. Irwin and Chen (1943) also indicate that, from their review of the literature to that time, they found five authors who report observing the vowels /ε, ɑ/ in birth cries, three who observed /æ/ and one other investigator who reported observing the vowel /ʌ/. They even report that some authors suggest that certain consonants can be found articulated in birth cries. In any case, it would appear that as long as parrots and similar classes of birds can be taught to produce intelligible speech, a variety of vocal tract configurations can be adapted for the purpose of producing speech-like sounds.

Finally, Ostwald et al. 1962, utilized a half-octave spectrum analyser to evaluate the vocalizations of 16 pairs of twins, all of whom were under the age of one month. These authors suggest that infant crying belongs to the mammalian pattern of mother-seeking and, hence, may have a genetic component. In any case, they report that in a previous study they found resonance peaks (formants?) in the frequency regions of 425-600 Hz and 1200-4800 Hz. In the case of the 32 subjects studied in this research, they report the first peak, or resonance region, to be in the area of 360-1430 Hz and the second to fall between 500 and 4000 Hz, depending upon which baby produced the cry.

In summary, it appears possible that neonates may exhibit different types of cries and that these cry classes might relate to some behavioral or physiological event/condition. Unfortunately, however, there is little or no quantitative (spectral) evidence to indicate what these cries might be or relative to how they might differ, one from another. While some additional research of this nature has been carried out on the utterances of older children, the procedures usually have been applied to their speech-like productions. Hence, the resulting data provide little guidance when the acoustic analyses of neonatal crying are to be considered. Thus, this area still is vulnerable to controversy and a substantial amount of research needs to be carried out in order to clarify relevant issues.

The Temporal Characteristics of Neonate Vocalizations

Typically, acoustic analyses of a signal of interest

would progress from evaluations of fundamental frequency to analysis of the signal's spectral characteristics and, thirdly, to estimations of observable energy levels. In the case of the present review, however, discussion of intensity will be omitted, partly because there is so little information available about it and partly because absolute intensity (or pressure) levels are very difficult to obtain for neonate vocalizations. This discussion will jump, rather, directly to temporal considerations. Moreover, since there is only a small amount of data available in this area, crying and vegetative vocalizations will not be considered separately.

Two studies provide some information about the amount of crying that can be expected from neonates. Aldrich et al.(1945) tracked the number of babies crying on a maternity ward (and the amounts of crying by newborns) for a period of 30 days. They calculated their data on the basis of a single instant, a single day, the whole month. For 720 "instants" recorded, there were no neonates crying for 232 of them but one or more (up to over 50) were crying at each of the other 488 "instants." Further, the average baby cried 1.3-11.2 minutes per hour or for a mean of 113.2 minutes (or 1.98 hours) per day. Brazelton (1962) also studied the extent of infant crying for babies 2-12 weeks of age. She found that the 80 babies cried, on the average, 1.75 hours per day at two weeks. They slowly increased their crying to a mean level of 2.75 hours per day at 6 weeks, with the amount dropping off to 0.80 hours per day at 12 weeks. From these data, it appears that a baby's cries not only provide him with an important tool for survival but also with a means for enhancing physiological development. That is, the amount of time the average infant cries each day provides him with an outstanding regimen of exercise and with ample opportunity to develop, especially, the aerodynamic/physiological support necessary for the subsequent development of speech and language.

Information about the typical durations of neonate and infant vocalizations may be found in Table 3. The table is roughly structured to reflect chronological age with the younger subjects coming first (at least, in most cases). Practically all of the data were generated via the analysis of cries; usually, the mean for a group is provided. If the observed patterns can be considered generalizable, it is possible to make some tentative statements about a possible trend.

Table 3. Observed durations of cries and vegetative vocalizations of neonates and infants.

Authors	Date	N	Age	Condition	Duration
Ringel/Kluppel	1964	10	4-40 hours	cry	1.50 sec (0.6-4.0 sec)
Wasz-Höckert et al.	1963	25	newborn⎫	cry	1.25 sec
		55	infants⎭	vegetative	1.25 sec
Prechtl et al.	1969	21	1-9 days	cry	0.4-0.9 sec
Prescott	1965	4	1-10 days	cry	1.23 sec
Sheppard/Lane	1968	2	1-141 days	cry	0.29 sec
Caldwell/Leeper	1974	26	2-4 days	cry	0.65 sec
Ringwall et al.	1965	40	3 days	cry	0.35 sec
Colton et al.	1977	32	1 week	cry	1.57 sec
Prescott	1965	10	4-6 weeks	cry	1.01 sec
Mallard/Daniloff	1973	1	4 months,	cry	2.05 sec
			3 weeks	vegetative	2.50 sec
Prescott	1965	10	6-8 months	cry	1.98 sec
		4	6-9 months	cry	1.19 sec
Lester	1975	12	12 months	cry	1.52 sec

First, it would appear (Ringel and Kluppel 1964; Wasz-Höckert et al. 1963) that newborns exhibit cry bursts of the magnitude of 1.25-1.50 sec. It then appears that the cry durations shorten rather dramatically and the new patterns continue through the rest of the neonatal period. Indeed, of the several authors cited, only Prescott's four 1-10 day-old neonates exhibited mean cry bursts of over 1 sec in length. Finally, as the baby grows into infancy, the duration of the cry bursts lengthen again to the levels cited for birth cries. Admittedly, this trend is not very easy to explain. However, since the data that support it are a little sparse, it would appear necessary, first, to confirm it. If it proves to be valid, an explanatory model will be developed at a later time.

Acoustic Predictors of Neonatal Health
    A number of authors have suggested that the birth cry and/or neonate/infant cries contain elements useful in predicting health states (Illingworth 1955; Truby and Lind 1965; Parmalee 1962). Some have reported that

they contrasted relevant groups of infants on the basis of acoustic data or descriptions. For example, Tenold et al. (1974), compared five 48-hour-old normal neonates with five babies born prematurely. They applied cepstral and stationarity analyses to the cries of these children and report that while f_o did not differentiate between the groups, spectral variability did. Colton and Steinschneider (1977) contrasted f_o and cry durations of one SIDS infant, who died at 63 days of age with parallel data for 32 normal infants. The temporal characteristics were found to be similar (SIDS: 1.59 sec; mean for normals:1.57 sec), but f_o differed somewhat. In this case, the SIDS infant exhibited an f_o of 411 Hz while the mean for the 32 normals was 487 Hz. This difference in fundamental frequency, while possibly contrastive, also may be more apparent than real as, it must be remembered, a level of 411 Hz falls within the cited range of cry levels for other normal neonates.[2]

Prechtl et al. (1969), contrasted seven normal neonates with nine transitory and five abnormal children on the basis of spontaneous crying as well as vocalizations resulting from a pinch. They report that the cries for the normal children were "shorter and more stable" and that they were more variable for the two abnormal groups. Ostwald and Peltzman (1974) also comment on such differences. In this case, however, they indicate that f_o for their normals centered in the 400-500 Hz frequency region, whereas those for the abnormals were on the order of 600-700 Hz.

Both Lenneberg et al. (1965), and Prescott (1965) studied the effects of hearing problems on infant vocalizations. In the Lenneberg et al. study, the productions by ten 1-3 month-old infants were contrasted with those of six 1-3 month-old children who had been born to deaf parents. Indeed, one of these infants showed a hearing loss also. However, these investigators did not find appreciable differences between the two groups. Prescott studied a single 6-month-old hearing-impaired child directly and contrasted his behavior with that of her four 6-9 month-olds and ten 6-8 month-old infants. She reports his mean f_o to be 436 Hz; those for the two normal groups to be 415 Hz and 496 Hz respectively. The differences among cry burst durations may be somewhat more revealing. In this case, the hearing impaired

[2]See also their chapter in this book.

child's cry bursts averaged 2.2 sec while the mean for the two normal groups was 1.2 sec.

That the duration of cry bursts may be a cue separating the normal child from infants who exhibit health problems also is suggested by Lester (1975). He compared 12 normal year-old infants with an equal number of children who had suffered from malnutrition. When he contrasted the two groups on the basis of f_o, cry burst duration and intensity, he found differences for all parameters. For the normals, the group means follows: f_o=308 Hz, D=1.5 sec and I=50 dB; for the malnourished infants, these values were: f_o=480 Hz, D=2.7 sec and I=38 dB. As can be seen, Lester's values provide a greater contrast between these two groups than do any of those reported for previously cited populations. In any event, he was able to conclude that, when an infant does not receive sufficient nourishment, his cry can be expected to be longer, weaker, and of higher pitch.

Finally, Karelitz and Fisichelli (1962) and Fisichelli and Karelitz (1963) have contrasted the behavior of normal and brain damaged infants on the basis of cry thresholds and latencies In the first study, a total of 293 children (230 normal, 63 abnormal) were studied variously at ages ranging from birth to over one year of age. Stimulus was a snap on the sole of the foot by a rubber band; the response criterion was one full minute of crying. The authors report that infants "with diffuse brain damage require more stimulation to produce ... a crying response than do normal infants." They also note, however, that normal infants younger than four days "may not cry as readily under this form of stimulation as older children do." The authors then studied the latency of responses to the snap of a rubber band for 117 normal infants and 69 exhibiting brain disorders; subjects ranged in age from one day to nearly three years. They report that there were group differences in the response times to the specified pain stimulus, with the brain damaged exhibiting delays in response that were significantly greater than those for normals (2.6 to 1.6 sec respectively). Moreover, the mean latency of 1.6 sec for the normals is in substantial agreement with the value of 1.5 sec reported by Caldwell and Leeper (1974) for a similar procedure. Finally, no sex differences were reported in either of the two studies cited above.

If all the investigations discussed are taken as a

group, it would appear that analysis of neonate and infant vocalizations could be useful in describing a number of childhood health states. However, as has been pointed out, there are so many specific impairments, conditions, and disorders that it is difficult to envision just how such measures could be used. Perhaps this confusion exists because there have been so few experiments carried out in this area and that they have been so diffused in their focus. Moreover, when the variability exhibited by neonates and infants for most of the measures is taken into account, it appears improbable that behavioral standards can be set that would permit the reasonable testing of a single child. That is, from the results available, it does not seem possible that acoustic/temporal data could be obtained that would be very useful in the diagnosis of a specific disorder. In any event, this area of inquiry appears to be one that requires a continued research thrust, at least if reasonable decisions are to be made in the future.

Cry Physiology

There exists in the literature a great deal of opinion about the physiological and aerodynamic bases of neonate/infant crying and vegetative vocalizations. Most of these opinions probably are reasonably accurate. However, they are based pretty much on research that has been carried out on older children and adults. Indeed, very few experiments have been carried out on the population of interest; a few of those that have been reported will be reviewed below.

The only study that has focused directly on babies in the neonatal category is that by Long and Hull (1961). They investigatged flow volumes for 14 newborns (aged 1-3 days) while they were crying. These investigators utilized average maximum flow and cry burst duration in their research and report that for inspiratory flow the mean values for these two measures were 161 ml/sec and 0.22 sec respectively. As expected, the maximum average flow for expiration was found to be somewhat lower (106 ml/sec) but, at 0.50 sec, duration was longer. The mean duration of the cries (as opposed to overall exhalation) was 0.40 sec, a value that pretty much agrees with those reported by Ringwall et al. (0.35 sec) and Caldwell and Leeper (0.65 sec) for similar aged neonates (see again Table 3). Further, these authors noted that, based on their measurements, neonates appear to engage in abnormally deep inspiration during crying.

Bosma and Smith (1961) report a generally descriptive study on groups of five neonates (1 day to 2 weeks in age) and five infants (4-6 months of age). They carried out cinefluoroscopic procedures in order to investigate the differences in the crying act between these two groups. Based on their observations, they indicate that, for the neonate, crying is part of a total body response to his or her environment. On the other hand, they suggest that, for the infant, crying is a discreet, specific event and that infants in this age category are capable of adding substantial variation to their (cry) vocalizations.

Finally, van Oordt and Drost (1963) studied the "physiological frequency range (PVR)" of two groups of normal children: the first group contained 45 individuals 0-5 years of age and the second group 81 subjects 6-16 years. For the very young (neonates and infants) they estimated PVR[3] from cry samples. While it is recognized that these authors may not have had many (or any) true neonates among their younger population, a few interpretations of their data can be made anyway. They report that none of their neonates/infants displayed a PVR of less than one octave. Further, it can be observed that two infants exhibited ranges of over three octaves and most subjects in this age range clustered between 2.5-3.0 octaves. They consider ranges of this magnitude to be "an appreciable achievement for the small larynx of the young child." Even though f_o ranges have been reported and are cited above, it is difficult to compare them to data such as these. Extreme frequencies are rarely reported and, even when they are, they are only roughly comparable because of major differences in the manner by which they are obtained and analyzed. For example, the Laufer/Horii (1977) data would only predict a PVR of about an octave; those reported by Murry et al. (1977) only about two octaves. However, the data reported by Fairbanks (1942) translates to a mean PVR of about 3.7 octaves, with a range of 2.5-5.0 octaves.

To summarize, not much is known -- except, perhaps, by inference -- about the basic physiology and neurophysiology of neonate cries and vegetative utterances. Yet, this area is an important one.

---

[3]PVR appears to functionally relate to the Phonational Frequency Range (PFR) procedure described in 1971 by Hollien, Dew and Phillips.

Substantially more research should be carried out on these and closely related issues.

SPEECH/LANGUAGE DEVELOPMENT OF NEONATES

When neonate crying is analysed relative to its speech/language components, it is obvious that the role such activity plays in the development of volitional communicative acts is tangential. Indeed, the cry is communicative in-and-of itself in that it signals the existence of the basic needs of the neonate. At this stage of life, however, it is almost accidental that the crying also results in gestures that exercise the vocal tract and its supporting mechanisms and permits the infant to "articulate" prelinguistic, or even phonemic, entities. Since the vegetative vocalizations of the neonate are of substantially lower communicative value than is crying, it might not be expected that they could provide very much in the way of support for speech/language development. Nevertheless, the possibility exists that, since some of the neonates' vegetative vocalizations can be speech-like, they may play some sort of a prelinguistic role in this process also.

Neonate Perception of Speech

One element in the process (discussed above) is that of a neonates' potential for perceiving, and the sensory processing of, speech-like sounds. Of course, there is a body of literature that reports the ability of babies to respond to a variety of auditory stimuli. However, for purposes of this discussion, only speech (or speech-like) sounds will be considered.

A number of authors have utilized nonnutritive sucking as a response indicator for the measurement of neonate perception of speech sounds. Two key studies among this group are those by Morse (1972) and Eilers and Minifie (1975). Morse studied 25 normal neonates 40-54 days of age; his stimuli consisted of CV combinations. Based on his results, Morse suggests that his subjects could discriminate acoustic cues for place of articulation and intonation, and that they behaved in a linguistically relevant manner. Eilers and Minifie investigated the behavior of 84 neonates/infants 4-17 weeks in age who were divided into three approximately equal experiment/control group combinations. These investigators report that their subjects were able to discriminate perceptually between the phonemes /s/ and /v/ and /s/ and /j/ but not between the unvoiced/voiced fricatives /s/ and /z/.

In a somewhat similar type of experiment, Eimas et al. (1971) studied 1-4 month-olds and were able to conclude that infants "as young as one month ... are not only responsive to speech sounds and able to make fine discriminations but are also perceiving speech sounds along the voicing continuum in a manner approximating categorical perception, ..." The differentiation that led to the last comment was between the unvoiced/voiced plosives /p/ and /b/. In studies that followed the Eimas et al. work, Trehub confirmed and extended their findings (Trehub and Robinovitch 1972; Trehub 1973). In the first experiment, 60 subjects 4-17 weeks in age were studied using the Eimas et al. stimuli. Trehub and Robinovitch found it possible to conclude that their neonates/infants were able to discriminate between /b/ and /p/ both for synthetic and natural stimuli, as well as between natural productions of /d/ and /t/. In the second investigation, Trehub extended the procedure to include vowels and sinusoids. Her 182 4-17 week-old infants were able to discrimate between /a-i/, /i-u/ and /ta-ti/ contrasts but not between certain sinusoids. Perhaps Mattingly (1973) best sums up this area of inquiry by suggesting that "the infants' 'technique for representing input signals' is a very robust process that is not easily upset by confusing, inconsistent, or fragmentary input." Although Mattingly was making this point in a slightly different context, it is a postulate that also has relevance for the previous discussion. That is, when even the few studies reported here are considered, it appears that the neonate is ready at a very early age to process speech-like signals for use in initial language learning.

Neonate Speech Development

Quite understandably, virtually all the research on speech development has been carried out on infants and young children, rather than on neonates. As is well known, it is not until after the neonatal period is complete and the infant has developed reasonable cognitive function that speech and language also can develop. Indeed, except for the reflexive aid-seeking calls (cries) exhibited by the neonate, few, if any, of his vocalizations can be classified even as prespeech. Perhaps some of the early cooing and/or laughter is communicatively imitative in nature, but a concept such as this is, of necessity, quite speculative.

Of course, controversy exists as to whether or not the neonate can and does produce any of the phonemes that ultimately will be found in his or her native language. The work of Irwin and his associates (see previous citations plus Irwin 1947 and 1948) appears relevant to this issue. He reports that neonates produce a number of identifiable vowels, as well as the vowels /ɛ, ɪ, ʌ/, in some quantity and, he adds, the vowel /ɛ/, if the infant is crying. Further, Irwin suggests that velar and glottal consonants can be heard among the vocal repertoire of the neonate and that it is possible to track both the addition of new consonants as they develop and the shifting proportions of consonantal use as the infant grows into and through infancy. Even though Irwin and his associates have gone to considerable length to demonstrate the reliabilty of their observations, they have been criticized both methodologically and for their interpretations of the data. Lynip (1951) was principal among their earlier critics. Basically, Lynip used a t-f-a spectrograph to acoustically analyse the tape recorded utterances of his child from birth until 56 weeks of age. He concluded that his infant did not produce any speech sounds that were the equivalent of adult phonemes, at least until near the end of the first year. Lynip was answered by Winitz and Irwin (1958) and by Winitz (1960) who used both judgments by panels of student phoneticians plus sound spectrographic analysis in refutation. Since that time, still others have criticized the Irwin data, primarily on the basis that he and his colleagues attempted to artificially force generally unspecific acoustic signals into a relatively detailed structure -- that of the International Phonetic Alphabet. On the other hand, other investigators (see for example, Ringel and Kluppel 1964; Stark et al. 1975 and 1976) have provided information suggesting that neonates do, indeed, produce phoneme-like utterances. Moreover, it is important to remember that the acoustic characteristics of phoneme-like sounds have to be extrapolated in order to take into account the size and configuration of the neonate larynx and vocal tract.

For example, the 1952 Peterson and Barney data demonstrated that children exhibit f_o and vowel formant regions that are different from those of adults. If the Peterson/Barney data can be accepted as valid, then it should be possible to extend the observed patterns to take into account the acoustic output of the neonate. Indeed, on this basis, it is curious that any investigator would require that the acoustic patterns of neonates and infants be similar to, or even parallel, those expected for adults. Rather, it is the reverse of this process that should be pursued. That is, if phoneme sounds can be reliably identified by valid perceptual measures, then the phonemes can be said to exist among a neonates' vocalizations. It is at this juncture that acoustic analysis of the signal should be carried out in order to determine the physical characteristics of the events that created the percept in the first place. Nor is the argument valid that a sound must be structurally linked to language in order that it exist. If the infant produces it, it does indeed exist, even though it is prelinguistic in nature. To summarize, it appears that neonates can, and do, produce speech-like sounds and these sounds must be considered as a facet of prespeech development.

Other projects which investigate the prelinguistic vocalizations of neonates and infants take different forms. For example, the research reported by Ringwall et al. (1965) provides insight into the manner by which distinctive features develop. Anderson et al. (1977) reported on how mother-infant interaction stimulates vocalizations by the child. By-and-large, however, the major thrust of research on language acquisition is for the infant period, i.e. 2 -24 months. Investigations of this type may involve empirical research (Cruttenden 1970; Oller et al. 1975; Oller and Smith 1977), model building (Dore et al. 1976) or in depth reviews (Crystal 1973; Rees 1972). The single attribute that all of these publications have in common is that their focus is on infant vocalizations rather than those produced by the neonate.

EPILOG

No attempt will be made to summarize this chapter. It would appear more important to combine the information presented here with that to be found in

other related sections of this volume and to synthesize
the total corpus. Moreover, it is difficult to
generalize from the variety of materials and
definitions provided by various investigators. As was
stated earlier, it is quite rare that there are more
than scattered, incomplete data available about any
issue. In addition, it is quite difficult to
synthesize and integrate the data that does exist. The
research approaches, definitions, populations, and
techniques vary so markedly from investigator to
investigator that it is difficult to make direct
comparisons. In short, it is understood that this
chapter has identified many more questions than it has
answered. It has also presented the reader with
sufficient "caveats" in order to understand and
interpret the data to be presented in the following
chapters. Methodological advances are apparent;
improved population selection and the introduction of
computer processing to assist in analysis of the infant
signals provide the basis for attacking the problems
associated with the study of infant communication.

It is hoped that the questions posed will lead to
additional research, to improved organization of the
available information and, ultimately, to a better
understanding of the rather important issues and
relationships found in this area of investigation.

REFERENCES

Aldrich, C.A., Sung, C., and Knop, C. 1945. The crying
of newly born babies. J. Pediat. 26:313-27.

Anderson, B.J. Vietze, P. and Dokecki, P.R. 1977.
Reciprocity in vocal interactions of mothers in
infants. Child Devel. 48:1676-81.

Bakeman, R. and Brown, J.V. 1977. Behavioral
dialogues: an approach to the assessments of mother-
infant interaction. Child Devel. 48:195-203.

Blair, R.G. 1965. Vargitis uterinus: crying in utero.
Lancet 2:1164.

Bosma, J.F. and Smith, C.C. 1961. Infant cry: a
preliminary study. Logos 4:10-18.

Brazelton, T.B. 1962. Crying in infancy. Pediat.
29:579-88.

Cairns, G.F. Jr. 1975. Longitudinal studies in infant
vocal production. Paper presented at the ASHA
Convention, Washington.

Caldwell, H.S. and Leeper, H.A. Jr. 1974. Temporal patterns of neonatal vocalizations: a normative investigation. Percept. Motor Skills 38:911-16.

Carney, R.J. 1961. A report on the pitch characteristics of two eighteen month males. In NIH Progress Report B-2162, University of Wichita, pp. 5-7.

Colton, R.H. and Steinschneider, A. 1977. The cry characteristics of an infant who dies of SIDS. Paper presented at the ASHA Convention, Chicago.

Cruttenden, A. 1970. A phonetic study of babbling. Brit J. Dis Comm. 5:110-18.

Crystal, D. 1973 Nonsegmental phonology in language acquisition: a review of the issues. Lingua 32:1-45.

Delack, J.B. 1975. Prosodic features of infant speech: the first year of life. Paper presented at Eighth International Congress Phonetic Sciences, Leeds, England.

Dore, J., Franklin, M.B., Muller, R.T. and Ramer, A.L.H. 1976. Transitional phenomena in early language acquisition. J. Child Lang. 3:13-28.

Eilers, R.E. and Minifie, F.D. 1975. Fricative discrimination in early infancy. J. Speech Hear. Res. 18:158-67.

Eimas, P., Siqueland, E., Jusczyhz, P. and Vigorito, J. 1971. Speech perception in infants. Science 171:303-06.

Fairbanks, G. 1942. An acoustical study of the pitch of infant hunger wails Child Devel. 13:227-32.

Fisichelli, V.R and Karelitz, S. 1963. The cry latencies of normal infants and those with brain damage. J. Pediat. 62:723-34.

Formby, D. 1967. Maternal recognition of infants' cry. Devel. Med. Child. Neurol. 9:293-98.

Hollien, P.A. and Hollien, H. 1976. Sex differences in SFF for prepubescent children. AAPS Newsletter 3:5(A).

Hollien, H. 1974. On vocal registers. J. Phonetics 2:125-43.

Hollien, H., Dew, D. and Philips, P. 1971. Phonational frequency ranges of adults. J. Speech Hear. Res 14:755-60.

Illingworth, R.S. 1955. Crying in infants and children. Brit. Med. J. 1:75-78.

Irwin, O.C. 1947. Infant speech: consonant sounds according to manner of articulation. J. Speech Dis. 12:402-04.

Irwin, O.C. 1948. Infant speech: development of vowel sounds. J. Speech Hear. Dis. 13:31-34.

Irwin, O.C. and Chen, H.P. 1943. A reliability study of speech sounds observed in the crying of newborn infants. Child Devel. 12:351-368.

Irwin, O.C. and Curry, E.T. 1941. Vowel elements in the crying vocalizations of infants under ten days of age. Child Devel. 12:99-109.

Jakobson, R. 1941. Kindersprache, a phasie, und allgemeine lautgesetze. Uppsala, Sweden: Almquist and Wiksell.

Karelitz, S. and Fisichelli, V.R. 1962. The cry thresholds of normal infants and those with brain damage. J. Pediat. 61:679-85.

Keating, P. and Buhr, R. 1978. Fundamental frequency in the speech of infants and children. J. Acoust. Soc. Amer. 63:567-71.

Laufer, M.Z. and Horii, Y. 1977. Fundamental frequency characteristics of infant nondistress vocalization during the first twenty-four weeks. J. Child Lang. 4:171-84.

Lenneberg, E.H. Rebelsky, F.G. and Nichols, I.A. 1965. The vocalizations of infants born to deaf and to hearing parents. Human Devel. 8:23-37.

Lester, B.M. 1975. Spectrum analysis of the cry sounds of well nourished and malnourished infants. Paper presented at the Biannual Meeting of the Society for Research in Child Development, Denver.

Lieberman, P., Harris, K.S., Wolff, P. and Russell, L.H. 1971. Newborn infant cry and nonhuman primate vocalization. J. Speech Hear. Res. 14:718-27.

Lind, J. Wasz-Höckert, O., Vuorenkoski, V. Partanen, T., Theorell, K. and Valanne, E. 1966. Vocal response to painful stimuli in newborn and young infants Ann Paediat. Fenn. 12:55-63.

Long, E C. and Hull, W.C. 1961. Respiratory volume flow in the crying of newborn infants. Pediat. 27:373-77.

Lynip, A. 1951. The use of magnetic devices in the collection and analysius of the preverbal utterance of an infant. Genet. Psycho. Mono. 44:221-62.

Mallard, A.R. and Daniloff, R.G. 1973. Glottal cues for parental judgment of emotional aspects of infant vocalizations. J. Speech Hear. Res. 16:592-96.

Massengill, R.M. 1968. Cry characteristics in cleft palate neonates. J. Acoust. Soc. Amer. 45:782-84.

Mattingly, I. 1973. Phonetic prerequisites for first-language acquisition. Haskins Laboratories, Status Report on Speech Research SR-34:65-69.

McCarthy, D. 1952. Organismic interpretations of infant vocalizations. Child Devel. 23:273-80.

McGlone, R.E. 1966. Vocal pitch characteristics of children aged one and two years. Sp. Mono. 33:178-81.

Michel, J.F. 1961. A pilot study of the pitch characteristics of hunger cries of neonates. In NIH Progress Report B-2162, University of Wichita, pp. 1-2.

Morse, P. 1972. The discrimination of speech and nonspeech stimuli in early infancy. J. Exper. Child Psych. Devel. 14:477-92.

Muller, E., Hollien, H. and Murry, T. 1974. Perceptual responses to infant crying: identification of cry types. J. Child Lang. 1:89-95.

Murry, T., Amundson, P. and Hollien, H. 1977. Acoustical characteristics of infant cries: fundamental frequency. J. Child Lang. 4:321-28.

Murry, T., Hollien, H. and Muller, E. 1975. Perceptual response to infant crying: maternal recognition and sex judgments. J. Child Lang. 2:199-204.

Oller, D.K. and Smith, B.L. 1977. Effect of final syllable position on vowel duration in infant babbling. J. Acoust. Soc Amer. 62:994-97.

Oller, D.K. Wieman, L.A., Doyle, W.I. and Ross, C. 1976. Infant babbling and speech. J. Child Lang. 3:1-11.

Olney, R.L. and Scholnick, E K. 1976. Adult judgments of age and linguistic differences in infant vocalization. J. Child Lang. 3:145-55.

Ostwald, P.F. 1972. The sounds of infancy. Devel. Med. Child Neurol. 14:350-61.

Ostwald, P.F. and Peltzman, P. 1974. The cry of the human infant. Scient. Amer. 230:84-90.

Ostwald, P.F., Freedman, D.G. and Kurtz, J H. 1962. Vocalization of infant twins. Folia Phoniat. 14:37-50.

Parmalee, A.H. Jr. 1962. Infant crying and neurologic diagnosis. J. Pediat. 61:801-02.

Peterson, G.E. and Barney, H.L. 1952. Control methods used in study of vowels J. Acoust. Soc. Amer. 24:175-84.

Prechtl, H.F.R., Theorell, K., Gramsbergen, A. and Lind, J. 1969. A statistical analysis of cry patterns in normal and abnormal infants. Devel. Med. Child. Neurol. 11:142-52.

Prescott, R. 1965. Infant cry sound: developmental features. J. Acoust. Soc. Amer. 57:1186-191.

Rees, N. 1972. The role of babbling in the child's acquisition of language. Br. J. Dis. Comm. 7:17-23.

Ringel, R.L. and Kluppel, D.D. 1964. Neonatal crying: a normative study Folia Phoniat. 16:1-9.

Ringwall, E.A., Reese, H.W. and Markel, N.N. 1965. A distinctive feature analysis of prelinguistic infant vocalizations. In The Development of Language Functions, ed. K F. Reejil. Ann Arbor: Center for Human Growth and Development pp: 69-78.

Rūke-Dravain, V. 1976. "Mama" and "papa" in child language. J. Child Lang. 3:157-66.

Sedláčková, E. 1964. Acoustic analysis of the voice of the newborn. Folia Phoniat. 16:44-58.

Sheppard, W.C. and Lane, H.L. 1968. Development of the prosodic features of infant vocalizing. J Speech Hear. Res. 11:94-108.

Sherman, M. 1927. Differentiation of emotional responses in infants: I. Judgments of emotional responses from motion picture views and from actual observations. J. Comp. Psych. 7:265-84.

Sherman, M. 1927. The differentiation of emotional responses in infants: II. The ability of observers judge the emotional characteristics of the crying of infants and of the voice of an adult J. Comp. Psych. 7:335-51.

Stark, R.E., Heinz, J.M. and Wright-Wilson, C. 1976. Vocal utterances of young infants J. Acoust. Soc. Amer. 60:S43(A).

Stark, R.E., Rose, S.N. and McLagen, M. 1975. Features of infant sounds the first eight weeks of life. J. Child Lang. 2:205-21.

Tenold, J.L., Crowell, D.H. Jones, R.H., Daniel, T.H., McPherson, D.F. and Popper, A.N. 1974. Cepstral and stationarity analysis of full term and premature infant cries. J. Acoust. Soc. Amer. 56:975-80.

Trehub, S. and Robinovitch, M. 1972. Auditory-linguistic sensitivity in early infancy. Devel. Psych. 6:74-77.

Trehub, S. 1973. Infants' sensitivity to vocal and contrasts. Devel. Psych. 6:74-77.

Truby, H.M. and Lind, J. 1965. Cry sounds of the newborn infant. Acta. Paediat. Scand. Suppl. 163:1-59.

Van Oordt, H.W.A. and Drost, H.A. 1963. Development of the frequency range in children. Folia Phoniat. 15:289-294.

Wasz-Höckert, O., Lind, J., Vuorenkoski, V., Partanen, T. and Valanne, E. 1968. The infant cry. Clin. Devel. Med. 29.

Wasz-Höckert, O., Partanen, T., Vuorenkoski, V., Michelsson, K. and Valanne, E. 1964. The identification of some specific meanings in infant vocalization. Experentia 20:154.

Wasz-Höckert, O., Partanen, T., Vuorenkoski, V., Valanne, E. and Michelsson, K. 1964. Effect of training on ability to identify preverbal vocalizations. Devel. Med. Child Neurol. 6:393-96.

Wasz-Höckert, O., Valanne, E., Vuorenkoski, V., Michelsson, K. and Sovijärvi, A. 1963. Analysis of some types of vocalization in the newborn and in early infancy. Ann. Paediat. Fenn. 9:1-10.

Weir, R. 1962. Language in the Crib. The Hague: Mouton.

Weir, R. 1966. Some questions on the child's learning of phonology. In The Genesis of Language, eds. I. Smith and G. Miller, Cambridge: MIT Press. pp: 153-68.

Winitz, H. 1960. Spectrographic investigation of infant vowels. J. Genet. Psych. 96:171-81.

Winitz, H. and Irwin, O.C. 1958. Infant speech: consistency with age J. Speech Hear. Res. 1:250-56.

Wolff, P. 1969. The natural history of crying and other vocalizations in early infancy. In Determinants of Infant Behavior IV, ed., B.W. Foss. London: Methuen and Co. pp. 81-111.

Zeskind, S. and Stein, K. 1975. Acoustic analysis of the cry response. Paper presented at the Meeting of the Southeastern Psychological Association, Atlanta.

CHAPTER 3

Pre-Speech Respiratory Behavior
During the First Year of Life

Aimee Langlois, Ronald J. Baken, and Carol N. Wilder

INTRODUCTION

The prime function of the respiratory system is to provide an unfailing source of the oxygen required by the body's metabolic processes and to ensure efficient disposal of one of the major waste products, carbon dioxide. To achieve this, land-dwelling animals have evolved gas-exchange interface structures-- the alveoli of the lungs. These, however, are internal and thus removed from effective contact with the atmosphere. This situation, in turn, has necessitated the development of mechanisms for supplying the pulmonary alveoli with a constantly renewed supply of fresh air. These mechanisms are the function of the ventilatory apparatus, the complex system that performs the visible actions of breathing.

Ventilation requires that the pressure within the lungs be periodically alternated from less than to greater than atmospheric. If the airway remains open, air will flow along the resulting pressure gradient, into and out of the lungs. The pressure changes are produced by modification of the volume of the thorax, a function performed by the action of the muscles of respiration, which change the position of the chest wall.

The speech signal is fashioned from a stream of pressurized air. For adequate speech production, the air supply must meet several criteria. First, it must be of sufficient capacity so that, when necesary, relatively long utterances may be produced without interruption. When recharging of the reservoir is required, it must be accomplished quickly in order that the unavoidable interruption of speech output be as short as possible. Further, the air supply must be appropriately pressurized, because a number of the acoustical characteristics of speech are sensitive to the magnitude of the air pressure (van den Berg 1957; Ladefoged and McKinney 1963; Isshiki 1964). Lastly, the air supply must be well regulated; that is, its pressure must be stable and essentially free of unwanted variations which would entail erratic changes in the speech signal.

Therefore, the ventilatory system is the servant of two masters: body metabolic requirements and speech production. Action that is sufficient to satisfy the former is inadequate to the demands of the latter, while the requirements of speech might well result in modifications that compromise tissue oxygenation (Otis and Clark 1968; Bunn and Mead 1971). Clearly, the metabolic needs of the body must always be satisfied, irrespective of any other needs. Speech thus requires that the individual develop acceptable strategies whereby both masters are served; speech breathing is the product of crucial respiratory compromises.

Mastery of the special control of the ventilatory system that permits the individual to power speech while avoiding significant derangement of tissue oxygenation is a critical prerequisite of speech development, yet it has received only scant attention by researchers. In the pages that follow, a summary is provided of what little seems to be understood about the infant's development of respiratory control for speech. This information indicates the significance of some of these insights for our understanding of language development and the speech skills of adults.

REVIEW OF RESPIRATORY DYNAMICS IN THE ADULT

Vegetative Breathing

Breathing for the purposes of life support (called vegetative breathing) is different in a number of ways from speech breathing. Given that the normal infant demonstrates adequate vegetative breathing ability from birth, a description of the salient differences that distinguish these types of breathing in the adult provides a short catalog of the skills that the infant must acquire.

Quiet vegetative breathing is accomplished by doing muscular work to elevate the ribs and flatten the diaphragmatic dome. Both of these actions enlarge the thoracic space and thereby cause the pressure in the lungs to drop below that of the surrounding atmosphere. Ambient air is then pushed into the lungs by the relatively higher atmospheric pressure. Expelling the air again is easy; it requires only that the muscles of the ventilatory system relax (Comroe 1965, p. 97). When they do, the relatively elastic chest wall, deformed to an expanded inspiratory posture, will collapse down to its smaller, resting size as a result of its own elasticity, gravitational forces, and the like. As it does, so the size of the thoracic cavity diminishes, and the pressure of the gas in the lungs rises to a level greater than atmospheric, forcing the air back out. Relevant characteristics of vegetative breathing are shown in Figure 1, which represents data as they might be gathered from a typical subject.

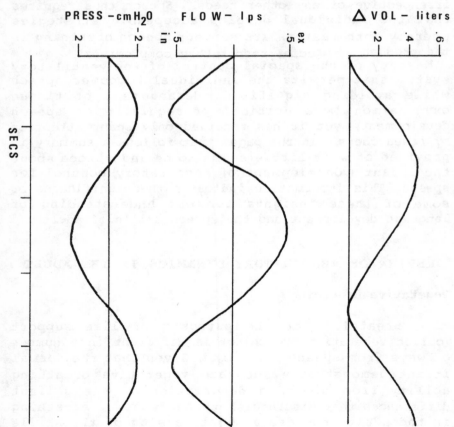

Figure 1. Schematic lung volume change, air flow, and pulmonary pressure as they might be observed during vegetative breathing in a normal adult.

Note that the pressures required to move the air in vegetative breathing are quite small, on the order of 2 cm H_2O (Comroe 1965, p. 102), and the quantity of air moved on each breath -- known as the tidal volume -- is also modest, about 450 ml. Reference to the time scale at the bottom of the figure shows that this person was breathing at a rate of about 18 breaths per minute (BPM), which is a typical value (Bunn and Mead 1971). Multiplying the ventilatory rate by the mean tidal volume tells us how much air is breathed per minute. For this subject, the "minute volume" is about 8.1 liters per minute.

The ventilatory needs of the resting body are met by breathing on the order of 500 ml of air about 15 to 18 times per minute. Doing so requires that pressures in the lung be varied from approximately +2 to about -2 cm H_2O, which can be achieved by using inspiratory muscles to enlarge the thorax and then relaxing those muscles to permit the chest wall to be returned to its original posture by passive recoil forces.

How well would this type of ventilation serve the needs of speech? Some idea can be gained by estimating how well one could sustain a vowel on a vegetative tidal breath. Average air consumption during production of /a/ has been found to lie in the range of about 90 to 110 ml/sec at the comfortable pitch and loudness level (Yanagihara and von Leden 1967; Hirano, Koike, and von Leden 1968; Koike and Hirano 1968). At that rate, phonation could only be carried on for about five seconds -- and many phonemes require higher flows -- meaning that the duration of a normal speech utterance would be even shorter, if only the vegetative tidal volume were available. It is clear that vegetative breathing does not fill the air reservoir enough for any but brief utterances.

The utility of vegetative breathing is limited even further by other considerations. The acoustic energy of speech is derived from the air pressure built up in the lungs. Adequate pressure is required to move the vocal folds for production of voice, to generate the small "explosions" characteristic of plosives, and to produce the air turbulence which provides for the characteristic "hissing" sound of the fricatives. The amount of air pressure varies, depending on the speech sound being produced. Normal children of age 10, for instance, typically use pressures as high as 8-9 cm H_2O for /t/ or as low as about 5 mm H_2O for /f/ (Subtelney, Worth, and Sakuda 1966; Arkebauer, Hixon, and Hardy

1967). Vegetative breathing does not involve positive pressures nearly high enough.

The inadequacy of vegetative breathing for speech does not end there. Reference to Figure 1 shows timing characteristics that are wholly unacceptable for communicative purposes. The respiratory rate for the few cycles shown is about 18 BPM. This implies that any spoken message would be interrupted 18 times per minute while inspiratory recharging of the air supply occurred. Even if one could arrange the linguistic structure of the intended message so that this rate of interruption could be tolerated, the timing *pattern* would be unacceptable. Note that, on the average, an inspiration in Figure 1 required 1.3 seconds. This would represent the average length of an inspiratory interruption in the flow of speech produced using this respiratory pattern. It is a long time in the comparison to the mean expiratory duration of about a second, which is the average time available for a string of speech events. The ratio of inspiratory time to the total duration of a respiratory cycle is known as I-fraction. For present purposes, the I-fraction represents the proportion of time not usable for speech because of inspiration In the sample shown, the I-fraction is about 0.4, which means that, even if all the other problems of vegetative breathing could be solved, this pattern could be used for speech no more than 60% of the total time available for talking.

Vegetative breathing does not store enough air during the inspiratory phase to permit any but short utterances, does not generate enough pressure to power a strong speech signal, and has too many interruptions of too great duration.

Speech Breathing

Clearly, another pattern of breathing is required to support speech. If the infant is to talk, he will have to master the necessary technique. Typical "speech breathing" is shown in Figure 2. Many of the differences between this pattern and that of vegetative ventilation are readily apparent, and some others are not so obvious.

The changes in ventilatory behavior during speech are just the ones that would be expected from a consideration of the inadequacies of vegetative breathing. The tidal volume has increased to about 750 ml, providing a larger reserve of air upon which the speaker draws during speech. The respiratory rate is considerably lower-- down to about 14 BPM (Bunn and Mead 1971) from the vegetative rate of 18 BPM. Equally significant is the relative rapidity of inspiration, especially when compared to the prolonged expirations. During vegetative breathing, our typical subject had a mean inspiratory time of 1.3 seconds and a mean expiratory time of 2 seconds. But, during speech, an average inspiratory time of less than 0.5 seconds provides enough air for a speech expiration whose

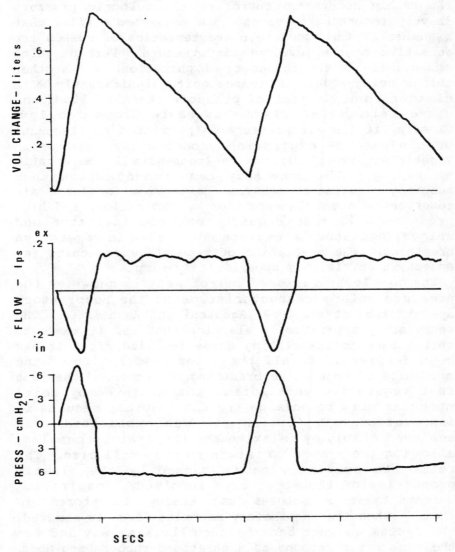

Figure 2. Schematic relationship of lung volume change, air flow, and pulmonary pressure during speech.

duration averages more than 3.5 seconds, giving an I-fraction of about 0.1. Thus, the alteration of ventilatory pattern has permitted the speaker to talk with fewer and much shorter inspiratory interruptions. The I-fraction indicates that the respiratory system is potentially available for speech about 90% of the time.

The air pressure generated in the lungs is also relatively high, about 8 cm H_2O. Note that despite the rapid changes in air flow that occur during speech production, the intrathoracic air pressure remains remarkably constant. Control of the pulmonic pressure is very important to speech. It was noted earlier that a number of the acoustic characteristics of speech are sensitive to the level of air pressure. Perhaps chief among these is the intensity of phonation, which other things being equal, decreases quite significantly with diminution of subglottal pressure (Isshibi 1964) and ceases altogether if the pressure drops too low. Clearly, if the air pressure is permitted to fluctuate or diminish as expiration proceeds (as it does in vegetative breathing), speech loudness will be erratic or fading. The constancy requirement means that adapting ventilatory behavior to provide for large air reserves, minimal interruption of expiration, and high pressure will also require some sophisticated and unique regulatory maneuvers not needed in vegetative breathing. The adaptation of vegetative breathing for speech, then, is only superficially simple.

The complexity arises out of what is known as the pressure-volume characteristics of the respiratory system (Rahn et al. 1964; Agostoni and Rahn 1960). The ventilatory apparatus is elastic; that is, it tends to spring back to its resting shape and size after it has been deformed. Recall the brief description of the mechanics of vegetative breathing. We stressed the fact that vegetative ventilation was achieved by doing muscular work to enlarge the thorax; this results in inspiration. Expiration, it was emphasized, was achieved simply by relaxing the inspiratory muscles, allowing the system to return to its small size. The return to smaller size is caused by the elastic properties of the structures involved. Inspiration deforms these structures and energy is stored in them. When the inspiratory muscular force is removed, the system springs back in much the same way and for the same basic reasons as a stretched rubber band does. The elastic recoil that results in a return to resting size causes a positive pressure to be created in the lungs-- a pressure that is due to passive recoil forces. This is know as the "relaxation pressure" and is demonstrated in Figure 3. Its magnitude is a function of the degree to which the thorax has been previously deformed. Put another way, the relaxation pressure is a function of the lung volume.

The rest position of the thorax is the position in which the various forces that act on the chest wall are in equilibrium and, hence, the gas pressure in the lungs is equal to the pressure of the atmosphere. Figure 3 shows that, in this position, the lungs contain roughly 40% of their total capacity. This volume is referred to as the "functional residual capacity" (FRC). It is from the FRC that we begin inspiration in quiet vegetative breathing, and it is to this volume that the elastic recoil forces of vegetative expiration return the system. As shown in Figure 1, quiet vegetative breathing is characterized by small tidal volume; Figure 3 demonstrates why the observed expiratory pressure is so small in vegetative breathing. Many, if not most, of our speech utterances require a reservoir that is about equivalent to a normal tidal inspiration in size (Hoshiko 1965), and a

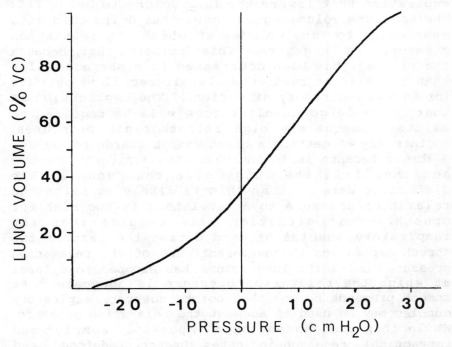

Figure 3.   Relationship of relaxation pressure to lung volume.   (From date of Rahn et al. 1946)

study recently completed (Froscher 1978) showed that normal males had a very strong tendency to use a mean tidal volume no greater than 13% of vital capacity on a set of reading tasks. The pressure-volume data show that at these volume levels the relaxation pressure is still somewhat lower than that required for speech. This means that speech expiration will require active contraction of the expiratory muscles to augment the relaxation pressure. The action of these muscles must be very carefully controlled to insure that the pulmonary pressure remains constant. This does not imply that a constant level of expiratory muscle activity is required, because as the lung volume falls during the utterance, the relaxation pressure also falls; therefore, the action of the expiratory muscles needs to be increased in a very precise way. It is this unseen activity that makes even ordinary speech breathing so complex.

If a long utterance is to be produced on a single expiration, the difficulties to be overcome increase very significantly. There are two ways to generate the requisite enlarged reservoir of air. One is to take a normally deep breath and then to speak on a large expiration that lowers the lung volume to below FRC. The pressure volume curve shows that doing this will mean going to lung volumes at which the relaxation pressure is negative. This indicates that, because the rib cage has been compressed to a shape smaller than its size at rest, the elastic recoil is *outward* (or in an inspiratory direction). The implication is that quite large muscle forces will be required to maintain adequately high intrathoracic pressures. Another way of getting a great enough charge of air for a long utterance is to increase the inspiratory volume and thus fill the lungs more than usual. The difficulty here is that this is likely to raise the relaxation pressure to a level that is too high for speech. This situation will require that the inspiratory muscles be used during the part of the speech expiration to counteract part of the relaxation pressure until the lung volume has dropped to a level at which the relaxation pressure is adequate. As speech proceeds beyond that point, however, expiratory muscles may be used to augment the relaxation pressure. While this process may seem impossibly complex and impractical, research indicates (Draper, Ladefoged, and Whitteridge 1959) that it is, indeed, routinely used by normal speakers.

What skills, then, must the infant develop in order to speak? First, it is necessary to negotiate inspiration of sufficient size to insure an adequate supply of air for the utterance intended, executed quickly enough to obtrude minimally into the flow of speech. Second, the infant must develop the ability to augment or diminish the relaxation pressure generated by the chest wall's elastic rebound following that inspiration and to constantly adjust the activity of the respiratory muscles, so as to maintain a relatively high intrathoracic pressure that remains constant throughout the duration of the utterance. Our own research and the work of several others has shed some light on the emergence of these skills.

DEVELOPMENTAL ASPECTS OF INFANT RESPIRATION DURING THE FIRST YEAR OF LIFE

Measurement Problems

Before discussing the development of respiratory patterns during the first year of life, we should briefly consider some of the problems inherent in measuring respiratory behavior, whether in the infant or the adult. Although current instrumentation permits very precise tracking of respiratory phenomena, much of it impinges upon the respiratory system to an extent that it might alter the activity under investigation. Further, many of the techniques used to assess air-volume, pressure, and flow are uncomfortable or invasive. These observational problems are compounded when infant respiration is to be studied. The phenomena to be observed may be of a much smaller magnitude than in the adult and typical respiratory patterns may be even more susceptible to alteration by external factors. For example, many measurement techniques described in studies of infant respiration involve such things as tightly-fitting face masks or neck seals, breathing into systems offering resistance to air flow, wrappings which severely restrict the infants' movements and/or externally-imposed atypical body postures (Deming and Washburn 1935; Long and Hull 1961; Truby et al. 1965). Some of these can be expected to result in struggle reactions, which may well involve the respiratory mechanism. Because the infant respiratory system is so highly compliant, respiration may be affected by methods offering relatively small amounts of external resistance, either to movement or to air flow. In addition, it is almost impossible to obtain informed parental consent for measurement techniques which might be considered in any way uncomfortable or invasive for the infant. (Even if parental consent for such techniques could be obtained, the resultant observations would almost certainly be limited to respiration during crying!) Therefore, interpretatons of all data on infant respiration, including those presented in this chapter, should be conditioned by an acknowledgment of the many problems and limitations inherent in assessing respiratory activity in the infant.

Fortunately, there are two types of instrumentation which avoid some of the above mentioned problems while still allowing for very precise tracking of respiratory movements: magnetometry, which measures changes in the antero-posterior diameter of the rib cage and abdominal walls, and impedance pneumography, which measures circumferential changes in these same structures. All of the respiratory information reported in this chapter for non-crying vocalizations (as well as most of the information for vegetative breathing and crying) was obtained via impedance pneumography. This method offers at least two major advantages for studying infant respiration: a) transducers (mercury-filled strain gauges) offer minimal mechanical loading of the chest wall and/or external resistance to respiratory activity, and b) they are completely noninvasive and may be worn without discomfort for long periods of time, in a variety of postures and activities. Within a very few moments after they have been fastened around the rib cage and abdomen, the infants appear to be unaware of the presence of the transducers.

In the adult, both impedance pneumography and magnetometry can be used to derive reliable estimates of lung volume without the necessity for a face mask or plethysmograph (Baken 1977; Hixon et al. 1976). Recent investigations using these techniques have led to a reconsideration of many aspects of adult speech breathing and have greatly expanded our knowledge about the relative contributions of the various components of the respiratory system to the generation and maintenance of air pressures for speech (Baken et al. 1978; Hixon, Mead, and Goldman 1976). These studies have also led to an appreciation of the fact that the influence of rib cage and abdominal wall movements upon speech respiration cannot be fully understood without reference to the lung volume prevailing at the time of movement. Unfortunately, the adult model for pneumographic lung volume estimation is not readily applicable to infants. Therefore, only the temporal parameters of infant respiration have been quantified by impedance pneumography. Other aspects of the respiratory pattern can be described qualitatively, but, in the absence of lung volume information, the relationships between respiratory movements and the generation/maintenance of air pressure for phonation cannot be specified with any degree of precision.

Vegetative Breathing

At the moment of his birth cry, the infant begins the automatic process of life-sustaining respiration. During the first year of life he gradually gains control over this automatic process and by doing so slowly acquires the ability to use his respiratory mechanism more effectively for both quiet and vocalized activities.

Time Factors

Respiratory rates (the speed with which one breathes) are extremely variable in infants. Not only do breathing rates evidence changing patterns with age, but at any given age an infant's breathing rate varies according to such conditions as health, activity level, and vocalizations. In normal infants who are awake, respiratory rates during quiet breathing show a definite decrease with increasing age (Peiper 1963). In other words a newborn infant breathes faster than a six month old who in turn still breathes faster than a year old child. The latest data on neonatal and infant (0 to 12 months) respiratory rates further support this statement (Langlois, Wilder, and Baken 1975). The following tabulation is abstracted from these data:

Age Levels (Months)	Breaths Per Minute (Rate)	Age Levels (Months)	Breaths Per Minute (Rate)
1	87	7	62
2	84	8	58
3	69	9	43
4	82	10	48
5	74	11	37
6	61	12	42
		13	43

Movement Patterns

In spite of the changes observed in breathing rates during quiet respiration in infants, most of the activity is observed in the abdominal area. This is caused by action of the diaphragm, which is the only muscle capable of effecting adequate lung inflation in very young infants. In early infancy the arrangement of the ribs is relatively perpendicular to the spine, making thoracic respiration practically impossible. The diaphragm in its downward motion pushes the abdominal content which causes the abdominal walls to expand. Breathing in infancy is therefore said to be of the diaphragmatic or abdominal type since the musculature of the ribs does not contribute to lung inflation.

After the sixth month of life, as the child develops control of an upright position (sitting and later pulling to standing), the anatomical relationship of the ribs to the spine begins to shift. Following the sixth month and the attainment of the erect posture, gravity exerts a downward pull on the ribs and the angle of the ribs in relation to the vertebral column becomes less than 90°. The chest expands downward and outward, and the consequent growth in the thoracic cavity facilitates the contribution of the rib musculature for respiration. From that point on, the child shows increasing activity of the rib cage during quiet breathing (Halverson 1941). Although the amount of abdominal activity remains greater through at least the end of the first year, the increased participation of the rib cage facilitates deeper breathing and the consequent decrease in rate described above.

Whether abdominal or thoracic, the movements during quiet breathing in infants are quite regular. Pneumographic tracings of these movements show that the respiratory cycle (the length of time it takes to draw a breath in and let it out) resembles a sine wave with expiration slightly longer than inspiration. Figure 4 shows pneumographic tracings of normal quiet respiratory activity in infants.

Other Aspects

Our knowledge of the development of respiratory parameters related to air volume and air flow rate in infants is minimal. The amount of air taken in the lungs during the inspiratory phase of a normal respiratory cycle (tidal volume) varies from 20 to 25 ml in normal fullterm neonates (Halverson 1941; Bosma

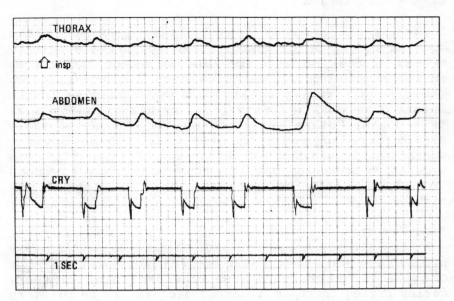

Figure 4. Pneumogram of a relatively simple respiratory pattern during crying.

1965; Frantz and Stark 1977). Although tidal volumes change considerably from infancy to adulthood, the proportion of lung volumes in the infant is about the same as in the adult. Tidal volumes of 20 to 25 ml comprise 10% of an infant's lung capacity, while the functional residual capacity of 75 ml is about 40% percent of the total (Avery and Normand 1965).

It is still not known how and when tidal volume changes as the infant gets older. However, it is logical to assume that the increased activity of the chest wall, which facilitates deeper breathing, results in higher tidal volumes in the growing infant. In addition, changes in children's size and weight which accompany growth may equally well account for increases in lung volumes.

The rate at which the air flows in and out of the lungs during a breath (air flow rate) is somewhat higher when the infant inhales than when he exhales. It appears that air flow rates reflect respiratory movement; their spirographic tracings in infants also "resemble a sine curve with a somewhat extended expiratory phase" (Bosma 1965). It can be hypothesized that the developmental changes in respiratory rate and depth are necessarily associated with modifications in air flow rate. However, data on air flow rate beyond the neonatal period can not be located.

Crying Respiration

The infant cries to signal his more obvious needs such as hunger or discomfort. At approximately three months of age, mothers are able to detect differences in the babies' cries which express different needs. The crying activity creates dramatic changes in the infant's overall activity level as his organism goes from a state of relative tranquility to one of acute discomfort, physical or otherwise. Some obvious variations in breathing occur as the child modifies his vegetative breathing pattern to accommodate his need for the lengthy vocalizations which signal his distress.

Time Factors

It has already been mentioned that the breathing rate of average normal infants varies according to the child's activity level and vocalizations. Indeed, during crying there is a marked decrease in respiratory rate. The drastic reduction in rate is apparent at all age levels during the first twelve months; it also becomes greater as the infant gets older. The following tabulation is abstracted from the works of Wilder and Baken (1974) and Langlois and Baken (1976):

Age Levels (months)	Quiet Breathing (BPM)	Crying (BPM)
1	87	50
2	84	40
3	69	37
4	82	35
5	74	34
6	61	31
7	62	29
8	58	24
9	43	26
10	48	27
11	37	23
12	41	23
13	42	19

It is of interest to note that by the end of his first year the respiratory rate of the crying infant falls within the range reported for adult speech.

The decrease in breaths per minute observed in crying results from the prolonged expiration needed by the infant to vocalize his discomfort. As he gets older, the exhalation phase of his crying cycle becomes longer, while the inhalation phase remains brief and sharp. The quick inspiration and the prolonged expiration of crying result in a ratio of inspiration to total respiratory time; this ratio, known as I-fraction, is relatively stable throughout the first year of life, as it only varies from .19 to .15 from birth to 12 months. This ratio is also comparable to that seen in adult speech, thus suggesting that at a very early age the infant can very well negotiate a short inspiration and a prolonged expiration.

Movement Patterns

The overall activity observed in the infant signaling his discomfort is reflected in added respiratory activity. As early as one month of age the thorax may participate in respiration during crying; different patterns of activity can be seen. In early infancy either the thorax and abdomen participate equally to the respiratory pattern or it is predominantly abdominal. After six months of age, the rib cage movements continue to be consistent but can become as great as and, in some cases greater than, the abdominal movements. The consistent participation of the costal musculature in crying makes deeper breathing possible; therefore, a lowering in rate occurs as reported above.

The movements of the rib cage and abdomen during crying reflect the brief inspiration and the prolonged expiration discussed earlier. Typical pneumographic tracings of this activity are presented in Figures 4, 5, and 6. In most cases (Figure 4), the general configuration of the respiratory movements is characterized by a brief and sharply defined inspiratory phase and a longer expiratory phase, the configuration of which is a simple steep slope. However, several variations can be noted during the expiration phase; these include longer and more complex waveforms which mark apparent subcycles and periods of fixation (Figures 5 and 6).

Another aspect of breathing observed during crying, but not seen in the quiet breathing of infants, concerns "asynchrony"[1] of the breathing movements. Whereas the participation of the rib cage during quiet

---

[1]The term "asynchrony" implies a disorganization and hints that events have become simultaneous but dissociated. Since it is clear that no such disruption occurs, the word "asynchrony" represents a poor descriptor. It is, unfortunately, current in the literature. Hence, we use it here with a firm caveat to the reader.

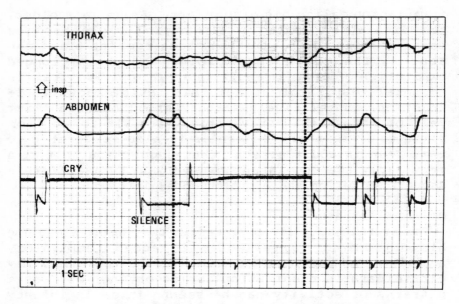

Figure 5.   Pneumogram showing respiratory behavior during several cry
bursts. The area within the dotted lines shows a single
respiratory cycle with subcycles during the expiratory
phase.

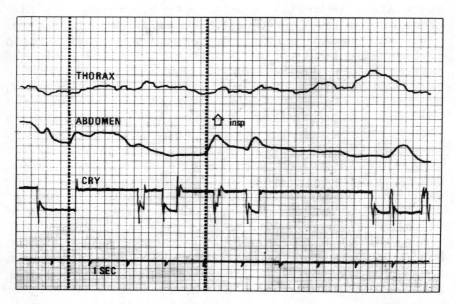

Figure 6.   Pneumogram showing respiratory behavior during several cry
bursts.   The cry signal produced during the single
respiratory cycle, marked off by dotted lines, contains
two silent intervals.

respiration is, for the most part, negligible, its movements are usually in synchrony with the abdomen's during this activity. That is, the chest and abdominal walls expand together for inspiration and similarly contract for expiration. This is modified, however, when the infant is crying, as the abdominal contraction leads the expiratory phase in the majority of respiratory cycles at any age level. This pattern, which is reminiscent of the asynchrony observed in adult speech, may reflect the infant's increasing ability to control the elastic recoil forces of expiration. This improved organization of thoracic activity appears to proceed in lock-step fashion with advances in the infant's developmental level from simple prone lying through aid-sitting posture, independent sitting, standing, and walking.

Other Aspects

There are no figures available on the amount of air inhaled during crying, but expiratory volumes of 56 to 110 ml have been reported for normal infants during a "hard cry" within 30 minutes of birth (Avery and Normand 1965). The amount of air exhaled during such a cry is believed to be the best available estimate of the infant's vital capacity. In addition, observations of crying infants have led to various reports that respiration during crying is characterized by a marked increase in the depth of inspiration and in the minute volume of inspired air (Deming and Washburn 1935; Halverson 1941). It can be assumed that the loudness of the cry and the need for a prolonged expiratory phase would be associated with changes in air volume in a similar fashion to the increase in the lung volume reported to occur in adult speech. It can be further hypothesized that the increase in duration of both the respiratory cycle and its inspiratory phase with age would also be associated with an increase in the amount of air intake preceding a cry.

Air Flow Rate

The changes in respiratory duration and depth which occur during crying are associated with changes in air flow rate. Figures reported for neonatal crying indicate a slow expiratory flow rate. Although data are not available for older infants, it is possible that flow rates remain lower during crying. This is inferred from the vocalizations of the infants that create a certain amount of glottal resistance. As opposed to adult speech, where the resistance to the air flow is offered both by the larynx and the articulators as they produce the sounds of speech, the decrease in flow rate suspected to occur in infant cry is mostly the result of extreme laryngeal constriction, since the lips and tongue do not participate actively to modify the airstream in crying.

In summary, a review of respiratory activity accompanying quiet vegetative breathing and crying behavior in infants reveals the following: a) there are developmental changes in the quiet vegetative respiration of infants through the first year of life, b) there are changes of infant vegetative patterns during crying, and c) for some respiratory parameters the modifications which occur during crying are quite different from the modifications which occur during adult speech.

Non-crying Vocalization

During the first year of life, the infant engages in a number of behaviors resulting in voicing. Some of these occur in association with vegetative functions (grunting, hiccuping, coughing) while others are related to emotional states (crying, laughing, fretting, etc.). However, the infant also engages in a third type of vocalization which is apparently produced volitionally. Initially, this type of vocal behavior consists primarily of relatively undifferentiated vowel and glide-type sounds. During the first year of life, these gradually evolve into a rather large repertoire of vocal tract adjustments resulting in a considerable range of more differentiated vowel and consonant-type sounds. There is disagreement in the literature about the precise nature of this developmental process, and consequently there are differences regarding descriptive terminology (Winitz 1969, p. 5-6). In this chapter, non-crying vocalization (NCV) will be used to refer to all such volitionally-produced, non-reflexive, prelinguistic utterances.

The development of the respiratory activity underlying NCV has received very little attention. However, the limited data available suggest that, during the first year of life, the respiratory activity supporting these utterances may occupy a middle ground between vegetative breathing and crying breathing. That is, while some modifications of vegetative breathing are apparent, they are different from and, in most cases, somewhat less extreme than those observed during crying.

Time Factors

The NCV's produced by the infants observed by the authors have typically been brief and sporadic, rarely occurring on more than a very few *consecutive* respiratory cycles. Therefore, a discussion of the respiratory *rate* for NCV's is not appropriate. However, it is possible to compare the respiration underlying NCV with vegetative breathing and crying on the basis of the duration of the inspiratory-expiratory cycle.

The mean duration of respiratory cycles during the production of NCV's generally falls between vegetative breathing and crying (Figure 7). Whereas there are rather clear developmental trends in respiratory cycle duration for the latter two activities, this is not the case for NCV. This is particularly evident in the

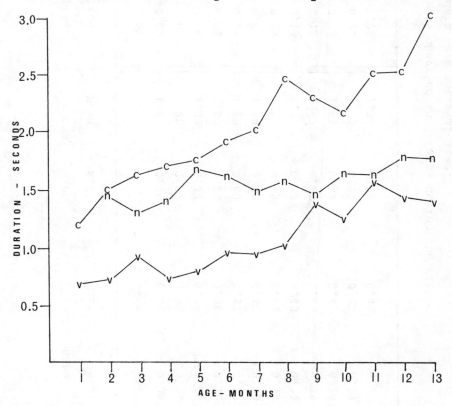

Figure 7. Mean duration of respiratory cycle during vegetative breathing (v), crying (c), and non-crying vocalization (N).

Table 1. Durational characteristics of the respiratory cycle and of the inspiratory phase during the non-crying vocalization.

| Age (mos) | CRY | | | | NON-CRYING VOCALIZATION | | | |
| | Total cycle Duration | | Insp. phase | | Total cycle Duration | | Insp. phase | |
	Mean	s.d.	Mean	s.d.	Mean	s.d.	Mean	s.d.
1	1.20	0.13	0.23	0.01	*	*	*	*
2	1.50	0.35	0.28	0.05	1.45	0.70	0.26	0.08
3	1.62	0.41	0.26	0.06	1.29	0.32	0.35	0.04
4	1.70	0.50	0.27	0.04	1.38	0.44	0.30	0.06
5	1.74	0.83	0.28	0.05	1.67	0.20	0.36	0.10
6	1.91	0.40	0.28	0.05	1.60	0.60	0.47	0.12
7	2.01	0.57	0.28	0.05	1.48	0.70	0.41	0.18
8	2.46	1.04	0.30	0.08	1.55	0.59	0.43	0.18
9	2.29	1.25	0.35	0.13	1.45	0.72	0.43	0.21
10	2.15	0.91	0.28	0.12	1.62	0.69	0.45	0.25
11	2.50	1.04	0.28	0.08	1.61	0.62	0.41	0.18
12	2.51	1.55	0.28	0.12	1.75	0.79	0.47	0.27
13	3.01	1.51	0.39	0.21	1.74	0.72	0.49	0.22

*Very few non-crying vocalizations were observed in infants during the first month of life and therefore these data were not evaluated.

76

comparison between crying and NCV. In crying, the mean duration of a respiratory cycle undergoes a 250% increase over the first year of life, from 1.20 to 3.0 seconds. In NCV, however, the mean duration fluctuates over a range of only 1.45 to 1.75 seconds (Table 1). It is also noteworthy that the standard deviation of the total cry breath duration increases at a faster rate than the mean, suggesting that as the infant matures, a greater variety of breath-group durations is used during crying. There is no comparable indication of increased variability for NCV.

The I-fraction for NCV also occupies a middle ground between crying and vegetative breathing (Figure 8). Further, during crying the mean duration of inspiration does not increase in proportion to the increase in the length of the total respiratory cycle. Clearly then, as the infant matures, he becomes increasingly adept at the essential skills of maximizing the proportion of the total cycle available for phonation, *at least during crying.* This particular skill, however, is not manifested as a typical respiratory adaptation in NCV.

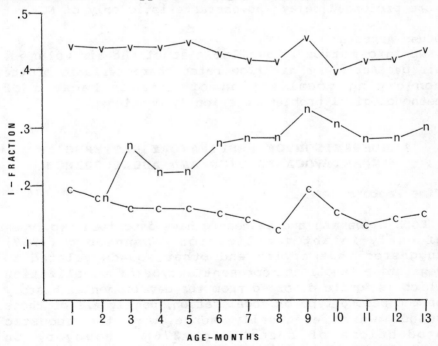

Figure 8. Mean I-fraction for respiration during vegetative breathing (v), crying (c), and non-crying vocalization (n).

Movement Patterns

It is relatively simple to differentiate between the gently sloping wave-form characteristic of vegetative breathing and the wave-form typical of crying with its rapid, sharply defined inspiratory phase and prolonged expiratory phase. The identification of NCV purely on the basis of respiratory wave-form is more difficult. At times, the movement pattern resembles vegetative breathing while at others it resembles crying. As was true for crying, there is increasing evidence of rib cage participation in respiratory movements. There is, however, one distinguishing characteristic of NCV respiratory movements which occurs in approximately half of these prelinguistic utterances: an extended delay between the onset of expiratory movement in the abdomen and the onset of expiratory movement in the rib cage. As mentioned earlier, the asynchrony between the initiation of abdominal and rib cage expiratory movements also occur during crying. However, the average duration of the delay in crying was only about .20 sec, whereas in NCV it was about .45 sec. This more prolonged delay was characteristic only of NCV.

Other Aspects

No information is available about the air volumes, air pressures, or air flow rates characteristic of the non-crying vocalization of infants because of methodological problems previously mentioned.

A COMPARISON OF RESPIRATORY PATTERNS IN INFANT VOCALIZATION AND ADULT SPEECH

Time Factors

Both Lieberman and Lenneberg have described two types of early infant vocalization. Lenneberg (1967) suggested that crying and other sounds related to vegetative functions represent a type of vocalization which is "quite divorced from the developmental history of the second type of vocalization, namely all of those sounds which eventually merge into the acoustic productions of speech" (p. 276). However, in describing a similar dichotomy between these two types of vocalization, Lieberman (1967) emphasized a close relationship between crying and adult speech breathing by suggesting that crying reflects an "innate referential breath-group" fundamental to the development of linguistic intonation. He also stressed the communicative nature of the crying act, noting that it is used to induce adults to minister to the infant in order to alleviate needs or distress. In that they do not appear to seek immediate adult attention, non-crying prelinguistic utterances could be said to have a lesser communicative urgency.

In adult speech, what might be called "communicative pressure" seeks to minimize the interruption of the flow of communication, thereby mandating that the time-out for inspiration be kept as short as possible. Given Lieberman's description of the communicative nature of crying, it is not difficult to imagine that some similar communicative exigency encourages the infant to shorten inspiration in order to lengthen the vocalization "duty cycle." And, indeed, the temporal characteristics of respiration during crying achieved over the first year of life was very similar to those reported for adult speech. This suggests that the infant respiratory system is capable of meeting those criteria for adult speech breathing which involve prolonging utterance and minimizing interruption. Only a weak approximation of these temporal characteristics may be manifested during NCV. This may be due, in part, to the lack of communicative pressure associated with these utterances. However, it may also be due to the fact that the NCV's produced by the normal infants observed by the authors were very short when defined in terms of syllables *per breath*, never exceeding a mean of 1.8 syllables per utterance. While these brief utterances were not superimposed on a simple tidal-breathing pattern, they also did not require the more profound temporal alterations typical of adult speech breathing. From either point of view then, the infants had little need to expend the extra energy required to produce very rapid inspiration and prolonged expiration.

Movement Patterns

In the absence of lung volume information, one can only speculate about the significance of the respiratory patterns observed in the infants and their possible relationship to adult speech breathing patterns. One possible hypothesis is that the abdomen/rib cage asynchrony, observed in both crying and NCV, is related to those volume shifts in adult speech breathing which seek to mechanically "tune" the respiratory system in order to provide a better fulcrum against which expiratory forces can work (Hixon, Mead, and Goldman 1976; Baken 1977). In NCV, this pattern of temporal asynchrony is exaggerated by the rather prolonged maintenance of the rib cage in an inspiratory posture, well after the onset of voicing. It might be hypothesized that this prolonged inspiratory posture reflects the infant's attempt to counteract a relaxation pressure which is too high. Insofar as either of these hypotheses might be correct, it would suggest that the infant is developing those aspects of the speech breathing pattern which are concerned with the generation and control of air pressure. However, it must be emphasized that, at this time, no conclusion can be drawn about this interesting aspect of the infant respiratory pattern.

Some Additional Development Considerations

If length of utterance is defined in terms of objective measures of respiratory activity, none of the infants observed by the authors can be said to have characteristically engaged in long strings of multi-syllabic babbling, even during the second six months of life. One possibility, perhaps remote, is that in spite of stringent selection and monitoring for normal development, the brevity of utterance was an idiosyncratic characteristic of the infants observed. Another possibility is that the NCV'S emitted during experimental sessions were atypical of the infant's usual behavior. However, the attending adult was always questioned about this, and almost always indicated that the vocalizations obtained were typical of the infant's production at that age. A more likely possibility is that previous descriptions of the "duration" of a babbling utterance have been concerned primarily with the acoustic product, with relatively casual, subjective assessment of respiratory boundaries.

It has been commonly accepted that "long" strings of babbling are a prominent developmental feature of prelinguistic utterances. However, in the absence of linguistic markers, how are the boundaries of an utterance to be determined? Many descriptions of babbling make no attempt to define what constitutes a *single* utterance. Most often, when boundaries are specified some sort of respiratory marker is used. For example, Van Riper described babbling as the "chaining and linking of sounds on one exhalation" (1978, p. 93), while the classic series of studies by Irwin and associates (reviewed in Winitz 1969) partitioned prelinguistic utterances in terms of "breath units." Unfortunately, respiratory markers in prelinguistic vocalizations have heretofore been determined by the observer's *subjective* evaluation of respiratory activity. However, the accuracy of subjective observations of infant respiratory activity is open to serious question. In the authors' experience, respiratory activity which was not otherwise visible or audible to an observer was readily apparent on instrumental monitors. If the length of a non-crying utterance had been determined by subjectively defined respiratory markers, many of these utterances would have been thought to be comprised of longer "strings" of babbling than they were when described in terms of objective respiratory measures.

This emphasizes the need to consider the motor activity underlying the acoustic product when studying infant vocalization. Truby et al. asserted that crying should be considered a "compound phenomenon--act plus sound," with the act consisting of "motor activity singularly involving the respiratory tract" (1965, p. 63). This concept was further confirmed in a study of infant cry, wherein it was demonstrated that both respiratory activity *and* the acoustic signal had to be taken into account in order to avoid erroneous assumptions about the temporal aspects of the cry (Wilder 1972) The concept of vocalization as "act plus sound" is equally relevant to non-crying vocalization and suggests that, in order to properly interpret the acoustic product, the underlying motor activity must be evaluated. While respiratory movements are only one component of this complex motor activity, at present they may represent the only component of that activity which is readily accessible to objective measurement in the infant. A better understanding of the developmental sequence of prelinguistic utterances may result if objective measures of respiratory events are used to define the boundaries of an utterance.

SUMMARY

Several characteristics of respiratory behavior show a variety of changes, depending on whether one is breathing for the purpose of life support or for speech purposes.

These modifications of respiratory activity which accompany a change from quiet breathing to speech breathing include a reduction in breaths per minute, an increase in tidal volume and air pressure generated in the lungs, and sophisticated muscular control of the pulmonic pressure.

Although the normal infant demonstrates adequate breathing for life support purposes from birth, his acquisition of respiratory control for speech is a process which is first demonstrated in his crying behavior. More specifically, during his first year, a child presents several changes in his respiratory behavior which are related to his increasing age. For vegetative breathing only, the basic respiratory rate changes. During crying not only does the respiratory rate consistently decreases but the rib cage steadily contributes to the movement. By the end of the first year of life, the respiratory rate, the length and degree of expiratory duration, and the muscular activity of both the rib cage and abdomen observed during crying closely approximate the reported characteristics of adult speech.

During non-crying vocalization, neither rate, expiratory duration, nor thoracic/abdominal activity ever approximate adult values. Yet, crying behavior clearly demonstrated the infants' ability to achieve a more "adult" respiratory performance. In short, a "respiratory matrix" for speech is probably established, but not manifested, at this age due to the brevity of the child's utterances It is hypothesized that the child's increased linguistic sophistication will call forth the established physiological potential for genuine speech.

REFERENCES

Agostoni, E. and Rahn, H. 1960. Abdominal and thoracic prssure at different lung volumes. J. Appl. Physiol. 15:1087-92

Arkebauer, H.S., Hixon, T.J., and Hardy, J.C. 1967. Peak intraoral air pressures during speech. J. Speech Hear. Res. 10:196-208.

Avery, M. and Normand, C. 1965. Repiratory physiology in the newborn infant. Anesthesiology 26:510-21.

Baken, R.J. 1977. Estimation of lung volume change from torso hemicircumferences. J. Speech Hear. Res. 20:808-12.

Baken, R.J., Cavallo, S.A., and Weissman, K.L. 1978. Chest wall preparation for phonation ASHA 20:759.

Bosma, J. 1965. Cry motions of the newborn infant. Acta Paediatr. Scand. Suppl. 163.

Bunn, J.C. and Mead, J. 1971. Control of ventilation during speech. J. Appl. Physiol. 31:870-72.

Comroe, J. 1965. Respiratory Physiology (2nd ed.) Chicago: Year Book Medical Publisher.

Deming, J. and Washburn, A. 1935. Respiration in infancy. American Journal of Diseases in Children 49:108-24.

Draper, M.H., Ladefoged, P., and Whitteridge, D. 1959. Respiratory muscles in speech. J. Speech Hear. Res. 2:16-27.

Frantz, I.D. and Stark, A. 1977. Effects of lung volume changes in respiratory control in newborn infants. In Breathing in the fetus and newborn. Mead Johnson Symposium on Perinatal and Developmental Medicine 12:13-16.

Froscher, M.M. 1978. The Effects on Respiratory Function of Sense-Group Duration. Ph.D. dissertation: Columbia University.

Halverson, H.M. 1941. Variations in pulse and respiration during different phases of infant behavior. J. Genetic Psychol. 59:259-330.

Hirano, M., Koike, Y., and von Leden, H. 1968. Maximum phonation time and air usage during phonation Folia Phoniat. 20:185-201.

Hixon, T.J., Mead, J., and Goldman, M.D. 1976. Dynamics of the chest wall during speech production: function of the thorax, rib cage, diaphragm, and abdomen. J. Speech Hear. Res. 19:297-356.

Hoshiko, M.S. 1965. Lung volumes for initiation of phonation. J. Appl. Physiol. 20:480-82.

Isshiki, N. 1964. Regulatory mechanism of voice intensity variation. J. Speech Hear. Res. 7:17-29.

Koike, Y. and Hirano, M. 1968. Significance of vocal velocity index. Folia Phoniat. 20:285-96.

Ladefoged, P. and McKinney, N.P. 1963. Loudness, sound pressure, and subglottal pressure in speech. J. Acoust. Soc. Am. 35:454-60.

Langlois, A. and Baken, R.J. 1976. Development of respiratory time factors in infant cry. Dev. Med. Child Neurol. 18:732-37.

Langlois, A., Wilder, C.N., and Baken, R.J. 1975. Pre-speech respiratory patterns in the infant. ASHA 17:668.

Lenneberg, E. 1967. Biological Foundations of Language. New York: John Wiley and Sons, Inc.

Liebermann, P. 1967. Intonation, Perception and Language. Cambridge, Mass.: M.I.T. Press.

Long, E.C. and Hull, W.E. 1961. Respiratory volume-flow in the crying newborn infant. Pediat. 27:373-77.

Otis, A.B. and Clark, R.G. 1968. Ventilatory implications of phonation and phonatory implications of ventilation. In Sound Production in Man, ed, A. Bouhuys. Annals of the New York Academy of Sciences, 155:122-28.

Peiper, A. 1963. Cerebral Function in Infancy and Childhood. New York: Consultants Bureau.

Rahn, H., Otis, A.B., Chadwick, L.E., and Fenn, W.O. 1946. The pressure-volume diagram of the thorax and lung. American Journal of Physiology 146:161-78.

Subtelney, J.D., Worth, J.J., and Sakuda, M. 1966. Intraoral pressure and rate of flow during speech. J. Speech Hear. Res. 9:498-518.

Truby, H., Bosma, J., and Lind, J. 1965. Newborn Infant Cry. Uppsala, Sweden: Almqvist and Wiksel.

van den Berg, J.W. 1957. Subglottic pressures and vibrations of the vocal folds. Folia Phoniat. 9:65-71.

Van Riper, C. 1978. Speech Correction: Principles and Methods. (6th Edition) Englewood Cliffs, N.J.: Prentice Hall.

Wilder, C.N. 1972. Respiratory Patterns in Infants: Birth to Eight Months of Age. Ph.D. dissertation: Columbia University.

Wilder, C.N. and Baken, R.J. Respiratory patterns in infant cry. Human Communication, Winter 1974-75: 18-31.

Winitz, H. 1969. Articulatory Acquisition and Behavior. New York: Appleton-Century Crofts.

Yanagihara, N. and von Leden, H. 1967. Respiration and phonation. Folia Phoniat. 19:153-66.

CHAPTER 4

Cry Characteristics
in Sound Spectrographic
Cry Analysis

Katarina Michelsson

INTRODUCTION

During the last decade research on the crying of
infants has interested many research centers all over
the world. Since cry analysis is a new area of
research, no standardized methods to measure different
cry characteristics have been available. Those
studying infant crying have had to develop their own
methods and criteria for describing normality and
abnormality. Thus, it is difficult, and at times
impossible, to compare the different works published.
A common vocabulary is urgently needed for use by all
those interested in this field in order to communicate
effectively with each other, benefit from previous
studies, and develop this area of study.

Infant crying can be dealt with from many different
aspects, and the aims of those scientists engaged in
cry studies is often different. There is interest in
the cry sound itself, in the complete cry act with
physiological or cinematography studies of the
laryngeal tract, or in the study of the means of
preverbal communication and child-mother interations.

For the past twenty years, a research group at the
University of Helsinki, Finland, has been developing
various means of cry analysis for the objective study
of the cry sound itself. Although aware that this area
of study is only a part of the entire cry research
field, this group believes it is important to have a
nomenclature for the objective measurements of the cry
sound that could be used by all scientists engaged in
cry analysis. Therefore, this chapter presents a
detailed description of the different cry

characteristics that have been analyzed. Throughout the years of study as the research progressed, some characteristics have been omitted and some have been added. The criteria for measurement of the different items have changed in some detail during this period. This chapter also presents a partial review of the analysis techniques used by other reseachers in this field.

TERMINOLOGY

Various terms used in the literature to describe the sound produced by small infants include cry, vocalization, utterance, phonation, articulation, and non-verbal communication. Many other terms are utilized which are not always exactly defined. Thus, it is difficult to compare the results of different authors. We agree with Crystal (1976) who suggests the term *vocalization* should be used to refer to any vocal sound produced by an infant. This includes crying, babbling, and all other early pitch patterns that the child uses. Crystal suggests, however, that the term vocalization should be used to denote all sounds which are non-linguistic in character. It is sometimes difficult to distinguish clearly between linguistic and non-linguistic function of a sound pattern.

The term *cry* has been classified in various ways. Most commonly, it is treated as referring to the audible performance so familiar to all (Truby and Lind 1965). However, they conclude that where there is sound there must be a motion or action from which the sound derives. Thus, the study of cry can be approached both acoustically and cinetically, differentiating between the *cry sound* and the *cry act*. Truby and Lind also describe the *cry cycle* to mean the total vocalization period, including sub-parts called alarm, arousal, approach, onset, attack, cruising, subdual, comfort, and peace.

Wasz-Höckert et al. (1968) have used the term *cry signal* to mean "the total vocalization occurring during a single expiration or inspiration." The term *phonation* has been used synonymously with *cry signal* (Michelsson 1971), as well as *utterance* (Prescott 1975). Thus, the terms cry signal, phonation, and vocalization have been used to refer to all sound produced during a single expiration or inspiration. Vocalization has additionally been used more widely to mean all sound produced by a child without any time limits.

In comparing the cry studies of different authors, it is confusing because the expirtory sounds can be discontinous and consist of many sub-parts of sound separated by silence. These sub-parts have been called phonations or signals. Other confusions arise because the segments of crying that are selected and investigated do not refer to a specific phase of respiration. This adds to the difficulty in making comparisons of different cry studies.

Stark, Rose, and McLagen (1975) used the term *vocalization series* or *cry cycle* to mean a group of vocalizations separated by all other groups by more than two inspiratory sounds in which no vocalization is produced. They used the term *vocalization segment* as a unit of vocalizations separated from all others by at least 0.05 sec of silence. Stark and Nathanson (1973) described a *breath unit* as the period between the beginning of one inspiration to the beginning of the next and a *cry unit* as the beginning of an inspiratory vocalization. The cry unit was divided into segments by periods of silence. The different vocalizations were classified as *cry sounds* (meaning those sounds produced in acute stress, such as pain or hunger), *discomfort sounds* produced in a lesser degree of discomfort (as when not reaching a toy), and *vegetative sounds* as coughs, burps, and sneezes).

Wasz-Höckert et al. (1968) have defined different *cry types* as signals with different meanings, such as the basic cry types of *birth*, *pain*, *hunger*, and *pleasure*. Wolff (1969) described three cry types: the *basic cry*, the *mad or angry cry*, and the *pain cry*. Lester and Zeskind (1978) and Murry, Gracco, and Gracco (1979) referred to *distress* and *non-distress vocalizations*.

Truby and Lind (1965) referred to three acoustic types of cry, including *phonation* (basic cry), *dysphonation* (turbulence), and *hyperphonation* (shift). A sudden presentation or loud noise employed in studies by Muller, Hollien, and Murry (1974) and Murry, Amundson, and Hollien (1977) was considered a *startle cry*.

The International Phonetic Alphabet has also been used for the description of infant vocalization (Flatau and Gutzmann 1906; Fisichelli et al. 1966; Sedláčková 1964 and 1967; Minnigerode 1968). Vowel and consonant sounds which have been developed for adult speech have not, in all instances, been applicable to utterances of small babies. Also, musical notes have been used in cry analysis (Gardiner 1838; Kiss et al. 1972; Mokoi et al. 1975).

Pitch is a phonetic term which refers to the perception of the fundamental frequency, but in cry research it has often been used to indicate the acoustically measurable fundamental frequency.

Thus, in the field of cry research, some basic vocabulary has been established. However, there remains an urgent need for uniform definitions of the acoustic characteristics which make up crying. A completely new vocabulary is not needed. Many of those phonetic terms which already exist are useful, but they need a clear definition that is understood and accepted by cry research groups and specialists in fields other than phonetics and the speech sciences.

Definitions of different cry charcteristics as found in the cry signals, mainly through the use of sound spectrography, are presented below. Additional cry characteristics are needed as the field of cry research develops. Also, the measurement of some cry characteristics can probably be omitted as less important when comparing cries from only healthy or only sick infants. In developing the definitions of the cry characteristics, the Helsinki group has changed or modified a few of them over the 20 years of the study.

SOUND SPECTROGRAPHY

In the objective analysis of the acoustical signal, a great advancement was made in 1947, when Potter et al. introduced their sound spectrograph. This apparatus was primarily intended for use in speech therapy for the deaf, but it was found to be too slow a process. Soon, the "Visible Speech" apparatus was found to be an efficient tool in phonetics and other areas concerned with the analysis and permanent visualization of the acoustical signal.

A systematic sound spectrographic study program was started in Helsinki, Finland, in 1961. A preliminary report was published by Wasz-Höckert et al. in 1962. In 1965, Lind and coworkers reported from the aspect of newborn physiology, sound spectrograms in connection with cineradiographic investigations. Other scientists using sound spectrography in the 1960's include

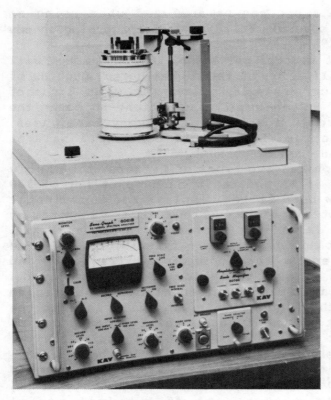

Figure 1.   The sound spectrograph 6061B.

Ostwald, Freeman, and Kurtz (1962); Ostwald, Phibbs, and Fox (1968); Ringel and Kluppel (1964); Sedláčková (1967); and Luchsinger et al. (1967).

In sound spectrography, the cry signals are converted to a permanent visualization where different parameters present in the cry signal can be measured. There are several brands of sound spectrographs available; however, the principles of operation are basically the same. We have mainly used the Kay Sona-Graph, which provides a sonagram for which the analyzing mode can be either time versus frequency or the amplitude versus frequency. The sonagraphic paper is attached on the analyzing drum of the apparatus (Figure 1). Approximately 2.4 sec of acoustical information can be displayed (Sona-Graph 6061B). When the drum rotates, a needle moves from the bottom of the drum to the upper part of it and burns the information onto the paper, with the time on the horizontal axis and the frequency distribution on the vertical axis. The intensity of every point in time is seen as a variation in the darkness of the traces. Longer signals than 2.4 sec can be analyzed when using an apparatus with several recording and reproducing speeds (Sona-Graph 7029A).

In the normal mode of operation, the Sona-Graph will provide a visualization of the signal up to 8000 Hz or 16000 Hz. In cry analysis, however, an upper limit of 4000 to 5000 Hz is usually sufficient to cover the frequency range in most cries. In very rare cases, especially in cries of sick infants, cry signals of more than 5000 Hz can be present.

The Sona-Graph has two types of filters, the narrow band filter of 45 Hz and the wide band filter of 300 Hz. The narrow band filter displays the fundamental frequency and its harmonic overtones on the sonagram as dark lines and is usually preferred in cry analysis. In the narrow band analysis, the first horizontal line in voiced cries is the fundamental frequency and represents the rate of vibration of the vocal cords. The harmonics are seen on the spectrogram as precise multiples of the fundamental. In analysis with the wide band filter, the fundamental frequency can be calculated from the number of vertical striations per second. However, in wide band analysis the resonance maxima, the formants, and the fundamental frequency and its harmonics often coincide and, thus, blur the trace, making accurate measurement of the fundamental impossible.

The disadvantage of sound spectrography is its relatively long, time consuming mode of operation and a certain inaccuracy in the measurement procedures, since measurements are done by hand. A blind cross check of the analyzed material has been done in our studies and has made the analysis more accurate. The time needed for this operation is often compensated for by the large amount of information received from the spectrograms.

The Cry Type

Since the first reports of birth, hunger, pain, and pleasure cries by Wasz-Höckert et al. (1963), the pain cry has been mainly used in comparing cries of healthy newborn and small infants, as well as in comparing infants with different diseases. In most studies, only the first cry signal following the application of a pain stimulus has been used. This has been defined as the entire vocalization during the first expiration or, in rare instances, the first inspiration after the pain stimulus. However, in later studies, also the second and third signals after the application of a pain stimulus have been analyzed.

True inspiratory cries are rare; most audible noise at inspiration is due to the anatomical structure of the airway and not to an intentional vocalization initiated from the central nervous system.

Pain cries have been used in cry analysis by Ringel and Kluppel (1964), Muller, Hollien, and Murry (1974), and Murry, Amundson, and Hollien (1977), while Fairbanks (1942) studied hunger cry. Stark and Nathanson (1973) and Stark, Rose, and McLagen (1975) analyzed spontaneous cry signals. Prescott (1975) omitted the first three cries in all recorded cry series, thus excluding "pain" cries in her analysis. Kittel and Hecht (1977) analyzed the first reflex cry after birth.

Similarities exist in different cries by the same infant (Truby and Lind 1965). Ringel and Kluppel (1964) state that different cries produced by the same infant do not differ significantly from each other with respect to fundamental frequency, sound pressure level, or duration. However, differences have been found, especially in the various cry types such as birth, hunger, and pain cries (Wasz-Höckert et al. 1963, 1968). In 1969, Wolff stated that the pain cry takes on the rhythmic morphology of the basic cry as the pain ceases. Blinick, Tavolga, and Antopol (1971) reported that when the vigor of the pain stimulus wore off, the cries became lower in amplitude with more harmonic form. Thodén and Koivisto (see Chapter 6) showed that differences exist between the first, second, and third cry signal after pain stimulus.

Therefore, when comparing cry signals in different studies, it should be stated which cry type and which signal have been studied in order to compare the results of different studies. We recommend use of the pain cry as a standard method when comparing cries of healthy and sick infants.

Recording Cries

In recording the cries of newborn and small infants, a high quality tape recorder and microphone are essential. In open reel recorders, a speed of 7½ in/sec (19 cm/sec) is preferred. Recently, we have used the Uher 4000 tape recorder and small high quality cassette tape recorders (Sony TC55 and TC155) which are easily transported and operated by the experimentor. Recorders with automatic sound level controls are not suitable for sound pressure analysis.

The type of microphone used depends on its recording properties. In collecting cries in obstetric and pediatric wards, we have used the AKG-D 58 200, which eliminated the unwanted background noise and echoes that are often present on the wards. Since this type of microphone is not very sensitive, it has to be held approximately 5 cm from the baby's mouth. Other scientists have used other types of microphones that are usually held about 20-25 cm from the infant's mouth (Ringel and Kluppel 1964; Lester and Zesking 1978). Contact microphones have been used by Lind et al. (1965) and Prescott (1975). Prescott found that when using a free field microphone or a contact microphone, the frequency pattern of the cries did not change.

State of wakefulness of the child at the time of the cry recording is also important. If the cries are recorded before feeding, the child is in a high, if not more labile, state than if tested after feeding (Lind et al. 1966). Differences exist in the durational features and, especially, in the latency period depending on whether the stimulus is applied when the child is deeply asleep or awake. Table 1 provides an effective means of defining the wakefulness of the child (Prechtl 1974).

Cry Characteristics

Latency

The latency period is defined as the time between the application of the pain stimulus and the onset of crying. In cry studies, the pain stimulus has been applied to the children in various ways including the following: vaccination (Vuorenkoski et al. 1966); pinching the infant's biceps (Wasz-Höckert et al. 1968; Michelsson 1971); snapping the ear (Michelsson et al. 1977); pulling the hair (Ringel and Kluppel 1964); stimulating the foot of the child (Tenold et al. 1974; Murry, Amundson, and Hollien 1977); snapping the sole of the foot (Fisichelli and Karelitz 1963; Fisichelli et al. 1974; Zeskind and Lester 1978).

We have measured latency by sound spectrography and with a direct writing oscillograph (Mingograph, Elema Schönander, Sweden). The latency has been measured from the middle of the word "now" said at the moment

Table 1. Five different behavioral states in newborn infants (H.F.R.
Prechtl 1974).

State 1   eyes closed, regular respiration,

               no movements.

State 2   eyes closed, irregular respiration,

               small movements.

State 3   eyes open, no movements.

State 4   eyes open, gross movements.

State 5   crying (vocalization)

---

the pain stimulus was applied to the onset of crying.
The rubber band apparatus provides an audible snap
from which the latency can be measured (Fisichelli et
al. 1974).

Sometimes, the very first sound emitted by the infant
is a cough-like signal. In the first cry studies by
Wasz-Höckert et al. (1968), these signals were not
included in the latency measurements The difference
in the latency period when measured from the stimulus
to the "main cry", instead of to the first audible
sound, is notable. For example, Ringel and Kluppel
(1964) took two measurements to determine the latency
period: the time from the stimulus to the first
response of the infant and the time from this first
short sound to the main signal.

It is important to establish a standard method of
measuring the latency period in order to compare the
various studies. The latency period is a good
indicator in evaluating abnormality in cries of infants
with various disorders, especially those affecting the
central nervous system.

The states of arousal and hunger can change the latency period. The latency period can also be influenced by the time during the respiratory cycle when the pinch is given (i.e. during inspiration or expiration).

Karelitz and Fisichelli (1962) have used the term "cry threshold" to describe the number of snaps required to elicit a cry.

Duration of the Cries

Cry duration has been thought to be the easiest part of the cry signal to measure objectively. Problems arise, however, because there are no definite rules describing which phonations should be measured. Wasz-Höckert et al. (1968) included in their measurements the total vocalization during a single expiration or inspiration. When the vocalization consists of one continuous signal, the duration of this signal is easily measured. In interrupted vocalizations, the time from the onset of the first to the end of the last phonation has been measured. In their first studies, Wasz-Höckert et al. did not measure signals with a duration of less than 0.4 sec if located at the beginning or the end of the phonation. Thus, if signals exceeding 0.4 sec occured, only the time from the onset of the first signal to the end of the last signal of 0.4 sec or more was included in the measurements. Currently, we have included all sound occurring during one vocalization in the measurements. Until now, neither the duration of the pauses in interrupted signals, nor the total time of vocalization have been measured.

It is easy to determine the onset of a phonation on the sound spectrogram because the intensity of the sound at the beginning of the signal is usually high. At the end of the cry signal, the print on the spectrogram can be characterized as a fade-out as the intensity decreases gradually (Figure 2). This can cause measuring problems as the signal still can be audible although no longer visible on the spectrogram. This is due to the limited dynamic range of the analyzing apparatus. The end of the vocalization can be visualized by increasing the reproduce level on the sound spectrogram.

The identification of the inspiration is often difficult on the spectrogram. Auditorily, the inspiration can be identified on the recording tape and a comparison of the auditory and visual impression

Figure 2. Pain cry of a healthy newborn infant.

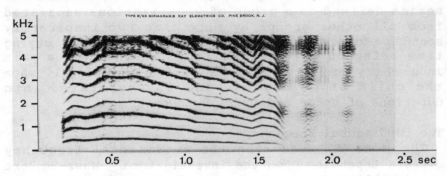

makes the recognition on the spectrogram possible. Sometimes, the inspiration is so weak that it cannot be recognized on a normally produced spectrogram. In these cases, it can be visualized by increasing the spectrograph reproduction level.

The Second Pause

The term "second pause" has been used with somewhat different explanations. Vuorenkoski et al. (1966) and Michelsson (1971) defined the second pause as the time between the first and second vocalization. Sirviö and Michelsson (1976) refer to the second pause as the time from the end of the vocalization to the next inspiration. Gleiss and Höhn (1968) used the term "seond interval" for the time between the short and prolonged crying.

In studies by Lind et al. (1966) and Michelsson (1971), the second pause was characterized as abnormal if it exceeded one second. Later, it has been preferable to have a precise measurement of the second pause in seconds, since it is also used for other durational cry characteristics.

When measuring durational features, it is obvious that a change in the measuring criteria for one attribute simultaneously changes the durational features of the others. For example, if very short phonations at the beginning of the vocalization are not included in the duration of the cry, the latency time is made longer.

The Crying Time

Crying time has been defined as the time from the onset of crying until the child stops crying. The crying time seems to be important, especially in studies with sick infants and in behavioral studies.

Stark, Rose, and McLagen (1975) studied vocalization series defined as a group of vocalizations separated from all other groups by more than two inspiratory sounds. In previous reports (Michelsson 1971), crying time referred to the time from the onset of a pain induced cry to the termination of the last signal when the child stops crying, and was separated into durations of under and over 30 seconds.

The Fundamental Frequency

The mode of measuring the fundamental frequency differs depending upon the investigators. Wasz-Höckert et al. (1968) measured the dominating pitch level in the cry, the *general pitch*. When the general pitch level was very unstable, the measurement was omitted. This characteristic is no longer in use. Two other characteristics, the *maximum pitch* and the *minimum pitch*, have been measured in all studies. the maximum pitch is the highest measurable voiced segment of the fundamental frequency, and the minimum pitch is the lowest measurable voiced segment. The maximum and minimum pitch, when possible, have been measured from the 4th and 5th harmonic overtone, which permits greater accuracy as the measuring error decreases. Occasionally, the lowest line on the spectrogram, the fundamental frequency, may not be seen due to low sound pressure, while the upper harmonics appear more clearly.

Ostwald et al. (1968) measured the fundamental frequency at the beginning and the end of the phonation and at the highest frequency in the middle of the cry signal.

A mean fundamental frequency has been noted by Luchsinger et al. (1967), Kittel and Hecht (1977), and Murry et al. (1977). Stark and Nathanson (1975), Lester and Zeskind (1978), and Lester (1978) have measured their mean fundamental frequency by computer analysis, which averages the frequency over time.

When the cry is voiceless or contains noise elements, the fundamental frequency cannot be determined. In glottal plosives and glottal roll, no fundamental frequency has been measured.

Shift

Shift denotes an abrupt upward and downward movement of the fundamental frequency. A shift part seems to be quite common in crying of healthy infants, appearing mostly at the beginning of the signals. Shift can also

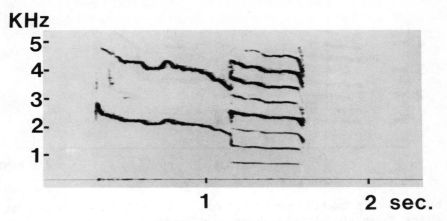

KHz

5-
4-
3-
2-
1-

1   2 sec.

Figure 3. Sonagram of a pain cry with shift. If the higher part of
fundamental is considered as shift, the first part of the
phonation is the shift. If the shorter part is considered
as shift, the last part is the shift part.

occur at the end of the phonation or in the middle,
where we see a kind of double shift. Shift parts occur
in almost every third pain cry. The shift part has
been included in the measurements when exceeding 0.1
sec (Michelsson et al. 1977a, b) or 0.2 sec (Wasz-
Höckert et al. 1968; Michelsson 1971).

The maximum pitch of the shift part has been measured
separately in studies by the Finnish research group.
The number of shifts, the pitch, the duration, and the
melody type of the shift part can be specific but has
not been investigated. Usually, the shift part is not
included in measures of fundamental frequency.

In studies by the Finnish research group, when a
shift part has been present in the cry signal, the
shorter part of the phonation has been regarded as the
shift. The determination of what should be considered
as the shift part needs further consideration.

Until now we have considered the shorter ones as the
shift part; this is in concordance with the audible
expression of the sound. Thodén and Koivisto (see
Chapter 6) state that in analyzing the cries of healthy
newborn infants, the higher part could be considered as
the shift irrespective of duration. A maximum pitch of
1500-2000 Hz in the shift part is not unusual in cries
of healthy infants.

Stark, Rose, and McLagen (1975) defined the shift as
a pitch break not due to halving or doubling of the
fundamental frequency. In our studies, we have noted
that when a shift occurs it is often due to an exact
halving or doubling of the fundamental and, because of

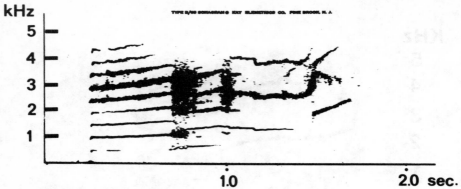

Figure 4. A cry with a rising melody type.

this, it is sometimes difficult to differentiate the shift from the double harmonic break.

Further consideration is needed in determining the location of the shift part. In cries of healthy infants, the cry often starts with a shift part, whereas, in cries of infants with CNS disorders, it seems as though shifts in the middle and the end of phonations are more common and that there is an overall instability of pitch.

If two or more shifts have occurred in the same cry signal, only the maximum frequency of the shift with the highest pitch has been measured. Truby and Lind (1965) call high pitched signals shift (hyperphonation) without any abrupt break in the pitch pattern. Thus, the term shift has been used with somewhat different meanings in cry analysis.

The Melody Type

The melody type of the fundamental frequency has been classified as falling, rising-falling, rising, falling-rising, and flat (Figure 4). When the frequency is very unstable, voiceless, or consists only of glottal plosives, often no melody type is detectable.

Wasz-Höckert et al. (1968) define the cry type as falling or rising when there is at least a 10% change in pitch level during more than 10% of the duration of the cry. Stark et al. (1975) have defined the melody as a flat, rising, or falling pitch contour, or a combination of these contours.

Continuity of the Signals

Cry signals have been classified as continuous or interrupted. More precise measurements of the number and duration of short signals in interrupted vocalizations are not available.

Voice Quality

Cries have been classified as voiced, half-voiced, or voiceless. If any voiceless part occurs in the signals, the signal has been noted as half-voiced. A standardization including a percentage definition would be more accurate. For example, a signal could be classified as half-voiced if 10% or more of the signal is voiceless.

Nasality

Nasality of the cry signal has previously been noted by Wasz-Höckert et al. (1968), who state that the nasal voice is poor in intensity and only the first harmonics are amplified on the spectrogram. Thus, this feature relies on the auditory perception of the sound and it cannot be objectively measured in high pitched cries. Futhermore, nasality is rare in pain induced cries, which constitute the standardized type of cry used in our cry studies.

Tenseness

The tenseness in cries was previously noted by Wasz-Höckert et al. (1968), who stated that tenseness increases the intensity of the upper harmonics. In very high pitched cries with no harmonics visible on the spectrogram, the tenseness could not objectively be noted and has, therefore, been omitted in later studies. Additionally, most pain cries are tense.

Glottal Roll

The glottal roll, or vocal fry, is a sound with very low pitched, voiced fundamental frequency and usually has a low intensity. Glottal roll occurs often at the end of the phonations. Duration measurements in cries which end with glottal roll can sometimes be difficult to determine due to the dynamic range of the sound spectrograph as the intensity of the glottal roll decreases. When appropriate, an increase of the mark level of the spectrograph makes the glottal roll visible on the spectrogram.

Vibrato

The glottal roll can be preceded by a vibrato or vibrato can occur solely Vibrato has been noted in the signals when at least four successive, rapid up and down vibrations have been noticed. There are no definite rules concerning the maximal or minimal period of time in which the pitch movements should take place

99

or in the extent of the pitch changes. Vibrato is characterized by frequency variations that appear more clearly in the upper harmonics.

Double Harmonic Break

Double harmonic break (or subharmonic break) defines a parrallel series of harmonics which have the same melody form as the fundamental frequency and occur simultaneously with the fundamental. There may be a double or treble series of parallel harmonics.

The double harmonic break gives an impression of roughness of the voice, but not of a pitch change (Stark, Rose, and McLagen 1975).

Bi-phonation

Bi-phonation, or diplophonation, is a double series of fundamental frequencies, but in comparing bi-phonation with the double harmonic break, the two or more series do not have a parallel melody form. One series can be falling while the other simultaneously can be rising. Bi-phonation has been included in the measurements when exceeding 0.1 sec (Michelsson et al. 1977a, b); however, 0.2 sec was used as a limit in previous studies (Wasz-Höckert et al. 1968).

Gliding, Glide

Gliding is a very rapid upward and/or downward movement of the fundamental frequency with a generally very short duration. The change in the fundamental frequency must be at least 600 Hz in 0.1 sec for gliding to be recorded (Wasz-Höckert et al. 1968). Stark, Rose, and McLagen (1975) have defined glide as a rapid pitch change of 100 Hz in 0.1 sec.

Gliding should be measured from the fundamental frequency, not from the harmonics. Gliding seldom occurs in cries of healthy infants (Figure 5).

Furcation

Furcation is a term denoting a "split" in the fundamental where a relatively strong cry signal suddenly breaks into a series of weaker ones, with each of them having its own fundamental frequency contour. This is also a feature which we have seen only in the crying of sick infants.

Noise Concentration

The term noise concentration was introduced to denote a clearly audible, high energy peak of 2000-2500

KHz

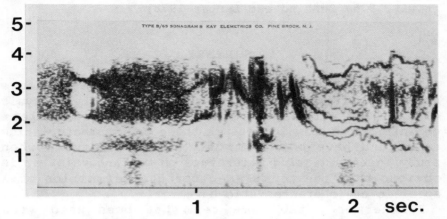

Figure 5. A pain cry from a newborn infant with hypoxia shows a voiceless part, a high fundamental frequency, and both bi-phonation and gliding.

Hz found both in voiced and voiceless parts of the signal. Noise concentration is uncommon in the cries of healthy babies.

Tonal Pit
Tonal pit refers to a rapid downward and upward movement in the fundamental frequency. This attribute has been included in the measurements when the fall in pitch exceeded 30% and occurred in less than 0.4 sec.

Glottal Plosives
Glottal plosives have been noted when present. The term is somewhat misleading because it denotes not only glottal plosives but also all other kinds of plosives. The fundamental frequency or other cry characteristics have not been measured from the plosives. In some studies by Wasz-Höckert et al. (1968), the glottal plosives were omitted from the durational measurements when appearing at the beginning or the end of the vocalization. The total number of glottal plosives or their location have not been reported.

Loudness
The loudness of the cry sound is displayed on the sound spectrogram as a darkness of the lines. The loudness of the cry sound is dependent on the distance from the microphone to the infant's mouth and is difficult to standardize on clinical pediatric wards.

Only a few studies are available on the sound pressure level in infant crying (Ringel and Kluppel 1964; Stark et al. 1975; Zeskind and Lester 1978).

SUMMARY

This chapter attempts to explain the nomenclature used for different cry characteristics in cry analysis of the newborn and small infant. Some clear definitions on how to measure these cry characteristics exist and have been commonly used However, when studying the existing literature on cry analysis, it is obvious that the terms used for the definition of a specific cry characteristic have varied.

Furthermore, the same term has been used with different meanings. Such variances in nomenclature make it difficult to compare the different studies published. Standardized methods used and understood by all scientists dealing with cry analysis are urgently needed.

ACKNOWLEDGMENT

This study has been supported by the Sigrid Jusélius Foundation.

REFERENCES

Blinick, G., Tavolga, W.N., and Antopol, W. 1971. Variations in birth cries of newborn infants from narcotic addicted and normal mothers. Am. J. Obstet. Gynecol. 110:948-58.

Crystal, D. 1976. Developmental Intonology. In Baby Talk and Infant Speech, ed. Raffler-Engel and Lebrun. Amsterdam: Suets & Zeitlinger.

Fairbanks, G. 1942. An acoustical study of the pitch of infant hunger wails. Child Dev. 13:227-32.

Fisichelli, V.R., and Karelitz, S. 1963. The cry latencies of normal infants and those with brain damage. J. Pediat. 62:724-34.

Fisichelli, V.R., Coxe, M., Rosenfeld, L., Haber, A., Davis, J. an Karelitz, S. 1966. The phonetic content of the cries of normal infants and those with brain damage. J. Psychol. 64:119-26.

Fisichelli, V.R., Karelitz, S., Fisichelli, R.M., and Cooper, J. 1974. The course of induced crying activity in the first year of life. Pediatric Research 8:921-28.

Flatau, T.S. and Gutzmann, H. 1906. Die stimme des sauglings. Arch. Laryng. Rhinol. 18:139-51.

Gardiner, W. 1838. The Music of Nature. Boston: Wilkins and Carter.

Gleiss, J. and Höhn, W. 1968. Das verhalten beim schreien nach konstanter schmertzreizung atemgesunder und atemgestörter neugeborener. Deutsche Zeitschr Nervenheilk 194:311-17.

Karelitz, S. and Fisichelli, V.R. 1962. The cry thresholds of normal infants and those with brain damage. J. Pediat. 61:679-85.

Kiss, P.G., Makoi, Z., Szöke, S.S., Sasvari, L., and Popper, P. 1972. Die für das lebensalter bezeichnenden eigenheiten des hunderweinens des säuglings. Acta Paediatr. Acad. Sci. Hung. 13:323-33.

Kittel, G. and Hecht, L. 1977. Der erste schrei - frequen-zanalytische untersuchungan. Sprache-Stimme-Gehör 1:151-55.

Lester, B.M. 1978. The organization of crying in the neonate. J. Ped. Psychol. 3:122-30.

Lester, B.M. and Zeskind, P. 1978. Brazelton scale and physical size correlates of neonatal cry features. Infant Behaviour and Development 1:393-402.

Lind, J., ed. 1965. Newborn Infant Cry. Acta Paediatr. Scand. Suppl. 163.

Lind, J., Wasz-Höckert, O., Vuorenkoski, V., Partanen, T.J., Theorell, K., and Valanne, E. 1966. Vocal reponse to painful stimuli in newborn and young infants. Ann. Paediatr. Fenn. 12:55-63.

Luchsinger, R., Dubois, C., Vassella, F., Joss, E., Gloor, R., and Wiesmann, U. 1967. Spektralanalyse des "miauens" bei cri-du-chat syndrom. Folia Phoniat. 19:27-33.

Makoi, Z., Szöke, Z., Sasvari, L., Kiss, P.G., and Popper, P. 1975. Das erste aufsschrei des neugeborenen nach vaginaler und nach Kaiser-schnitt-Entbindung. Acta Paediatr. Acad. Sci. Hung. 16:155-61.

Michelsson, K. 1971. Cry analysis of symptomless low birth weight neonates and of asphyxiated newborn infants. Acta Paediatr. Scand. Suppl. 216.

Michelsson, K., Sirviö, P., and Wasz-Höckert, O. 1977a. Sound spectrographic cry analysis in infants with bacterial meningitis. <u>Dev</u>. <u>Med</u>. <u>Child</u> <u>Neurol</u>. 19:309-15.

Michelsson, K., Sirviö, P., and Wasz-Höckert, O. 1977b. Pain cry in fullterm asphyxiated newborn infants correlated with late findings. <u>Acta Paediatr</u>. <u>Scand</u>. 66:611-16.

Minnigerode, B. 1968. Klinische und vergleichend-anatomische untersuchungen zur erzeugung der hohen schrilltöne menschlicher säuglings. <u>Archiv</u>. <u>Ohren-usw Heilk u Z Hals-usw Helik</u> 181:208-15.

Muller, E., Hollien, H., and Murry, T. 1974. Perceptual response to infant crying: identification of cry types. <u>J</u>. <u>Child</u> <u>Lang</u>. 1:89-95.

Murry, T., Amundson, P., and Hollien, H. 1977. Acoustical characteristics of infant cries: fundamental frequency. <u>J</u>. <u>Child</u> <u>Lang</u>. 4:321-28.

Murry, T., Gracco, V., and Gracco, C. 1979. Infant vocalization during the first twelve weeks. Paper presented at American Speech and Hearing Ass'n, November, 1979, Atlanta, Ga.

Ostwald, P.F., Freeman, D.G., and Kurtz, J.H. 1962. Vocalization of infant twins. <u>Folia</u> <u>Phoniat</u>. 14:37-50.

Ostwald, P.F., Phibbs, R., and Fox, S. 1968. Diagnostic use of infant cry. <u>Biol</u>. <u>Neonat</u>. 13:68-82.

Potter, R., Kopp, G.A., and Gren, H.C. 1947. <u>Visible Speech</u>. New York: Van Nostrand.

Prechtl, H.F.R. 1974. The behavioural states of the newborn infant (a review). <u>Brain</u> <u>Res</u>. 76:185-212.

Prescott, R. 1975. Infant cry sounds: developmental features. <u>J</u>. <u>Acoust</u>. <u>Soc</u>. <u>Am</u>. 57:1186-90.

Ringel, R.L. and Kluppel, D.D. 1964. Neonatal crying: a normative study. <u>Folia</u> <u>Phoniat</u>. 16:1-9.

Sedláčková, E. 1964. Analyse acoustique de la voix de nouveau-nes. <u>Folia</u> <u>Phoniat</u>. 16:44-58.

Sedláčková, E. 1967. Composition acoustique des manifestations vocales des enfants dans la periods de lallation. <u>Folia</u> <u>Phoniat</u>. 19:351-58.

Sivriö, P. and Michelsson, K. 1976. Sound-spectrographic cry analysis of normal and abnormal newborn infants. <u>Folia</u> <u>Phoniat</u>. 28:161-73.

Stark, R.E. and Nathanson, S.N. 1973. Spontaneous cry in the newborn infant: sounds and facial gestures. In <u>Fourth</u> <u>Symp</u>. <u>on</u> <u>Oral</u> <u>Sens</u>. <u>and</u> <u>Percept</u>., ed. J.F. Bosma. p. 323-52.

Stark, R. E., Rose, S. N., and McLagen, M. 1975. Features of infant sounds: the first eight weeks of life. <u>J</u>. <u>Child</u> <u>Lang</u>. 2:205-21.

Tenold, J.L., Crowell, D.H., Jones, R.H., Daniel, T.H., McPherson, D.F., and Popper, A.N. 1974. Cepstral and stationarity analysis of fullterm and premature infants' cries. J. Acoust. Soc. Am. 56:975-80.

Truby, H.M. and Lind, J. 1965. Cry sounds of the newborn infant. Acta. Paediatr. Scand. Suppl. 163-59.

Vuorenkoski, V., Lind, J., Partanen, T.J., Lejeune, J., Lafourcade, J., and Wasz-Höckert, O. 1966. Spectrographic analysis of cries from children with maladie du cri-du-chat. Ann. Paediatr. Fenn. 12:174-80.

Wasz-Höckert, O., Vuorenkoski, V., Valanne, E., and Michelsson, K. 1962. Tonspektrographische untersuchungen des säuglingsgeschreis. Experientia 18:583.

Wasz-Höckert, O., Valanne, E., Vuorenskoski, V., Michelsson, K., and Sovigärvi, A. 1963. Analysis of some types of vocalization in the newborn and in early infancy. Ann. Paediatr. Fenn. 9:1-10.

Wasz-Höckert, O., Lind, J., Vuorenkoski, V., Partanen, T., and Valanne, E. 1968. The Infant Cry. A Spectrographic and Auditory Analysis. Clinics in Developmental Medicine No. 29. Lavenham, Suffolk: Spastics International Medical Publications.

Wolff, P.H. 1969. The natural history of crying and other vocalization in early infancy. In Determinants of Infant Behaviour IV, ed., B.M. Foss. London: Methuen & Co., Ltd.

Zeskind, P.S. and Lester, B.M. 1978. Acoustic features and auditory perceptions of the cries of newborns with prenatal and perinatal complications. Child Dev. 49:580-89.

CHAPTER 5

Acoustic Characteristics
of the First Cries of Infants

Thomas A. Gardosik, Patti Jayne Ross,

and Sadanand Singh

INTRODUCTION

The cries of a newborn infant are its first vocalizations. Emitted in response to the rigors of birth, the birth cry appears to be merely a forcible expiration, random and undirected. Later neonatal cries seem to be reflexive responses to distress or hunger. If interpretation of their meaning were possible, these early cries may be found to contain a great deal more information than is commonly supposed. There need not be any intention on the part of the infant to actively communicate with those around him. Communication takes place if the cry can be shown to be a reflection of the infant's physical or neurological state.

In order to determine if various messages contained in an infant's prevocal verbalizations exist, the cry has been the subject of extensive research. Three aspects of its nature have been given primary attention: the cry's meaningfulness as a direct communication of the immediate cause of distress, its usefulness as a diagnostic tool of central nervous system abnormality and/or degree of development, and its developmental progress as a prelude to speech and verbal intelligence. Since this data is extensively discussed in other chapters, each of these areas shall be reviewed primarily in relation to the birth cry. Modest new evidence that the cry is, indeed, a complex signal containing subtle information and that this information is available as early as the first cry emitted at birth will be presented.

Cry Meaningfulness

A common pretheoretical assumption has been that "...
the cry of the newly born is a reflexive protective
mechanism used to signal need to whoever may attend
him" (Aldrich, Sung, and Knop 1945b, p. 94). In this
view, the cry is an elicitor of parental behavior,
acting to bring the infant into close physical contact
with his mother. It is at first reflexive and only
gradually becomes goal-directed (Murray 1979). This
ethological interpretation is supported by evidence
indicating that crying can be reduced by additional
nursing care (Aldrich, Sung, and Knop 1945a,b,c;
Aldrich et al. 1946) and that it lessens in importance
as other forms of communication are developed (Bell and
Ainsworth 1972). The work of Bell and Ainsworth also
demonstrates that physical contact is the most
effective method of ending crying immediately, and that
consistent, prompt response to an infant in the first
quarter of the first year reduces the amount of crying
thereafter. Proximity of the caretaker may induce the
infant to develop other forms of communication,
rendering crying less important in the infant's
behavioral repetoire.

An indication of the specific nature of the distress
which provokes a given bout of crying can be obtained
with a lesser degree of confidence. Perceptual
identification of the cry signal in an experimental
situation is sensitive to the method of presentation of
the cry. Several investigators (Murry, Hollien, and
Muller 1975; Muller, Hollien, and Murry 1974) report
that recognition of a cry signal does not extend beyond
the mother's ability to recognize the sound of her own
infant. Given acoustically balanced, excerpted
portions of cries elictied by hunger, pain, or
startling, most cries are classifed as hunger cries.
The ability to differentiate among cry types is
restricted or absent when cries are presented in this
manner.

However, this recording and test procedure may
eliminate the acoustic cues normally available in a
cry. For example, the intensity of a cry resulting
from painful stimulation may be the major aoustic
factor differentiating it from a cry arising from
hunger-- as if the distress of pain were more acute
and immediate than that of hunger. In a series of
studies, Wasz-Höckert and colleagues (1968) have found
that in a more natural setting, (complete cry signals

107

presented) perceptual identification of the cry type is possible, and that experience in child care improves this ability. Women experienced in child care were significantly more accurate in their judgments of the cause of the cry than were inexperienced women. The magnitude of the training effect can best be seen in identification of birth cries. In general, these were the most poorly recognized cries, usually mistaken for pain or hunger cries. The birth cry must be considered relatively rare since few people have the opportunity to become familiar with it. In the Wasz-Höckert studies, midwives who were exposed regularly to the birth cry found it no more difficult to identify than pain or hunger cries.

The Wasz-Höckert group supplemented their perceptual studies with spectrographic analysis of the four signal types (birth, pain, hunger, pleasure). These spectrograms were submitted to analysis to identify acoustic attributes present in each cry. Factor analysis then permitted the generation of objective classification rules, with melody form and length of cry emerging as the best predictors of signal class for the ages of 0-1 month and melody form, nasality, and presence or absence of pitch shift predicting signal class of cries of infants aged 1-7 months. Intraclass variability limits the accuracy of this method to 71% and 82% respectively for the two age groups. This is a highly respectable level of prediction, but the analysis did not extend to the group of cries which must be classified as "other" (the importance of which will be discussed below). If this were done, it is possible that prediction would become less accurate as more acoustic variables are shared among the various cry signals.

Previous research does not provide unequivocable support for the contention that the vocalizations of an infant are sufficient to specify the cause of distress. This has been shown only in a forced choice situation where the cry is known to belong to one of four signal classes. In a non-laboratory environment, there are always additional cues as to the nature of the cry-provoking situation. Every cry is not necessarily induced by hunger or some immediately obvious external cause. Aldrich (Aldrich et al. 1946) recorded diaries of infant cries over eight-day post-natal nursery stays and found that unknown causes accounted for as many crying spells as hunger and that, together with the hunger cries, they accounted for a large majority of all crying. The importance of these unknown causes diminished substantially when the infants were taken home and given (presumably) more individualized care. If difficulties arise in specifying the exact cause of a cry, even with the observer's knowledge of the circumstances of the cry-provoking situation, inferring the probable cause of a cry must be even more difficult without that additional knowledge. The task may become impossible if, as was suggested above, neonatal crying is initially an innate mechanism that serves primarily to promote proximity.

Diagnostic Aspects of Cry

The information communicated to the trained observer goes beyond an indication of momentary distress. In addition to focusing attention on the infant's immediate needs, the cry can serve as an index of the condition of the central nervous system.

> Everyone responsible for the care of newborn babies recognizes the high pitched cry of the baby with cerebral damage, and many pediatricians are conversant with the cry of the cretin, the growling low pitched cry of the Cornelia de Lange syndrome, the feeble cry of the severely hypotonic infant, the cri du chat, the whimper of the seriously ill child, or the hoarse cry of the child with a laryngeal infection. (Illingworth, in Wasz-Höckert et al. 1968, preface.)

The anecdotal importance of the use of the sound of a cry for the diagnosis of CNS distress is supported by recent work, indicating that the cry of an abnormal infant is, in many cases, audibly different from that of a normal infant. Differences have been documented for Down's Syndrome (Fisichelli et al. 1966), trisomy 13-15 (Ostwald et al. 1970), cleft palate (Massengill 1969), cri du chat, hyperbilirubinemia (Wasz-Höckert et al. 1971), cerebral insult (Karelitz and Fisichelli 1962, Karelitz, Karelitz, and Rosenfeld 1960), and severe malnutrition (Lester 1976, Juntunen, Sirviö, and Michelsson 1978). These differences may be manifested in pitch, pitch shift, melody, latency of onset, nasality, stimulation necessary to produce crying, and lack of pre-speech sounds in abnormals. There may also be differences in average duration of the individual cry signal (Prechtl et al. 1969), although this has been disputed (Ostwald, Phibbs and Fox 1968).

In every case cited, analysis of the cries was conducted after diagnosis of abnormality. It has not been shown that the audible signal alone can be indicative of anything more than the presence of gross abnormality. In practice, without further specification of norms, the sound of an infant can signal disorder, but other diagnostic methods are necessary to specify the distress (Ostwald 1972; Sirviö and Michelsson 1976).

Most of the work on infant cry has been aimed at defining its use as an indicator of immediate or chronic distress. Much less emphasis has been placed on studying the normal development of the infant voice. Fairbanks (1942) recorded the hunger wails of one infant over a period of nine months and found a tendency of increasing fundamental frequency with age, especially during the first half of that period. Subsequent analysis of the cries of normal infants have shown no such developmental trends during early infancy (Prescott 1975; Stark, Rose, and McLagen 1975; Laufer and Horii 1977). In their book, Wasz-Höckert et al. (1968) report that characteristics of the cry are established within the first seven days of life and remain stable until the age of seven months. The exception to this is in the 'pleasure signal', which is not a cry as such, but is a babbling sound that progressively approaches speech sound. Developmental studies have concentrated on the gradual appearance of recognizable phonemes and their relationship to language acquisition (Lewis 1959) and on the developing understanding and use of intonation and stress to convey meaning (Lewis 1959; Crystal 1973). Discussion of phonemic development and language acquisition, however, is beyond the scope of this chapter. (For a review of the area, see McNeill 1970.)

Finally, it has been suggested that the complexity of the cry-sound can be a predictor of adult intelligence. Cameron (1967) tested 74 infants with the California First Year Mental Scale at one month intervals. Their progress was followed longitudinally by testing yearly from the age of 6 to 26 years. Cameron was able to isolate a seven-item vocalization factor which was significantly correlated with later I.Q. of females at 11 of the 21 ages tested. Karelitz et al. (1964) judged complexity of the cry sound by the number of individual sounds emitted during the most active 20-

second portion of the signal. Karelitz was able to show that complexity of the cry correlates with Stanford-Binet I.Q. at the age of three years for the group. However, the relationship was not strong enough for individual prediction. With further isolation of relevant cry-variables, it may be possible to stipulate both the relationship between early vocalizations and later intelligence and the sequence of development that underlies both. It is not yet clear that such a relationship exists.

The discussion of these three general areas of research in the broader area of infant cry draws toward the same tentative conclusion. A promising diagnostic tool cannot yet be applied outside of the experimental laboratory. It does, however, provide a posteriori support to neurological findings. Aberrations cannot be specified any more than the degree of normality has been specified. Definitions of parameters is a prerequisite to the use of the cry signal as a diagnostic aid and to an understanding of the perceptual ability to recognize the content of the information the infant is conveying. Whether or not the cry is 'intended' to be communication, it seems clear that there is information to be gained from the signal if these preverbalizations can be understood.

Cry as a Prelude to Speech

Because the infant vocal tract does not lend itself to traditional formant analysis, a problem arises in the attempt to relate pre-speech sound to the acoustics of speech. In the adult human, formant frequencies reflect the resonant characteristics of the vocal tract. In vowel production, the formant loci specify articulatory movements necessary to produce given patterns (Fant 1970). However, the infant vocal apparatus is significantly different from that of the adult, both in relative position of the various organs and in absolute mobility.

At birth, the position of the larynx is higher than in adulthood and the only movements during cry are gross manuevers of the larynx up or down (Truby, Bosma, and Lind 1965). The epiglottis is at the level of the first cervical vertebrae and the inferior border of the cricoid is at the level of the fourth cervical vertebrae. (In the adult, these positions are in the third and sixth vertebra, respectively.) The thyroid cartilage is contiguous to the hyoid bone, which places the epiglottis near the velum and the root of the tongue in the oral cavity. The pharyngeal region cannot vary in cross-sectional area and there is no dorsal or posterior wall to the epipharynx. Gradually, through the age of four years, the root of the tongue and the larynx descend into the pharynx, and the upper pharynx is oriented superoanteriorly, rather than anteroposteriorly as in the infant.

Thus, at birth, the supralaryngeal vocal tract most closely resembles a uniform cross-section tube, open at both ends during production of sound. It approximates the vocal tract of non-human primates more so than that of human adults and is incapable of the full range of human speech sounds (e.g. Lieberman et al. 1971; Crelin 1976). For a more complete anatomical description, see Bosma and Fletcher (1961).

Although vowel sounds cannot be isolated in neonatal infant cry, the sounds produced must still reflect the characteristics of the vocal tract. Formant loci are evident which show some similarity to the vowels (ae) and (ʌ) (Ringel and Kluppel 1964). Sound spectrographic analysis of formant frequencies reported in the work of Lieberman et al. (1971) provides one of the first attempts to identify the characteristics of the transfer function of the vocal tract. Visual analysis of the spectrograms of the cries of 20 healthy infants places the first three formant ranges at 1-1.25 kHz, 3-3.3 kHz, and 5-5.8 kHz. These frequencies are an averaged approximation of the center of each formant band. Lieberman maintains that they are predictable, from the assumption that the infant oral cavity is a 7.5 cm uniform cross-section tube open at one end.

This chapter presents an analysis of the use of a combined procedure of sound spectrographic and computer analysis in determining the fundamental frequency and resonance frequencies of an infant's vocalizations in a standardized situation. The birth cry is used since it is caused by known distress, and no insupportable assumptions need be made about the evoking situation.

Since formant frequencies serve as a perceptual cue in sexual identification of adult voices (Murry, Hollien, and Muller 1975; Brown and Feinstein 1977) and of children (Hasek, Singh, and Murry in press), a fine-grained analysis of the signal may differentiate male and female infants on the basis of formant frequencies since no sex-related differences have been found in the fundamental frequency of infant voices (Murry, Amundson, and Hollien 1977). In addition, variations

in the length of gestation permit the consideration of
developmental trends as they relate to acoustic
information.

A STUDY OF THE BIRTH CRY

The subjects of this study were 55 male and 53
female infants born to 106 women in Houston Texas.
This included one set of triplets. The average
gestational age was 277.6 days with a standard
deviation of 15.99. The gestational age (GA) range was
203 to 308 days for female infants and 227 to 308 days
for male infants. There were 52 white, 41 black, 1
oriental, and 14 Latin infants. Medical records were
collected for both the mothers and the infants.

Recording Procedure

A high fidelity Uher 4000 Report L tape recorder with
a flat frequency response from 40 to 20,000 Hz was used
to record the cries. This is a portable machine
weighing approximately 12 pounds and was carried under
the gown of the experimenter,supported by a shoulder
strap. A hand held Uher microphone was used to allow
recording of the cry at a distance of approximately 6
inches. The birth cry was recorded for a minimum of 10
seconds and a maximum of 15 seconds. Birth cry is
defined here as a cry within the first 5 minutes after
birth. At the time of the recording, a silence
compatible with the demands of delivery was maintained
by the delivery staff. The recording was done by a
medical student at The University of Texas Medical
School at Houston.

Acoustical Analysis

Acoustic analysis of these samples was done to
determine intra- and inter-subject variability of the
distribution of energy as a function of frequency via
fast Fourier analysis (FFT) and sound spectrographic
analysis.

A measure of fundamental frequency was obtained by
submitting three arbitrarily selected 500 msec samples
of each cry to an FFT routine with a band width
characteristic of Hz at a rate of 20,000 samples per
second. Frequency by amplitude histograms was thus
obtained for each sample. The first prominent peak to

appear on the histograms was assumed to be the f_o for that sample, and the median value of the three samples was assumed to be the f_o for that infant. Sound spectrographic measurements were obtained separately by processing cry samples on a Voiceprint VII series 700 Sound Spectrograph. Frequency values were judged independently by three experimenters and were accepted when agreement was reached If these values were in agreement with FFT measures, they were accepted as the fundamental frequency. The process was repeated in cases of discrepancies until reliable measures were obtained.

Measures of formant frequencies were also obtained by using this combined procedure. Samples were submitted to FFT analysis at two band width characteristics, 160 Hz and 320 Hz A line with a slope of −6 dB per octave was drawn from the f_o peak across the histogram display. Energy peaks above that line were assumed to be the result of vocal tract resonance and curves of best fit were drawn above those peaks. The high point of the first curve beyond f_o was considered to be the central frequency of the first formant. The high point of the second curve was judged to be the central frequency of the second formant. As with the measure of f_o, the median value of three formant measures was taken to be representative of a given infant. In addition, broadband (300 Hz) and narrowband sound spectrograms were obtained at a reduced playback speed (1/2) to minimize the possibility of mistaking harmonics for formants (Fant 1968). Frequency values were accepted when agreement was reached among the three experimenters of the FFT and broadband spectrographic measures. The outcome of the narrowband sound spectrogram was to aid in the determination of wideband measurements in the event of gross ambiguity.

RESULTS

Incomplete medical information was collected on four infants and a fifth did not cry within the first five minutes following birth. These five cases were excluded from further analysis. The results are displayed in Table 1 and are based on 103 cases, 53 males and 50 females.

Table 1 shows the f_o, F_1, and F_2 values for the combined group of subjects for males and females separately. The male f_o was 467.2 Hz (s.d.=79.2), as

114

Table 1. Means and standard deviations (Hz) of fundamental frequency and formant frequency measures.

		Combined	Male	Female
F_0	x	462.5	467.2	457.5
	s.d.	72.4	79.2	64.8
F_1	x	1550.8	1573.2	1527.0
	s.d.	460.0	496.5	421.6
F_2	x	3108.8	3106.5	3111.2
	s.d.	612.8	646.9	581.0
	n	103	53	50

compared with the female F_1 of 1527.0 (s.d.=421.6). The male F_2 was 3106.5 (s.d.=646.9), compared to the female value of 3111.2 Hz (s.d.=581.0). Differences between these pairs of means were not significant (p>.25).

The regression lines for fundamental frequency and formant frequencies as a function of gestational age are shown in Figure 1. As can be seen from the figure, f_0 remained unchanged across GA but both F_1 and F_2 tended to decrease with increased GA. The main effect of age was a significant predictor of both $F_1 (F_{(1,99)}=7.95$, p < .01) and of F_2 ($F_{(1,99)}=9.96$, p<.01). No other effects or interactions were statistically significant.

An interesting trend is suggested by the patterns of the regression lines shown in Figure 1. Formant frequencies tended to decrease with increasing gestational age for both males and females, but the decrease was more accelerated for females than for males. The female sample shows higher formant frequency values than the male sample at short GA (less than 260 days) and lower values at fullterm GA and beyond. Although this sex-related interaction did not reach conventional levels of statistical significance, it does hold some interest for future study.

DISCUSSION

Although this method of analysis is a departure from traditional spectrographic analysis of fundamental frequency, the f_0 values obtained are in general

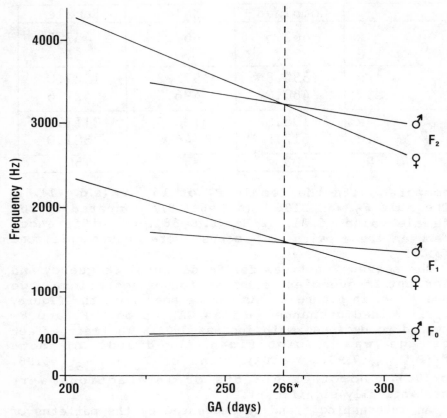

Figure 1. Fundamental frequency and formant frequencies as a function of gestational age (GS). (*Age of full-term birth.)

agreement with values reported by other investigators. Table 2 presents a comparison of f_o measures reported in the literature. Comparison between studies is made difficult by differences in reporting measures, but the range of values reported encompasses those obtained here.

There have been few previous attempts to identify the formant frequencies of infant vocalizations. Table 2 includes reports of two studies. The values of Ringel and Kluppel (1964) are estimated from Figure 2 of their report. Based on a sample of 20 neonates (not birth cries), these estimated ranges fall within the frequency ranges reported here.

For the measure of first formant frequency, the Ringel and Kluppel values are statistically the same as those of the female infants in this study and with the male infants, with the exception of one extreme case. Exclusion of that one case from this report would

Table 2. Comparison of f_o and formant values obtained in this study with other reported values. Values reported as means and ranges unless otherwise noted.

Study	cry	n/sex	F_o	F_1	F_2
Current Study	birth	53♂	467.2(327-669)	1573.2(937-3281)	3106.5(1719-4375)
	birth	50♀	457.5(356-664)	1527.0(900-2400)	3111.2(1875-4375)
Ringel & Kluppel(1964)	pain 4-40 hours	20	413.13(290-508)	approx.(925-2000)	approx.(1700-3200)
Lieberman et al(1971)	birth	10♂	400	1100	3300
Ostwald et al(1970)	pain 6d Trisomy 13-15	1♀ 13-15	(100-680)		
Fairbanks(1942)	hunger 9m longitudinal	10♂	556		
Juntunen et al(1978)	normal kwashiorkor marasmus 7m-2y	15 1 4	(310-520) (290-460) (330-1650)		
Lester(1976)	spontaneous normal malnourished	12 12 12	308.0 479.77		
Ostwald et al(1968)	normal possibly impaired abnormal	5 5 3	(280-614) (200-2875) (240-1833)	'pitch range'	
Prescott(1975)	1-10d 6-9m 6m (hearing impaired)	4 4 1	384 415 436 436		
Sirvio-Michelsson(1976)	full-term premature cleft-palate asphyxia	50 75 13 70	(390-620) (450-770) (340-570) (470-1120)		
Wasz-Hockert et al(1968)*	birth pain hunger pain hunger	77 60 75 60 75	500(450-550) 530(410-650) 470(390-550) 530(380-680) 500(420-520)	0-1m 1-7m	

*Fundamental frequency values given as median 'general pitch' and median values of individual ranges.

reduce the range of F_1 to 900 to 2488 Hz. The range of reported F_2 frequencies shows less complete agreement. Ringel and Kluppel's sample falls roughly into the lower half of the range of values of this study. Lieberman et al. (1971) reported on one subject only; the only observation is that the one value falls within the limits of these findings.

The difficulty of obtaining accurate formant frequencies in voices with a high fundamental frequency has contributed to the lack of information about formant patterns in infant vocalizations. In addition, the absence of recognizable speech sounds raises questions concerning the existence of identifiable formant bands. To this point the identifiable energy bands representing the resonant characteristics of the vocal tract have been referred to as formants. This is not to imply identity with formant bands associated with speech sounds. A phonetic transcription may result in the neutral vowel suggested by Fant (1968). Due to inherent measurement difficulties, what has been identified as the second formant may be a harmonic of the first formant. In any case, it is felt that the first formant (at least) does reflect vocal tract parameters since "the vocal tract transfer function depends almost exclusively on the shape of the air cavities of the vocal tract" (Fant 1968, p. 192).

Accepting the validity of the measurement techniques employed, a return to the original hypotheses is in order. These findings are in agreement with prior studies showing no early developmental trends in fundamental frequency. The hypothesis of no developmental changes in the acoustic characteristics of the birth cry, however, is not confirmed.

The pattern of lowered formant frequencies with increased gestational age may suggest that, in terms of the positioning of the larynx in its relationship to the supralaryngeal vocal tract, fullterm infants may be more developed than those born prematurely. The less developed sound production system of short GA infants implies higher positioning of the larynx, causing a functional shortening of the vocal tract and thereby resulting in higher F_1 and F_2 frequencies for these infants This developmental trend is not seen if newborn infants are considered to be all the same age.

An alternative explanation postulates that the degree of neurological development is associated with the length of gestation. Lieberman (1971) suggests that vocal limitations are, to some degree, the result of "deficiencies in central control of the vocal apparatus...", and that the first four months of life are a period of cortical inhibition of vocal behavior (McNeill 1970). It is only during the second half of this period that the infant can produce true speech sounds. This period of rapid neurological development should be accompanied by concomitant development of finer control of the vocal apparatus. As the infant becomes able to control tongue and laryngeal movements, he becomes able to vary the functional length and cross-sectional area of the vocal tract, thereby altering (lowering) resonant frequencies of the sounds he produces. This is, however, purely speculation. If increased control of the vocal mechanism was responsible for differences in formant frequencies, it would be expected that there would be occurrences of higher formant frequencies also, since tongue movements of repositioning could effectively decrease the length of the vocal tract.

Since the decreased formant frequency can result either from vocal tract growth or (less plausibly) from neurological development, subsequent research will investigate other physical parameters, such as birth weight and head diameter. If changes in formant frequencies can be attributed to development of the vocal tract, acoustic analysis of an infant's preverbalizations may serve as an index of physical maturity. If these changes result from increased central control of the musculature of speech production, an infant's first cry would contain information about neuromuscular maturity. In either case, characteristics of phonation would have increased diagnostic value.

The early hypotheses of no sex-related differences in the acoustic characteristics receives support from the current data. Although it must be stressed that the sex-related trends in decreasing formant values were not statistically significant, the measures were sufficiently consistent to invite further work. The tendency of other investigators to study combined groups masks sex-related differences, as does the great variability in infant's voices. In addition, if these differences are seen only in longitudinal trends, care must be taken in stipulating the age of a newborn. As can be seen from Figure 1, at 38 weeks GA, the age of normal fullterm birth, these differences are minimized.

This chapter presents acoustic mappings of the first vocal output of an infant and integrates it with previous analyses of neonatal cries. Much of the concluding remarks are speculative in nature, but point toward a direction of further research.

Progress in the acoustic analysis of cry can be furthered by longitudinal rather than cross-sectional study. The infants who participated in this project are now approximately one year old, and an assessment of their overall health, specifically auditory and language functions, would contribute toward determining the usefulness of acoustic analysis preverbal vocal behavior as a diagnostic tool. Study of those individual cases which were 'deviant' in either vocal output or gestational age presents an opportunity to a *priori* target possible abnormalities.

A final word must be added about the complexity of an infant's cry. Increasingly subtle analysis shows that increasingly subtle distinctions can be made. A synthesis of the various techniques considered above will permit delineation of the interrelationships between structure and function and between function and behavior.

ACKNOWLEDGMENTS

The study upon which this chapter is centered is based on data collected by Gary Duncan, a student at The University of Texas School of Medicine. The authors also gratefully acknowledge the assistance of Dr. Charles E. Lincoln, Research Fellow at the Speech and Hearing Institute; Dr. John W. Black, Visiting Distinguished Professor at the Speech and Hearing Institute; Dr. David F. Barr, University of Central Florida; and Dr. Samuel Brown, Assistant Director of Academic Affairs at the Institute for Advance Study of the Communication Processes.

REFERENCES

Aldrich, C.A., Sung, C., and Knop, C. 1945a. The crying of newly born babies, I. The community phase. J. Pediat. 26(4):313-26.

Alrich, C.A., Sung, C., and Knop, C. 1945b. The crying of newly born babies, II. The individual phase. J. Pediat. 27(2):89-96.

Aldrich, C.A., Sung, C., and Knop, C. 1945c. The crying of newly born babies, III. The early period at home. J. Pediat. 27:428-35.

Aldrich, C.A., Norval, M.W., Knop, C., and Venegas, F. 1946. The crying of newly born babies, IV. A follow-up study after additional nursing care has been provided. J. Pediat. 28:665-70.

Bell, S.M. and Ainsworth, M.D.S. 1972. Infant crying and maternal responsiveness. Child Dev. 43:1171-90.

Bernal, J. 1972. Crying during the first 10 days of life and maternal responses. Dev. Med. Child Neurol. 14:362-72.

Bosma, J.F. and Fletcher, S.G. 1961. The upper pharynx, a review, part 1, embryology, anatomy Annals of Otology, Rhinology and Laryngology 70:953-73.

Brown, W S., Jr. and Feinstein, S.H. 1977. Speaker sex identification utilizing a constant laryngeal source. Folia Phoniat. 29:240-48.

Cameron, J., Livson, N., and Bayley, N. 1967. Infant vocalizations and their relationship to mature intelligence. Science 157:331-33.

Crelin, E.S. 1976. Development of the upper respiratory system. Clinical Symposia 28(3):1-30.

Crystal, D. 1973 Linguistic mythology and the first year of life. British Journal of Disorders of Communication 8:29-36.

Fairbanks, G. 1942. An acoustical study of the pitch of infant hunger wails. Child Dev. 13:227-32.

Fant, G. 1968. Analysis and synthesis of speech processes, in Manual of Phonetics, ed. B. Malmberg. Amsterdam: North-Holland Publishing Co.

Fant, G. 1970. Acoustic Theory of Speech Production. Paris: Mouton.

Fisichelli, V.R., Haber, A., Davis, J., and Karelitz, S. 1966. Audible characteristics of the cries of normal infants and those with Down's Syndrome. Perceptual and Motor Skills 23:744-46.

Hasek, C.S., Singh, S., and Murry, T. Acoustic attributes of preadolescent voices. J. Acoust. Soc. Am., in press.

Juntunen, K., Sirviö, P., and Michelsson, K. 1978. Cry analysis in infants with severe malnutrition. Eur. J. Pediatr. 128-41.

Karelitz, S. and Fisichelli, V. 1962. The cry thresholds of normal infants and those with brain damage. J. Pediat. 61:679-85.

Karelitz, S., Fisichelli, V., Costa, J., Karelitz, R., and Rosenfeld, L. 1964. Relation of crying activity in early infance to speech and intellectual development at age three years. Child Deve. 35:769-77.

Karelitz, S., Karelitz, R., and Rosenfeld, L.S. 1960. Infant's vocalizations and their significance. In Proceedings of the First International Conference on Mental Retardation, eds. P.W. Bowman and H.V. Mautner. New York: Grune and Stratton.

Laufer, M.Z. and Horii, Y. 1977. Fundamental frequency characteristics of infant non-distress vocalizations during the first twenty-four weeks. J. Child Lang. 4:171-84.

Lester, B.M. 1976. Spectrum analysis of the cry sounds of well-nourished and malnourished infants. Child Dev. 237-41.

Lewis, M.M. 1959. How Children Learn to Speak. New York: Basic Books.

Lieberman, P., Harris, K.S., Wolff, P., and Russell, L.H. 1971. Newborn infant cry and nonhuman primate vocalization. J. Speech Hear. Res. 14:718-27.

Massengill, R.M. 1969. Cry characteristics in cleft-palate neonates. J. Acoust. Soc. Am. 45:782-84.

McCarthy, D. 1952. Organismic interpretation of infant vocalizations. Child Dev. 23:273-80.

McNeill, D. 1970. The development of language. In Carmichael's Manual of Child Psychology, ed. P.H. Mussen. New York: John Wiley.

Muller, E., Hollien, H. and Murry, T. 1974. Perceptual responses to infant crying: identification of cry types. Child Lang. 1:89-95.

Murray, A.D. 1979. Infant crying as an elicitor of parental behavior: An examination of two models. Psychol. Bull. 86:191-215.

Murry, T., Amundson, P., and Hollien, H. 1977. Acoustical characteristics of infant crys: fundamental frequency. J. Child Lang. 4:321-28.

Murry, T., Hollien, H., and Müller, E. 1975. Perceptual responses to infant crying: maternal recognition and sex judgments. J. Child Lang. 2:199-204.

Ostwald, P. 1972. The sounds of infancy. Dev. Med. Child Neurol. 14:350-61.

Ostwald, P. and Peltzman, P. 1974. The cry of the human infant. Scientific American 230:84-90.

Ostwald, P., Peltzmann, P., Greenberg, M., and Meyer, J. 1970. Cries of a trisomy 13-15 infant Dev. Med. Child Neurol. 12:472-77.

Ostwald, P.F., Phibbs, R., and Fox, S. 1968. Diagnostic use of infant cry. Biol. Neonat. 13:68-82.

Prechtl, H.F R., Theorell, K., Gramsbergen, A., and Lind, J. 1969. A statistical analysis of cry patterns in normal and abnormal newborn infants. Dev. Med. Child Neurol. 11:142-52.

Prescott, R. 1975. Infant cry sound: developmental features. J. Acoust. Soc. Am. 57:1186-90.

Ringel, R.L. and Kluppel, D.D. 1964. Neonatal crying: a normative study. Folia Phoniat. 16:1-9.

Sirviö, P. and Michelsson, K. 1976. Sound-spectrographic cry analysis of normal and abnormal newborn infants. Folia Phoniat. 28:161-73.

Stark, R.W., Rose, S.N., and McLagen, M. 1975. Features of infant sounds: the first eight weeks of life. J. Child Lang. 2:205-21:

Stark, R.E. and Nathanson, S.N. 1973. Spontaneous cry in the newborn infant: sounds and facial gestures. In Fourth Symposium of Oral Sensation and Perception: Development in the Fetus and Infant, ed. J.F. Bosma. DHEW Pub. No. 73-546.

Tanner, J.M. 1970. Physical growth. In Carmichael's Manual of Child Psychology, third edition. New York: John Wiley.

Truby, H.M., Bosma, J.F., and Lind, J. 1965. Newborn Infant Cry. Acta Paediatr. Scand. Suppl. 163.

Wasz-Höckert, O., Lind, J., Vuorenkoski, V., Partanen, T., and Valanne, E. 1968. The Infant Cry: A Spectrographic and Auditory Analysis. Clinics in Developmental Medicine No. 29. Lavenham, Suffolk: Spastics International Medical Publications.

Wasz-Höckert, O., Partanen, T., Vuorenkoski, V., Valanne, E., and Michelsson, K. 1964. Effect of training on ability to identify preverbal vocalizations. Dev. Med. Child Neurol. 6:393-96.

Wasz-Höckert, O., Koivisto, M., Vuorenkoski, V., Partanen, T.J. and Lind, J. 1971. Spectrographic analysis of pain cry in hyperbilirubinemia. Biology of the Neonate 17:260-71.

CHAPTER 6

Acoustic Analysis
of the Normal Pain Cry

Carl-Johan Thóden and Maila Koivisto

INTRODUCTION

Surprisingly few prospective investigations have been published concerning cry in children with normal development. The cry research group in Finland, which has concentrated on the study of cry for many years, has recognized the need for such a study. The aim of the present investigation is to create by sound spectrography normative pain cry data in 0-6 months old infants.

The most important previous results on normative data for infant cry are summarized in Tables 1-3. There are difficulties in comparing the results due to differences in definitions of the cry features and heterogenity in the groups of children included in the investigations. Some groups have concentrated on the durational features of the cry; others have concentrated on the cry fundamental frequency.

SOUND SPECTROGRAPHIC ANALYSIS OF PAIN CRY

The material for this research was collected at the Department of Pediatrics, University of Oulu, Finland, and included 38 children who fulfilled the strict criteria for normality set in this investigation. The criteria were: a normal gestational period, a normal delivery at term, an Apgar score of 8 or more at 5 minutes, an appropriate weight and length for gestational age, a normal perinatal period, a normal development up to the age of one year, a repeatedly normal EEG, and a normal chromosomal karyotype. The 38 infants in this investigation had a mean gestational age of 39.8 weeks, a mean birth weight of 3,460 g, and a mean Apgar score of 9.7 at 5 minutes.

The pain cries were recorded at 1 day, 5 days, 3 months, and 6 months of age when the infants were examined by an experienced pediatrician. An EEG examination was performed at the same ages. Occasionally, the child could not attend one of the examinations because of illness, etc. Thus, there are different numbers of cries in the age groups. All children were examined, however, at 1 year of age, which assured that the development was normal during the first year of life.

The total sample comprises 401 signals from 140 cry series and is displayed in Table 4.

Methods

The pain cry was induced by pinching the arm, and, with a few exceptions, the cry was elicited by the first pinch. At the moment of stimulation, the children were awake and thus in state 3 or 4 as defined by Prechtl and Beintema (1964). The cries were recorded with an AKG 200 dynamic microphone, at a distance of abut 5 cm from the mouth, on a Nagra tape recorder.

The sonagrams were made on a Kay Sona-Graph 7029A provided with a narrow band filter using a frequency range of 40-4000 Hz. When this frequency range was used, the duration of the sonagram was approximately 4.8 seconds.

The sonagrams were interpreted according to defintions by Sirviö and Michelsson (1976), with the exception that when a cry included a shift, the part of the signal with the higher frequency was chosen as the shift part and the highest point of this part was regarded as the maximum pitch of the shift. In this investigation, the term signal denotes the phonated part of a cry between two inspirations; the signals are numbered as the first, the second, and the third signal after the pain stimulus. In previous investigations on pain cry, usually only the first cry signal has been measured. However, in this study we have measured the second and third signals in order to increase the amount of information. All cries in this investigation were expiratory cries.

The following cry features were noted and defined as follows:

Authors	No. of children	Age	Latency (sec)	Type of cry
Fisichelli, 1963	44	1-808 d	1.6 ± 0.75	pain
Gleiss & Höhn, 1968	39	1-4 w	0.92-6.44 (range)	pain
Michelsson, 1971	50	1-10 d	1.8 (median) 1.2-2.5 (Q_1-Q_3)	pain
Fisichelli et al., 1974	158	0-12 m	$1.41 \pm 0.39 - 2.18 \pm 0.89$	pain
Lester, 1977	12	Newborn	1.56 ± 0.46 (mean)	pain
Zeskind & Lester, 1978	24	2 d	1.369 ± 0.62 (mean)	pain

Table 1. Summary of latencies from previous studies.

Authors	No. of children	Age	Duration (sec)	Type of cry
Ringel & Kluppel, 1964	10	4-40 h	1.47 ± 0.62 (mean)	pain
Wasz-Höckert el al., 1968	60	0-7 m	2.7 ± 1.1 (mean)	pain
Gleiss & Höhn, 1968	39	1-4 w	0.6 - 4.0	pain
Ostwald et al., 1968	5	1 d – 6 m	1.3 ± 0.8	pain
Wolff, 1969	1	3 d	4.1	pain
Michelsson, 1971	50	1-10 d	2.0 (median) 1.6-3.6 (Q_1-Q_3)	pain
Prescott, 1975	10	4-6 w	1.007 ± 740 (mean)	spontaneous
	10	6-8 m	1.194 ± 426 (mean)	spontaneous
Lester, 1976	12		1.52 ± 0.39 (mean)	spontaneous
Lester, 1977	12	newborn	4.85 ± 2.84 (mean)	pain
Lester & Zeskind, 1978	40	1-2 d	2.54 ± 2.23 (mean)	pain
Zeskind & Lester, 1978	24	2 d	6.448 ± 3.623 (mean)	pain

Table 2. Summary of durations from previous studies.

Authors	No. of children	Age	Frequency (Hz)	Type of cry
Flatau & Gutzman, 1906	30	0-5 w	a' - d''	spontaneous
Ringel & Kluppel, 1964	10	4-40 h	413.13 ± 30.5 (mean)	pain
Wasz-Höckert et al., 1968	60	0-7 m	520 ± 80 (mean)	pain
Ostwald et al., 1968	5	1 d – 6 m	540 ± 120 (mean)	pain
Michelsson, 1971	50	0-10 d	620 (median) 580-690(Q_1-Q_3)	pain
Tenold et al., 1974	9	48 h	518 (median)	pain
Prescott, 1975	10	4-6 w	453 ± 67 (mean)	spontaneous
	10	6-8 m	495 ± 53 (mean)	spontaneous
Murry et al., 1977	8	3-6 m	441.0 (mean)	pain
Kittel & Hecht, 1977	50	0 d	425 (mean)	birth
Lester, 1976	12		308 ± 32.18 (mean)	spontaneous
Lester, 1977	12	newborn	466.67 ± 83.15 (mean)	pain
Lester & Zeskind, 1978	40	1-2 d	606.25 ± 301.97 (mean)	pain
Zeskind & Lester, 1978	24	2 d	468.3 ± 53.8 (mean)	pain

Table 3. Summary of fundamental frequencies from previous studies.

Table 4. Number of signals in different groups.

Age	Signal I	Signal II	Signal III	Total
1 d	38	37	36	111
5 d	37	35	29	101
3 m	37	36	34	107
6 m	28	28	26	82
	140	136	125	401

latency period - the time between when the stimulus was applied and the onset of crying.
duration - the time between the onset of crying and the end of the signal.
maximum pitch of the fundamental frequency - the highest point of the fundamental frequency. This feature was measured excluding the shift parts of the fundamental frequency.
minimum pitch of the fundamental frequency - the lowest point of the fundamental frequency.
shift - a rapid up or down movement of the fundamental frequency.
maximum pitch of the shift - the highest point of the shift.
melody type - four main groups of melody including 1) falling and rising-falling, 2) rising and falling-rising, 3) flat, and 4) no type melodies.
continuity - an uninterrupted signal.
voicing of the signal - grouped in three main types including 1) voiced, 2) half-voiced, and 3) voiceless signals.
double harmonic break - a parallel series of harmonics which have the same melody form as the fundamental frequency.
vibrato - at least four rapid up and down movements of the fundamental frequency.
glottal roll - a sound of very low intensity which is still periodic.
glottal plosives - short, not voiced signals, generated by closure of the glottis.
gliding - very rapid up and down movements of at least 600 Hz in 0.1 seconds.

Table 5. Latency period (sec).

Age	Signal I	Signal II	Signal III	p
1 d				
X ± SD	1.4 ± 0.8			
Md	1.1			
Range	0.4 - 3.6			
5 d				
X ± SD	1.4 ± 0.7			
Md	1.2			
Range	0.4 - 3.2			
3 m				
X ± SD	1.2 ± 0.6			
Md	1.2			
Range	0.1 - 2.8			
6 m				
X ± SD	1.2 ± 0.5			
Md	1.2			
Range	0.2 - 2.3			
p	N.S.			

$p \leq 0.05$ +, $p \leq 0.01$ ++, $p \leq 0.001$ +++
mean and standard deviation = X±SD
median = Md

bi-phonation - a double series of the fundamental frequencies which do not have a parrallel melody form.
furcation - a split in the fundamental frequency where the cry signal breaks into a series of signals.
noise concentration - a clearly audible high energy peak at 2000-2300 Hz.

The durational features were measured with an accuracy of 0.1 sec and frequency with an accuracy of 10 Hz. When possible, the maximum and minimum pitch of the fundamental frequency was measured from the third harmonic.

In the statistical work, the Wilcoxon test for two samples was used because of the need to use non-parametric tests as the frequencies were not normally distributed. For testing the frequency of the occurrence of different features, the Chi square test

Table 6.   Duration (sec).

Age	Signal I	Signal II	Signal III	p
1 d				
X $\pm$ SD	5.0 $\pm$ 2.8	1.8 $\pm$ 0.9	1.2 $\pm$ 0.8	I -II +++
Md	4.9	1.6	1.1	I -III +++
Range	0.5 - 12.2	0.6 - 4.0	0.3 - 4.3	II-III ++
5 d				
X $\pm$ SD	5.2 $\pm$ 2.3	1.6 $\pm$ 0.7	1.3 $\pm$ 0.8	I -II +++
Md	5.6	1.4	1.1	I -III +++
Range	0.9 - 10.4	0.5 - 3.6	0.5 - 3.7	II-III N.S.
3 m				
X $\pm$ SD	4.2 $\pm$ 2.5	1.7 $\pm$ 0.8	1.6 $\pm$ 1.0	I -II +++
Md	4.2	1.5	1.2	I -III +++
Range	0.3 - 9.9	0.5 - 3.6	0.5 - 4.4	II-III N.S.
6 m				
X $\pm$ SD	4.1 $\pm$ 2.2	2.0 $\pm$ 1.1	1.5 $\pm$ 0.8	I -II +++
Md	3.6	1.9	1.3	I -III +++
Range	1.5 - 10.4	0.4 - 5.1	0.7 - 3.6	II-III N.S.
p	N.S.	N.S.	N.S.	

$p \leq 0.05$ +, $p \leq 0.01$ ++, $p \leq 0.001$ +++
mean and standard deviation = X $\pm$ SD
median = Md

with Yeates correction coefficient was used. When this test could not be applied because of the low expected frequencies, the Fisher exact test was used. All tests were used as two-tailed tests. In the tables the mean as well as the median value for the frequencies are given.

Results

Latency Period

The mean of the latency shown in Table 5 in the different age groups was between 1.2 and 1.4 sec. The corresponding median values were between 1.1 and 1.2 sec. No significant differences between the means of the different age groups could be found, although the latency period was somewhat longer in the first week of

Table 7. Maximum pitch (Hz, excluding shift).

Age	Signal I	Signal II	Signal III	p	
1 d					
X $\pm$ SD	660 $\pm$ 280	560 $\pm$ 80	550 $\pm$ 130	I -II	N.S.
Md	570	550	530	I -III	N.S.
Range	400 - 1540	400 - 750	350 - 1040	II-III	N.S.
5 d					
X $\pm$ SD	630 $\pm$ 440	580 $\pm$ 190	550 $\pm$ 150	I -II	N.S.
Md	560	530	530	I -III	N.S.
Range	340 - 3130	350 - 1500	390 - 1210	II-III	N.S.
3 m					
X - SD	570 $\pm$ 150	590 $\pm$ 140	640 $\pm$ 320	I -II	N.S.
Md	560	560	560	I -III	N.S.
Range	310 - 1060	420 -1060	420 -1870	II-III	N.S.
6 m					
X $\pm$ SD	630 $\pm$ 250	600 $\pm$ 240	560 $\pm$ 150	I -II	N.S.
Md	560	540	530	I -III	N.S.
Range	150 -1440	390 -1460	410 -1110	II-III	N.S.
p	N.S.	N.S.	N.S.		

$p \leq 0.05$ +, $p \leq 0.01$ ++, $p \leq 0.001$ +++,
mean and standard deviation = X$\pm$SD
median = Md

life. The range of the latency was also wider in the first week of life and at 3 months than at 6 months.

Duration

The duration of the three first cry signals was measured. The mean duration of the first cry signal was between 4.1 and 5.2 sec; that of the second signal between 1.6 and 2.0 sec, and of the third signal between 1.2 and 1.6 sec as shown in Table 6. The first signal was of significantly longer duration than the second and third signals in all age groups. The second signal was also significantly longer than the third signal at the age of 1 day. The median values for signal I were between 3.6 and 5.6 sec, for signal II between 1.4 and 1.9 sec, and for signal III between 1.1 and 1.3 seconds.

Table 8. Maximum pitch (Hz, including shift).

Age	Signal I	Signal II	Signal III	p	
1 d					
$X \pm SD$	860 ± 480	650 ± 290	590 ± 230	I -II	N.S.
Md	600	580	550	I -III	++
Range	400 -2250	400 -1850	350 -1290	II-III	N.S.
5 d					
$X \pm SD$	1080 ± 740	780 ± 650	640 ± 290	I -II	N.S.
Md	680	600	590	I -III	++
Range	410 -3130	400 -3420	390 -1480	II-III	N.S.
3 m					
$X \pm SD$	690 ± 320	750 ± 380	790 ± 500	I -II	N.S.
Md	580	600	600	I -III	N.S.
Range	400 -1670	420 -2170	420 -2500	II-III	N.S.
6 m					
$X \pm SD$	830 ± 500	700 ± 460	760 ± 360	I -II	N.S.
Md	580	550	570	I -III	N.S.
Range	390 -2750	390 -2630	410 -1920	II-III	N.S.
p	N.S.	N.S.	N.S.		

$p \leq 0.05$ +, $p \leq 0.01$ ++, $p \leq 0.001$ +++
mean and standard deviation = $X \pm SD$
median = Md

Maximum Pitch of the Fundamental Frequency

The mean of the maximum pitch, when excluding the shift parts of the signal, varied between 550 and 660 Hz; the corresponding median values were between 530 and 570 Hz. The data in Table 7 show that no significant differences between the means of the maximum pitch could be found between the different age groups or the order of the signal.

When the maximum pitch of the cry was measured at the highest point of the fundamental frequency, irrespective of whether it consisted of a shift part or not, the mean of the maximum pitch was between 590 and 1080 Hz as seen in Table 8. The corresponding median values were between 550 and 680 Hz. The change was obvious in the first signal at 1 and 5 days of life where statistically significant differences to signal III were reached.

131

Table 9. Minimum pitch (Hz).

Age	Signal I	Signal II	Signal III	p
1 d				
X $\pm$ SD	390 $\pm$ 120	370 $\pm$ 80	370 $\pm$ 110	I -II N.S.
Md	380	360	330	I -III N.S.
Range	190 - 770	130 - 550	240 - 830	II-III N.S.
5 d				
X $\pm$ SD	350 $\pm$ 100	370 $\pm$ 90	380 $\pm$ 140	I -II N.S.
Md	340	380	350	I -III N.S.
Range	190 - 570	190 - 580	240 -1020	II-III N.S.
3 m				
X $\pm$ SD	340 $\pm$ 120	390 $\pm$ 140	410 $\pm$ 160	I -II N.S.
Md	320	380	360	I -III N.S.
Range	170 - 630	180 - 920	180 - 830	II-III N.S.
6 m				
X $\pm$ SD	330 $\pm$ 100	380 $\pm$ 120	390 $\pm$ 610	I - II +
Md	350	350	380	I - III ++
Range	150 - 490	190 - 810	290 - 520	II- III N.S.
p	1 - 6 ++	N.S.	N.S.	

p 0.05 +, p$\leq$0.01 ++, p$\leq$0.001 +++
mean and standard deviation = X$\pm$SD
median = Md

Minimum Pitch of the Fundamental Frequency

Table 9 presents the measures of minimum pitch at the lowest visible point of the sonagram. The lowest point is not always very easily documented because of the fading out of the sonagram at the end of the signal. The mean of the minimum pitch was between 330 and 410 Hz. The corresponding median values were between 320 and 380 Hz.

Shift

Shift occurred in 14 to 38% of the cries (Table 10). No statistically significant differences could be found, although in the first week of life there seemed to be a tendency for the first signal to include a shift part more often. No such tendency could be seen at 3 and 6 months of age. The mean of

Table 10. Shift (%).

Age	Signal I	Signal II	Signal III	p
1 d				I - II N.S.
	26	19	22	I - III N.S.
				II - III N.S.
5 d				I - II N.S.
	38	29	21	I - III N.S.
				II - III N.S.
3 m				I - II N.S.
	16	22	21	I - III N.S.
				II - III N.S.
6 m				I - II N.S.
	32	14	38	I - III N.S.
				II - III N.S.
p	N.S.	N.S.	N.S.	

$p \leq 0.05$ +, $p \leq 0.01$ ++, $p \leq 0.001$ +++

the maximum pitch of the shift was between 750 and 1740 Hz. The corresponding median values shown in Table 11 were between 590 and 1650 Hz. During the first week of life, the mean of the maximum pitch of the shift of the first signal was significantly higher than that of signal III. No such differences were seen at 3 or 6 months of age.

Melody Type
  The falling and rising-falling melody type was the predominant type for all age groups and in all signals and occurred in 73 to 97% of the signals as summarized in Table 12. The lowest percentage was seen in the first signal at all ages, except at the age of 5 days, when the second signal showed the smallest percentage. The difference in occurrence of this melody type

Table 11. Maximum pitch of the shift (Hz).

Age	Signal I	Signal II	Signal III	p	
1 d					
X $\pm$ SD	1460 $\pm$ 450	960 $\pm$ 500	750 $\pm$ 320	I -II	N.S.
Md	1600	630	590	I -III	++
Range	640 -2250	580 -1850	540 -1290	II-III	N.S.
5 d					
X $\pm$ SD	1740 $\pm$ 530	1450 $\pm$ 950	1070 $\pm$ 370	I -II	N.S.
Md	1650	1320	1110	I -III	++
Range	900 -2630	470 -3420	640 -1070	II-III	N.S.
3 m					
X $\pm$ SD	1230 $\pm$ 410	1280 $\pm$ 490	1260 $\pm$ 750	I -II	N.S.
Md	1240	1160	1080	I -III	N.S.
Range	520 -1670	730 -2170	540 -2500	II-III	N.S.
6 m					
X $\pm$ SD	1210 $\pm$ 680	1500 $\pm$ 810	1080 $\pm$ 450	I -II	N.S.
Md	1040	1340	1050	I -III	N.S.
Range	510 -2750	690 -2630	450 -1920	II-III	N.S.
p	N.S.	N.S.	N.S.		

$p \leq 0.05$ +, $p \leq 0.01$ ++, $p \leq 0.001$ +++
mean and standard deviation = X $\pm$ SD
median = Md

between signal I and signal II was significant at the age of 3 months. When comparing signal I with the combined signal II and III, significant differences were found at the ages of 1 day and 3 months of life. Rising and falling-rising melodies were seen in 0 to 11% percent of the signals, and the number decreased with increasing signal number (Table 13). The signals of the fifth day, however, behaved in a different manner, with the percent of rising and falling-rising melody being lowest in the first signal and higher in the following two signals.

As the number of signals in the flat melody type group was small, no significant differences could be found, although there seems to be a tendency for the flat signals to increase in number in the second and third signals (Table 14). Table 15 shows the opposite

Table 12. Falling and rising-falling melody (%).

Age	Signal I	Signal II	Signal III	p	
1 d	82	97	94	I - II	N.S.
				I - III	N.S.
				II - III	N.S.
5 d	86	80	93	I - II	N.S.
				I - III	N.S.
				II - III	N.S.
3 m	73	86	94	I - II	N.S.
				I - III	N.S.
				II - III	N.S.
6 m	79	89	96	I - II	N.S.
				I - III	N.S.
				II - III	N.S.
p	N.S.	N.S.	N.S.		

$p \leq 0.05$ +, $p \leq 0.01$ ++, $p \leq 0.001$ +++

tendency in the group with no type, where the percent of no type melody was highest in the first signal and decreased in the second and third signals.

Continuity of the Signal

As shown in Table 16, at all ages the first signal was significantly less often continuous when compared to the second and third signals. Between the second and third signals, there were no significant differences. The first signal was continuous in 32 to 66% of the cries and 68 to 92% of the second and third signals were continuous.

Voicing of the Signals

Between 57 and 94% of all signals were voiced (Table 17). The number of voiced occurrences increased with

135

Table 13. Rising and falling-rising melody (%).

Age	Signal I	Signal II	Signal III	p
1 d				I – II N.S.
	8	0	0	I – III N.S.
				II– III N.S.
5 d				I – II N.S.
	3	11	7	I – III N.S.
				II– III N.S.
3 m				I – II N.S.
	11	6	3	I – III N.S.
				II– III N.S.
6 m				I – II N.S.
	11	4	0	I – III N.S.
				II– III N.S.
p	N.S.	N.S.	N.S.	

p≤0.05 +, p≤0.01 ++, p≤0.001 +++

increasing order of the signal. Half-voiced and voiceless cries were less abundant in signals two and three than in signal one, as shown in Tables 18 and 19.

Double Harmonic Break

Double harmonic break was seen quite frequently at all ages and occurred in 29 to 42% of the first signals. Table 20 indicates that the number decreased in the second and third signals at all ages except at the age of 6 months, where it seemed to remain constant in all signals.

Vibrato

A vibrato was often noted at the end of the signal; the frequency declined with increasing age and order of the signal. In the first signal, vibrato occurred in 25 to 68%, in the second signal in 11 to 29%, and in the third signal in 8 to 25% of the signals (Table 21).

Table 14. Flat melody (%).

Age	Signal I	Signal II	Signal III	p
1 d				
				I - II N.S.
	0	0	6	I - III N.S.
				II- III N.S.
5 d				
				I - II N.S.
	3	6	0	I - III N.S.
				II- III N.S.
3 m				
				I - II N.S.
	0	3	0	I - III N.S.
				II- III N.S.
6 m				
				I - II N.S.
	4	4	8	I - III N.S.
				II- III N.S.
p	N.S.	N.S.	N.S.	

$p \leq 0.05$ +, $p \leq 0.01$ ++, $p \leq 0.001$ +++

Glottal Roll

Table 22 presents the results of glottal roll. Glottal roll was seen in 18 to 30% of the first signals at all ages and less in the second and third signals.

Glottal Plosives

Glottal plosives were most abundant in the first signal where they were found in 5 to 32% of the cries. The frequency of glottal plosives increased somewhat with increasing age. As Table 23 shows, only at 3 and 6 months of age could significant differences between the first signal and the following signals be found.

Rarely Seen Cry Features

Glide, bi-phonation, and furcation, which are usually regarded to be pathological cry features, were rarely seen. Glide was found at the age of 3 months in one infant in signal II and III. Bi-phonation and furcation were seen in one signal each, in the first signal at the age of one day and in the third signal at

137

Table 15. No type melody (%).

Age	Signal I	Signal II	Signal III	p
1 d				I - II N.S.
	11	3	0	I - III N.S.
				II- III N.S.
5 d				I - II N.S.
	8	3	0	I - III N.S.
				II- III N.S.
3 m				I - II N.S.
	22	11	9	1 - III N.S.
				II- III N.S.
6 m				I - II N.S.
	11	7	0	I - III N.S.
				II- III N.S.
p	N.S.	N.S.	N.S.	

p$\leq$0.05 +, p$\leq$0.01 ++, p$\leq$0.001 +++

5 days of life. Noise concentration was not seen in this material.

Discussion

In spite of the recent computer techniques suggested for cry analysis (Tenold et al. 1974; Lester 1976), we feel that the sonagram made with narrow band filter has some great advantages for visualizing the cry. It is easy to recognize noise or other disturbing signals on the sonagram which may be difficult to identify or control in computerized techniques. Another advantage of spectrography is that a larger portion of the information included in the cry can be used to identify cry features. The computer at the present time does not recognize these and is limited to short segments. This seems to be especially true when working with the cries of sick infants since since the pathological findings are often features other than duration or

Table 16. Continuous signals (%).

Age	Signal I	Signal II	Signal III	p	
1 d					
	66	89	92	I - II	+
				I - III	+
				II- III	N.S.
5 d					
	32	86	86	I - II	+++
				I - III	+++
				II- III	N.S.
3 m					
	43	75	82	I - II	++
				I - III	++
				II- III	N.S.
6 m					
	36	68	88	I - II	+
				I - III	+++
				II- III	N.S.
p	1 - 5 ++	N.S.	N.S.		
	1 - 6 +				

$p \leq 0.05$ +, $p \leq 0.01$ ++, $p \leq 0,001$ +++

frequency. Therefore, we believe that the more tedious work with spectrography is necessary.

Latency Period

Our latency results, with a mean latency between 1.2 and 1.4 sec and a range of 0.1 to 3.6 sec, is in agreement with the results of other investigations. Fisichelli et al. (1974) report a mean latency of 1.41 $\pm$ 0.39 to 2.18 $\pm$ 0.89 sec in a prospective study of infants up to the age of one year. In an earlier study in 1963, the same group reports a latency period of 1.6 $\pm$ 0.75 sec in newborn infants. Gleiss and Höhn (1968) report a latency range of 0.92 − 6.44 sec with 74 percent of the cries in the range between 1.1 − 2.0 sec, a result which is in agreement with Michelsson (1971), who gives a median value of 1.8 sec for the latency with 50 percent of the latencies being between 1.2 and 2.5 sec. Our median values for the latency were between 1.1 and 1.2 sec. In a recent report by

Table 17. Voiced signals (%).

Age	Signal I	Signal II	Signal III	p	
1 d					
	79	84	94	I - II	N.S.
				I - III	N.S.
				II- III	N.S.
5 d					
				I - II	N.S.
	78	94	90	I - III	N.S.
				II- III	N.S.
3 m					
				I - II	N.S.
	57	61	62	I - III	N.S.
				II- III	N.S.
6 m					
				I - II	+
	57	89	77	I - III	N.S.
				II- III	N.S.
p	N.S.	5-3 ++	1-3 ++		
		3-6 +	5-3 +		

p$\leq$0.05 +, p$\leq$0.01 ++, p$\leq$0.001 +++

Zeskind and Lester (1978), a mean value of 1.369 $\pm$ 0.62 sec with a range of 0.7 and 6.44 sec was reported.

The agreement between the latency results shows that the pinch method used to elicit the cry yields results that are comparable to the results of those who utilize some special device for the pain stimulus (Karelitz and Fisichelli 1962; Ringel and Kluppel 1964; Gleiss and Höhn 1968; Zeskind and Lester 1978). This finding also supports the view of Parmelee (1962), who states that the pain cry is a maximal type of response. From our results, a tendency for the latency to become shorter with increasing age is seen. This tendency is also noted in the work of Lind et al. (1966).

Duration
Our results on the duration of the pain cry with a mean duration of the first signal of 4.1 to 5.2 sec, the second signal of 1.6 to 2.0 sec, and the third

Table 18. Half voiced signals (%)½

Age	Signal I	Signal II	Signal III	p
1 d				
	18	16	6	I - II N.S. I - III N.S. II- III N.S.
5 d				
	19	6	7	I - II N.S. I - III N.S. II- III N.S.
3 m				
	30	31	29	I - II N.S. I - III N.S. II- III N.S.
6 m				
	32	11	23	I - II N.S. I - III N.S. II- III N.S.
p	N.S.	5 - 3 +	1 - 3 +	

$p \leq 0.05$ +, $p \leq 0.01$ ++, $p \leq 0.001$ +++

signal of 1.2 to 1.6 sec clearly show that the first
signal is very different from the following signals
because of a much longer duration (Table 6).   Also,
between signals two and three a tendency for the third
signal to be the shorter one is seen.   This difference
between the first and the following signals has not
been clearly stressed in earlier investigations   The
duration obtained for the first signal agrees with the
results reported by Lester (1977), who reported a mean
duration of 4.85 $\pm$ 2.84 sec.   The duration of the
second and third signals is similar to the data
reported by Prescott (1975) for the mean duration of
signals 4 to 6 during the first ten days of life and
between 6 and 9 months of age which were 1.234 $\pm$ 0.55
and 1.978 $\pm$ 0.95 sec, respectively.   Ringel and Kluppel
(1964) give a mean value of 1.47 $\pm$ 0.62 sec after pain
stimulus.   This value is a mean of many cries after the
stimulus, and the order of the signals measured is not
reported.

Table 19. Voiceless signals (%).

Age	Signal I	Signal II	Signal III	p
1 d				
	3	0	0	I - II N.S. I - III N.S. II- III N.S.
5 d				
	3	0	0	I - II N.S. I - III N.S. II- III N.S.
3 m				
	16	8	9	I - II N.S. I - III N.S. II- III N.S.
6 m				
	11	0	0	I - II N.S. I - III N.S. II- III N.S.
p	N.S.	N.S.	N.S.	

$p \leq 0.05$ +, $p \leq 0.01$ ++, $p \leq 0.001$ +++

Lester (1976) reports a mean duration for spontaneous cry of 1.52 $\pm$ 0.39 sec. Ostwald's results in 1968, with a mean duration of about 1.3 $\pm$ 0.8 sec, agree with our results for signals two and three. There are some differences between our results and those of Lind et al. 1966) and Wasz-Höckert et al. (1968), who report a mean duratin of 2. $\pm$ 1.5 sec and 2.6 $\pm$ 1.5 sec under one month of age and 2.7 $\pm$ 1.1 sec between 1 month and 7 months of age. This difference might partly be explained by the cry sample. In the present investigations, all features of a duration of 0.1 sec or more were measured, whereas Lind and Wasz-Höckert measured only features of 0.4 sec or more. Our results show the importance of defining which signal is used when reporting durational features of the cry because there are significant differences in the duration of at least signals one to three.

Table 20. Double harmonic break (%).

Age	Signal I	Signal II	Signal III	p
1 d	42	27	14	I - II N.S. I - III + II- III N.S.
5 d	30	11	0	I - II N.S. I - III +++ II- III N.S.
3 m	38	14	6	I - II + I - III ++ II- III N.S.
6 m	29	25	23	I - II N.S. I - III N.S. II- III N.S.
p	N.S.	N.S.	1 - 5 + 5 - 6 ++	

p≤0.05 +, p≤0.01 ++, p≤0.001 +++

Maximum Pitch of the Fundamental Frequency

Our results on the maximum pitch are in agreement with those of Wasz-Höckert et al. (1968), who reported a mean maximum pitch of 650 Hz during the first month of life and 680 Hz between 1 and 7 months of age. Ostwald, Phibbs, and Fox (1968) report a mean maximum pitch of 540 Hz. Other investigators usually report a mean value for the pitch based on the mean frequency of the whole cry, which is, naturally, somewhat lower than our values. This value varies in diffferent reports between 308 and 606 Hz (Kittel and Hecht 1977; Lester 1977; Flatau and Gutzmann 1906). In some investigations, the median has been reported instead of the mean. Tenold et al. (1974) report a median of 518 Hz; Michelsson (1971) gives a median value of 620 Hz. The median for the maximum pitch in the present investigation was between 530 and 570 Hz and 550 and 680 Hz, depending on whether the shift was included or not in the measurement of the maximum pitch. In the

Table 21. Vibrato (%).

Age	Signal I	Signal II	Signal III	p	
1 d				I - II	+++
	68	22	25	I - III	+++
				II- III	N.S.
5 d				I - II	++
	65	29	10	I - III	+++
				II- III	N.S.
3 m				I - II	++
	49	11	9	I - III	+++
				II- III	N.S.
6 m				I - II	N.S.
	25	14	8	I - III	N.S.
				II- III	N.S.
p	1 - 6 ++	N.S.	N.S.		
	5 - 6 ++				

p≤0.05 +, p≤0.01 ++, p≤0.001 +++

future, when this normal material is used for the evaluation of pathological cries, a decision can be made on how the maximum pitch should be measured.

Minimum Pitch of the Fundamental Frequency

There are only a few reports on the minimum pitch of the fundamental frequency; these reports are mainly from the Finnish cry research group. Wasz-Höckert et al. 1968) reported a mean minimum pitch of 410 Hz under 1 month of age and 420 Hz over 1 month of age. In her thesis, Michelsson (1971) reported a median minimum pitch of 390 Hz. These results show that there is better agreement for the minimum pitch values than for the maximum pitch.

Shift

Shift was seen in the present data in 14 to 38% of the cries, as indicated in Table 10, which agrees with

144

Table 22. Glottal roll (%).

Age	Signal I	Signal II	Signal III	p		
1 d						
	29	5	0	I – II	+	
				I – III	+++	
				II– III	N.S.	
5 d						
	24	3	0	I – II	+	
				I – III	++	
				II– III	N.S.	
3 m						
	30	3	3	I – II	++	
				I – III	++	
				II– III	N.S.	
6 m						
	18	7	4	I – II	N.S.	
				I – III	N.S.	
				II– III	N.S.	
p	N.S.	N.S.	N.S.			

$p \leq 0.05$ +, $p \leq 0.01$ ++, $p \leq 0.001$ +++

the results of Wasz-Höckert et al. (1968), where 28 to 32% of the signals included a shift Stark and Nathanson (1973) reported a lower incidence of shift in the spontaneous cry in four babies where the fequency of shifts was between 0 to 31%. Michelsson (1971) reported a shift in 32% of the cries. The mean of the maximum pitch of the shift was, in our investigations, between 750 and 1740 Hz and the median was between 590 and 1650 Hz, as shown in Table 11. Wasz-Höckert et al. reported a median value of 1100 Hz. In their investigation, the maximum pitch of the shift was measured in a somewhat different manner than in ours and this may account for the differences in the results. (For additional information, refer to the Methods section of this chapter.)

Melody Form
    The melody form of the pain cry has been studied primarily by the Finnish cry research group. In this

Table 23. Glottal plosive (%).

Age	Signal I	Signal II	Signal III	p	
1 d					
	5	14	8	I – II	N.S.
				I – III	N.S.
				II– III	N.S.
5 d					
	27	9	7	I – II	N.S.
				I – III	N.S.
				II– III.	N.S.
3 m					
	32	11	9	I – II	N.S.
				I – III	+
				II– III	N.S.
6 m					
	25	14	0	I – II	N.S.
				I – III	++
				II– III	N.S.
p	N.S.	N.S.	N.S.		

$p \leq 0.05$ +, $p \leq 0.01$ ++, $p \leq 0.001$ +++

investigation, the predominant melody form was the
falling and rising-falling melody type as described in
Table 12.   Its occurrence in the first signal was
between 73 and 86%, which agrees with the 85%
reported by Wasz-Höckert et al. (1968).

We saw a higher number of rising and falling-rising
and no type melody forms (Tables 13-15) than Wasz-
Höckert and Michelsson, who reported 7-8% rising and
falling-rising melody forms and 5-14% no type melody
forms.   There was a similar proportion of flat melodies
in our investigations as in their investigations.   One
feature that is clearly seen is that the no type,
rising, and falling-rising melody forms occur less
often in the second and third signals.   This, once
again, shows the uniqueness of the first signal.
However, the cry at 5 days of age is an exception as
higher frequencies of rising and falling-rising
melodies are found in the second and third signals.

Stark and Nathanson (1975) have reported on the melody form of spontaneous cry, which they call a pitch contour. They studied three types of pitch contours--flat, rise and fall, or a combination of these three. Out of a total of 95 cries, they found a rising pitch in 11 signals and a falling pitch in 12 signals. Their results are not comparable with our results as we have used the pain induced cries and a different definition of melody form features.

Continuity of the Signal

Comparing our results for the continuity of the pain cry signal with the results of others, some differences can be noted. Wasz-Höckert et al. (1968) reported 70% continuous signals in a 0-1 month group and 73% continuous signals in a 1-7 months group. Sirviö and Michelsson (1976) reported 68% continuous signals in fullterm newborn infants. In our data, the percentage varied between 32 and 68% in the first cry signal. To some extent, this difference can be explained by the difference in the measuring techniques used. We have measured all features with a duration of 0.1 sec or more, whereas Wasz-Höckert et al. measured only features longer than 0.4 sec. The frequency of continuous signals in the second and third signals in our material was between 68 and 92%, which exceeds the numbers given by Wasz-Höckert et al. and Sirviö and Michelsson for the first signal.

Voicing of the Signals

There is agreement between the results of voicing in our investigations and the investigations of Wasz-Höckert et al. (1968). The respective numbers in signal one were 57 to 79% versus 65% for voiced signals, 18 to 32% versus 28% for half-voiced signals, and 3 to 16% versus 7% for voiceless signals. Michelsson (1971) and Sirviö and Michelsson (1976) reported voiced signals in 66% of the cries. In signals two and three, the number of voiced signals increased to 61 and 94%. In no other investigation could values for the second and third signals be found. Corresponding to the increase in voiced signals, the frequency of half-voiced and voiceless signals decreased in the second and third signals.

Double Harmonic Break

We observed double harmonic break somewhat less often than Wasz-Höckert et al. (1968). In this investigation

double harmonic break was found in 29 to 42% of the
first signals, compared to 48 to 62% reported by Wasz-
Höckert et al. The occurrence of double harmonic break
seems to decrease with increasing signal number,
except at the age of 6 months, when the frequency is
stable.

Vibrato and Glottal Roll

Vibrato was seen quite often in this study compared
to the frequencies reported by other investigators.
This might be due to the difficulties of separating
vibrato from glottal roll. This is revealed by the
fact that vibrato occurred in our data 25 to 68%
of the first signals, which agrees with the values for
glottal roll reported by others. For example, Wasz-
Höckert et al. (1968) reported 63 to 73% vocal fry and
Sirviö and Michelsson (1976) reported 60% glottal
roll. Stark et al. (1975) noted about 40% fry in
their data of two girls 0-8 weeks of age. In this
investigation, we held to a stricter definition for
glottal roll than has been used in most other
investigations. It occurred in the first signal
between 18 to 30%. Most often, the glottal roll was
preceeded by a vibrato. In signals two and three,
glottal roll was seldom seen.

Glottal Plosives

The incidence of glottal plosives in the first signal
was between 5 to 32% and was lower than that of Wasz-
Höckert et al., where glottal plosives were found in
50% of the cries. The difference was caused by the
fact that Wasz-Höckert et al. regarded short voiced
signals to be glottal plosives.

Rarely Seen Cry Features

A small number of cry features, such as bi-phonation,
glide, and furcation, were found in our investigations.
These features are thought to be found mainly in
pathological cries. This shows that if material is
chosen in a specific way, these features occur. This
does not mean that the data is not normative, but
rather that single so-called pathological features have
little or no predictive value regarding the long time
prognosis of the infant. On the other hand, we have
not excluded temporary disturbances in the homeostasis
of the children.

CONCLUSIONS

This investigation has revealed some new information on pain cry. It can be seen that pain induced cry signals differ from one another depending on the order of the signal. This is clearly noted in the duration of the signal, melody form, continuity of the signal, double harmonic break, vibrato, glottal roll, and also partly in the maximum pitch of the fundamental frequency. Therefore, it is important to define which signal is used when results on pain cry are reported. This new normative data will be extremely helpful in the future evaluation of pain cry in sick or at risk infants.

ACKNOWLEDGMENTS

The findings presented in this chapter have been supported by the Foundation for Pediatric Research in Finland and the Sigrid Jusélius Foundation.

REFERENCES

Fairbanks, G. 1942. An acoustical study of the pitch of infant hunger wails. Child Dev. 13:227-32.

Fisichelli, V.R. and Karelitz, S. 1963. The cry latencies of normal infants and those with brain damage. J. Pediat. 62:724-34.

Fisichelli, V.R., Karelitz, S., Fisichelli, R.M., and Cooper, J. 1974. The course of induced crying activity in the first year of life. Pediatric Research 8:921-28.

Flatau, T.S. and Gutzmann, H. 1906. Die stimme des säuglings. Arch. Laryng. Rhinol. 18:139-51.

Gleiss, J. and Höhn, W. 1968. Das Verhalten beim schreien nach konstranter schmertzeizung atemgesunder und atemgestörter neugeborener. Deutsche Zeitschr Nervenheilk 194:311-17.

Karelitz, S. and Fisichelli, V.R. 1962. The cry thresholds of normal infants and those with brain damage. J. Pediat. 61:619-85.

Kittel, G. and Hecht, L. 1977. Der erste schrei-frequenzana-lytische untersuchunger. Sprache-Stimme-Gehör 1:151-55.

Lester, B.M. 1976. Spectrum analysis of the cry sounds of well-nourished and malnourished infants. Child Dev. 47:237-41.

Lester, B.M. Maternal nutrition and fetal outcome. The pollution of the fetus. Symposium presented at the meeting of the American Psychological Association, August 1977, San Francisco.

Lester, B.M. and Zeskind, P. 1978. Brazelton scale and physical size correlates of neonatal cry features. Infant Behaviour and Development 1:393-402.

Lind, J., Wasz-Höckert, O., Vuorenkoski, V., Partanen, T.J., Theorell, K., and Valanne, E. 1966 Vocal response to painful stimuli in newborn and young infants. Ann. Paediatr. Fenn. 12:55-63.

Michelsson, K. 1971. Cry analyses of symptomless low birth weight neonates and of asphyxiated newborn infants. Acta Paediatr. Scand. Suppl. 216.

Murry, T., Amundson, P., and Hollien, H. 1977. Acoustical characteristics of infant cries: fundamental frequency. J. Child Lang. 4:321-28.

Ostwald, P.F., Phibbs, R., and Fox, S. 1968. Diagnostic use of infant cry. Biol. Neonat. 13:68-82.

Parmelee, A.H. 1962. Infant crying and neurologic diagnosis. J. Pediat. 61:801.

Prechtl, H.F.R. and Beintema, D. 1964. The Neurological Examination of the Fullterm Newborn Infant. Clinics in Developmental Medicine No. 12. Lavenham, Suffolk: Spastics International Medical Publications.

Prescott, R. 1975. Infant cry sound: developmental features. J. Acoust. Soc. Am. 57:1186-91.

Ringel, R.L. and Kluppel, D.D. 1964. Neonatal crying: a normative study. Folia Phoniat. 16:1-9.

Sirviö, P. and Michelsson, K. 1976. Sound-spectrographic cry analysis of normal and abnormal newborn infants. Folia Phoniat. 18:161-73.

Stark, R.E. and Nathanson, S.N. 1973. Spontaneous cry in the newborn infant: sounds and facial gestures. In Fourth Symposium on Oral Sensation and Perception, ed. J.F. Bosma, Department of Health, Education, and Welfare No. 73-546:323-52.

Stark, R.E., Rose, S.N., and McLagen, M. 1975. Features of infant sounds: the first eight weeks of life. J. Child Lang. 2:205-21.

Tenold J.L., Crowell, D H., Jones, R.H., Daniel, T.H., McPherson, D.F., and Popper, A.N. 1974. Cepstral and stationarity analyses of fullterm and premature infants' cries. J. Acoust. Soc. Am. 56:975-80.

Wasz-Höckert, O., Lind, J., Vuorenkoski, V., Partanen, T., and Valanne, E. 1968. The Infant Cry. A

150

<u>Spectrographic</u> <u>and</u> <u>Auditory</u> <u>Analysis.</u> Clinics in
Developmental Medicine No. 29. Lavenham, Suffolk:
Spastics International Medical Publications.
Wolff, P H. 1969. The natural history of crying and
other vocalization in early infancy. In <u>Determinants</u>
<u>of</u> <u>Infant</u> <u>Behaviour</u> <u>IV,</u> ed. B.M. Foss. London:
Methuen & Co., Ltd.
Zeskind, P.A. and Lester, B.M. 1978. Acoustic features
and auditory perceptions of the cries of newborns
with prenatal and perinatal complications. <u>Child</u>
<u>Dev.</u> 49:580-89.

CHAPTER 7

The Value of Cry Analysis
in Neonatology and Early Infancy

Katarina Michelsson and Ole Wasz-Höckert

INTRODUCTION

The infant cry sound has interested researchers of different disciplines for over a century. In 1838, Gardiner studied infant crying by means of musical notes and concluded that the tones of infant crying were between the A and E in the middle of the piano keyboard. In 1855, Darwin made notes on screaming and weeping of infants. He was mainly concerned with the local anatomy and developmental physiology of speech in relation to the expression of emotion.

The first cry studies were based on auditory analysis only. The development of instrumentation which enabled both a permanent recording and a more objective measurement of sound motivated scientists to study different kinds of preverbal vocalization. At the beginning of this century, the graphophone and the gramophone were used. Later, tape recorders for collecting the cry sounds and direct writing oscillographs for different kinds of cry analysis were used.

The development of the sound spectrograph by Potter et al. in the 1940s made remarkable progress in phonetic sciences. This apparatus was used for phonetic research first by Joos in 1948 and for the analysis of infant vocalization by Lynip in 1951. The most progress in cry research has been developed during the last 20 years by scientists from many parts of the world. Cooperative studies from different disciplines -- pediatrics, neurology, physiology, phonetics, phoniatrics, and behavior sciences-- are needed to further develop the field of cry research.

In addition, a standardized nomenclature that is understood and used by all scientists in the field is urgently needed. In the future, the development of new technical equipment will benefit cry research.

This chapter describes the crying of infants in the newborn period utilizing mainly sound spectrographic measurements of the cry sound. Cry characteristics of infants with various diseases will be given, especially those which typify diseases involving the central nervous system. Cry analysis can be helpful in evaluating both clinical diagnosis and prognosis of diseases in the newborn period.

AUDITORY INVESTIGATIONS

Identification of Cry Types

The auditory investigations of infant vocalization have been mainly observations of when, why, and how much babies cry.

Crying, according to Illingworth, (see Chapter 1), can be attributed to many different causes, including underfeeding, overfeeding, tension in the family, tiredness of the baby, colic, allergy, hypertonia, gastric flatulence, etc. The cry also has been said to have physiological usefulness in the early days of neonatal adjustment, such as improving pulmonary capacity in the first days of life (Long and Hull 1961) or being a defense mechanism to increase body temperature (Watson and Lowrey 1951).

Sherman (1927) is often referred to as stating that neonatal crying has little intent or meaning. She tested auditory identification of infant cries. The infants were placed behind a curtain and the cries were evoked with different kinds of stimuli, such as coldness, hunger, and anger. Sherman found that graduate students in psychology, medical students, and nurses were unable to differentiate the various emotional cries of infants. The test situation in Sherman's study, however, was not the best possible. Other authors have found differences in infant crying varying with stimuli (Bayley 1932, Fairbanks 1942, McCarthy 1952).

Wasz-Höckert and his research group began their systematic studies of infant crying in the early 1960's with analysis of four different basic cry types: birth, hunger, pain, and pleasure. The cries were identified both auditorily (Wasz-Höckert et al. 1964b, 1968) and with sound spectrography (Wasz-Höckert et al. 1962, 1963). This research group constructed an experimental listening tape with 24 selected short cry samples from normal, healthy children. The cries were auditorily typical birth, pain, hunger, and pleasure cries.

When these cries were played to 483 adults, it was found that those who had various degrees of experience in child care (349 adults) could identify the cries more accurately than those who had no previous experience of infant cries (134 adults). Due to their ability to recognize the birth cries, midwives obtained the highest percentage of correct responses. Additionally, it was found that training increased the ability to recognize different kinds of cries (Wasz-Höckert et al. 1964a).

The abiity of mothers to recognize the vocalizations of their own infants has been confirmed by Valanne et al. (1967), Formby (1967), and Murry, Hollien, and Muller (1975). Murry, Amundson, and Hollien (1977) noticed that an infant's sex could not be reliably identified using an auditory identification paradigm.

Auditory differences between the crying of sick infants compared to healthy ones have often been recognized in various pediatric textbooks. Illingworth (1955) stated that "a clinician recognizes the hoarse, gruff cry of cretinism, the hoarse cry of laryngitis, the shrill cry of hydrocephalus, meningitis, or cerebral irritability, the grunting cry of pneumonia, the feeble cry of amyotonia or a severely debilitated infant, and the whimper of the seriously ill child." Partanen et al. (1967) found that audible differences were recognizable when comparing the neonatal-period cries of healthy newborn infants and those with asphyxia, brain damage, jaundice, or Down's syndrome. The test tape included 20 pain cry signals representing eight normal and three cries each from the diagnosis groups. Forty-five pediatricians and 37 medical students were tested. A few months training improved the ability of medical students to recognize cry types.

From the existing research, there are audible differences in the crying of healthy infants. Furthermore, differences occur in the crying of sick infants when compared to healthy ones.

Cry Duration

The amount of crying by small babies has also interested scientists. Aldrich et al. (1945a,b,c) measured the amount of crying in 50 newborn babies. The average crying time during the first eight days of life was 117 min/day with a range of 48.2 min/day. Less crying occurred in infants with more nursing care. In the home situation, the baby had four prolonged crying spells in contrast to 11.9 for babies in the nursery. The main cause for crying was defined as hunger.

Brazelton (1962) studied 80 mothers of normal newborn infants, keeping daily records of the infant's fussing for the first 12 weeks of life. He found an average of 2¼ hours crying per day during the first seven weeks, with less crying each week thereafter, and daily peaks of crying in the evenings.

Greenberg et al. (1967) found that 7 newborn babies who were clamped early after delivery were more alert and cried more than 7 late-clamped infants.

Bell and Ainsworth (1972), in a longitudinal study of 26 infant-mother pairs, showed that promptness of maternal response was associated with a declined frequency and duration of infant crying. Close physical contact was the most effective in terminating the cry.

Rebelsky and Black (1972) found that 1-3 week old infants cried 14-34 min/day during a 7-8 hour period. The amount of crying increased during the first six weeks of life from an average 22 min/day to 34 min/day and decreased thereafter. The number of hours in which there was some crying did not change much between 1 and 13 weeks of age.

Bernal (1972) studied the crying behavior during the first ten days of life. In 77 babies, the peak in crying was observed between 6 p.m. and midnight. Breastfed babies showed more marked 24 hour patterns of crying with more crying after feeds than did bottle fed babies. Second babies cried less than first babies as mothers responded more quickly and more often by feeding the crying baby. In a controlled study, de Chateau (1976) reported less crying per day in a group of newborn infants when the baby received "early stimulation" and breast sucking a few minutes after delivery.

While there is a rather large amount of information concerning cry duration, most of the research lacks sufficient controls to generalize to normative growth and development patterns. Additional research will require more stringent controls to identify patterns of cry duration.

Studies on Cry Latency

In many studies the cry latency, the time between the pain-inducing stimulus and the onset of crying, has been measured. Fisichelli and Karelitz (1963) measured the latency period from the stimulus with a rubber band apparatus to the onset of crying. The study was composed of 117 normal infants and 69 infants who suffered from brain disorders. Eighty-eight percent of the normal infants and 54% of the abnormal ones responded to the first rubber band pinch. When latencies of more than 4 seconds were excluded from the measurements, Fisichelli and Karelitz found a mean latency of 2.6 sec for the abnormal group of infants and 1.6 sec for the normal group. Additionally, it was determined that infants with diffuse brain damage require a greater stimulus to produce one minute of crying (Karelitz and Fisichelli 1962).

In the analysis of 50 prematures (39 health and 11 with pulmonary disorders), Gleiss and Höhn (1968) found latency variations from 0.9 to 6.0 sec. The latency period decreased with repeated stimulation. A second interval, between the first short phonation and prolonged crying, was observed in 41% of the premature infants.

Cry latencies have been measured in studies of healthy infants by the Wasz-Höckert research group (Lind et al. 1966) and in connection with sound spectrogrphic cry analysis in both healthy infants and those with pathological conditions (Wasz-Höckert et al. 1968; Michelsson 1971; Michelsson et al. 1975; Michelsson and Sirviö 1976).

Fisichelli et al. (1974) reported on cry latencies during the first year of life and found latencies for the whole period between 1.41 sec and 2.18 sec. The crying activity was relatively stable from 2 days of age to 12 weeks of age and diminished thereafter. At 5 hours of age, the crying activity was somewhat depressed.

Additional studies on latencies in both healthy and sick infants are needed, however, to correlate the latency to the mode of stimulus, to age parameters, and also to the state of the infant, as defined by Prechtl

(1974). A neonate being in state 1 (deep sleep) might react to the stimulus in another way than the fully awake infant in state 3 or 4.

Cry Stimulus

The mode of stimulus to elicit the cry has varied from the use of a rubber band apparatus to pinches and snaps. Parmelee (1969) stated that the cry is always the maximum type of response to a stimulus and the mode of stimulation is, therefore, of less importance. This has also been stated by Murry, Hollien, and Muller (1975), who did not find any changes in the cries when correlated to different types of stimuli.

SOUND SPECTROGRAPHY

Cry research entered a new era when the sound could be transferred from tape to a spectrogram. The sound spectrograph provides a visualization of the sound, showing the time on the horizontal axis and the frequency (Hz) on the vertical axis. As described in Chapter 4, more than 20 different cry characteristics can be measured on the spectrograms.

The characteristics of cry can be divided into durational features, such as latency, duration, continuity of the cries, and the second pause, and in features related to the fundamental frequency. There are measurements of the pitch, the shift, melody type, and the voice quality. From the fundamental frequency, the maximum and minimum frequency, as well as the range of the fundamental or a percent change in time, can be measured. The occurrence of double harmonic break, glottal roll, vibrato, bi-phonation, gliding, furcation, noise concentration, tonal pit, and glottal plosives can also be noted. Figure 1 shows a schematic sonogram with some of the cry characteristics measurable by sound spectrography.

CRY IN HEALTHY INFANTS

Cry analysis of healthy newborn infants is described in Chapter 4 and will not be discussed in detail here.

Since Flatau and Gutzman (1906) found a fundamental frequency of 440 Hz in the crying of healthy neonates, many other researchers have confirmed these results.

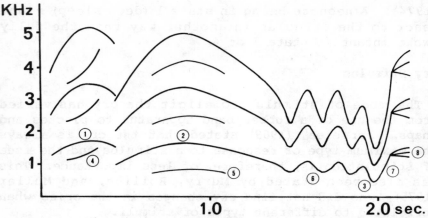

KHz

Figure 1.   Schematic sonagram displaying some cry characteristics:
1.   Maximum pitch of shift; 2.   maximum pitch of the
fundamental frequency; 3. minimum pitch of the
fundamental frequency; 4. bi-phonation; 5. double
harmonic break; 6. vibrato; 7. gliding; 8. furcation.

In most of the first cry studies, only the fundamental
frequency has been noted.   In later studies, other cry
characteristics have been found to be important,
especially in clinical work when comparing groups of
children with different diseases.
   As described in Chapter 4, the fundamental frequency
in crying of healthy infants varies between 350 Hz and
650 Hz.   The cry in healthy infants often has a falling
or rising-falling melody type with a stable pitch and a
duration of approximately 2 sec (Table 1).   Shifts with
a higher pitched frequency occur mainly at the
beginning of the signals and especially in pain cries
in which almost every third cry has a shift part.
Occurrence of glottal roll is quite common at the end
of the phonations, and vibrato sometimes precedes the
glottal roll part (Figure 2). Bi-phonation and gliding
are rare.   The signals are voiced and continuous in
about two-thirds of the cries.

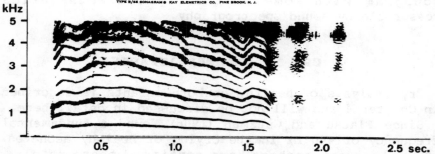

Figure 2.   Pain cry of a healthy newborn baby.

158

Table 1. Cry analysis of healthy full-term, small for gestational age and asphyxiated premature infants (Michelsson 1971).

	CONTROLS	LOW BIRTH WEIGHT			ASPHYXIATED PREMATURES	
		small for age	prema-ture	prema-ture	periph. asphyxia	central asphyzia
Gestational weeks	38-40	38-40	35-37	34	37	37
No of infants	50	30	35	40	40	55
No of cries analyzed	50	30	35	40	40	55
Age, days	0-10	0-10	0-10	0-10	0-3	0-3
Duration, sec.						
mean	2.6	4.4	3.0	2.6	3.3	2.9
median	2.0	3.8	3.1	2.4	3.4	1.7
standard deviation	1.6	2.2	1.8	1.8	2.3	2.4
Minimum pitch, F_0, Hz						
mean	400	340	480	570	700	880
median	390	330	460	450	490	720
standard deviation	90	90	240	340	470	580
Maximum pitch, F_0, Hz						
mean	650	640	1010	1360	1450	1730
median	620	550	740	1040	1590	1700
standard deviation	110	390	750	950	760	930
Occurrence of shift,%	32	13	43	28	20	31
Maximum pitch of shift,%						
mean	1170	1650	2030	1900	1560	1730
median	1100	1830	1830	1200	1540	1540
standard deviation	340	730	940	950	530	930
Maximum pitch, whole cry,Hz						
mean	810	760	1450	1590	1610	1950
median	680	550	870	1470	1650	1890
standard deviation	330	570	1010	1010	690	850
Continuous signals, %	68	63	66	69	50	62
Voiced phonations, %	66	50	49	53	60	53
Melody type, %						
falling, rising-falling	85	94	83	85	85	54
rising	0	0	3	5	7	15
falling-rising	7	3	3	7	3	22
flat	3	3	11	3	3	7
no type	5	0	0	0	2	2
Double harmonic break,%	44	33	29	25	13	20
Bi-phonation, %	0	0	14	5	25	27
Gliding, %	0	0	11	13	13	11
Vibrato, %	0	7	6	3	13	2
Glottal roll, %	60	57	43	43	40	26
Glottal plosives, %	40	13	9	3	15	5

The pain cry has been the type of cry selected by our reasearch group for the analysis of cries in different diseases. In many of the studies, only the first phonation after the pain stimulus was used. Later studies additionally include the second and the third phonation after stimulus application.

CRY IN VARIOUS CONDITIONS AND DISEASES

Classic pediatric textbooks have mentioned the cry as one attribute which changes according to different pathological conditions. Parents have often noticed that when their child is ill, the cry changes. The cry can be wailing when the child has a high fever. In more serious diseases, the cry can be helpful in making a diagnosis. The main purpose of our research group has been to show that cry analysis is an aid in making a diagnosis, especially in the newborn period and in diseases which have affected the central nervous system.

When a child is sick and the cry changes from normal to abnormal, it can be caused by disturbances in the larynx or in the oral cavities. It can, however, also reflect the function of the brain as the neural impulses to the voice-producing organs originate in the brain. Parmelee (1962) stated that crying "reflects the capacity of the nervous system to be activated and also the ability of the nervous system to inhibit or modulate this activation. The differences in the ability of different nervous systems to respond could be in the peripheral sensory receptors, but it seems more likely that these differences are in the more complex activating systems of the brain." Thus, for our research group, one of the main purposes of cry analysis has been not only to evaluate in which diseases the cry pattern is different from the normal, but also which characteristics can be caused by abnormality or disease in the larynx and oral cavities only and which are caused by disturbances in the function of the central nervous system. Additionally, our goal has been to know what kind of cry characteristics are typical of certain specific diseases, especially in the newborn period when diagnosis is not always easy. Any method to assist in assessing diagnosis and prognosis during this period is important and should be further developed.

High-pitched "shrill" cries have often been associated with diseases involving the brain. With advances in cry research, it has been demonstrated that pitch pattern is not the only indicator of abnormality. For instance, the high-pitched characteristic of the cry is not the only indicator of pathology in infants with brain damage. Other features, such as variations in the latency in pain stimulated cries, duration of the phonation, an abnormal melody type, or a more frequent occurrence of gliding and bi-phonation, are involved.

Additional basic research is needed when correlating variations of the different cry characteristics with specific diseases. In clinical studies, the cry analysis can be compared with the EEG which can give specific clues to diagnosis. However, the EEG can be nonspecific in diseases involving the central nervous system. Cry analysis is already beneficial in assessing both diagnosis and prognosis in the newborn period. We have, therefore, repeatedly pointed out the need for reasearch by teams of physicians and phoneticians to obtain basic facts. The analysis of sonagrams is by no means more difficult to master than are the EEG or ECG data. It is only a question of attitude for the medical profession to adapt phonetic techniques and skills.

CRY IN NEWBORN LOW BIRTH WEIGHT INFANTS

In 1971, spectrographic studies were made of the crying of newborn low birth weight infants (Michelsson 1971). Cry samples of 105 symptomless low birth weight infants were analyzed, of which 30 were small for gestational age and 75 truly premature. All the small for gestational age infants were born after 38-40 gestational weeks and their birth weights were below the 10 percentile curve for normal birth weight distribution. The first phonation after a pain stimulus was applied, was analyzed for each child. The results showed that the cry of the small for age infants did not change much from the crying of 50 healthy fullterm infants with normal birth weights. In both groups, the melody type was predominantly falling or rising-falling, and neither bi-phonation nor gliding were seen. The mean of the maximum fundamental frequency in the small for gestational age infants was 640 Hz (Table 1).

In 1978, Lester and Zeskind found that the cries of fullterm but underweight infants had a shorter duration (2.0 sec) and a higher fundamental frequency (740 Hz) than babies of normal birth weight (4.9 sec and 467 Hz, respectively).

The truly premature infants, in the study by Michelsson, were divided into two groups: those born at 35-37 gestational weeks (35 infants) and those born at 34 gestational weeks or earlier (40 infants). The

161

Figure 3. Pain cry of premature infants:

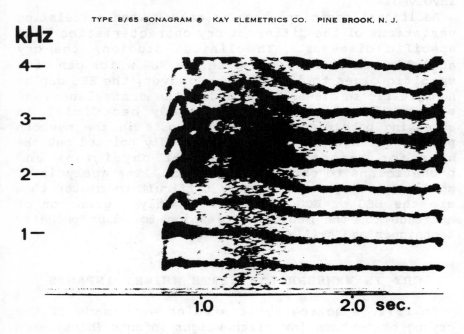

TYPE B/65 SONAGRAM ® KAY ELEMETRICS CO. PINE BROOK, N. J.

kHz

4—

3—

2—

1—

1.0   2.0 sec.

a. b.w.2,150g, 36g.w.;

SONAGRAM ® KAY ELEMETRICS CO. PINE BROOK, N. J.

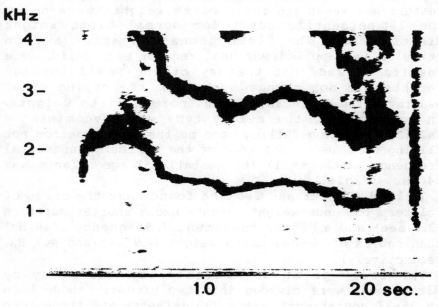

kHz

4 -

3 -

2 -

1 -

1.0   2.0 sec.

b. b.w.1,560g., 32g.w.

162

results showed that the younger infants cried with higher pitched sounds than those born at 35-37 gestational weeks (Table 1). Figure 3 displays sonagrams of 2 premature infants' cries. The fundamental frequency was highest in the smallest prematures with a mean of maximum pitch of 1360 Hz and a minimum pitch of 590 Hz. Greater variations and lower fundamental frequencies occurred in the cries of the very small prematures. These variations may be due to immaturity or to prenatal risk factors not thought of when the cry samples were collected. This latter notion is supported by the study of Zeskind and Lester (1978), who found pitch differences in the crying of healthy fullterm infants when compared to healthy newborns with maternal or parturital risk factors.

The dominating melody type in all premature infants was falling or rising-falling, similar to that seen in the controls. Both bi-phonation and gliding occurred in the cries of the prematures 5-14 percent of the time. No significant changes were seen in the continuity and voicing of signals, neither in the occurrence of double harmonic break nor in the second pause It was found, additionally, that the cry changed with the increasing age of the premature infant. At the time when the baby should have been born according to the gestational age, the cry was similar to that of a healthy child born at term.

Tenold et al. (1974) found a median fundamental frequency of 752 Hz for 5 premature infants and 518 Hz for 9 term infants.

Cry in Chromosome Abnormalities

The first systematic sound spectrographic studies on the crying of infants with chromosome abnormalities were performed by Lind et al. in 1970. They studied 120 cry samples of infants 0-8 months old (30 infants with Down's syndrome, 21-trisomy). The results show that when compared to the cries of 120 healthy infants of corresponding age, the cries in Down's syndrome often had a long duration with a mean of 4.5 sec. In addition, they were lower pitched with a mean maximum pitch of 510 Hz and a mean minimum pitch of 210 Hz. The melody was flat in 63% of the samples, bi-phonation occurred in 23%, and stuttering in 53%. Figure 4a shows a cry signal in Down's syndrome.

Figure 4. Pain cry in chromosome abnormalities: a. Down's syndrome,

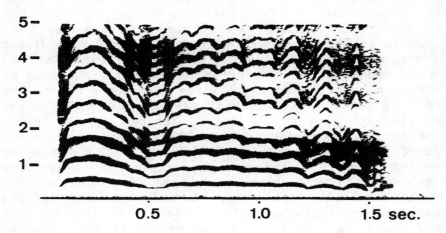

kHz

SONAGRAM ® KAY ELEMETRICS CO. PINE BROOK, N. J.

b. Cri-du-chat syndrome.

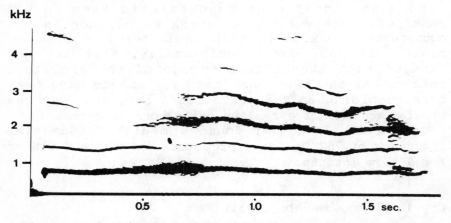

The cry of children with a deletion of chromosome 5, the "cri du chat" syndrome, has been studied by Vuorenkoski et al. (1966), Luchsinger et al. (1967), and Bauer (1968). Vuorenkoski et al. noticed a general pitch of 860 Hz in 44 cries of 8 children 4-48 months old. They also found a flat melody type in 36% of the cries and a rising melody type in 23%. Approximately the same values of the fundamental fequency in the "cri du chat" infants have been found by Kittel and Hecht in 1977 and Michelsson et al. in 1980. A sonagram of a cry signal in the "cri du chat" syndrome is seen in Figure 4b. Bauer found a fundamental frequency of 800 Hz in the "cri du chat" syndrome when compared to 400-500 Hz in the control group. Luchsinger et al. found a fundamental frequency

164

between 600-100 Hz in one infant with "cri du chat" syndrome; whereas in a control group the fundamental frequency was 290-440 Hz. Kittens, but not adult cats, have a "cry" with a similar sonagram (Vuorenkoski et al. 1966).

The cry of one infant with 13-trisomy has been reported by Ostwald et al., in 1970. In 9 cries from this infant, a peak was noted in the fundamental frequency of 405-680 Hz, and the crying resembled that of Down's syndrome more than that of the "cri du chat" syndrome.

In 1980, Michelsson et al. analyzed 135 cries of 14 infants aged 0 days to 7 months who exhibited various chromosome abnormalities, excepting Down's syndrome (Table 2). Two of the infants had the "cri du chat" syndrome, two a deletion of chromosome 4, three had 13-trisomy, and three had 18-trisomy, and one case each of abnormalities of chromosomes 1, 2, 8, and 20. In both 13-trisomy and 18-trisomy, the cries were low pitched and the perception of the cries as low pitched was accentuated because shift parts were absent and glottal roll occurred frequently at the end of the phonations.

In all infants with a deletion of chromosome 4 or 5 and in one infant with a translocation of chromosomes 1 and 4, more higher pitched cries were noted than in the control group. Cries with a pitch above 800 Hz were not seen in any other cases with a chromosome abnormality. No bi-phonation occurred in the samples of chromosome abnormality and in the 135 cry samples studied, only one showed gliding. This was also the case in the cry of an infant who additionally had low Apgar scores at birth.

A flat melody type was common in the "cri du chat" syndrome; flat or no melody type was common in 13-trisomy. The dominating melody type in cries of the other chromosome abnormalities was falling or rising-falling.

Cry in Newborn Infants with Asphyxia

Studies were made of the crying of infants with asphyxia (oxygen deficiency) in the newborn period (Michelsson 1971). Cries from 205 infants during the infants' first three days of life were collected. Only the first phonation after pain stimulus was used for analysis, and only one cry from each child was obtained. The children were divided into two groups whether the asphyxia was of mainly pulmonic or cerebral

Table 2. Cry analysis of full-term infants with asphyxia, meningitis, marasmus and kwashiorkor (Michelsson 1971, Michelsson et al. 1977, Juntunen et al. 1978).

| | ASPHYXIA | | | MENINGITIS | MALNUTRITION | |
	peripheral	central	Apgar ≤ 6 at 5 min.	meningitis	marasmus	kwashiorkor
No of infants	40	70	45	14	4	1
No of cries analyzed	40	70	115	115	26	4
Age,						
Duration, sec.						
mean	4.8	3.7	2.5	1.7	2.0	2.1
median	4.5	3.7	2.3	1.2	1.8	2.0
standard deviation	2.9	2.3	1.9	1.5	0.8	0.2
Minimum pitch, F_0, Hz						
mean	430	640	580	560	730	290
median	390	470	440	410	650	270
standard deviation	240	460	440	400	370	80
Maximum pitch, F_0, Hz						
mean	1000	1320	1080	1100	1340	460
median	640	1120	1100	750	1390	470
standard deviation	940	910	850	890	650	50
Occurrence of shift, %	20	39	26	25	19	0
Maximum pitch of shift,%						
mean	1870	1840	1490	1200	1110	–
median	1600	1450	1350	970	1890	–
standard deviation	720	910	820	710	520	–
Maximum pitch, whole cry, Hz						
mean	1210	1460	1290	1200	1370	460
median	640	1420	1040	840	1400	470
standard deviation	1020	930	890	910	610	50
Continuous signals, %	53	63	79	75	85	100
Voiced phonations, %	47	51	68	45	85	100
Melody type, %						
falling, rising-falling	65	50	59	50	73	0
rising	7	13	16	9	4	0
falling-rising	8	17	11	15		0
flat	20	20	9	15	23	100
no type	0	0	5	11	0	0
Double harmonic break,%	28	26	20	8	27	25
Bi-phonation, %	20	26	34	49	23	0
Glide, %	3	14	5	11	0	0
Vibrato, %	3	6	32	8	0	0
Glottal roll, %	50	26	20	25	0	0
Glottal plosives, %	33	13	16	0	0	0

origin. Since it has been shown that newborn premature infants cry differently than fullterm infants, the infants with asphyxia were divided into two groups according to gestational age. The cry characteristics of the asphyxiated infants were compared to the crying of 50 healthy fullterm or 75 premature infants, depending upon whether the neonate with asphyxia was fullterm or premature at birth. In both gestational age groups, the cry was found to be more abnormal in those infants in which the asphyxia was considered to

Table 3. Cry in cleft palate, hypothyroidism and chromosomal abnormalities (Michelsson and Sirviö 1976, Michelsson et al. 1975, 1980).

	Cleft palate	Hypothyr- oidism	delet. chr. 4	Cri du chat	13- trisomy	18- trisomy
No of infants	13	4	2	2	3	3
No of cries analyzed	52	40	22	18	26	32
Age,						
Duration, sec.						
mean	4.5	2.5	1.6	2.7	3.3	1.6
median	3.5	2.4	1.3	1.9	1.7	1.0
standard deviation	2.1	1.5	1.1	1.9	2.8	1.7
Minimum pitch, F_o, Hz						
mean	360	290	430	680	350	300
	340	280	380	680	350	280
			100	150	190	70	60
Maximum pitch, F_o, Hz						
mean	710	470	740	980	480	550
median	570	470	600	840	470	540
standard deviation	280	130	370	500	70	60
Occurrence of shift, %	21	7	18	6	0	0
Maximum pitch of shift,%						
mean	1970	910	1020	900	–	–
median	1700	740	1430	900	–	–
standard deviation	900	320	920	–	–	–
Maximum pitch,whole cry,%						
mean	1010	520	910	990	480	570
median	590	490	610	900	480	540
standard deviation	800	180	580	500	70	60
Continuous signals, %	54	74	82	94	41	88
Voiced phonations, %	67	74	73	94	46	76
Melody type, %						
falling, rising-falling	8	76	86	17	42	75
rising, falling-rising	9	12	0	17	0	6
flat	4	12	9	60	23	19
no type	0	0	5	6	35	0
Double harmonic break, %	29		9	17	19	19
Bi-phonation, %	9	0	5	6	0	0
Glide, %	10	0	5	0	0	0
Vibrato, %	47	5	14	6	19	13
Glottal roll, %	49	57	14	6	27	16
Glottal plosives, %	4	10	14	6	19	6

be of cerebral origin as can be seen in Tables 1 and 3.
In particular, the pitch was higher in infants with asphyxia but other characteristics differentiated the crying in these infants from normal infant crying (Figure 5). In the fullterm infants with cerebral asphyxia, the mean of the maximum pitch was 1320 Hz; the minimum pitch 640 Hz. In the prematures with cerebral asphyxia, the corresponding values were 1730 Hz and 930 Hz. Bi-phonation occurred in 26% of the fullterm and in 27% of the prematures and gliding in 14% and 11% respectively. In the central type of asphyxia, rising and fall-rising types of melody were increased.

Figure 5. Cry in hypoxia.

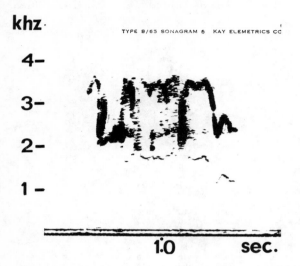

In addition, it was found that in those cry characteristics where the asphyxiated infants differed significantly from the controls, the differences were often more marked in the newborn that had suffered more severely from asphyxia. Thus, of the 42 neonates with central asphyxia in the study group who either died or were found to have symptoms of brain damage at a follow-up examination, only eight had the cry signal characteristic of a healthy infant.

The cry changes were often so obvious that we have good reason to use the cry analysis as an additional tool in neonatal neurological examinations. This has been confirmed in a follow-up study in 1977 (Michelsson et al.) which demonstrated that cry analysis had prognostic value when asphyxia was concerned. One hundred and fifteen pain induced cries of 45 fullterm newborn infants with Apgar scores of 6 or less at 5 minutes were analyzed. The results showed that in infants who retrospectively were found to be neurologically damaged at the check-up at 2-8 years, the cry characteristics were more abnormal, as can be seen in Table 3. The signals were shorter, the maximum and minimum pitches were higher, bi-phonation and gliding were more common, and the melody type was more often abnormal. Thus, it is indicative that cry analysis not only has diagnostic but also prognostic value.

Cry in Other Metabolic Disturbances

The cry of newborn infants with *jaundice*, caused by hyperbilirubinaemia, has been reported by Wasz-Höckert et al., (1971). One cry each from 45 infants with jaundice was studied. When the cry sample to be analyzed could be chosen from many different signals, the most abnormal one was selected. The mean of the maximum of the fundamental frequency was found to be 2120 Hz. The mean of the minimum pitch was 960 Hz. Bi-phonation occured in 49% of the cries and furcation in 42%. Furcation seems to be a specific feature in pain cries of infants with jaundice. Figure 6 shows cry in hyperbilirubinaemia.

A cry score rating system that was developed by Vuorenkoski et al. (1971) has also been used in analyzing cries of the 45 infants with hyperbilirubinaemia. Each of the 13 cry features was assigned a weight of 0 to 4, and the cry score was the sum of these ratings. A score of 0-3 was defined as normal, and a score of 4-50 was defined as abnormal. When applied to hyperbilirubinaemia, a mean score of 4.4 was found as compared to a score of 1.4 in the group fo control infants. Only one of the 45 infants with jaundice had a normal score.

Tardy-Renucci and Appaix (1978) found in four infants with hyperbilirubinaemia a mean fundamental frequency of 630 Hz. This was higher than in the other groups of infants with various disorders in the neonatal period, as well as in the control group (470 Hz).

A preliminary report on the crying of newborn infants with low blood sugar, *hypoglycaemia*, was presented by

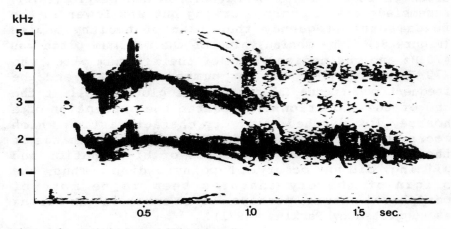

Figure 6. Cry in hyperbilirubinemia.

Figure 7. Cry in hypoglycaemia.

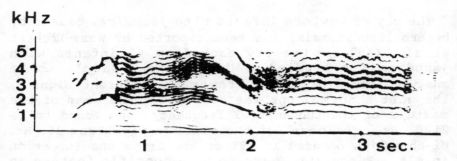

Koivisto et al. in 1974. In 17 cries from 15 fullterm infants with hypoglycaemia, a median maximum pitch of 1600 Hz was noted with a minimum pitch of 610 Hz. The beginning of the phonation was often unusually high-pitched as seen in Figure 7. Vibrato was seen in 11, bi-phonation in 10, and gliding in 3 of the 17 cries studied. In analyzing cries of newborn *infants of diabetic* mothers, Thoden and Michelsson (1979) found higher fundamental frequency with a mean maximum pitch of 1180 Hz. The maximum pitch was still higher when the child in the neonatal period additionally had hypoglycaemia (1520 Hz) or hyperbilirubinaemia (1790 Hz) or both simultaneously (1980 Hz). The minimum pitch in cries of infants of diabetic mothers was 510 Hz. When the babies additionally had both hypoglycaemia and hyperbilirubinaemia, the minimum pitch was 690 Hz. The study clearly shows that the cry analysis is an indicator of the severity of the diseases in the neonatal period.

The cry in *congenital hypothyroidism*, studied in 40 cries of four infants by Michelsson and Sivriö (1976) resembled that of normal crying but was lower in the fundamental frequency than that of healthy babies (Figure 8). The median value of the maximum pitch was 470 Hz and the median value of the minimum pitch was 270 Hz (Table 3). The low number of shifts and the frequent occurrence (57 percent) of glottal roll at the end of the phonation accentuated the perception of a hoarse, low pitched cry. Cry characteristics which occur in brain damaged infants, such as the change in the melody type and occurrence of bi-phonation and gliding, did not occur in hypothyroidism. Thus, the origin of the cry features seem to be more of peripheral nature, perhaps due to edema in the larynx as suggested by Perkins (1971).

Figure 8. Cry in hypothyroidism.

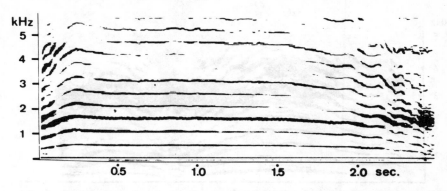

Cry characteristics in one child with hypothyroidism have been studied by Vuorenkoski et al. (1973) with a Cry Analyser. This apparatus (Vuorenkoski et al. 1970) differentiates between cries with a pitch greater or less than 1000 Hz. Even at the age of eight months, the child did not show any tendency to use a pitch 1000 Hz.

Cry in Cleft Palate Infants

Sound spectrographic cry analysis of *cleft palate* infants has been performed by Michelsson et al. (1975) and is displayed in Table 3. The purpose of this study was mainly to find out what kind of changes in the cry characteristics are caused by anatomical defects in the sound producing oral cavities and if these changes are different from those seen in infants with central nervous system involvement.

Fifty-two cries from 13 infants with cleft palate were analyzed. No changes were noted in the fundamental frequency, melody type, and duration in association with these anatomical defects when compared to controls. One feature which did not occur in the crying of the control groups was the "tonal pit," e.g., a sudden change of fundamental frequency during a short time interval (Figure 9). Tonal pit occurred in 22%. Abnormal characteristics occurring in infants with central nervous system involvement, such as an occurrence of bi-phonation, gliding, and a change in the melody type, did not occur in infants with cleft palate. The results indicate that the cry characteristics are different depending on whether the

171

Figure 9. Cry in cleft palate.

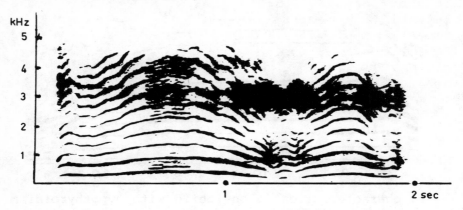

brain or the articulators are affected. This observation shows that the cry evaluation in central nervous system conditions has a diagnostic value.

Cry in Central Nervous Diseases

The crying of 14 infants with *bacterial meningitis* aged 4 days to 6 months was investigated by Michelsson et al. in 1977. The crying in meningitic infants was found to be abnormal in respect to fundamental frequency. The cries were higher pitched and the mean of the maximum pitch was 1100 Hz and of minimum pitch was 560 Hz in the 110 cries studied (Table 2). The dominating melody type, which in healthy infants is falling or rising-falling, was seen in only every other cry in meningitic babies. Bi-phonation occurred in

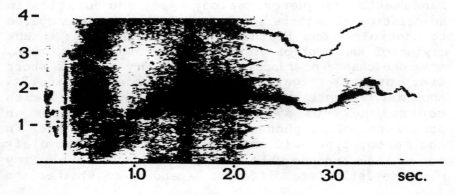

Figure 10. Cry in bacterial meningitis.

49%, gliding in 11%, and glottal roll in 25%. Figure 10 shows cry characteristics in meningitis. Those infants with meningitis who at a later time were abnormal also had more abnormal cry characteristics. Especially noted was an increase in rising, falling-rising, and flat melody types (68% versus 37% in the meningitis babies without sequelae and 15% in the controls).

The crying of infants with *herpes virus encephalitis* has been studied by the Finnish research group (Michelsson and Sirvio 1976 and Pettay et al. 1977). When analyzing the cries of these infants, a voiceless fricative noise was noted in the frequency region of 2000-2500 Hz and was seen in both voiced and voiceless parts of th signals (Figure 11). The meaning and specificity of the noise concentration is still unknown. Since it has occurred in almost half of the signals in herpes encephalitis that were studied, the cry analysis is used in clinical work when herpes encephalitis is suspected.

Lind et al. (1965) reported a cry analysis of one infant with *brain damage from a birth injury*. They found in ten pain cries a fundamental frequency of 450-2070 Hz as compared to 280-900 Hz of a group of 20 controls.

The cry in *hydrocephalus* has been analyzed by Michelsson et al., in 1980. Cries with the highest pitch, mean of maximum pitch over 1000 Hz, were noted in those infants who in addition to the hydrocephalus had congenital malformations of the brain (porencephalus or hydranencephalus). It was also noted that the cry changed to a more normal one after the shunt operation for hydrocephalus when the increased intracranial pressure was normalized.

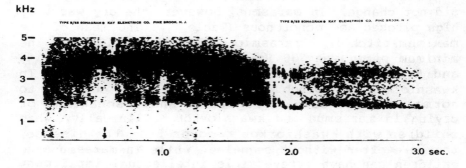

Figure 11. Cry in herpes virus encephalitis.

kHz

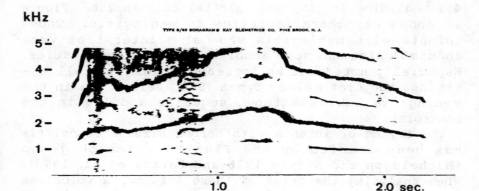

Figure 12. Cry in malnutrition: a. marasmus; b. kwashiorkor.

kHz

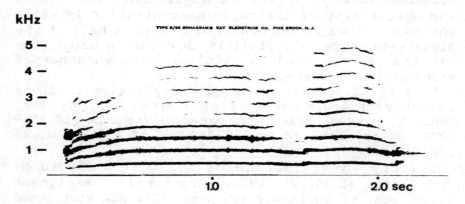

Cry in Malnutrition

Infants suffering from severe malnutrition (marasmus and kwashiorkor) were studied by Juntunen et al. (1978). In 30 cry samples from 5 infants in North Nigeria who had kwashiorkor, the cry characteristics did not change. In marasmus, however, the cry was very high pitched and monotonous (Table 2). The mean of the maximum pitch in 4 marasmic children was 1340 Hz; the minimum pitch was 730 Hz; bi-phonation occurred in 6; and 6 of the 26 cries had a flat melody type. In kwashiorkor, the pitch was 290-460 Hz which compares to normal control cases. Figure 12 shows sonagrams of crying in marasmus and kwashiorkor. Clinically, when children with kwashiorkor recover from the disease, they are often without sequelae, while in marasmus the children can have irreversible intellectual impairment and organic brain dysfunction (Stoch and Smythe 1967). Therefore, an important feature in the analysis was

174

that the cry did not change in kwashiorkor, but was abnormal in marasmus.

Lester (1976) studied the cry sounds of 12 well-nourished infants and 12 malnourished infants and found that the cry sounds of the 12 well-nourished infants were longer, 2.66 sec versus 1.52 sec for the controls. The malnourished infants also showed higher pitch, 480 Hz versus 308 Hz for the controls.

Cry in Various Disorders

In 1968, Ostwald et al. determined how two acoustical features, duration and pitch, had a relationship to clinical diagnosis ratings. Altogether, 355 cries from 13 subjects were analyzed. The children were divided into three groups; 5 normal infants, 5 questionably impaired, and 5 abnormal. Duration measurements showed no differences between the groups. Pitch measurements showed a marked increased of fundamental frequency among infants rated as impaired or abnormal in which cries with a high frequency of 300-2875 Hz occurred, compared to the normal group, 360-785 Hz.

Blinick et al. (1971) stated that 11% of 338 normal infants and 50% of 31 newborn infants of narcotic addicted mothers showed abnormal birth cries, with a higher fundamental frequency being the most striking abnormality.

Stark and Nathanson (1975) suggested that infant cry analysis might aid in the understanding of some of the mechanisms underlying SIDS (sudden infant death syndrome). A retrospective study of a four day old fullterm, normal baby, who at six months suddenly died, showed that the cry in SIDS had a higher frequency, more shifts, and more extremes in frequency. Andersson-Huntington and Rosenblith (1976) also mentioned abnormal cries in their retrospective report of babies who died of SIDS. Further information on this subject is reported in Chapter 8 by Colton and Steinschneider.

Kittel and Hecht (1977) found that the cry in one child born to a mother with floride syphilis had a fundamental frequency of 206 Hz compared to 425 Hz in 50 healthy newborns.

Tardy-Renucci and Appaix (1978) found a mean fundamental frequency of 512 Hz in a group of 68 infants with various neonatal disorders, such as hyperbilirubinaemia, malformation syndromes, anoxia, and respiratory disorders. They defined the cry as a "reflex motor action under the dependency of the nervous centers" and further stated that the cry "can be modified by diverse physiologic and pathologic processes." The highest mean fundamental frequency was noted in four infants with jaundice, 630 Hz, and in three who had been resuscitated after birth, 613 Hz. The mean fundamental frequency in 9 control infants was 470 Hz.

In 1978, Lester and Zeskind found a mean pitch of 814 Hz in the crying of 24 healthy newborn infants with *maternal and parturital risk factors* when compared to 468 Hz for 24 healthy newborn infants without pre- or perinatal complications. Additionally, they found that the infants with risk factors required more snaps (3.2) to elicit the cry compared to controls (1.3). The latency to the onset of crying was longer for those with the risk factors (2.1 sec versus 1.4 sec). The infants at risk cried less in total time (13.7 sec cmpared to 21.3) than the low complication infants.

One of our study programs investigates the cry in various *malformation syndromes*. Many of the syndromes are very rare; therefore, it takes considerable time to collect a sufficiently large enough series of infants with the same syndrome. In three infants with *Krabbe's* disease, 30 cries were analyzed by Thodén and Michelsson (1979). A mean maximum pitch of 1120 Hz and a mean minimum pitch of 590 Hz was noted. The control infants compared had a mean maximum pitch of 520 Hz and a mean minimum pitch of 370 Hz. There were significantly less falling and rising-falling melody types in the Krabbe group, and these children also produced continuous signals less often.

SUMMARY

Cry analysis has been performed for many diseases and conditions in the newborn period. The results of these investigations imply that cry analysis is an additional method of diagnosis and prognosis during the newborn period. Further research is needed to correlate different cry characteristics with various states and infants' diseases. The examples presented in this chapter are only one aspect of possible investigations. Knowledge of the physiological and anatomical defects which change the cry pattern is still limited. The development of new measuring equipment and data computing analysis will profit future cry research.

ACKNOWLEDGMENTS

This research has been supported by grants from the Sigrid Jusélius Foundation.

REFERENCES

Aldrich, C.A., Sung, C., and Knop, C. 1945. The crying of newly born babies I. The community phase. J. Pediat. 26:313-27.

Aldrich, C.A., Sung, C., and Knop, C. 1945. The crying of newly born babies II. The individual phase. J. Pediat. 27:89-95.

Aldrich, C.A., Sung, C., and Knop, C. 1945. The crying of newly born babies III. The early period at home. J. Pediat. 27:428-35.

Andersson-Huntington, R.B. and Rosenblith, J.J. 1976. Central nervous system damage as a possible component of unexpected deaths in infancy. Dev. Med. Child Neurol. 18:480-92.

Bauer, H. 1968. Phoniatrischer Beitrag zum cri-du-chat syndrom. HNO 6:185-87.

Bayley, N. 1932. A study of the crying of infants during mental and physical tests. The Pedagogical Seminary and J. Genetic Psychol. 40:306-29.

Bell, S.M. and Ainsworth, M.D.S. 1972. Infant crying and maternal responsiveness. Child Dev. 43:1171-90.

Bernal, J. 1972. Crying during the first 10 days of life and maternal responses. Dev. Med. Child Neurol. 14:362-72.

Blinick, G., Tavolga, W.N., and Antopol, W. 1971. Variation in birth cries of newborn infant from narcotic-addicted and normal mothers. Am. J. Obstet. Gynecol. 110-948-58.

Brazelton, T.B. 1962. Crying in infancy. Pediat. 29:579-88.

de Chateau, P. 1976. Neonatal Care Routines. Influences on maternal and infant behavior and on breast feeding. Academic dissertation, University of Umeå, Sweden.

Darwin, C. 1872. The Expression of Emotion in Man and Animals. New York: Appleton.

Fairbanks, G. 1942. An acoustical study of the pitch of infant hunger wails. Child Dev. 13:227-32.

Fisichelli, V.R. and Karelitz, S. 1963. The cry latencies of normal infants and those with brain damage. J. Pediat. 62:724-72.

Fisichelli, V.R., Karelitz, S., Fisichelli, R.M., and Cooper, J. 1974. The course of induced crying activity in the first year of life. Pediatric Research 8:921-28.

Flatau, T.S. and Gutzmann, H. 1906. Die stimme des sauglings. Arch. Laryng. Rhinol. 18:139-51

Formby, D. 1967. Maternal recognition of infant's cry. Dev. Med. Child Neurol. 9:293-98.

Gardiner, W. 1838. The Music of Nature. Boston: Wilkins & Carter.

Gleiss, J. and Höhn, W. 1968. Das verhalten beim schreien nach konstanter schmertzreizung atemgesunder und atemgestörter neugeborener. Deutch Z Nervenheilk 194:311-17.

Greenberg, M, Vuorenkoski, V., Partanen, T.J., and Lind, J. 1967. Behavior and cry patterns in the first two hours of life in early and late clamped newborn. Ann. Paediatr. Fenn. 13:64-70.

Illingworth, R.S. 1955. Crying in infants and children. Brit. Med. J. 1:75-77.

Joos, M. 1948. Acoustic phonetics. Language Monographs 23:1.

Juntunen, K., Sirviö, P., and Michelsson, K. 1978. Cry analysis of infants with severe malnutrition. Eur. J. Pediatr. 128:241-46.

Karelitz, S. and Fisichelli, V.R. 1962. The cry thresholds of normal infants and those with brain damage. J. Pediat. 61:679-685.

Kittel, G. and Hecht, L. 1977. Der erste schrei-freqvenzanalytische untersuchugen. Sprache-Stimme-Gehör 1:151-55.

Koivisto, M., Michelsson, K., Sivriö, P., and Wasz-Höckert, O. 1974. Spectrographic analysis of pain cry of hypoglycemic newborn infants. Proc. XIV International Congress of Pediatrics, Buenos Aires. p. 250.

Lester, B.M. 1976. Spectrum analysis of the cry sounds in well-nourished and malnourished infants. Child Dev. 47:237-41.

Lester, B.M. and Zeskind, P. 1978. Brazelton scale and physical size correlates of neonatal cry features. Infant Behavior and Development 1:393-402.

Lind, J., Wasz-Höckert, O., Vuorenkoski, V., and Valanne, E. 1965. The vocalization of a newborn, brain-damaged child. Ann. Paediatr. Fenn 11:32-37.

Lind, J., Wasz-Höckert, O., Vuorenkoski, V., Partanen, T.J., Theorell, K., and Valanne, E. 1966. Vocal response to painful stimuli in newborn and young infants. Ann. Paediatr. Fenn 12:55-63.

Lind, J., Vuorenkoski, V., Rosberg, B., Partanen, T.J., and Wasz-Höckert, O. 1970. Spectrographic analysis of vocal response to pain stimuli in infants with Down's syndrome. Dev. Med. Child Neurol. 12:478-86.

Long, E.C. and Hull, W.E. 1961. Respiratory volume-flow in the crying of newborn infants. Pediat. 27:373-77.

Luchsinger, R., DuBois, C., Vassella, F., Joss, E., Gloor, R., and Wiesmann, U. 1967. Spektralanalyse des "miauens" bei cri-du-chat syndrome. Folia Phoniat. 19:27-33.

Lynip, A.W. 1951. The use of magnetic devices in the collection and analysis of the preverbal utterances of an infant. Genet. Psychol. Monogr. 44:221-62.

McCarthy, D. 1952. Organismic interpretation of infant vocalizations. Child Dev. 23:273-80.

Michelsson, K. 1971. Cry analysis of symptomless low birth weight neonates and of asphyxiated newborn infants. Acta Pediatr. Scand. Suppl. 216.

Michelsson, K., Sirviö, P., Koivisto, M., Sovijäri, A., and Wasz-Höckert, O. 1975. Spectrographic analysis of pain cry in neonates with cleft palate. Biol. Neonat. 26:353-58.

Michelsson, K. and Sirviö, P. 1976. Cry analysis in congenital hypothyroidism. Folia Phoniat. 28:40-47.

Michelsson, K. and Sirviö, P. 1976. Cry analysis of newborn infants with herpesvirus honinis encephalitis. 5th Eur. Congress of Perinatal Med. 212: (abs).

Michelsson, K., Sirviö, P., and Wasz-Höckert, O. 1977. Pain cry in full-term asphyxiated newborn infants correlated with late findings. Acta Paediatr. Scand. 66:611-16.

Michelsson, K., Sirviö, P., and Wasz-Höckert, O. 1977. Sound spectrographic cry analysis of infants with bacterial meningitis. Dev. Med. Child Neurol. 19:309-15.

Michelsson, K., Tuppurainen, N., and Aula, P. 1980. Cry analysis of infants with karotype abnormality. Neuropädiatrie (in press).

Michelsson, K. and Thodén, C.J. Pain cry analysis of infants with hydrocephalus. Unpublished report.

Murry, T., Hollien, H., and Muller, E. 1975. Perceptual responses to infant crying: maternal recognition and sex judgments. J. Child Lang. 2:199-204.

179

Murry, T., Amundson, P., and Hollien, H. 1977. Acoustical characteristics of infant cries: fundamental frequency. J. Child Lang. 4:321-28.

Ostwald, P.F., Phibbs, R. and Fox, S. 1968. Diagnostic use of infant cry. Biol. Neonat. 13:68-82.

Ostwald, P., Peltzman, P., Greenberg, M., and Meyer, J. 1970. Cries of a trisomy 13-15 infant. Dev. Med. Child Neurol. 12:472-77.

Parmelee, A.H. 1962. Infant crying and neurologic diagnosis. J. Pediat. 61:801-02.

Partanen, T.J., Wasz-Höckert, O., Vuorenkoski, V., Theorell, K., Valanne, E.H., and Lind, J. 1967. Auditory identification of pain cry signals of young infants in pathological conditions and its sound spectrographic basis. Ann. Paediatr. Fenn 13:56-631.

Perkins, W.H. 1971. Speech Pathology. St. Louis: Mosby.

Pettay, O., Donner, M., Michelsson, K., and Sirviö, P. 1977. New aspects on the diagnosis of herpes simplex virus (HSV). XV International Congress of Pediatrics, New Delhi, 1977.

Potter, R., Kopp, G.A., and Green, H.C. 1947. Visible Speech. New York: van Nostrand.

Prechtl, H.F.R. 1974. The behavioral states of the newborn infant (a review). Brain Res. 76:185-212.

Rebelsky, F. and Black, R. 1972. Crying in infancy. J. Genet. Psychol. 121:49-57.

Sherman, M. 1927. The differentiation of emotional responses in infants. J. Comp. Physiol. Psychol. 7:335-51.

Stark, R.E. and Nathanson, S.N. 1975. Unusual features of cry in an infant dying suddenly and unexpectedly. In Development of Upper Respiratory Anatomy and Function, eds, J. Bosma and J. Showacre. Department of Health, Education, and Welfare No. 75-941, Washington, D.C.

Stock, M.B. and Smyth, P.M. 1967. The effect of under-nutrition during infancy on subsequent brain growth and intellectual development. S. Afr. Med. J. 41:1027-30.

Tardy-Renucci, M. and Appaix, A. 1978. Etude sur l'analyse sonographique de cris de nouveau-nés. Folia Phoniat. 30:1-12.

Tenold, J.L., Crowell, D.H., Jones, R.H., Daniel, T.H., McPherson, D.R., and Popper, A.N. 1974. Cepstral and stationarity analyses of full-term and premature infants' cries. J. Acoust. Soc. Am. 56:975-80.

Thodén, C.J. and Michelsson, K. 1979. Pain cry in newborn infants of diabetic mothers (in Swedish). Proc. XIX Scandivian Congress of Pediatrics, Gothenburg.

Thodén, C.J. and Michelsson, K. 1979. Cry analysis in Krabbe's disease. Dev. Med. Child Neurol. 3:400-02.

Valanne, E.H., Vuorenkoski, V., Partanen, T.J., Lind, J., and Wasz-Höckert, O. 1967. The ability of human mothers to identify hunger cry signals of their own newborn infants during the lying-in-period. Experientia 23:768.

Vuorenkoski, V., Lind, J., Partanen, T.J., Lejeune, J., Lafourcade, J., and Wasz-Höckert, O. 1966. Spectrographic analysis of cries from children with maladie du cri du chat. Ann. Paediatr. Fenn 12:174-80.

Vuorenkoski, V., Kaunisto, M., Tjernlund, P., and Vesa, L. 1970. Cry detector, a clinical apparatus for surveillance of pitch and activity in the crying of a newborn infant. Acta Pediatr. Scand. Suppl 206:103-04.

Vuorenkoski, V., Lind, J., Wasz-Höckert, O., and Partanen, T.J. 1971. A method for evaluating the degree of abnormality in pain cry response of the newborn and young infant. STL-QPSR 1:68-75.

Vuorenkoski, L., Vuorenkoski, V., and Anttolainen, I. 1973. Cry analysis in congenital hypothyroidism: an aid to diagnosis and clinical evaluation. Acta Pediatr. Scand. Suppl. 236:27-28.

Wasz-Höckert, O. Vuorenkoski, V., Valanne, E., and Michelsson, K. 1962. Tonspektrophische untersuchungen des säuglingschreis. Experientia 13:583.

Wasz-Höckert, O., Valanne, E., Vuorenkoski, V., Michelsson, K., and Sovijärvi, A. 1963. Analysis of some types of vocalization in the newborn and in early infancy. Ann. Paediatr. Fenn 9:1-10.

Wasz-Höckert, O., Partenan, T., Vuorenkoski, V., Valanne, E., and Michelsson, K. 1964a. Effect of training on ability to identify preverbal vocalizations. Dev. Med. Child Neurol. 6:393-96.

Wasz-Höckert, O., Partanen, T., Vuorenkoski, V., Valanne, E., and Michelsson, K. 1964b. The identification of some specific meanings in infant vocalization. Experientia 20:154.

Wasz-Höckert, O., Lind, J., Vuorenkoski, V., Partanen, T., and Valanne, E. 1968. The Infant Cry. A Spectrographic and Auditory Analysis. Clinics in

Developmental Medicine No 29. Lavenham, Suffolk: Spastics International Medical Publications.

Wasz-Höckert, O., Koivisto, M., Vuorenkoski, V., Partanen, T.J., and Lind, J. 1971. Spectrographic analysis of pain cry in hyperbilrubinemia. _Biol. Neonat._ 17:260–71.

Watson, E.H. and Lowrey, G.H. 1951. _Growth and Development of Children_. Chicago: Year Book Med.

Zeskind, P.S. and Lester, B.M. 1978. Acoustic features and auditory perceptions of the cries of newborns with prenatal and perinatal complications. _Child Dev._ 49:580–89.

CHAPTER **8**

Acoustic Relationships of
Infant Cries to the
Sudden Infant Death Syndrome

R. H. Colton and Alfred Steinschneider

THE CRY AND HEALTH

It is said many times that the human infant cry reflects his physiological state. Pediatricians, nurses, and mothers associate the biological health of an infant with the "healthiness" of his cry. For the most part, the "healthiness" of his cry is based on perception and not necessarily on the acoustic characteristics of the cry.

There has been increasing interest in relating the acoustic features of an infant's cry to the state of his health. It is not the purpose of this chapter to review the available literature relating acoustics to the infant's general biological state. Such reviews may be found in the earlier chapters of this book and elsewhere. Few experimental investigations have been reported relating the acoustic aspects of an infant's cry to the infant's physiological behavior. One important work, however, was that of Bosma, Truby and Lind (1965), who related the acoustic features of the infant cry to the dynamic motions of the vocal tract in the same infant.

At present, sufficient evidence exists to conclude that certain acoustic features of a cry are related to different neurological and/or pathological states (Fisichelli and Karelitz 1963; Karelitz and Fisichelli 1962, 1969). Acoustic analysis of the cry would seem to be a valuable adjunct tool to utilize for the evaluation of the physiological integrity and development of the infants. In view of the apparent relationship between the cry and the infant's health, it is surprising that acoustic analysis of cries is not a routine procedure in every program of early infant care. Failure to utilize the infant cry may reflect the unavailability of a simplified technique for acoustic cry analysis. There are numerous acoustic variables which require adequate time for proper analysis. The lack of routine clinical use may reflect the insufficient data on the acoustic characteristics of infant cries. It is apparent that important information can be gained from the analysis of infant cries, a procedure that is noninvasive and does not interfere with the infant's routine.

THE CRY AND SIDS

Attempts to understand the Sudden Infant Death Syndrome (SIDS) have led to considerable interest in the infant's cry. Mothers, fathers, pediatricians, and nurses have often remarked that the cries of infants who eventually succumbed to SIDS sounded unusual. The cries of these children were strange or different in some way when compared to their siblings or other infants (Naeye et al. 1976). This observation has led to speculation that the acoustic characteristics of a SIDS infant cry may help to differentiate a potential SIDS infant from other infants.

Objective studies of the acoustic characteristics of the cries of SIDS victims have been meager. Stark and Nathanson (1975) reported the results of an extensive analysis of the cries of one male infant who died of SIDS at the age of six months. In general, these investigators found that the cries of the SIDS infant differed from those of four non-SIDS infants' cries on several acoustic features. First, the cries of the SIDS infant were much shorter and weaker than those of the control infants. Furthermore, a high proportion of the cries exhibited by the SIDS victim was associated with glottal voicing, higher fundamental frequency levels, and evidence of sudden shifts or breaks in the pitch level. Based on their acoustic studies, Stark and Nathanson reported that the SIDS infant exhibited more instances of vocal tract constriction; the back of the tongue touched the soft palate and briefly created an obstruction in the vocal tract. Voiced inspiratory sounds were also characteristic of the SIDS infant.

From the data of Stark and Nathanson, it can be concluded that the acoustic features of cry may reflect the anatomical/physiological state of the upper airway

184

in the potential SIDS infant. Presumably, the cries which result from vocal cord vibration reflect the physiological state of this important part of the respiratory system. It has been hypothesized that the SIDS infant exhibits a high degree of respiratory instability (Steinschneider 1972, 1974, 1977) as manifested by frequent and severe episodes of diaphragmatic apnea and/or upper airway obstruction (Guilleminault et al. 1975, Steinschneider and Rabuzzi 1976). Thus, the unusual features of the cry may be another manifestation (albeit several stages removed) of poor respiratory control.

In summarizing these various studies, there seems to be a relationship between an infant's cry and the state of his health. The infant's crying behavior is reflected in the acoustic characteristics of his cry. It has been hypothesized, and existing evidence suggests, that there is a relationship between the cry and SIDS. There is a lack of information about the acoustic characteristics of infants thought to be at "risk" for SIDS. Can the cry be used to help identify these infants? Indeed, can the cry help differentiate normal infants from potential SIDS victims?

THE CRY AND POTENTIAL SIDS

Since the statistical incidence of SIDS is low (0.1 - 0.3%, Showacre 1975), a very large number of infants must be studied in order to identify those infants who may be at risk for SIDS. One group of infants (subsequent siblings of a SIDS victim) is known to be at increased risk for SIDS (Froggatt 1970). It is assumed that the siblings of a SIDS infant possess, to some degree, an anatomical/physiological state similar to that found in SIDS victims. It is possible, therefore, that the cries of SIDS siblings may also reflect this physiological or anatomical difference. Included in our investigations were infants who were siblings of SIDS victims. A total of 22 fullterm subsequent siblings (SIBS) were studied which included 13 males and 9 females. Incidently, both parents of the infants studied were the same as those of the SIDS victim.

Two other infant groups were included in this investigation. All of these infants were born in a hospital adjacent to the Upstate Medical Center, Syracuse, New York.

The first group (N=66) consisted of infants who were born at term, having a birthweight greater than 2500 grams. They will be referred to as the normal newborn group (NNB). The other group of infants (N=58) had a birthweight less than 2500 grams. For discussion purposes, these infants will be referred to as the premature group (PRE).

The infants were all participants in a larger, multifaceted study. During the first week of life an attempt was made to obtain a recording of the infants' cry, measures of cardiorespiratory activity during nutritive sucking and complete napping, and an examination of a variety of neonatal behaviors (Brazelton 1973). Similar studies, excluding the Neonatal Assessment Scale, were repeated within the fourth week of life. The present chapter is limited to the cries recorded within the first week of life.

OBTAINING THE CRY SAMPLES

The infants were studied in an environmentally quiet, constant temperature room. The infant was placed in a crib with a microphone (Teledyne Electret) affixed to the crib side and prepared for the feeding and sleep study. Surface recording electrodes were taped to the infant, which usually resulted in a period of crying (a situation somewhat akin to maternal handling during a diaper change). The cry was recorded with the infant's head placed perpendicular to and about nine inches from the microphone. About two to three minutes of cry samples were recorded on a Nakamichi 550 cassette tape deck. On those occasions when the infant did not cry sufficiently when handled, he was recorded again at the conclusion of the nap when the various electrodes were removed. The recorder was placed in a state of readiness should the infant awake during the nap and cry.

ANALYSIS OF THE CRY SAMPLES

Five cry segments were selected from the entire repertoire of recorded cries. The five cries selected were all produced on expiratory air flow, were at least 500 milliseconds in duration, and were separated from another cry segment by at least 100 milliseconds. The following acoustic characteristics of the cries were analyzed:

1) fundamental frequency (f_o)
2) overall sound pressure level (SPL)
3) duration (sec)
4) center frequency of the first formant (F1)
5) center frequency of the second formant (F2)
6) center frequency of the third formant
7) energy in the frequency range 50-4000 Hz (spectral band #1)
8) energy in frequency range 4000-8000 Hz (spectral band #2)
9) energy in frequency range 8000-16000 Hz (spectral band #3)

Fundamental frequency was measured from narrow band spectrograms (45 Hz), whereas, duration and formant frequencies were analyzed from wide band (450 Hz) spectrograms. All spectrograms were made on a Voiceprint Series 700 Sound Spectrograph. The overall sound pressure levels of the cries were analyzed using a General Radio 1523 graphic level recorder. The acoustic spectrum of the cries was filtered to obtain the average sound pressure levels in three spectral bands and represents a very rudimentary spectral analysis. The SPL in each spectral band was obtained from measurements made on graphic writeouts from the General Radio Graphic Level Recorder.

Analytic Strategy

The ultimate purpose of this project was the identification of those acoustic cry variables that could differentiate infants in each of the three subject groups. In all analyses conducted, birthweight was retained because of the possible, but unknown relationship, between birthweight and the other nine variables. Relationships between the cry and infant groups could be confounded with the birthweight/cry relationships.

Two major analytic stategies were undertaken. In the first, the relationships between birthweight, the nine cry variables, and infant groups were explored. In the second strategy, the number of cry variables was reduced and the relationships between the cry and infant group were reanalyzed.

The analysis of intergroup relationships was conducted using the statistical technique of multiple regression. Of primary interest was the prediction of infant group (dependent variable), given birthweight, and the nine cry variables (independent variables).

However, prior to consideration of these intergroup relationships, an analysis of the individual cry variables for each infant group was conducted. Of special interest was the formant frequency relationships for the infants in each group.

In the second analytic strategy, an attempt was made to reduce the number of cry variables in the analyses without, at the same time, substantially reducing the contributions of the cry variables to the prediction of infant group. In the hope of improving the predictive power of the acoustic cry variables, a principal components analysis was conducted for the total infant group using the nine cry variables. In this analysis, intercorrelations among the cry variables were analyzed in order to group these variables that are in common and to identify the number of different groups of variables that are present in the data. Finally, the various infant group differences were assessed with the reduced model, using a multiple regression as previously done with the full ten variable model.

RESULTS

Birthweight

The average birthweight for each infant group subdivided according to sex is presented in Table 1.

Table 1. Birthweight summary statistics for three infant groups (data reported in grams).

Group	N	Mean	SD
Normal Newborn	66	3396.45	482.86
Males	35	3453.03	538.45
Females	31	3332.58	410.63
Prematures	58	2144.28	309.78
Males	20	2236.20	244.75
Females	38	2095.89	327.43
Siblings	22	3378.91	573.38
Males	13	3220.15	526.08
Females	9	3641.13	621.51

The mean birthweights of the male and female infants for each group appear very similar, an observation supported by statistical tests. When analyzed by group, the birthweights of the normal newborn group and SIBS group are very similar. A large difference exists between the premature group and both other infant groups; a difference not unexpected since the criterion for the identification of premature infants is low birthweight.

Birthweight was not related to any of the nine cry variables for either the premature or SIBS groups. For the normal newborn groups, however, the correlations between birthweight and overall sound pressure level and birthweight and spectral band No. 1 are greater in magnitude than those expected by chance. For this group, there is a tendency for larger infants to produce slightly louder cries than smaller infants.

Normal Newborn Cries

A summary of the results for each of the nine cry characteristics of the normal newborn infant group is presented in Table 2. From the data in this table, there is little difference in the cries of male and female newborns. The results of a multiple regression analysis relating the nine cry variables and birthweight to infant sex reveals a statistically non-

Table 2. Summary statistics for 9 acoustic cry variables for 35 male and 31 female newborn infants.

Acoustic Parameters	Males		Females	
	Mean	SD	Mean	SD
Fundamental Frequency (Hz)	503.26	91.74	522.94	101.07
Duration (sec)	1.20	0.39	1.23	0.31
F1 Center Frequency (Hz)	1592.46	396.80	1653.06	322.50
F2 Center Frequency (Hz)	3223.80	585.40	3274.61	486.95
F3 Center Frequency (Hz)	5337.20	863.64	5368.19	785.82
Sound Pressure Level (dB)	74.34	6.79	73.72	7.36
Spectral Band #1 (dB) (50 - 4 kHz)	73.63	7.00	72.58	8.06
Spectral Band #2 (dB) (4K - 8 kHz)	62.85	10.40	65.11	8.85
Spectral Band #3 (dB) (8K - 16 kHz)	45.40	8.09	46.35	8.40

significant multiple correlation of 0.28. Thus, no male-female distinction is revealed in the acoustic characteristics of the cries studied.

Premature Cries

Table 3 presents the results for the nine cry variables for the premature infant group. Inspection of this table suggests that male infants tend to exhibit greater variability of fundamental frequency than female infants. This difference is statistically significant. Female infants exhibit slightly lower fundamental frequencies than the male premature infants. This male/female difference of fundamental frequency is not, however, statistically significant. Furthermore, there are no statistically significant male/female differences of any of the eight remaining acoustic cry variables.

The results of the multiple correlations analysis relating the nine cry variables, birthweight, and sex revealed a non-significant correlation of 0.44. Thus, like the normal newborns, there appears to be no male/female difference in the acoustic cry characteristics investigated.

Table 3. Summary statistics on 9 acoustic cry variables for 20 male and 38 female premature infants.

Acoustic Parameters	Females		Males	
	Mean	SD	Mean	SD
Fundamental Frequency (Hz)	522.60	129.61	500.87	71.35
Duration (sec)	1.27	0.49	1.21	0.35
F1 Center Frequency (Hz)	15 36.20	292.85	1703.76	387.89
F2 Center Frequency (Hz)	3373.35	574.61	3542.34	600.39
F3 Center Frequency (Hz)	5562.25	1076.42	5769.68	1275.74
Sound Pressure Level (dB)	72.43	7.51	73.38	7.19
Spectral Band #1 (dB) (50 4 kHz)	71.72	6.41	72.57	7.22
Spectral Band #2 (dB) (4K - 8 kHz)	64.77	9.22	64.93	8.73
Spectral Band #3 (dB) (8K - 16 kHz)	46.59	8.33	47.28	8.79

190

SIDS SIBS Cries

The cry characteristics of the siblings of SIDS victims are presented in Table 4. In general, males exhibit lower magnitude on several of the nine cry variables that were analyzed. However, none of these differences are statistically significant.

A multiple correlation of 0.66 resulted from the analsysis in which the nine cry variables, birthweight, and sex were correlated. This correlation, although high, is not statistically significant due to the small number in the SIDS sibling group (13 males vs 8 females). Again, there is no difference between male and female cries for the sibling group.

Among adult speakers, males have lower fundamental frequencies than females. This difference reflects the different laryngeal and vocal fold sizes. Among one week old infants, there are no male/female differences in fundamental frequency nor in the eight other acoustic cry measures. Presumably, the size of the larynx/vocal folds is very similar for young male and female infants.

Table 4. Summary statistics for 9 acoustic cry variables analyzed in the cries of 13 male and 8 female siblings of SIDS infants.

| Acoustic Variable | Male | | Female | |
	Mean	SD	Mean	SD
Fundamental Frequency (Hz)	466.07	71.67	480.75	47.90
Duration (sec)	1.10	0.25	1.44	0.43
F1 Center Frequency (Hz)	1614.71	74.09	1770.00	414.69
F2 Center Frequency (Hz)	3364.93	616.62	3473.00	703.38
F3 Center Frequency (Hz)	5338.14	996.96	5445.50	1456.38
Sound Pressure Level (dB)	75.59	6.00	78.14	4.40
Spectral Band #1 (dB) (50 - 4 kHz)	73.70	5.53	77.51	4.39
Spectral Band #2 (dB) (4K - 8 kHz)	68.41	8.55	71.89	5.47
Spectral Band #3 (dB) (8K - 16 kHz)	48.08	6.75	50.24	4.74

Intragroup Cry Analysis

The average values for each of the nine cry variables, pooled across males and females for each infant group, are reported in Table 5. The infant groups exhibit differences on several cry variables including fundamental frequency, formant 2 center frequency, formant 3 center frequency, and the four variables relating to sound pressure level. Before condidering the possibility that these infant groups can be differentiated on the basis of their cry, an analysis of the cry variables was conducted.

Fundamental Frequency

In the present study, the average fundamental frequency (f_O) of the first week infant cries is similar to the average f_O reported by Wasz-Höckert et al. (1968) for 87 newborn cries. Michelsson (1971) analyzed the f_O in the cries of 50 fullterm and 75 premature infants. The median minimum f_O for fullterm newborns was 390 Hz, for prematures 450 Hz. The median maximum pitch was 620 Hz for the newborns and about 850

Table 5. Summary statistics for 9 acoustic cry variables for 66 normal newborn, 58 premature infants and 22 siblings of SIDS victims.

Acoustic Parameter	Normal Newborn Mean	SD	Premature Mean	SD	SIDS Siblings Mean	SD
Fundamental Frequency (Hz)	512.50	95.99	508.36	94.93	471.41	63.19
Duration (sec)	1.21	0.35	1.23	0.40	1.22	0.36
F1 Center Frequency (Hz)	1620.92	362.35	1645.98	364.29	1671.18	387.04
F2 Center Frequency (Hz)	3247.66	537.91	3484.07	592.13	3404.23	634.92
F3 Center Frequency (Hz)	5351.75	821.83	5698.16	1205.22	5377.18	1151.13
Sound Pressure Level (Hz)	74.05	7.01	73.05	7.25	76.52	5.50
Spectral Band #1 (dB) (50 - 4 kHz)	73.13	7.47	72.28	6.91	75.08	5.38
Spectral Band #2 (dB) (4K - 8 kHz)	63.91	9.69	64.87	8.82	69.68	7.62
Spectral Band #3 (dB) (8K - 16 kHz)	45.85	8.19	47.04	8.57	48.87	6.07

Hz for the prematures. An average f_O of approximately
500 Hz for the newborns and 650 Hz for the prematures
can be estimated from these data. Other authors report
average fundamental frequencies lower than the present
series. Ringel and Kluppel (1964) reported an average
f_O of 413 Hz for their 10 newborn infants. Prescott's
(1975) four infants had an average f_O of 384 Hz.

Some of the differences of fundamental frequency
reported may reflect the different ages at which the
cry was recorded. Wasz-Höckert et al. (1968) note that
their infants, when recorded at or before one month of
life, had an average f_O of 500 Hz. When cries from the
same infants wee analyzed at a later age (1-7 mos), the
average f_O was 530 Hz. Perhaps, very young infants (as
in the Ringel and Kluppel study, 4-40 hrs) exhibit
lower f_O than do older infants. Another variable that
may affect the f_O of a cry is the type of cry produced
by the infant. Laufer and Horii (1977) reported a mean
f_O of 317 Hz for four infants, four weeks or less in
age, emitting non-distress, non-vegetative vocalizations. It appears very important to specify the type
of cry an infant produced before comparing its f_O to
normative data.

Duration

The average duration of the cries in the present
study is very similar to cry durations previously
reported (Prescott 1975; Wasz-Höckert 1968; Ringel and
Kluppel 1964). The median duration of the newborn
cries recorded by Michelsson (1971) was 2 sec, by
Prechtl et al. (1969) less than 1 sec. Cry duration
seems to be dependent on a variety of factors, includng
the ability to produce a steady egressive airflow,
environmental factors, the stimulus used to elicit cry,
etc. Thus, many factors could account for the
interstudy differences of infant cry duration.

Formant Frequencies

Very little data have been reported in the literature
with respect to the formant frequencies of infant
cries. Ringel and Kluppel (1964) measured the center
frequencies of the first two formants in the cries of
their 10 infants. No average data were given, but,
rather, the data were reported as a scatter plot
relating F1 and F1. It appeared from the F1/F2 plot
that the center frequency of F2 was approximately twice
that of F1. Most of the first formant center

frequencies reported by Ringel and Kluppel seem to be 1400–1500 Hz.

Lieberman et al. (1971) also considered the resonant charcteristics of fullterm infant cries and reported that the formant frequencies of the cries in their sample were similar to those formant frequencies predicted from acoustic theory. According to this theory, an infant's vocal tract functions acoustically as a one-quarter wavelength tube resonator of specified length. For example, a tube 8.08 cm long and closed at oneend would produce resonant frequencies (formants) at 1095, 3285, and 5475 Hz.[1] Many of the cries that Lieberman et al. analyzed exhibited similar formant frequencies. Collapsing across all three infant groups, the average formant frequencies for these infants is 1646 Hz (F1), 3379 (F2), and 5475 (F3). The major difference between the observed and the predicted (from the Acoustic Theory) formant frequencies occurs at the first formant, where the center frequency is much higher than expected.

The ·finding of a higher F1 center frequency does not necessarily mean that the vocal tracts of the infants in this series were behaving contrary to acoustic theory. It is possible that the higher first formant frequency may be the consequence of a lowered mandible resulting in a greater opening at the front of the vocal tract. Bosma, Truby and Lind (1965), on the basis of their cineradiographic films, reported that many infants (but apparently not all) lowered their mandible during the cry. Lindbloom and Sundberg (1971) predict from their acoustic model of the vocal tract that an estimated 10 mm increase of jaw opening could result in a first formant frequency increase of approximately 100 Hz. Fant (1970) showed that in the case of a vocal tract of gradually increasing area (posterior to anterior), a four-fold increase in frontal area could result in approximately a 50% increase of formant 1 frequency. Fant points out, however, that the center frequency of both formant 2 and formant 3 would remain approximately the same provided that this increase of front cavity was gradual. Does the phenomena of mandibular lowering account for the increased first formant frequency in the infant cries of this study? In the attempt to analyze this possibility, individual scatter plots of the F1/F2 data were prepared and are shown in Figures 1–3.

[1]Formant = $\frac{(2K-1)C}{4\ell}$ where C = 35390 cm/sec (velocity of sound at, 98.6°F), ℓ = length of vocal tract and K $\geq$ 0.

194

Figure 1.   Scatter plot of Fl/F2 data for individual
infants in the normal newborn group1

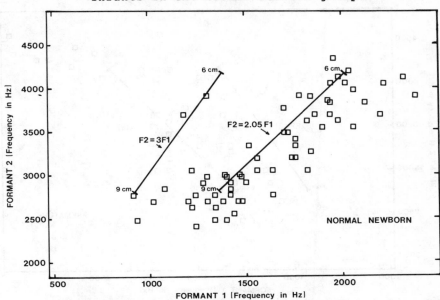

Individual Fl/F2 data for the normal newborn group
are plotted in Figure 1.   In addition to the individual
data points, two prediction lines are drawn on this
figure.   The line labeled F2 - 3Fl[2] predicts formant 2
frequency data, given that the vocal tract is acting as
a simple one-quarter wavelength resonator with no major
variations of cross sectional area.   The line labeled
F2 = 2.05 F2 represents the predicted relationship
between Fl and F2, given that there is a 51%
increase of Fl due to lip/jaw opening.   In Figure 1,
the data from three newborns fit the unperturbed one-
quarter resonator model very well.   A large number of
the infants' Fl/F2 data cluster about the line labeled
F2 = 2.05 Fl.   Inspection of Figure 1 suggests that
other groups of individual data points could fit with
straight lines if different degrees of jaw openings are
postulated.   For example, the four individual data
points below and to the right of the line labeled F2 =
3Fl show approximately a 14% increase of formant 1
frequency over that frequency redicted by F2 = 3Fl.
This relationship suggests these infants used only a
small amount of jaw opening.   The data points which lie
to the extreme right and lower portions of the figure
could be predicted with the assumption of a 66%
increase of formant 1 frequency, an acoustic result
consistent with a larger amount of jaw opening.   It

[2]From the equation given in footnote 1, if K = 1, then 2K-1 = 1. If K = 2, then 2K-1 = 3.
Consequently, the equation would result in the relationship F2 = 3Fl.

Figure 2. Scatter plot of F1/F2 data for individual infants in the premature group.

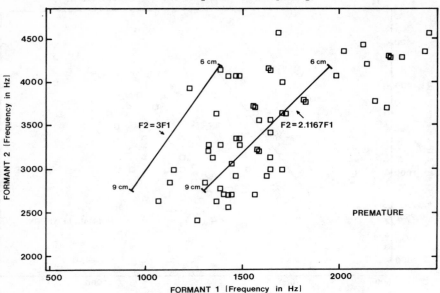

should be pointed out that on this and subsequent figures, the prediction lines shown are for vocal tract lengths thought to be appropriate for first week infants (Lieberman et al. 1971). Thus, the start of the line labeled F2 = 3F1 (lower left) is for a vocal tract of 9 cm, whereas, the end (upper right) of this line represents a 6 cm length. For the normal newborn infants shown in Figure 1, the individual vocal tract length was approximately 8.27 cm, only slightly longer than that reported by Lieberman.

The F1/F2 data for the 58 premature infants are plotted in Figure 2. Analysis of these data suggests that the average first formant frequency increased by about 44% above that predicted from simple resonator theory. It is also obvious that there is more scatter and, therefore, variability of the data points for the premature infant group. This would be expected since premature infants tend to exhibit greater variability in their physiological maturation. In their study of premature infants, Bosma, Truby, and Lind (1965) noted more instability of tongue, pharynx, and mandible position and movement.

Several of the infants in this group exhibited formant frequencies similar to that predicted from the one-quarter resonator theory (line labeled F2 = 3F1). Most of the data, however, fit the line labeled F2 =

196

Figure 3.   Scatter plot of F1/F2 data for individual
            infants in the SIDS SIBS groups.

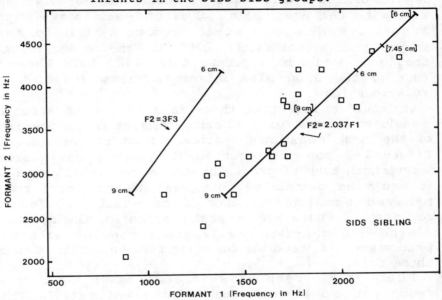

2.1167 F1, representing approximately a 44% increase
of formant 1 frequency.

The SIDS SIBS formant data are plotted in Figure 3.
The first formant frequency is about 55% higher than
that predicted and would result in the relationship
F2 = 2.037 F1. In these data, no individual subject
possesses F1/F2 frequencies predicted from an
unperturbed one-quarter wavelength resonator model.

From the data presented in the three figures, it was
observed that some infants exhibit F1/F2 data that
could be predicted assuming a half-wavelength resonator
model. In fact, the relationship F2 = 2.037 F1
reported for the sibling data is very similar to a
resonator wherein F2 is predicted to be twice that of
F1. Such a relationship would result if the vocal
tract operated acoustically as a one-half wavelength
resonator.[3] However, the magnitude of the actual
frequencies would be much higher than for the one-
quarter resonator model. For the data in Figures 1–3,
this means that the F1/F2 frequencies would be shifted
right along the prediction line. The extent of this
shift is indicated on Figure 3 by the vocal tract

---

[3]The equation for determining the resonant frequencies of a one-half wavelength tube is
given as $f = \frac{kc}{2\ell}$ where c is the velocity of sound, k is the resonant frequency desired
and ℓ is the length of the tube. In the present discussion, this would result in the
relationship, F2=2F1.

length given within the parenthesis. For the average length of the vocal tract of these infants (7.45 cm) and with the assumption of a one-half wavelength acoustic model, one would predict a first formant frequency of approximately 2200 Hz; the second formant frequency would be approximately 4400 Hz. Three or four of the SIDS SIBS infants do show these F1/F2 relationships.

It would appear that there is a choice of acoustic models to choose for predicting formant frequency data of the first week infant cries. Most of the data in Figure 1-3 can be acounted for with a one-quarter wavelength tube of gradually increasing frontal area or it could be postulated that the infant's vocal tract behaved acoustically like a one-half wavelength resonator. There are several reasons for the adoption of the one-quarter wavelength resonator with the phenomenon of mandible lowering for the explanation of these data.

First, it has been shown that a basic one-quarter resonator model provides a good estimate of the observed formant frequencies in the adult vocal tract. It would be expected that all human vocal tracts, young or old, would behave acoustically to some degree in a similar way.

Second, the presence of a glottal sound source generally results in the vocal tract behaving as if it were closed acoustically at the glottis. A half-way resonator may occur when the sound source (noise) is located elsewhere in the vocal tract and the glottis is open. In this case, the vocal tract is open at both ends and would behave as a one-half wavelength resonator.

Third, the one-quarter resonator model accounts for the data of a greater number of infants as shown in Figures 1 - 3. In Figure 3, it is estimated that the one-half wavelength resonator model accounts for less than half of the total number of infants shown. If one assumes changes in vocal tract length, the one-quarter wavelength resonator model seems to encompass 70-80% of the individual data points.

Accounting for the increased first formant frequency on the basis of jaw opening seems to be very reasonable and appealing. Furthermore, it is reasonable to expect approximately a 50% increase of vocal tract area in the anterior vocal tract with this amount of mouth opening. The increased frontal area could theoretically account for all or most of the increase of first formant frequency. For these reasons, it seems apparent that frequencies of first week infant cries in this investigation were most probably produced by a vocal tract acting like a one-quarter wavelength resonator tube model with the increase of formant 2 frequency most likely due to mandibular lowering.

Sound Pressure Level

As expected, analysis of the four variables concerned with sound pressure level reveals that most of the energy of an infant's cry is present in the lower frequencies, although reasonably high energy levels can be measured in frequencies up to 8,000 Hz. The average overall SPL is about 75 dB, a value somewhat lower than that reported by Ringel and Kluppel (1964) for 10 infants. In addition to the difference of sample sizes, Ringel and Kluppel's procedure for eliciting the cry was by pinching. Wasz-Höckert et al. (1968) report several acoustic differences between so called "pain" cries and "discomfort" cries. Perhaps "pain" cries also result in higher sound pressure levels than do "discomfort" cries. Furthermore, it appears that Ringel and Kluppel obtained a single estimate of SPL at the mid-point of the cry. In the present investigation, the SPL level of a cry represents the average level throughout the entire cry (excluding the extremes). These differences of methodology may account for the difference of sound pressure level.

It is interesting to note that the average SPL's of the sibling cries are higher than either the normal newborns or premature groups. Additionally, the siblings have greater energy in the frequency band between 4 and 8 kHz. These results suggest that the cries of the SIDS siblings are louder than comparable newborns.

Intergroup Cry Analysis

One of the major objectives of the present study was to determine if the nine cry variables, collectively or individually, could differentiate the three infant groups and, specifically, if the SIDS siblings exhibit differences with respect to the cry. The data shown in Table 5 suggest intergroup differences for the cry variables of fundamental frequency, formant 2, and formant 3 center frequencies. In order to investiage the power of these nine cry variables to differentiate

199

the three infant groups, a multiple regression analysis was performed. In this analysis birthweight was always included to investigate its effect and to complete the statistical model. Actually, two separate multiple regression analyses were performed with the dependent variable being two of the three possible infant groups. In the first analysis, the normal newborn and premature groups comprised the dichotomous dependent variable; in the second analysis, the normal newborn and SIDS siblings were used.

Normal Newborn/Premature
The regression analysis employing the ten variable model revealed that a significant proportion of the original variance could be accounted for by birthweight and formant 1. Note in Table 5 that the average F1 frequency is 1621 Hz for the NNB group and 1646 Hz for the premature group. It would appear from this analysis that premature infants have slightly higher formant frequencies than the NNB infants. Higher F1 center frequencies may be the acoustic consequence of increased mouth opening on the part of the premature infant.

NNB/SIDS SIBS

The results of the multiple regression analysis revealed that the normal newborns and SIDS SIBS infants can be additionally differentiated on the basis of their birthweight and/or cry.

Analysis of the individual variables revealed that fundamental frequency and the sound pressure level in the frequency band 4 - 8 kHz (Spectral Band #2) were the most important variables in descriminating the SIDS SIBS infants from NNB. In general, the SIDS infant sibling cries exhibited lower fundamental frequencies and higher sound pressure levels in the frequency range from 4 -8 kHz than did the fullterm infants.

Other Intergroup Analyses

It was extremely interesting to find that some of the cry variables analyzed in this investigation were related to the infant group type. It was somewhat disappointing that other cry variables did not reflect differences of infant groups in a similar way. Since several cry variables seem to be related to each other, one would expect that these variables would also contribute to the prediction of different infant groups in the same way as the actual predictive variables. For example, the four measures of sound pressure level are interrelated, and, to some degree, the three formant frequencies. In an attempt to investigate the relatedness of the different cry variables, intercorrelations among the nine cry variables were computed. The results of the correlation analysis are shown in Table 6.

Analysis of Table 6 suggests interrelationships among the center frequencies for formant one, two, and three. For the most part, the highest relationship is between the center frequency of F2 and F3 (R = 0.88). Fl and F2 center frequency are also related (R = 0.75). Further analysis of Table 6 reveals tha the overall SPL and three spectral bands exhibit high correlations. For example, the overall sound pressure level and the sound pressure level in spectral band #1 (50 - 4000 Hz) have a correlation of 0.95. The overall SPL and spectral band #2 correlation is 0.81; overall and spectral band #3 have a correlation of 0.75.

Factor Analysis of the Ten Cry Variables

Because of the cry variable interrelationships, a principal components analysis was conducted and factors were identified in the cries of the infants. The results of this analysis are shown in Table 7.

Table 6. Correlation coefficient matrix for 9 cry variables for 146 newborn infants.

Variable	fo	dur	F1	F2	F3	AP	SB#1	SB#2
dur	-0.32							
F1	-0.11	0.14						
F2	-0.13	0.21	0.75					
F3	-0.09	0.20	0.63	0.88				
AP	0.17	0.04	0.08	0.03	0.01			
SB#1	0.16	0.04	0.09	0.06	0.05	0.95		
SB#2	0.18	0.09	0.19	0.10	0.09	0.81	0.75	
SB#3	0.23	0.15	0.13	0.10	0.13	0.75	0.70	0.75

Two of the factors (III and IV) had high correlations with only a single variable: Factor III with duration, Factor IV with fundamental frequency. Duration and fundamental frequency are, therefore, important variables to retain in any subsequent analyses. The other two factors had significant correlations with three or more of the remaining variables.

The first factor has very high correlations with the overall SPL and three spectral bands and is obviously a "Level" factor. The highest correlation is between the factor and the overall SPL variable whereas the lowest correlation is with spectral band #3. In general, most of the energy in the infant cries resides in the lower frequencies.

Factor 2 loaded highest on formant frequency 2, followed by formant frequency 3, and, finally, formant frequency 1. This factor apparently reflects the resonant characteristics of the infants' vocal tract and has been labeled the "Resonant" factor. Interestingly, F2 and F3 have the highest correlations with this factor. It may be that F2 and F3 best reflect the overall resonant characteristics of the vocal tracts of these infants, whereas F1 exhibits more individual subject variation due to mouth opening as noted previously.

Table 7. Results of principal components analysis performed on the 9 cry variables for 146 infants.

| Variable | Loadings For | | | |
	Factor I	Factor II	Factor III	Factor IV
fo	0.14	-0.08	-0.18	0.96 *
dur	0.06	0.12	0.96 *	-0.17
F1	0.11	0.86*	-0.03	-0.09
F2	0.03	0.96*	0.09	-0.04
F3	0.01	0.91*	0.13	0.03
A Pass	0.97*	-0.01	-0.03	0.01
SB#1	0.94*	0.02	-0.06	-0.02
SB#2	0.89*	0.10	0.04	0.08
SB#3	0.84*	0.09	0.18	0.21
% Variance	37.00	28.00	11.00	11.00
Multi R*	0.99	0.99	0.96	0.96

* These variables comprised the independent variables in a multiple regression analysis with the factor score as the dependent variable.

The results of the principal components analysis indicate that four factors are sufficient to adequately account for the data of these three infant groups. These factors are estimated from the original variables by the normalized regression weights given in Table 8. In subsequent analyses, the factor sources were expressed in standardized form.

Intergroup Analysis for Four Cry Factors

A multiple regression model was utilized to determine if the reduced variable set (i.e. 4 factors) distinguished the three infant groups equally or better than the original nine individual cry variables. From the original five factors (birthweight, f_o, duration, level, resonance), the set of the best factors that discriminated the three infant groups was retrieved. Birthweight was always included as a fifth variable. These analyses were performed separately for the normal newborns versus prematures and the normal newborns versus SIDS siblings.

Normal Newborns Versus Prematures

The results of the regression analysis showed that no cry variable is an important discriminator of the normal newborn/premature distinction.

Normal Newborns Versus SIDS SIBS

The reduced variable model retained its ability to

Table 8. Normalized regression weights for estimating scores for the level and resonance factors (in standard form).

Factor	Variable	Weight
Level	All Pass	0.3530
	Spectral Band #1	0.2809
	Spectral Band #2	0.2547
	Spectral Band #3	0.1891
Resonance	Formant 1	0.3495
	Formant 2	0.3706
	Formant 3	0.3665

discriminate normal newborns from SIDS siblings. Further analysis revealed that the most important discrimination variables were fundamental frequency and level. Birthweight contributed very little discriminative power to the statistical model. Addition of the variables f_o and level resulted in an insignificant increase of discriminative power. The contribution of the two most important cry discriminators was insignificant statistically beyond the 0.01 level. The results of this analysis for the reduced variable model are presented in Table 9. Only level and f_o are present; birthweight was always retained in any analysis performed.

The regression analysis presented in Table 9 confirms the results of the previous ten variable regression analysis, in which the important variables for distinguishing normal newborn from SIDS SIBS was f_o and SPL in the frequency band 4 - 8 kHz. Thus, the reduced variable model retains the essential information originally contained within the acoustic variables initially considered.

Table 9. Results of multiple regression analysis for normal newborn vis SIDS SIBS.

Analysis of Variance

Source	DF	SS	MS	F
Model	3	2.0262	0.6754	3.92*
Error	84	14.4738	0.1723	
Total	87	16.500		

*P = 0.0114

Regression

Parameter	Estimate	T for H_o	Prob
Intercept	1.2427	2.89	0.0049
Birthweight	0.0000	-0.83	0.4075
Level	0.1394	2.82	0.0060
Fund. Freq.	-0.0015	-2.81	0.0061

IMPLICATIONS

Two major generalizations can be drawn from the result of the work reported in this chapter. The first generalization is that the cry may be related to the phenomenon of the Sudden Infant Death Syndrome. The second generalization is that the cry may suggest some of the underlying anatomical/physiological variants that are related to the cause of the Sudden Infant Death Syndrome.

Some of the acoustic characteristics of the cry have been shown in this chapter to be related to SIDS siblingship. *A priori*, SIDS SIBS are suspected of possessing the same, or similar, anatomical or physiological characteristics that eventually lead to SIDS. Consequently, these data add further support to the hypothesis that cry characteristics are related to risk status for SIDS.

The study of the acoustic characteristics of infant cries may also lead to hypotheses regarding the anatomical and/or physiological characteristics of the infant who dies of SIDS. As has been shown, analysis of the formant frequencies in a cry can lead to inferences about the length of the vocal tract as well as the dynamics of the articulator movements. Further, the spectral characteristics of the cry may lead to predictions about the vibratory motion of the vocal cords. As Stark and Nathanson (1975) have shown, analysis of the acoustic characteristics of the cry can lead to inferences about the degree and location of any vocal tract constrictions within the cry. Inferences about relationships between the acoustics and the physiology of a cry are possible because of the work by Fant (1960), Stevens and House (1961), and others. The relationships established by these investigators resulted in the formulation of the Acoustic Theory of Speech Production. Predictions of the acoustic behavior of the human vocal tract made possible by the theory seem to have no less validity for very young infants.

Consider, for example, the following potential relationship between acoustic cry data and physiology. In 1974, Tonkin reported on several infants who showed abnormal posterior displacement of the mandible during sucking activities. She attributed this phenomenon to greater mobility of the head of the mandible, which she claimed is much freer in early infancy than in adulthood. In the SIDS infant, perhaps, greater mandible mobility, especially in the posterior direction, could result in airway occlusion and asphyxiation.

If, indeed, some infants exhibit greater mobility of the mandible, it is possible that during the cry these same infants tend to open their mouth more than a normal newborn. Greater mouth opening would yield higher first formant frequencies. In the present study, the sibling group exhibited greater F1 frequencies. Perhaps they also exhibit greater mobility of the mandible. Although speculative, there does seem to be some consistency between the hypermobile mandible hypothesis of Tonkin and the SIDS sibling formant frequency data reported here.

Two general areas of inquiry seem appropriate in future work on the cry and SIDS. First, analysis of the acoustic characteristics of the cry should be developed to determine if this technique, alone or in combination with other measures, can identify potential SIDS victims. Second, we should continue analysis of the cry in order to generate viable hypotheses about the dynamics of the upper respiratory system in young infants and specifically in infants who are at risk for SIDS.

ACKNOWLEDGMENTS

The research reported in this chapter was supported in part by a contract (N01-HO-5-2853) and a research grant (1-R01-HD-07460) from the National Institute of Child Health and Human Development.

The authors would like to thank Dr. John Gleason, Department of Psychology, Syracuse University, for his assistance and advice with the statistical analyses reported here. We also benefited from the discussions with Dr. Martin Rothenberg, Department of Electrical Engineering, Syracuse University, who helped us gain insights into the strange world of infant cries.

REFERENCES

Bosma, J. F., Truby, H.M., and Lind, J. 1965. Cry motions of the newborn infant. In Newborn Infant Cry, ed., J. Lind. Uppsala: Almqvist and Wilkins.
Brazelton, T.B. 1973. Neonatal behavioral assessment scale. Clinics in Development Medicine. #50.

Fant, G. 1960. Acoustic Theory of Speech Production. The Hague: Mouton.

Fisichelli, V.R. and Karelitz, S. 1963. The cry latencies of normal infants and those with brain damage. J. Pediat. 62:724-34.

Froggatt, P. 1970. Epidemiologic aspects of the Northern Ireland study. In Sudden Infant Death Syndrome, eds., A. Bergman, J.E. Beckwith, and C.G. Ray. Seattle: University of Washington Press. p. 32-46.

Guilleminault, C., Peraita, R., Souquet, M., and Dement, W. 1975. Apneas during sleep in infants: possible relationships with sudden infant death syndrome. Science 190:677-79.

Karelitz, S. and Fisichelli, V.R. 1962. The cry thresholds of normal infants and those with brain damage. J. Pediat. 61:679-85.

Karelitz, S. and Fisichelli, V. 1969. Infants' vocalizations and their significance. Clinical Proc. Child Hosp. 25:345-61.

Laufer, M.Z. and Horii, Y. 1977. Fundamental frequency characteristics of infant non-distress vocalization during the first twenty-four weeks. J. Child Lang. 4:171-84.

Lieberman, P., Harris, K., Wolff, P., and Russell, L. 1971. Newborn infant cry and nonhuman primate vocalization. J. Speech Hear. Res. 14:718-27.

Lindblom, B. and Sundberg, J. 1971. Acoustical consequences of lip, tongue, jaw and larynx movement. J. Acoust. Soc. Am. 50:1166-79.

Michelsson, K. 1971. Cry analyses of symptomless low births weight neonates and of asphyxiated newborn infants, Acta Paediatr. Scand. Suppl. 216.

Naeye, R.L., Messmer, III, J., Specht, T., and Merritt, T.A. 1976. Sudden infant death syndrome temperament before death. J. Pediat. 88:S11

Prechtl, H.F.R., Theorell, K., Gramsbergen, A., and Lind, J. 1969. A statistical analysis of cry patterns in normal and abnormal newborn infants. Dev. Med. Child Neurol. 11:142-52.

Prescott, R. 1975. Infant cry sound: developmental features. J. Acoust. Soc. Am. 57:1186-91.

Ringel, R.L. and Kluppel, D.D. 1964. A normative study. Folia Phoniat. 16:1-9.

Showacre, J. 1975. Introductory Comments. In Symposium on Development of Upper Respiratory Anatomy and Function: Implications for Sudden Infant Death Syndrome, ed. J. Bosma and J. Showacre. U.S.

Department of Health, Education and Welfare.

Stark, R.E. and Nathanson, S. 1975. Unusual features of cry in an infant dying suddenly and unexpectedly. In Development of Upper Respiratory Anatomy and Function. Implications for Sudden Infant Death Syndrome, eds. J. Bosma and J. Showacre. Washington: U.S. Department of Health, Education, and Welfare. pp. 233-49.

Steinschneider, A. 1972. Prolonged apnea and the sudden infant death syndrome: clincial and laboratory observations. Pediat. 50:646-54.

Steinschneider, A. Laboratory sleep apnea and the identification of the infant at risk. Presented at the Research Planning Workshops on the Sudden Infant Death Syndrome: 7. Recognition of Infants at Risk for Sudden Infant Death: An Approach to Prevention, 19-20 Feb. 1974. NICHHD, Bethesda, Md.

Steinschneider, A. and Rabuzzi, D. 1976. Apnea and airway obstruction during feeding and sleep. Laryngoscope 86:1359-66.

Steinschneider, A. 1977. Prolonged sleep apnea and respiratory instability: a discrimination study. Pediat. 59:962-70.

Stevens, K. and House, A. 1961. An acoustical theory of vowel production and some of its implications. J. Speech Hear. Res. 4:303-20.

Tonkin, S. 1974. Airway occlusion as a possible cause of SIDS. In SIDS 1974, ed. R.R. Robinson. Canadian Foundation for the Study of Sudden Infant Death, pp. 73-74.

Wasz-Höckert, O., Lind, J. Vuorenkiski, U., Partanen, T., and Valanne, E. 1968. The Infant Cry: A Spectrographic and Auditory Analysis. Clinics in Development Medicine No. 29. London: Spastics International Med. Pub. Heinemann.

CHAPTER 9

Patterns of Fundamental Frequency and Vocal Registers

Patricia Keating

INTRODUCTION

This chapter reports observations on vocal register use and register shifts in young children. It also reports on the fundamental frequency (f_o) values observed in the speech of four children before the appearance of their first words. The goal of this chapter is to add to our knowledge about normal children's speech vocalizations and ultimately to develop a model of the acquisition of prosodic features.

There are few sources of data on the range of f_o in young children's speech. Studies reporting average f_o for reading include Peterson and Barney (1952), Fairbanks, Wiley, and Lassman (1949), and Fairbanks, Herbert, and Hammond (1949); these averages vary from about 250 to 300 Hz. Other studies, such as Sheppard and Lane (1968), report infant f_o for continuous vocalization, including cries. Average f_o for 95-sec samples of two infants over a five-month period varied from 398 to 438 Hz. Still other studies, such as Fairbanks (1942), Prescott (1975), and Murry, Amundson, and Hollien (1977), treat only infant cries. In such studies, average f_o typically ranges from 410 to 585 Hz. Keating and Buhr (1978) provide information on f_o and vocal register use in the speech of children ages 33 to 169 weeks. In their study, f_o ranged from a low of 30 Hz to a high of 2500 Hz. Each sample for each child had a f_o range of at least several hundred Hz, with some children showing extreme f_o variation. No longitudinal trends were apparent in the range of f_o used. In addition, utterances were analyzed as containing one or more of three registers: fry, modal, and high. (See below for descriptions of these registers.) In fry register, f_o values ranged from 30 to 250 Hz; in modal register, from 150 to 700 Hz; and in high, from 380 to 2500 Hz. These values cover a much wider range than had previously been reported for child speech.

The present chapter, using the methodology of Keating and Buhr (1978), offers a number of advantages for the study of speech acquisition. First, this methodology excludes f_o values of cries and vegetative sounds (e.g., spitting and burping) which provide data on the inherent properties of the larynx but are of unknown relevance to speech. Second, the data are derived from spontaneous speech recorded in a natural, familiar setting over an extended period of time. This is particularly true in the present study. Since these children were recorded from such an early age, recording sessions became a normal part of life for them. Third, the data are presented as overall ranges as well as averages. Fourth, the data are classified by vocal register, giving some indication of longitudinal trends in register use.

METHODOLOGY

The data reported are drawn from tape recordings of child speech in the Brown Phonetics Laboratory, directed by Philip Lieberman. These recordings are of several children playing at home, usually with their mothers, and were recorded approximately every two weeks using a Nagra 4.2 tape recorder and either an AKG or Sony ECM-50PS microphone. Ages range from ten days to over five years in this corpus; substantial longitudinal data are available, although no single child has been recorded over this entire period of time.

The samples were chosen to span at least two of three speech acquisition stages, which are described below. Such longitudinal data were available for four children. Table 1 includes a listing of the samples. It should be noted that the third sample for child JD, at 53 weeks, was the last before clearly recognizable words appeared; child LS did not produce such words for some time after the session at 66 weeks; the sample for child RC at 69 weeks is the last in her corpus.

There are clear phonetic differences characterizing

Table 1. Overall f_0 range for each sample for each child.

Child	Sex	Ages (weeks)	f_0 Ranges
JD	F	16	30 – 600
		33	80 – 2500
		53	? – 900
LS	M	16	15 – 1250
		33	25 – 1000
		66	55 – 1150
GM	M	16	20 – 1440
		36	25 – 2750
RC	F	33	80 – 500
		69	55 – 900

the three stages for these infants. Before 12 weeks, there are few speech-like sounds during any one session. By 16 weeks, breathy vowel-like sounds [ae, ε, ʌ] begin to occur loudly and often enough for anlaysis. These vowels occur alone, in groups of phonetically similar vowels, or in syllables with glottal stops or [h]. After 20 weeks, longer strings of various vowels occur. During this period, CV syllables also begin to appear, but they do not occur consistently until after 40 weeks. It is these long sequences of syllables with consonants such as nasals and stops which emerge in the period around 40 weeks and that are typical of what is called babbling. After this period, until the use of recognizable words, these babbled utterances develop so that they more closely correspond to possible English words. In particular, they shorten to one- or two-syllable forms, sometimes with glides or final consonants.

Samples were chosen for each child at 16 and 33 weeks, where possible, and prior to recognizable words. A sample consists of the first 50 vocalizations in each session, with some exceptions.

The following types of vocalizations were eliminated: cries or vegetative noises, utterances with interfering noise in the background, low-volume utterances, ingressive and voiceless utterances. The end of an utterance was taken to be the point at which the child took a breath. This point was generally easy to determine by listening to the tape since our recordings are made by holding a sensitive directional microphone within a few inches of the child's mouth, thereby emphasizing breathy noise.

Spectrograms were made on a Kay Songraph, model 6061B. The input was recorded at high speed (160-16,000 Hz), so that there was an effective narrow bandwidth of 90 Hz and an effective wide-bandwidth of 600 Hz. Various settings on the 6076C scale magnifier were used as appropriate; setting the upper limit to 50% displays 8000 Hz on the spectrograms, while setting it to 40% displays 6400 Hz. Fundamental frequency was measured from narrow band spectrograms at the fifth harmonic (or the next highest one possible if the fifth was absent or obscured) to the nearest 25 Hz. Values below about 200 Hz were determined by counting striations per unit of time on wide band spectrograms.

DATA

Table 1 lists the samples available for each child and the total f_o range for each sample. In several cases, this range is quite wide. Table 2 divides f_o values in each utterance into three vocal registers: fry, modal, and high. The lowest and highest f_o values within each register were noted for each utterance. The range within each register is presented, as well as the mean low and high values and their standard deviations. Assignment of an utterance, or portion of an utterance, to a register was conservative; it would be considered "modal" unless there was a clear indication to the contrary. Thus, there may actually be more instances of vocal fry and high register use than are tabulated here.

The lower f_o values are found in fry register, also known as "creaky voice" (Ladefoged 1971; Hollien 1974). Fry register is associated with widely and irregularly spaced striations on wide band spectrograms. Generally, fry register for this age group occurs at f_o values below approximately 250 Hz. Often, a few fry pulses occur at the onset of phonation for about 50 or

Table 2. f_o range (in Hz), mean lowest value, and mean highest value for each vocal register for each sample (child and age in weeks).

Sample & Register	N	Overall Range	Range of Lows	Mean Low (+ S.D.)	Range of Highs	Mean High (+ S.D.)
JD - 16						
FRY	12	30- 290	30- 135	73 (37)	165- 290	215 (38)
MODAL	50	150- 415	150- 300	242 (37)	225- 415	299 (50)
HIGH	4	400- 600	400- 500	463 (48)	475- 600	534 (57)
JD - 33						
FRY	6	80- 330	80- 110	94 (13)	240- 330	293 (34)
MODAL	48	150- 575	150- 425	315 (60)	300- 575	424 (70)
HIGH	13	350-2500	350-1000	545 (178)	500-2500	990 (621)
JD - 53						
FRY	1	?	?	?	?	?
MODAL	50	200- 600	200- 325	281 (34)	275- 600	380 (68)
HIGH	6	400- 900	400- 550	467 (61)	450- 900	625 (175)
LS - 16						
FRY	40	15- 300	15- 160	72 (45)	160- 300	219 (41)
MODAL	50	175- 575	175- 350	251 (46)	300- 575	372 (43)
HIGH	11	500-1250	500- 850	640 (98)	540-1250	835 (213)
LS - 33						
FRY	24	25- 340	25- 215	103 (51)	160- 340	267 (50)
MODAL	50	200- 490	200- 400	303 (43)	300- 490	382 (38)
HIGH	6	400-1000	400- 750	549 (169)	420-1000	677 (260)
LS - 66						
FRY	10	55- 340	55- 180	127 (46)	160- 340	253 (66)
MODAL	45	220- 575	220- 450	323 (46)	300- 575	359 (53)
HIGH	5	500-1150	500- 940	698 (172)	500-1150	777 (246)
GM - 16						
FRY	16	20- 340	20- 200	94 (57)	140- 340	219 (54)
MODAL	49	150- 575	150- 400	276 (63)	275- 575	388 (68)
HIGH	6	450-1440	450- 790	622 (143)	575-1440	878 (297)
GM - 36						
FRY	16	25- 290	25- 160	96 (44)	140- 290	199 (59)
MODAL	40	150- 500	150- 425	260 (85)	250- 500	365 (60)
HIGH	16	350-2750	350-2000	645 (387)	500-2750	907 (540)
RC - 33						
FRY	8	80- 290	80- 160	104 (30)	120- 290	216 (66)
MODAL	48	120- 500	120- 450	280 (57)	250- 500	388 (52)
HIGH	0	-	-	-	-	-
RC - 69						
FRY	9	55- 290	55- 225	116 (62)	160- 290	236 (43)
MODAL	50	200- 650	200- 450	305 (71)	250- 650	434 (93)
HIGH	5	350- 900	350- 900	545 (244)	375- 900	570 (239)

100 msec. Less often, an entire utterance will move in and out of fry register. At any given age, children differ in how much fry they use, and a child may use different amounts of fry at different ages. For this reason it is difficult to make statements about trends in the use of fry during speech development. The implications of this data for speech acquisition are discussed below.

It should be noted that the measurement of "highest fry" and "lowest modal" values is problematical since one register often changes smoothly into the other. If no obvious shift was evident, the lowest modal value was taken to be the lowest one measurable from the narrow-band spectrogram, and the highest fry value was set arbitraily at 10 Hz below that. Computer waveform displays of fry and modal phonation show the continuous pattern of modal phonations, even at low f_o values, versus the interrupted pattern of fry phonations. For example, Figure 1a shows narrow and wide band spectrograms of an utterance containing both fry and modal registers. Figure 1b shows the waveform of the utterance in fry register, and Figure 1c shows the waveform of the same utterance in modal register at approximately the points indicated in Figure 1a. Presumably, some criterion to differentiate the two types of waveforms could be devised, possibly on the basis of the pause between glottal pulses in fry

Figure 1a.   Narrow- and wide-band spectrograms of utterance by RC at
             33 weeks of [ɛ], containing both fry and modal
             registers.

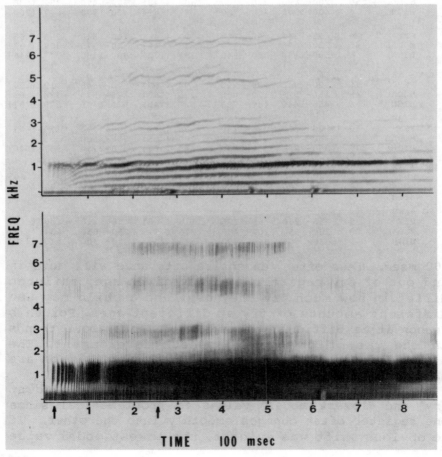

Figure 1b. Waveform from first arrow in 1a (16 msec); 1 point = .05 msec.

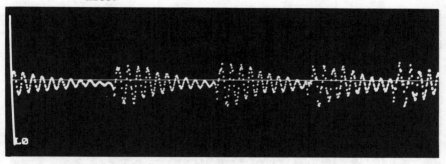

Figure 1c. Waveform from second arrow in 1a (246 msec).

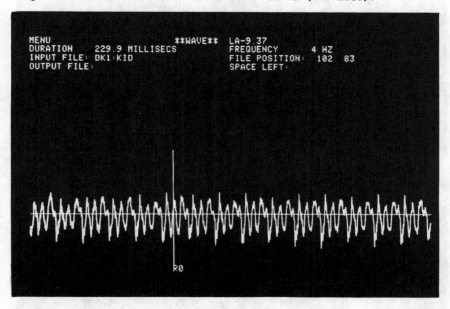

register. Another criterion might be the spectra in each register. Figures 1d and 1e show the Discrete Fourier Transforms of the portions of the utterance shown in Figures 1b and 1c, respectively. In addition, the sophisticated computer editing techniques available on the PDP-11/34 allow a waveform to be arbitrarily segmented and individual segments listened to. With practice, such segmentation of a few pitch periods might permit perceptual categorization of individual portions of an utterance.

Utterances containing modal register comprise the bulk of the samples for each child. The range of f_o values in this register alone is wider than that previously thought to characterize non-cry

Figure 1d. Discrete Fourier Transform (DFT) corredsponding to 1b;
            Hanning window is 25.6 msec wide with center at 28 msec.

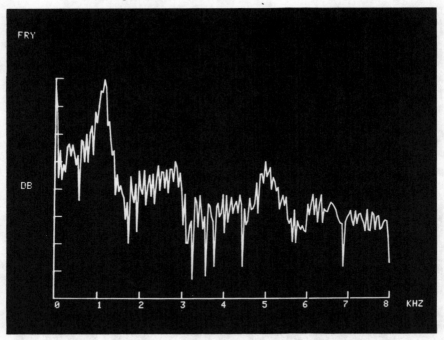

Figure 1e. DFT corresponding to 1c, with center at 258 msec.

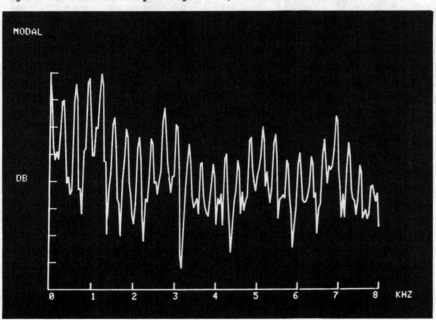

vocalizations. In order to give some indication of the frequency of occurrence of the higher f_o values in modal register, Table 3 presents a breakdown of the peak modal f_o values. The highest modal value of each utterance containing modal register was put into one of six f_o ranges.

"High" register is not to be confused with these higher modal values. Our term "high" is probably equivalent to "falsetto," but that term has been avoided since it has connotations of a false voice quality, which these children do not seem to be using. Additionally, it is unclear exactly how many registers are involved in these high f_o utterances; therefore, a single neutral term is preferred. It is quite likely that the very high and relatively uncommon f_o values included in "high" register are actually due to some fourth register, as their perceptual quality is somewhat shriller and more piercing. In general, high

Table 3. Breakdown of peak modal f_o values -- No. per f_o range.

Sample	200-99	300-99	400-99	500-99	600-99
JD - 16	25	19	6	-	-
33	-	14	26	7	1
53	1	32	14	2	1
LS - 16	-	39	9	2	-
33	-	29	21	-	-
66	-	35	9	1	-
GM - 16	1	23	21	4	-
36	1	27	10	2	-
RC - 33	1	19	26	2	-
69	2	14	18	12	4

register is characterized by high pitch and a thin quality. High register is usually associated with a discontinuity (or "shift") in the f_o contour on narrow band spectrograms, although this is not always the case. Additional shifts are sometimes seen at the higher f_o values which may then be further evidence of a fourth vocal register.

DISCUSSION

A number of interesting phenomena that can be observed in the spectrograms should be mentioned. In a very few cases, every n^{th} (for example, fifth) harmonic will be much darker than the others. This pattern seems to be the result of the child's having her vocal folds separated enough for that end of the vocal tract to be considered open. With the mouth also open, the formant frequencies generated will be spaced at equal intervals, and so individual evenly-spaced harmonics near these formants will appear darkened.

Another result of the vocal folds not being brought close together is the breathiness of much of the speech in these samples. When the vocal folds do not come together completely as they vibrate, air can pass through. In addition, the aerodynamic conditions that allow phonation to continue are affected such that the f_o is rather low, but there are few harmonics in the glottal source spectrum. In this case only the first one or two formants are periodically excited; higher formants are noise-excited.

In a few instances, what appears to be rapidly alternating fry and high register is seen on spectrograms. That is, in between the glottal pulses associated with fry, there are harmonics at multiples of about 1000 Hz. This f_o may be vibration of the edges of the vocal folds coupled to the supralaryngeal vocal tract at the first formant frequency. These edge vibrations would generate their own harmonics, even as the vocal folds as a whole vibrate in fry register. The slackness of the folds in fry may facilitate independent edge vibration.[1]

Usually fry and high register occur in utterances which also contain modal register phonation. There is generally a noticeable shift between modal and high register on spectrograms which may, in fact, be

[1]P. Lieberman: personal communication.

218

considered one criterion for the identification of high register in infants' speech. It is less obvious exactly where a shift between modal and fry registers occurs, although one register is clearly differentiated from the other. One indication of a register shift seems to be harmonic 'doubling', described by Buhr and Keating (1977).[2] In the case of doubling, extra harmonics appear on the spectrograms, evenly spaced between the harmonics of the fundamental and often fading in and out. The perceived pitch does not change, but the voice quality is quite distinctive, being somewhat raw and harsh. Although this quality is similar to that of cries or shrieks, these utterances are neither. In older children the doubling occurs during normal word and sentence production.

Table 4 indicates how often and in what registers doubling occurs. Only clear instances of doubling are tabulated, so the actual rate may be slightly higher. Both the upper and lower ranges of modal register seem to be characterized by doubling, especially in conjunction with register shifts. High register also shows the phenomenon in the absence of any apparent register shift. Figure 2a shows the narrow-band spectrogram of an utterance in high register with extended doubling. Figure 2b shows the Fourier Transform centered at the first arrow; the f_o is clearly about 900 Hz. Figure 2c shows the Fourier Transform centered at the second arrow. The harmonics through 5 kHz are multiples of 500 Hz, but there is no fundamental actually at 500. Figure 2d shows the

Table 4. Number of utterances per sample showing doubling, and in which register or between which registers each instance occurs.

Sample	Total	Fry-Modal	Modal	Modal-High	High
JD - 16	13	–	13	–	–
33	8	3	5	–	–.
53	2	–	1	1	–
LS - 16	10	7	3	–	–
33	23	7	14	3	1
66	4	–	3	–	1
GM - 16	5	1	3	–	1
36	15	1	9	1	4
RC - 33	6	–	6	–	–
69	6	–	6	–	–

[2] 'Doubling' appears to be the same phenomenon as the 'diplophonia' described in Monsen (1979) and Monsen, Engebretson, and Vemula (1979).

waveform of this portion. The pitch period is 1 msec, which corresponds to a f_o of 1000 Hz. A few msec later, however, there is an abrupt change in pitch period to 2 msec, which corresponds to a f_o of 500 Hz. Figure 2e shows the Fourier Transform centered at the third arrow of 2a with a weak fundamental at 500 Hz. A few msec later, the Fourier Transform shows a clear 500 Hz fundamental (Figure 2f). Later in the utterance, the process repeats itself in reverse until by 465 msec the f_o is again clearly 1000 Hz. The doubling phenomenon will be discussed further in the next section.

The use of wide f_o ranges, multiple vocal registers, and even register shifts involving doubling by the four normal infants of this study indicates that care should be taken in interpreting specific acoustic attributes of the vocal production of impaired children. High f_o has been observed in the cries of deaf (Jones 1965) and retarded (Ostwald, Phibbs, and Fox 1968) infants. In

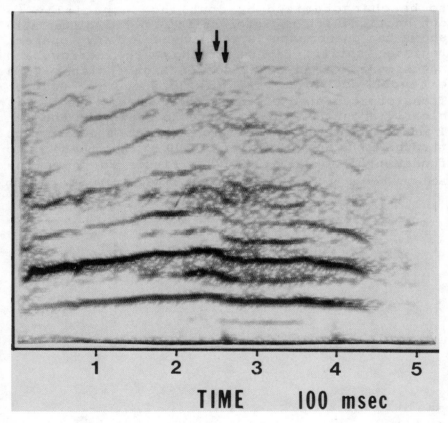

Figure 2a. Narrow-band spectrogram of utterance by GM at 36 weeks of [ae], showing extended doubling in high register.

Figure 2b. DFT centered at first arrow in 2a (230 msec).

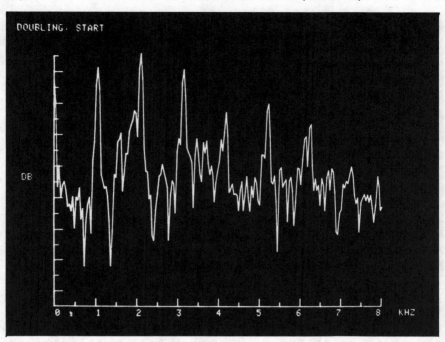

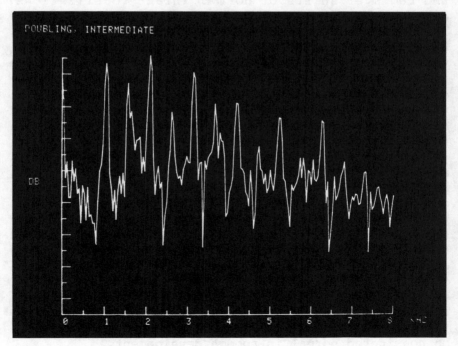

Figure 2c. DFT centered at second arrow in 2a (250 msec).

221

Figure 2d. Waveform corresponding to 2c.

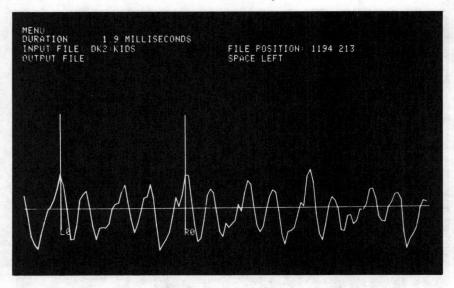

the latter study, spectrograms of supposedly "abnormal" cries show the sudden pitch changes characteristic of the register shifts of normal infant vocalizations. Also showing these shifts are spectrograms of "hyperphonation" in Truby and Lind (1965). Hyperphonation is their term for the very high f_o values, breathy phonation, and prominent formant 1 with its own harmonics that sometimes occur in cries. Truby and Lind also mention abrupt f_o shifts, suggesting that they are unique to newborn cries. The data presented here, however, indicate that all of these features are found in infant speech.

In particular, breathy phonation and abrupt f_o shifts are common for children as old as 169 weeks (Keating and Buhr 1978). Stark and Nathanson (1975) reported a greater incidence of high f_o in the cries of an infant who later died of Sudden Infant Death Syndrome than in those of normal infants. Again, the data presented here indicate the need for caution in making such connections. Neither fry register nor extremely high f_o values per se necessarily indicate the presence of any pathological condition or anomaly. The study of variation in normal infant speech production leads to the conclusion that a wide array of vocal output must be considered normal in speech development.

Figure 2e. DFT centered at third arrow in 2a (258 msec).

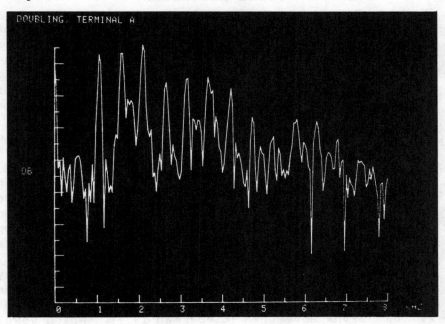

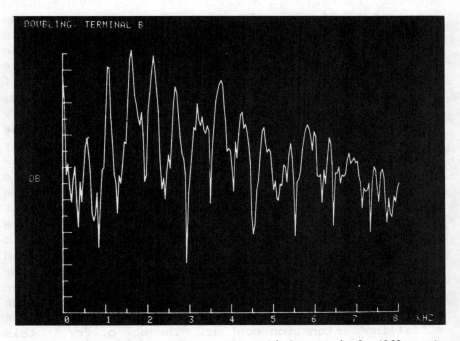

Figure 2f. DFT centered 5 msec after third arrow in 2a (263 msec).

223

During the first year, children use a wide range of f_o values and at least three vocal registers in their prelinguistic speech. It is tempting to hypothesize that, in some sense, the children are experimenting with their larynxes to determine both the range of possible outputs and the linguistic meaning that can be attached to them.

Before 20 weeks, the children's vocalizations are mostly characterized by laryngeal maneuvers. The vegetative noises, such as coughing and burping, involve closing the glottis. The nonvegetative noises that I have called "speech" are similar in that there is usually an initial glottal stop [?], followed by an indeterminate vowel, followed by another glottal stop or [h]. The vowels most used [ae, ɛ, ʌ, U] are "indeterminate" because they cannot be uniquely specified by a particular tongue position. They involve minimal changes from the rest position and the proper formant frequencies can occur as the result of lip and larynx movements (Lieberman 1977). Which vowel actually is heard in a given utterance may be quite accidental, simply a function of whatever position these articulators happen to be in. The large proportion of fry register and breathiness in these utterances would be the result of only the interarytenoid muscles contracting. This type of contraction closes only the rear part of the glottis, so the vibration of the folds is slow and with very little tension (van den Berg 1968a). This is the vibratory pattern of fry register -- slow and irregular pitch pulses.

Fry register can have two quite different linguistic uses. One is as a segmental feature of either vowels or consonants. Ladefoged (1971) says that Chadic languages, such as Housa, Bura, and Margii, have "laryngealized" stops and semivowels, while Nilotic languages, like Ateso and Lango, have laryngealized vowel phonemes. Laryngealization is Ladefoged's term for the use of fry (creaky voice) in a segment. The other use is prosodic; fry register can be used at the end of a breath group to effect the f_o drop required in a "falling" intonation contour. The use of fry in this way, of course, enhances the pitch drop. Atkinson (1973) derived f_o contours for a number of speakers reading different sentence types. In several cases, the f_o fell to a fry register value at the end of declarative sentences. In addition, our tape recordings reveal varying, but substantial, use of fry by parents, especially at the end of a breath group. However, fry register seems to be used intermittently throughout discourse by a speaker to produce an effect of overall lower f_o, for example, by women or by men with naturally high f_o's. The study of the social conditions under which this happens would be an interesting one.

Leaving aside this last suggestion, we can consider our data in light of adult use of fry phonemically and prosodically. It may be the case that all infants babble in fry register, but that for some infants this fry register use serves as preparation for linguistic manipulation later on. It would be interesting to gather data on the use of fry by children learning languages such as those cited above to see how similar the early babbling is, as well as how the phonemic use of fry comes in later. In this regard, the use of fry over very brief portions of an utterance by our infants is relevant, because this kind of fry may be channeled into a segmental distinction more easily than utterance-long fry. Prosodically, children's fry often occurs as they begin and end modal phonation as if they are unable to do so smoothly. Observation of older children speaking in sentences suggests that both fry register and sudden voicelessness (even of vowels) are used to ensure the correct f_o contour. These phenomena may, in some sense, be "mistakes" on the children's part, yet they produce the desired effect. Further work on speech acquistion should include some study on how fry register comes to be used within an intonation system.

The production of different vocal registers is discussed by van den Berg (1968 a,b) and Hollien (1974) among others. Van den Berg is concerned primarily with the particular muscles that contract for each register; Hollien has focused more on vocal fold length and thickness. Van den Berg's description of "falsetto" register in adults is especially relevant to our data. In this register the vocal ligaments are maximally tense as a result of medial compression and contraction of the interarytenoid and cricothyroid muscles. Only the edges, not the body, of the vocal folds vibrate and the glottis does not close completely. The resulting signal should be almost a pure sine wave.

Figure 3a shows the narrow band spectrogram of an utterance with peak f_o of about 1000 Hz. Figure 3b

Figure 3a. Narrow-band spectrogram of utterance by JD at 33 weeks of [eheh], with peak FF of about 1000 Hz.

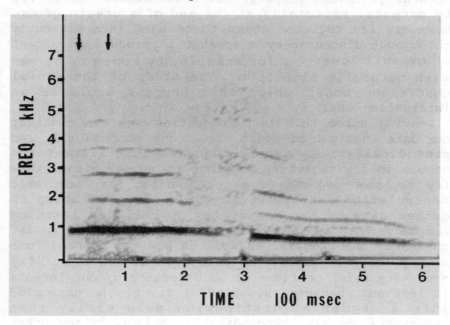

Figure 3b. DFT centered at first arrow in 3a (25 msec).

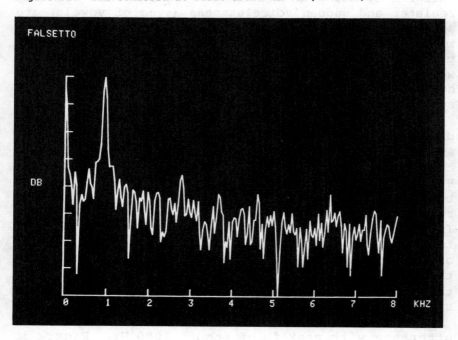

Figure 3c. Waveform corresponding to 3b.

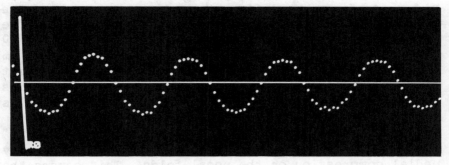

Figure 3d. DFT centered at second arrow in 3a (72 msec).

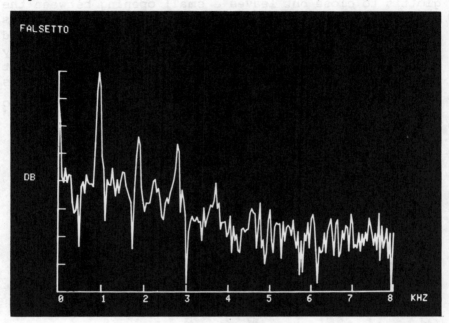

shows the Fourier Transform at the point marked by the
arrow in 3a. This display shows that, at the beginning
of the utterance, the signal is indeed almost a pure
sine wave since there is a fundamental but no
harmonics. The sinusoidal form is also apparent in
Figure 3c, the waveform of the same portion of the
utterance. The computer display has been stretched out
for this picture; each point still represents .05 msec.
Figure 3d shows the Fourier Transform of the portion
centered at 72 msec in 3a. By this point in the
utterance, three harmonics have been added in the
glottal source. Note the large amplitude decrease
across these harmonics; the source spectrum normally
falls off more rapidly in high register than in modal.

227

The utterance with a peak f_O of 2500 Hz shown in Figure 4a is quite different in these respects. The waveform shown in Figure 4b is not sinusoidal. The pitch period of .4 msec corresponds to a f_O of 2,500 Hz. This f_O is also clear in the Fourier Transform shown in Figure 4c. Note that the harmonics do not fall off as they do in Figure 3d. These differences may be further evidence that a different register is involved in such utterances.

Van den Berg describes a "whistle" or "flute" register, in which the cricoarytenoid muscles supply medial compression on the vocal folds. This causes the glottis to close but leaves a small opening between the arytenoids. The vocal folds do not vibrate in this register; rather, air vibrates in the small cavity and so the f_O generated depends on the resonance frequency of this cavity. In van den Berg's excised adult larynges, this f_O went as high as 2500 Hz. This mechanism may be responsible for the very high f_O values in our data. Interestingly, van den Berg offers

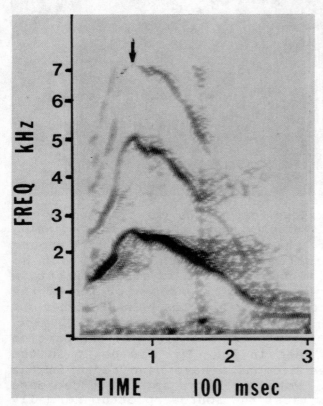

Figure 4a. Narrow-band spectrogram of utterance by JD at 33 weeks of [ae ɪ ə], with peak FF of about 2,500 Hz.

Figure 4b. Waveform from arrow in 4a (70 msec).

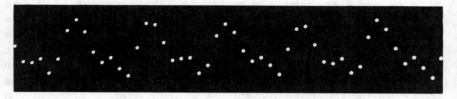

Figure 4c. DFT corresponding to 4b.

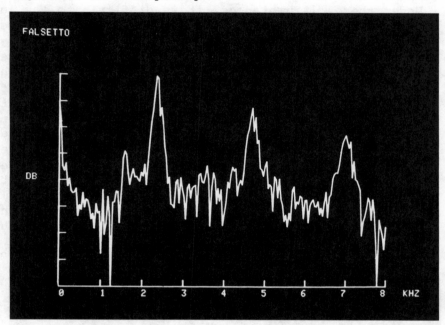

a way of determining-- in theory-- when this mechanism is used. Since the f_O is a resonance frequency, it would vary with the sound velocity of the gas medium used. The frequency of vocal fold vibration is not affected by breathing helium, for example, while formant (resonance) frequencies are doubled. If the f_O were to reach values such as 5000 Hz while an infant was breathing helium, then we could guess that it was not generated by vocal fold vibration.

A number of utterances involving what I have called doubling were analyzed with the Discrete Fourier Transform (DFT) analysis implemented on the Phonetic Laboratory's PDP-11/34 computer. The DFT displays corresponding to various points in time in an utterance usually show a consistent pattern: first a clear f_O at a high value, later a few relatively low-intensity harmonic peaks emerging from between the harmonics

229

(especially between 1 and 3 kHz), then clear harmonics of a f_o half that of the original one, *except that the fundamental itself is missing*, finally optionally a clear f_o at the halved value. In the intermediate stages there are invariably some displays for which it is difficult to determine the f_o. Measuring the pitch period from the waveform will usually put the f_o at the lower value in these cases. However, even the waveform is sometimes ambiguous in this regard.

Under these circumstances, it is difficult to say in what way and at what moment the f_o has changed. There is no auditory impression of a pitch drop, but it may be that it is so brief that it is not perceived. Since so many instances of doubling are associated with register shifts, it would be strange if the f_o went from, for example, a high modal value to half that value and then to a high register value. Still, in some parts of most doubling utterances one would measure the f_o as being halved. It is primarily the fact that the doubling harmonics do not continue throughout the utterance but, rather, fade in and out that led us to consider doubling a separate phenomenon. Even when the lower fundamental is present, the even numbered harmonics assert themselves in the pitch

Figure 5. Example of waveform with main and secondary pitch periods.

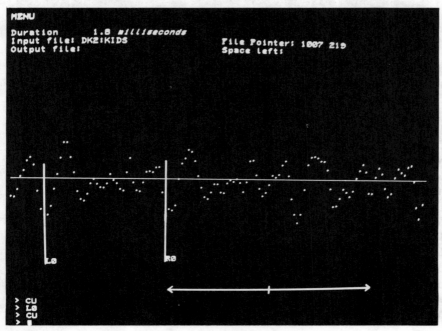

period. Figure 5 shows a typical waveform display of this sort. The duration from peak to peak is 1.8 msec, corresponding to a f_o of 550 Hz, but there is also a secondary peak in this period. The duration from main peak to secondary peak is exactly half of that, .9 msec.

Possible mechanisms to account for doubling include sympathetic vibrations of some structure (e.g. the false vocal cords) with the vocal folds at certain unstable frequency regions. Alternatively, van den Berg (1968a, p. 24) noted that "thick and firmly adducted" vocal folds were sometimes observed to vibrate such that the body of the folds had a frequency twice that of the glottis. It is possible that such a phenomenon is involved here. However, the most likely mechanism is an alternating pattern of vocal fold vibration described for deaf speech by Monsen et al. (1979). For normal children, the question remains whether certain phonetic contexts, utterance positions, or similar factors contribute to the occurrence of doubling.

This chapter is intended as a suggestion for future work to be done in the area of register use in speech. Both the study of register use in adult speech and its development in children's speech are inviting areas that deserve further investigation.

ACKNOWLEDGMENTS

This research was carried out while the author was a graduate research assistant in the Linguistics Department at Brown University and was supported by National Institute of Child Health and Human Development grant #5R01HD09197 to Brown University. I wish to thank Philip Lieberman for his advice and assistance, Robert Buhr for his part collaborations with me in this project; Cathy Kubaska and Howard Golub for helpful discussions; John Mertus for computer programs used in the analysis; and the mothers and children who volunteered for the study.

REFERENCES

Atkinson, J. 1973. Aspects of Intonation in Speech: Implications from an Experimental Study of Fundamental Frequency. Ph.D. Dissertation. Storrs: University of Connecticut.

Buhr, R. and Keating, P. 1977. Spectrographic effects of register shifts in speech production. J. Acoust. Soc. Am. 62:S25(A).

Fairbanks, G. 1942. An acoustical study of the pitch of infant hunger wails. Child Dev. 13:227-32.

Fairbanks, G., Herbert, E.L., and Hammond, J.M. 1949. An acoustical study of vocal pitch in seven- and eight-year-old girls. Child Dev. 20:71-79.

Fairbanks, G, Wiley, J.H., and Lassman, F.M. 1949. An acoustical study of vocal pitch in seven- and eight-year-old boys. Child Dev. 20:62-69.

Hollien, H. 1974. On vocal registers. J. Phonetics 2:124-43.

Jones, M.C. 1965. An investigation of certain acoustic parameters of the crying vocalizations of young deaf chldren. Ph.D. Dissertation. Ann Arbor, Michigan: University microfilms.

Keating, P. and Buhr, R. 1978. Fundamental frequency in the speech of infants and children. J. Acoust. Soc. Am. 63:567-71.

Ladefoged, P. 1971. Preliminaries to Linguistic Phonetics. Chicago: University of Chicago Press.

Lieberman, P. 1977. Speech Physiology and Acoustic Phonetics: An Introduction. New York: Macmillan & Co.

Monsen, R.B. 1979. Acoustic qualities of phonation in young hearing-impaired children. J. Speech Hear. Res. 22:270-88.

Monsen, R.B., Engebretson, A.M., and Vemula, N.R. 1979. Some effects of deafness on the generation of voice. J. Acoust. Soc. Am. 66:1680-90.

Murry, T., Amundson, P., and Hollien, H. 1977. Acoustical characteristics of infant cries: fundamental frequency. J. Child Lang. 4:321-28.

Ostwald, R.F., Phibbs, R., and Fox, S. 1968. Diagnostic use of infant cry. Biol. Neonat. 13:68-82.

Peterson, G.E. and Barney, H.L. 1952. Control methods used in a study of the vowels. J. Acoust. Soc. Am. 24:175-84.

Prescott, R. 1975. Infant cry sound: developmental features. J. Acoust. Soc. Am. 57:1186-91.

Sheppard, W.C. and Lane, H.L. 1968. Development of the prosodic features of infant vocalizing. J. Speech Hear. Res. 11:94–108.

Stark, R.E. and Nathanson, S. 1975. Unusual features of cry in an infant dying suddenly and unexpectedly. In Development of Upper Respiratory Anatomy and Function: Implications for Sudden Infant Death Syndrome, eds. J.F. Bosma and J. Showacre. Washington, D.C.: U.S. GPO. p. 237.

Truby, H.M., and Lind, J. 1965. Cry sounds of the newborn infant. In Newborn Infant Cry, ed. J. Lind. Uppsala: Almqvist and Wiksell. Chapter 1.

van den Berg, J. 1968a. Sound production in isolated human larynges. Ann. N.Y. Acad. Sci. 155:18–27.

van den Berg, J. 1968b. Register Problems. Ann. N.Y. Acad. Sci. 155:129–34.

CHAPTER **10**

Cry and Maturation

Robin Prescott

RATIONALE FOR THE STUDY OF CRY

The rationale for the study of maturation in infant cry is its potential clinical usefulness in the diagnosis of pathological, particularly neuropathological, states and also its possible function in speech and language development. Acoustic measures of cry performances are the principal topic of discussion in this chapter. Also considered are the methods used in the study of cry and a review of findings explaining these methods.

Although the conventional linguistic approach to child language is the analysis of a corpus of child speech (Bloom 1973, Brown 1973), Bruner observes that analysis of a corpus of child speech, no matter how brilliant, cannot illuminate processes by which the child acquires a set of "broadly transferrable or generative skills...which, appropriately coordinated, yield linguistic performances" (Bruner 1975, p. 256). If, as Bruner advises, investigations of the constituent skills of language must begin well before the language begins, then it is possible that developmental norms in infant cry patterns could contribute to a better understanding of some processes underlying language acquisition. Lieberman hypothesized that infant cry constitutes an "innate referential breath group" which provides "the universal acoustic properties of the normal breath group that is used to segment speech into sentences..." (Lieberman 1967, p. 42). Wolff observed developments in infant vocalization, which appear related to changes in the fussing which precedes cry if not to changes in cry

234

itself (Wolff 1969). Monkeys, as Darwin observed in the last century, do not cry like human infants.

ACOUSTIC PARAMETERS

Acoustic parameters of human infant cry which have been analyzed are the *frequency spectra* (including fundamental tone, pitch patterns and resonant characteristics), *relative intensities*, and *temporal patterns* (including frequency of production, response latency and rhythmic patterns within series).

Frequency Spectra

Fundamental Tone
Perhaps more than any other single feature, the pitch of infant cry has been reported. Using an ingenious variety of techniques for determination of the fundamental tone, observers have located average f_o measures of 'normal' cry at about 440Hz during the first half year of life. Murry, Amundson, and Hollien (1977) summarize a number of these investigations.

The clinical issue regarding pitch is that central nervous system pathology is associated with high pitched cry. Cri du chat syndrome, a chromosomal abnormality with extremely poor prognosis for growth and development, was named for the high, flat sound of its cry. Observers report that objective measures of the f_o's of cry sounds of infants with a variety of neurological deficits tend to be higher than those of normal controls. This has been described thoroughly in the earlier chapters of this book.

Longitudinal studies of cries of normally developing infants all found slightly higher f_o's for older infants (Fairbanks 1942; Prescott 1975; Sheppard and Lane 1968). However, a possible trend to slightly higher pitch with increased age is not particularly impressive when examined against variability in infant cry performance.

Pitch Patterns
Wasz-Höckert and his colleagues demonstrated that rising-falling patterns are a principal melody type in neonatal cry (1968). Lack of conformity to principal melody types of rising-falling or falling is said to characterize cry of asphyxiated newborns, meningitic babies with neurological sequelae, and others. These

characteristics are fully described by Michelsson and Wasz-Höckert in Chapter 7. Michelsson (1971) reports that babies who died of cerebral hemorrhage "had very high frequencies and odd melodies."

The 'melody types' referred to above are not to be confused with a phenomenon variously referred to as

Figure 1. Fundamental frequencies of cry utterances by well babies at two age levels.

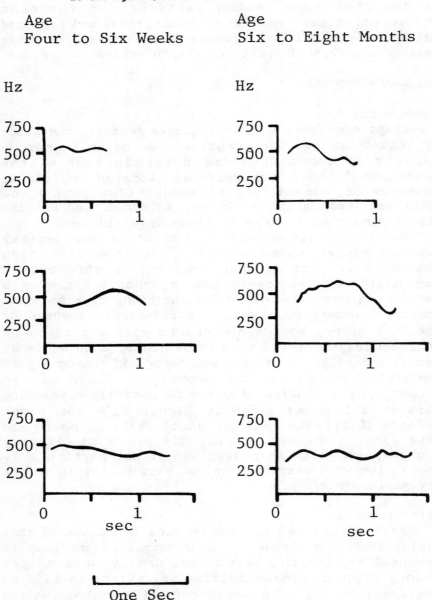

"hyperphonation" (Wasz-Höckert et al. 1971) and
"extreme pitch glides" (Stark and Nathanson 1973).
Although sudden pitch glides occur in the cries of all
infants, their frequency of occurrence is said to be
greater in pathological states.

Evidence for the infant's developing control of his
cry melodies is summarized in Figure 1 and Table 1.
The tracings of fundamental frequencies for single cry
utterances in Figure 1 illustrate small elaborations on
a theme which are made by more mature voices. Table 1
presents evidence that variability in the pitch of
older cries if found *within* utterances and is obscured
when data are pooled across utterances (Prescott 1975).
Fairbanks (1942) reported a bimodal distribution of f_o
values for cry during the second half of the first year
of life, a finding which may support growth of
complexity of cry melodies with advancing age. During
the second year of life, cry may include articulations
with obvious speech referents (Karelitz, Karelitz, and
Rosenfeld 1966). The adult proclivity for attributing
vowel and consonant characteristics to all cry sound
(Winitz 1960) does not dominate the approach to this
subject, as the present volume testifies.

Classification of Overtones and Unvoiced Sounds

The presence of unvoiced components in newborn cry
are described as turbulence, cough, choking, and
constrictive silence (Truby and Lind 1965). Systematic
use of cough may be used to initiate a cry series
(Wolff 1967). Stark and Nathanson (1973, p. 334)
propose a set of features which include turbulence,
vocal fry, "closure of the vocal tract above the
glottis," i.e. combinations of movements which do not

Table 1. Variability of the fundamental tone in cry utterances of
well babies at two age levels.

SAMPLES	Mean F_o All Utterances		Standard Deviation All Utterances		Standard Deviation Within Utterances	
	≤ 6 wks.	6-9 mos.	≤ 6 wks.	6-9 mos.	≤ 6 wks.	6-9 mos.
Longitudinal (N = 4)	384 Hz	415 Hz	38 Hz	39 Hz	28 Hz	53 Hz
Matched (N = 20)	453	473	67	53	30	53
$\bar{x}$	418	444	52	46	29	53

include tongue tip or bilabial closure, and "forceful expulsion of air," which is perceived as alternation of voiced and voiceless portions of cry and is observed to be associated with spasmodic movements of the diaphragm. Broad categories of 'cry,' 'discomfort,' and 'vegetative sound' have been proposed by Stark, Rose, and McLagen (1975) for initial classifications of the infant's sound. Their selection rules are determined by visual and auditory impressions of the infant.

A few longitudinal studies of cry compare frequency spectra in terms of visual impressions (Lynip 1951; Sedláčková 1964; Tonkova 1969). Deviance from normal resonance patterns is reported for pathological states, but not well quantified. One example of a 'deviant' resonant phenomenon is that of a frequency spectrum showing unrelated sets of harmonics. Truby and Lind (1965, p. 55) state the case for the potential importance of this phenomenon:

> The manner of performance of a source mechanism generating *periodic* or *quasiperiodic* stimulus is of considerable neuro-physiological import, while the *manner of response*, the "resonance system" (i.e. here of the respiratory tract), is of no more than secondary significance.

Stark and Nathanson hypothesize that spectra showing more than one set of harmonics are related to multiple sound sources. They describe a low f_o of 100 Hz or less, which changed pitch at a rate varying independently from the concurrent melody of the normally voiced portion of the cry, and suggest that the low frequency sound could relate to motion at the aryepiglottic folds or the ventricular folds (Stark and Nathanson 1973). Michelsson and her colleagues associate "biphonation" or "furcation of the f_o" with hyperbilirubinemia, streptococcal meningitis, and other diseases. The frequency of occurrence of this phenomenon is unclear, but reports of its occurrence were found only for newborns and pathological conditions (Sirvio and Michelsson 1976).

Relative Intensity in Cry Sound

Ostwald reported that cry sound is usually at least 20 dB more powerful than other vocal sounds (Ostwald 1963). Greater variability in the output levels of cries by brain injured babies is well known (Truby and Lind 1965). The separation of normal and pathological

238

cry recordings by averaging output levels in given units of time (Fisichelli et al. 1961) did not lead to standard measures (Fisichelli et al. 1974).

Stark and Nathanson evaluated their auditory impressions of 'low' cries in reference to graphic level recordings and found the 'low' cries were reliably 10 dB or less in peak intensity than the principal portion of a series of newborn cries. A feature of cry designated as 'low' was accordingly defined as $\geq$ 10 dB below average intensity. Relatively more 'low' cries characterized the newborn cries of a fullterm, normally delivered infant, who died suddenly at six months (Stark and Nathanson 1975).

Measures of the relative voltage levels of cry sound are probably most profitably evaluated in relation to pitch contours and temporal data. A program of computer analysis of intensity vs time in relation to frequency measures is discussed in the methodology section of this chapter.

Temporal Patterns in Cry

Frequency of Production

As the child matures, he cries less. In the normal course of events, the total amount of crying varies inversely with age (Aldrich et al. 1946; Brazelton 1962; Fisichelli et al. 1974). School-aged children with I.Q's less than 38 and with impoverished language, laughed *and* cried more than a control group of the same age (Norris 1971). While this finding might suggest that severely mentally retarded children substitute laughing and crying for speech, the question of the communicative function of cry must be approached cautiously. Decerebrate infants cry (Blanton 1917).

Wolff (1967) found that the effect of masking noise upon crying neonates, if they continued to cry at all, was no variation in rhythms and sounds of crying. Wolff argues, however, that intrinsically regulated time sequences of cry are of theoretical significance for cognition and language, even though cry itself may, at least at the early stages, be an autonomic function (Wolff 1969).

Response Latency

The application of a painful stimulus is a basic procedure in cry studies of the 1960's and 1970's. The response latency time from stimulus application to onset of first cry sound can be routinely measured.

Brain injured children were found to have longer and more variable response latencies than controls in many studies. A longitudinal study of 158 infants during the first year of life demonstrated that, for normally developing infants, response latency times remained constant during the first year (Michelsson 1971).

The Respiratory Cycle

Inspiratory voicing is typical in newborn cry but decreases with age (Fisichelli et al. 1974). Darwin was interested in those series of inspirated, unvoiced, or largely unvoiced sounds, which he designated as 'sobbing' and which he observed in children from about four months of age and onward. In older children and adults, sobbing may occur without expiratory voicing (Darwin 1896).

The duration of the expiratory segments of cry cycles varies with chronological age. During steady, 'cruising' type of cry, the duration of the expiratory portion of the cycle increases month by month with remarkable regularity throughout the first eight months of life. Wilder and Baken (1978) report that duration of inspiratory periods, on the contrary, remained constant during the first eight months of life at about 280 msec, a figure agreeing well with 220 msec reported by Long and Hull for newborns (1961). Long and Hull also describe a 100 msec inertial period following the inspiration.

Stark and Nathanson (1973) use the breath group to describe temporal organization of newborn cry. The breath group constitutes the framework for analysis of a cry unit. They present data both for series of cry units and for combinations of series, giving both the number of cry units and the number of breath units—including "empty" breath units. It may be that Stark and Nathanson achieve a more rigid definition of respiratory boundaries than a number of other investigators. A number of cry studies assume that respiratory boundaries are intact even though procedures for their specification are not well described.

Silences within expiratory utterances constitute another temporal feature of cry. In the early period these are long, highly variable, and lacking predictable rhythms. In the second half-year, expiratory silences begin to be patterned. The "boo hoo" of American comic strip babies is determined by within utterance silences of approximately 70 msec

(Prescott 1975). A single expiratory utterance may have more than one such silence, thus becoming (in the comic strip) "boo hoo hoo" or even "boo hoo hoo hoo." Karelitz et al. (1966) called this the 'ae hae' phenomenon. Maturational changes in within utterance silences (shown in Table 2) are increases in frequency of occurrence, decreases in duration, and decreases in the variability of duration time. The frequency of occurrence of within utterance silence patterns is not known. The sample in Table 2 is small (41). Following hypodermic injections, older babies did not produce within utterance silences even in cry series lasting 30 sec or longer (Prescott, unpublished observations).

The 'boo hoo' or 'ae hae' phenomenon is unlike Darwinian sobbing in that it is expiratory rather than inspiratory. Comparisons of temporal features in 'ae hae' and sobbing have not been made, nor have the rhythms of newborn patterns of alternating egressive and ingressive sound been systematically compared to later more elaborate on-off egressive patterns.

METHODOLOGICAL CONSIDERATIONS IN CRY STUDIES

There are inherent problems involved in sampling, recording, analyzing, and treatment of data from infant cry studies. While recent investigations have demonstrated increased technical rigors, additional considerations to the stimulus and infant states remain a major concern in the study of infant vocalization.

Table 2. Number and duration of silences within cry utterances of well babies at two age levels.

AGE	No. of Silences	Duration of Silences	
		X̄	SD
1-10 days	21	150 msec	70 msec
6-9 months	101	73	43

Stimulus Definition

Selection of cry samples has frequently been determined by the specification of a stimulus application. Lind, et al. (1966) noted that following application of a painful stimulus, the first three cries had distinct acoustic properties. Fisichelli et al. (1961) employed a rubber band of a given weight and snapped it against the infant's foot from a specified distance. A controlled 'foot stick' was used by Golub (1979), while Stark and Nathanson (1973) studied the natural arousal of the baby and his cry. Bosma (Stark and Nathanson 1973, p. 347) states that Stark and Nathanson's "demonstrations of ... the sounds accompanying the graduations of spontaneous arousal are more meaningful than ... studies of cry elicited by imposed pain or sensory disturbance..."

Uniform stimulus specification has distinct limitations in maturational studies. Older infants observed in several well-baby clinics had a repertoire of vocal responses to hypodermic injections ranging from the emission of a single brief vocalization to production of high intensity cry performances of several minutes' duration.

Stimulus defintion does not necessarily determine state. Aldrich et al. (1945) found that the "most clear cut result of our study of the causes of neonatal crying is the demonstration of the importance of unknown reasons," and that barometric pressure bore more relation to crying than weight gain or food intake.

Defining the Respiratory Cycle

When the cry utterance is defined as one expiratory segment, maturational changes are seen both in f_0 variability within utterances and in duration of utterances (Prescott 1975; Wilder and Baken 1978). Studies which failed to make consistent identifications of the breath cycle report no maturational differences, and this is true of both crossectional and longitudinal investigations (Michelsson 1971; Sheppard and Lane 1968; Wasz-Höckert et al. 1968).

The respiratory boundaries in infant cry have been determined by various techniques 1) volume flow measures, 2) measures of the infant's torso movements, 3) inspection of cry spectrograms in combination with auditory perception of the investigators, and 4) three-step computer analysis of acoustic records in combination with auditory perception of the investigators. The strengths and limitations of the above approaches warrant consideration.

_1._ Volume flow measures in combination with acoustic measures of neonatal cry found a 220 msec 'violent' inspiration, followed by an inertial period of approximately 100 msec, which preceded the generation of expiratory sound. "High expiratory volume flow was also of extremely short duration and continued to fall because of partial closure of the glottis during production of sound (Long and Hull 1961, p. 376). In newborn cry, turbulent opposition in the flow from the lungs may exceed critical volume just as in adult coughing (Long and Hull 1962).

Measures of 'crying vital capacity' by reverse plethysmography employ a technique by which known volumes of air are injected into a 're-breathing chamber' and calibrated to deflections of a pen and paper recorder. Very low volumes can be determined in this manner and the function of 'crying vital capacity' for gestational age, postnatal age, and body length is predictable in newborns (Kraus et al. 1973). The function of 'crying vital capacity' and chest circumference differentiated infants with hyaline membrane disease from those with transient tachypnoea (Chiswick and Milner 1976).

Although stroke volume and volume flow measures in combination with acoustic measures (Long and Hull 1961) yield precise information, the instrument problems presented by this method are considerable and include problems such as resonances of cry emitted in a plastic bag, problems related to gas exchange during the recording period, and so forth. Spirometric/cry data for infants older than ten days is not available. Defensive reactions of older infants to the face seal can well be imagined.

_2._ Measures of the amplitude of thoracic and abdominal movements of infants are achieved by attaching one or more mercury tube strain gauges to the infant. The strain gauges are connected to an impedance bridge which is calibrated to a pen and paper recorder (Baken and Matz 1973; Jones 1965). Movements of the infant which are unrelated to his breathing are monitored by the observers and excluded from the data. Wilder and Baken calculated durations of respiratory cycles from phase relations of abdominal and thoracic movements of crying infants aged two days to eight months (Wilder and Baken 1978). Analyses were made for pneumographic and not for acoustic records. The principal difficulty encountered in this technique is that the excursion of the strain gauge can change when the infant is still exhaling.

3. Independent listener judgments of acoustic records, such as spectrograms and/or graphic level recordings, have also been used for determination of respiratory boundaries. Stark and Nathanson (1973) state that spectrographic records provide "an increased number of visual cues signalling the onset of inspiration." The drawbacks of this method, aside from the time involved in spectrographic analysis, is that low intensity cries and/or respiratory sounds may fail to be resolved in the spectrogram. As in the strain gauge method, the respiratory boundaries most easily detected by spectrograms and by ear are those associated with rhythmic 'cruising' type of cry; more complex cries may produce ambiguous records by any of the above methods.

4. A computer based system analyzing frequency and intensities in cries of normal and premature infants was used by Tenold and his colleagues (1974). Acoustic data was subjected to two analyses (cepstral and stationarity), and then summarized by pen and ink recorder. Tenold found higher pitch and greater variability in cries by premature infants, but the measures did not reach the level of statistical significance. Similar findings have been reported for traditional spectrographic analyses.

A computer based system using three independent programs of intensity-frequency-time analyses has been applied to infant cry analysis by Golub (1979). The analysis proceeds from root mean square intensity vs time, to fundamental frequency vs time, to peak resonance curves vs time. The signature of inspiratory segments employed in this method is a combination of temporal duration and, if voicing is present, rising pitch within given constraints of time. Golub's fourth procedure involves the comparison of the computer obtained results to auditory impressions of the investigators. Listener judgments produced a 2-3% rate of disagreement with the computer analysis of utterance boundaries for about 900 cry utterances of normal neonates and by neonates with known pathologies.

Golub assumes that large aoustic differences are explainable by small differences in muscle control. Muscle tensions are hypothesized to control speech musculature in a quantal fashion and cry, therefore, can be a measure of muscle control maturation. In Golub's model, Truby cry types of *phonation*, *dysphonation*, and *hyperphonation* have direct relations to mode of laryngeal action.

Golub emphasizes that his physiological model formed the basis for his selecton of acoustic parameters, and that he employs an acoustic theory of cry for his operations, taking care, for example, to treat sound source as separate from resonance characteristics. Interpretations of the program outputs do not depend upon the physiological model.

Golub's outputs give detailed information on the frequency of occurrence of critical features as well as considerable detail about the features themselves. Since the programs were derived from those developed for adult speech production and were modified for infant voice, it seems possible that the variables intervening between cry and speech may eventually be described with the assistance of computer analysis.

Concurrent Behaviors in Addition to Respiration

Bosma, et al. (1965) described 'square mouth' and other cry motions by conventional motion pictures and cineradiography. Gestures in the region of the larynx and pharynx, documented by cineradiography, include the observation that, following effortful inspiration, large boluses of air were sometimes swallowed into the esophagus and trachea (Bosma and Lind 1962). Stark, Rose, and McLagen (1975, p. 207) recommend that non-vocal behaviors distinguish 'cry' from 'distress'. They state that in cry "the mouth is wide open, eyes closed at least some of the time, frowning: stiffness of trunk and limbs. These behaviors are sustained for long periods of time, often as long as 30 seconds." Stark and Nathanson (1973) reported that 24 frame-per-second sound film showed that face, mouth, and body gestures corresponded to acoustic features, such as turbulence. In addition, they agreed with Bosma that the end of the expiratory phase of a cry preceded the elevation of tongue and jaw. The expense of both production and analysis of visual records constitutes a major obstacle to their routine use in studies of cry behavior.

Acoustic Recording

The usual recording problems of noise, response

characteristics of the recording system, and positioning of the microphone are present in infant cry recording. The dynamic range of the infant's sound creates particular problems for cry recording as final portions of expiratory cries and 'vegetative' sounds of various origins may have significantly less power than the main portions of the cry. Management of the dynamic range by automatic gain control devices buries some intensity information and has other effects upon the spectrum. Truby and his colleagues (1965) used a contact microphone placed on the infant's neck for one channel and a conventional microphone on the second channel. No spectrographic differences were found for f_os and silences recorded in a quiet environment by the Truby "auscophone" and a conventional microphone (Prescott 1975). The advantage of the contact microphone is improved signal to noise ratios in most clinical environments.

Acoustic Analysis

Graphic level recordings and spectrograms were the principal analytical tools for cry studies from 1951–1979. In the future, analyses of acoustic records of cry may be expected to be increasingly computer based. Programs for pitch extraction, for example, are well known (Lauger and Horii 1977; Tenold et al. 1974). A promising three-step program based on a physiological model of newborn cry is said to identify significant acoustic parameters, including respiratory markers (Golub 1979). Computer analysis is economical, enabling the introduction of large amounts of raw data to a system which identifies and quantifies acoustic features and then performs the prescribed analytical operations. Theoretically, a computer program can also be fine-tuned to different response characteristics of particular recording systems, can identify changes in signal to noise levels in the data, and can apply these to estimates of confidence levels for the output.

SUMMARY OF FINDINGS

In the course of normal development, consistent maturational change in infant cry appears to include a decreasing number of total cry utterances with increasing age, a decreasing number of inspiratory cries, as well as decreases in the durations of within utterance silences. Maturational changes are also characterized by increases in the durations of single utterances, increases in the number of silences within utterances, increases in pitch and pitch variability within, but not between, utterances. There appears to be no change in the response latency time for 'pain cries' nor in the duration of the inspiratory segment.

Cries by infants with central nervous system pathologies have repeatedly been demonstrated to deviate from those of normal infants. Relatively small measurable differences may be significant, as shown in the records of the newborn cries of an infant with Sudden Infant Death Syndrome at age six months. Cries by cleft palate infants and those with peripheral respiratory disease deviated less from normal cry sounds than those of premature infants and/or those with CNS disorders. A few observations of cries by deaf children in the second half-year of life (Jones 1965; Prescott 1975) suggest that more extreme pitch glides and less patterning of melodies may be characteristic of features in crying by those with congenitally impaired hearing. In the cries of pathological infants, the available data indicate large differences within subjects. Therefore, it is necessary to study more than one or two infants in these categories.

The potential diagnostic power of cry analysis appears assured. If, as recently reported, a computer can reliably identify breath groups in cry, then quantification of the developmental features of infant cry will improve through the use of computer assisted acoustic analyses of infant cry.

REFERENCES

Aldrich, C.A., Sung, C., Knop, C., Stevens, G., and Burchell, M. 1945. The crying of newly born babies I. The community phase. J. Pediat. 26:313-26.

Aldrich, C.A., Norval, M.A., Knop, C., Venegas, F., and Belle, H. 1946. The crying of newly born babies IV. A follow-up study after additional nursing care. J. Pediat. 28:665-70.

Baken, R.J. and Matz, B.J.A. 1973. A portable pneumograph. Human Communications 2:28-38.

Blanton, M.G. 1917. The behavior of the human infant during the first 30 days of life. Psychol. Rev. 24:456-83.

Bosma, J. and Lind, J. 1962. Upper respiratory mechanisms of newborn infants. Acta Pediatr. Suppl. 135:32-44.

Bosma, J., Truby, H.M., and Lind, J. 1965. Cry motions of the newborn infant. Acta Paediatr. Scan. Suppl 163:61-92.

Bloom, L. 1973. One Word at a Time: The Use of Single Word Utterance before Syntax. The Hague: Mouton.

Brazelton, T.B. 1962. Crying in infancy. Pediat. 29:579-88.

Brown, R. 1973. A First Language, the Early States. Cambridge: Harvard University Press.

Bruner, J.S. 1975. From communication to language: a psychological perspective. Cognition 3:255-87.

Chiswick, M.L. and Milner, R.D.G. 1976. Crying vital capacity: measurement of neonatal lung function. Archives of Disease in Childhood 52:22-27.

Darwin, C. 1896. The Expression of the Emotions in Man and Animals. New York: Appleton. p. 157.

Fairbanks, G. 1942. An acoustical study of the pitch of infant hunger wails. Child Dev. 13:227-32.

Fisichelli, V.R., Karelitz, S., Eichbauer, J., and Rosenfeld, L.S. 1961. Volume-unit graphs: their production and applicability in studies of infants' cries. J. Psych. 52:423-27.

Fisichelli, V.R., Karelitz, S., Fisichelli, R.M., and Cooper, J. 1974. The course of induced crying activity in the first year of life. Pediatric Research 8:921-28.

Golub, H. 1979. A physioacoustic model of the infant cry and its use for medical diagnosis and prognosis. J. Acoust. Soc. Am. 65:525(A).

Jones, M.C. 1965. An investigation of certain acoustic parameters of the crying vocalization of young deaf children. Ph.D. Dissertation, Northwestern University.

Karelitz, S., Karelitz, R.F., and Rosenfeld, L.S. 1966. Infants' vocalizations and their significance. Proc. First International Conference on Mental Retardation. New York: Grune & Stratton.

Krauss, A.N., Klain, D.B., Dahms, B.B., and Auld, P.A.M. 1973. Vital capacity in premature infants. Am. Rev. of Respiratory Dis. 108:1361-72.

Laufer, M.Z. and Horii, Y. 1977. Fundamental frequency characteristics of infant non-distress vocalization during the first 24 weeks. J. Child Lang. 4:171-84.

Lieberman, P. 1967. Intonation, Perception and Language. Cambridge: MIT Press.

Lind, J., Wasz-Höckert, O., Vuorenkoski, V., Partanen, T.J., Theorell, K., and Valanne, E. 1966. Vocal responses to painful stimuli in newborn and young infants. Ann. Paediatr. Fenn 12:55-63.

Long, E.C. and Hull, W.E. 1961. Respiratory volume flow in the crying newborn infant. Pediat. 27:272-77.

Long, E.C., Hull, W.E., and Gebel, E.L. 1962. Respiratory dynamic resistance. J. Appl. Physiol. 17:609-12.

Lynip, A.W. 1951. The use of magnetic devices in the collection and analysis of pre-verbal utterances in an infant. Genetic Psychology Monographs 44:221-62.

Michelsson, K. 1971. Cry analysis of symptomless newborn infants. Acta Paediatr. Scand. Suppl. 216.

Murry, T., Amundson, P., and Hollien, H. 1977. Acoustical characteristics of infant cries: fundamental frequency. J. Child Lang. 3:321-28.

Norris, D. 1971. Crying and laughing in imbeciles. Dev. Med. Child Neurol. 13:756-61.

Ostwald, P. 1963. Soundmaking. The Acoustic Communication of Emotion. Springfield, Illinois: Charles C. Thomas.

Prescott, R. 1975. Infant cry sound: developmental features. J. Acoust. Soc. Am. 57:1186-91.

Sedláčková, E. 1964. Analyse acoustique de la voix de nouveau-nés. Folia Phoniat. 16:48-58.

Sheppard, W.C. and Lane, H.L. 1968. Development of the prosodic features of infant vocalizing. J. Speech Hear. Res. 11:94-108.

Sirviö, P. and Michelsson, K. 1976. Sound-spectrographic cry analysis of normal and abnormal newborn infants. Folia Phoniat. 18:161-73.

Stark, R.E. and Nathanson, S.N. 1973. Spontaneous cry in the newborn infant: sounds and facial gestures. In Oral Sensation and Perception, Fourth Symposium, ed., J.F. Bosma. Department of Health, Education and Welfare No. 75-547:323-52.

Stark, R.E. and Nathan, S.N. 1975. Unusual features of cry in an infant dying suddenly and unexpectedly. In Development of Upper Respiratory Anatomy and Function, ed., J.F. Bosma and J. Showacre, U.S. Government Printing Office No. 617 046 00033 1:233-49.

Stark, R.E., Rose, S.N., and McLagen, M. 1975. Features of infant sounds: the first eight weeks of life. J. Child Lang. 2:205-21.

Tenold, J.L., Crowell, D.H., Jones, R.H., Daniel, T.H., McPherson, D.F., and Popper, A.N. 1974. Cepstral and stationarity analyses of fullterm and premature infants' cries. J. Acoust. Soc. Am. 56:975-80.

Tonkova Iampolskaiia, R.V. 1969. Development of speech intonation in infants during the first two years of life. Sov. Psychol. 7:48-54.

Truby, H.M. and Lind, J. 1965. Cry sounds of the newborn infant. Acta Paediatr. Scand. Suppl. 163.

Wasz-Höckert, O., Lind, J., Vuorenkoski, V., Partanen, T., and Valanne, E. 1968. The Infant Cry: A Spectrographic and Auditory Analysis. Clinics in Developmental Medicine No. 29. Lavenham, Suffolk: Spastics International Medical Publications.

Wasz-Höckert, O., Koivisto, M., Vuorenkoski, V., Partanen, T.J., and Lind, J. 1971. Spectrograpic analysis of pain cry in hyperbilirubinemia. Biol. Neonat. 17:260-71.

Wilder, C.N. and Baken, R.J. 1978. Some developmental aspects of infant cry. J. Genetic Psychol. 132:225-30.

Winitz, H. 1960. Spectrographic investigation of infant vowels. J. Genetic Psychol. 96:171-81.

Wolff, P.H. 1967. The role of biological rhythms in early physiological development. Bull. Menninger Clinic 31:197-218.

Wolff, P.H. 1969. The natural history of crying and other vocalizations in early infancy. In Determinants of Infant Behavior IV, ed., B.M. Foss. London: Metheun & Co.

CHAPTER 11

Perceptual and Acoustic Characteristics of Infant Cry Types

Thomas Murry

INTRODUCTION

The infant's cry is generally thought to be an acoustic manifestation of a complex motor act in response to a stimulus. The birth cry itself has been regarded as the commencement of a stimulus-response bond between the child and his new environment. It serves as an effective force in the reorganization of cardiorespiratory function and represents the infant's first use of the vocal mechanism. Whether the cry is a specific behavioral response to indicate change or part of a generalized body response, it provides the child with a communicative link to other people in his environment. Preverbal crying may be the infant's most effective and immediate method of communicating (Borgguist 1906). During the early months of life, motor reactions to stimuli (internal and external) are total body responses. As a result, it was suggested that the acoustic character of the cry is without specification (Eisenson, Auer, and Irwin 1963). However, there is evidence to show that, as early as two weeks of age, acoustic parameters may be associated with specific cry evoking situations (Murry, Gracco, and Gracco 1979).

Infant cries have been of interest both as a psychomotor and as a neuromotor phase of development. As Parmelee (1962) suggested, "...crying behavior reflects the central nervous system's capabilities to activate, to inhibit, or to modulate the action of crying. At a more peripheral level, certain respiratory, laryngeal, or resonator activities are reflected in the acoustic characteristics of the vocal output."

Infant cries are informative to clinicians as supplementary criteria for the evaluation of physiologic functions. Various genetic anomalies (e.g. Down's Syndrome), neurologic disorders (e.g. 'Cry du Chat' Syndrome), and respiratory conditions (e.g. Respiratory Distress Syndrome of newborn infants) have been detected and characterized by particular cry sounds (Karelitz, Karelitz, and Rosenfeld 1960; Parmelee 1962; Ostwald, Freedman, and Kurtz 1962).

Analysis of the acoustic characteristics of the infant cry is noninvasive and easily obtained. With appropriate interpretation, the cry may provide diagnostic or communicative information. One of the acoustic parameters available for analysis of cry is fundamental frequency (f_o). It has been shown in the past that fundamental frequency reflects not only the physical characteristics about an individual's identify (e.g. age, sex) but also his emotional state (e.g. fear).

The fundamental frequency characteristics of non-speech vocalization, such as cry, are somewhat variable, as shown in earlier chapters. However, these studies have furthered the understanding of the acoustical structure of infant cry sounds.

The majority of the perceptual investigations of infant crying have attempted to demonstrate whether or not meaningful crying exists by using listener judgments of various cry evoking stimuli. The literature tends to provide conflicting information concerning the relative informational value of the cry. There appears to be more agreement concerning the ability of listeners to identify an individual infant auditorily (Illingworth 1955; Formby 1967; Murry, Hollien, and Muller 1975) than to identify the information contained in the cry. If it postulated that the anatomic features that contribute to the production of vocal output are undifferentiated during infancy and only at some later stage in life (i.e. puberty or old age) change to account for the acoustic differences between male and female vocalization, one might expect to find no difference in the cries of infants.

This chapter describes the acoustic characteristics of cries of male and female infants and the perceptual information associated with the cries. The scope of this review is concerned primarily with the acoustic and perceptual characteristics of the infant cry. Brief mention will first be made of cry as "preverbal communication", and as a manifestation of central nervous system integrity. The latter notion is perhaps responsible for the acknowledgment and increasing awareness of the clinical importance of the infant cry.

CRY AS A MODE OF COMMUNICATION

Illingworth (1955) suggested a role for crying in the general developmental scheme. Crying has been considered to have a definite biological utility as a 'distress signal' from the infant to his surroundings. It is thought to be initially a reflexive behavior in response to either an internal stimulus, such as hunger or pain, or to an external stimulus, such as noise or cold. "...Later, with repeated parental response, crying becomes operant and more purposeful. As the infant's speech development progresses, sounds imitative of words appear in the cry and soon, syllables, then real words...allowing for more complex communication with the environment..." (Karelitz, Karelitz, and Rosenfeld 1960). Miller (1951) disputed the notion of meaningful cry by pointing out that, like normal infants, those born without a cerebrum produce crying. Lenneberg, Rebelsky, and Nichols (1965) found that normal infants born to deaf parents had a similar emergence pattern for vocalizations, including cry, when compared to normal infants born to hearing parents. These two studies suggest that the infant possesses an inherent mode of primitive communication, despite the presence or absence of parental response. However, it has been argued that the primitive reflexive cry may acquire purpose and the rate of development of the infant's meaningful cries may depend on the existence of an intact central (and peripheral) nervous system (Karelitz et al. 1960; Parmelee 1962). Karelitz and coworkers found that the progressive evolution from cry to speech was delayed in 'brain-damaged' children when compared to normal children of the same ages. Thus, while there seems to be some agreement as to the necessity of neurologic integrity for the acquisition of language skills, the role of crying in language development is still uncertain.

Phoneticians, such as Irwin and Chen (1941), have suggested that infant cry sounds are 'prespeech', since they are characterized predominantly by vowel sounds. Ringel and Kluppel (1964) cited additional evidence for the phonetic interpretation of cry sounds. When they spectrographically analyzed neonatal cries, the formant patterns were similar to those generally associated with the /æ/ (cat) and /ʌ/ (but) vowels. The roentgenographic findings of infant laryngeal movements during crying by Bosma, Lind, and Truby (1964) were also felt to be in agreement with the 'phonetic' observations of the articulatory musculature during pronunciation of /æ/ and /ʌ/ vowels (Ringel and Kluppel 1964). However, Truby and Lind (1965) and others argue that crying is not like speech and can, therefore, have no phonological classification. While certain phonological elements exist in the early cry, few patterns coincidental with later language have as yet to be found.

CRY AS A MANIFESTATION OF NEUROLOGIC INTEGRITY

Diagnostic significance has been attached to infant cries characteristic of certain diseases affecting the nervous system. Among those described by Illingworth (1955), Ostwald, Phibbs, and Fox (1968) and others are: the 'hoarse', 'gruff' cry of cretinism, the 'shrill' cry of meningeal irritation or hydrocephalus, the 'Cri-du-Chat' (cat-like cry) Syndrome, and the 'feeble', 'high-pitched' cry of Down's Syndrome. Some of these cries have been acoustically characterized. For example, Vuorenkoski et al. (1966) demonstrated a fundamental frequency elevated significantly above 600 Hz for 8 children aged 4 to 12 months suffering from the 'Cri-du-Chat' Syndrome. Formants above 4000 Hz were noted as being typical of this disease entity (Luchsinger, et al. 1967). Ostwald and Peltzman (1974) utilized sound spectrography to show that the 'distress' cries of several neurologically abnormal neonates exhibited a significantly higher f_o when compared to the 'distress' cries of normal neonates. However, the specific nature of the abnormality was not discernable from the spectrographic patterns of the infant cries. Karelitz, Karelitz, and Rosenfeld (1960) demonstrated differences between normal and brain-damaged children (aged birth to 2 years) with respect to the cry stimulus response patterns. The abnormal infants tended to cry more as they grew older, requiring less stimulation. Furthermore, the abnormal infants' cries were irregular and of short duration when compared to the rhythmic, sustained cries of normal infants of the same age range.

Colton (see Chapter 8) has shown that infants who are siblings of Sudden Infant Death Syndrome (SIDS) babies have elevated f_o when compared to a normal population. These infants and those who subsequently died as the result of SIDS showed a high, rather flat f_o with higher intensity peaks than normal infants.

Although specification has not yet reached the level of prediction, there is substantial data demonstrating significant differences in the acoustic characteristics (f_o and duration) of abnormal and normal infant cry sounds.

PERCEPTUAL ASPECTS OF INFANT CRIES

Identification of Cry Types

Much of the controversy surrounding the notion of cry as a meaningful mode of communication stems from early perceptual studies of infant vocalizations. As early as 1927, Sherman attempted to elicit distinctive emotional responses from neonates. Four stimuli (restraint of the head, pricking with a needle, withholding feeding, and suddenly dropping toward a table top) were used to elicit the crying responses. Sherman found that both 'trained' observers (nurses, medical students, and graduate psychology students) and 'untrained' observers (college freshman) were unable to correctly match the emotional response with the cry evoking stimulus. Sherman argued that based on this study the nature of the discomfort which elicits a cry cannot be distinguished by the type of resultant vocalizations. However, Sherman's techniques for testing the two observer groups did not allow for the separation of the visual and auditory components of the infants' cry responses. Nor were their judgments based solely on the auditory perception of the cry sounds. Aldrich and coworkers (1945) found no 'clear-cut' answers as to the cause of infant crying. Illingworth (1955) stated "... it would seem...to be obvious that the cry of hunger or loneliness is quite different from the cry of pain..." Wasz-Höckert, et al. (1964a) tested the notion that different types of infant vocalizations are perceptually distinguishable. Recordings of vocalizations "typical" to the situations of 'birth,' 'pain,' 'hunger,' and 'pleasure' were obtained from normal neonates. Eighty nurses trained in the care of young children listened to the randomized cry recordings and were able to identify the type of vocalization 67 percent of the time. In a followup study, Wasz-Höckert et al. (1964b) used the same experimental method to examine the effect of training on the ability of the listener to identify the cry evoking stimulus. Training was defined as having the experience of caring for children from birth to two years of age for more than two weeks. It was shown that the trained listeners were better able to identify the types of cry evoking stimuli than the untrained listeners.

It is noteworthy that the mothers of the infants tested were not included in the studies by Wasz-Höckert, Sherman, and Aldrich. Yet, for a long time, it has been assumed that mothers can differentiate the cause of their infant's cry (Illingworth 1955).

The results of these studies may not be generalized to the efficacy of the cry as a communicative like between parent and infant because they included the birth cry as well as non-cry sounds. In addition, the investigators pre-selected "typical" samples which may have biased the perceptual responses. Also, the duration of the cry, the age of the infants, and the manner of obtaining the samples were not well controlled.

Muller, Hollien, and Murry (1974) reported on the perceptual responses of mothers to the cries of their children. They elicited three types of cry from four male and four female infants aged three to five months. All infants were healthy and the samples were obtained in an experimental setting. Three distinct cry samples were obtained: pain -- this sample was elicited by snapping an elastic band against the sole of the infant's foot; startle -- this was elicited by a single clap of two large wooden blocks slammed together (the intensity of the noise burst was 95 dB SPL at the infant's ear); and hunger -- food was withheld after several seconds of feeding (if the infant stopped crying when feeding was resumed, the sample was accepted as a hunger cry). Cries elicited by pain and auditory stimulation were recorded in a sound-treated booth with the infant's mother, the experimenter, and the tape recorder outside the infant's visual field. The recording of cries in response to hunger stimulation was performed in the infant's home while the mother was feeding the child. All cries were recorded for approximately 90 seconds from the time of stimulus application.

After all recordings were made, the first and third 15-second segments of each of the 24 recordings (8 infants by 3 stimulus conditions) were extracted and a duplicate recording of these samples was made. Thus, for all infants there were six cry-sample types represented; i.e., the initial 15-second segments of cries evoked by pain, hunger, and startle (auditory) stimuli (referred to as P_1, H_1, and S_1 respectively) and the third 15-second segments of cries elicited by the three stimulus conditions (P_3, H_3, and S_3 respectively). Two groups of listeners were utilized. Group A consisted of the mothers of the eight infants recorded in the study. They were asked to indicate on their answer sheets whether the stimulus which originally evoked the cry was either pain (P), hunger (H), or startle (S). The mothers, however, were never told by the experimenter which of the cry samples were produced by their own infant. Group B was 10 mothers of children whose ages were comparable with the infants recorded in the study but who had no previous contact with the eight recorded infants. Subjects in Group B were asked to also indicate whether the cry sample was P, H, or S.

Each group was given a brief description of the cry evoking stimuli and told to use this description as the basis for their judgment. In order to familiarize the mothers with the type of samples they were to hear, 10 samples (selected at random) were presented prior to the listening session.

The response of mothers judging cry samples produced by infants with whom they were unfamiliar (i.e. all responses of Group B, as well as Group A's judgments on those cry samples that were not produced by their own infants) are reported in Table 1 as a function of cry-sample types. The data in this table are reported in percentages of judgments falling into into each of the three response categories (P, H, or S). The percentage of correct responses to each sample type are underlined and appear along the diagonals in the table. Using a statistic that was based on the normal approximation to the binomial distribution, each percentage was tested in order to ascertain whether it was significantly greater than a chance level of 33.3% confidence level. This test indicated that some of the hunger cry samples were correctly identified a significant number of times; in Group A, samples H_1 and H_3, and in Group B, sample type H_1. However, a number of other samples were also incorrectly identified as

Table 1. Responses of mothers of cry samples produced by all infants except their own. The percentage of judgments falling into each of the three response categories is indicated as a function of cry-sample type.

Response Type	Cry-Types						
	H_1	H_3	P_1	P_3	S_1	S_3	Total
Group A							
H	44.7*	43.8*	41.1*	44.6*	56.3*	46.4*	56.1*
P	33.0	24.1	32.1	26.8	19.6	19.7	25.9
S	22.3	32.1	26.8	28.6	24.1	33.9	28.0
Group B							
H	44.4*	37.5	37.5	43.8	42.5	39.9	40.9
P	32.5	28.1	36.3	33.7	36.3	31.3	33.0
S	23.1	34.4	26.2	22.5	21.2	28.8	26.1

*Significantly greater than chance at 0.05 level.

hunger cries a significant percentage of time. While superficially these results indicate that the mothers were able to correctly identify only some of the hunger cry-sample types, this conclusion is confounded by the large number of hunger responses. Therefore, it must be concluded that the mothers incorrectly perceived an excessive number of the samples as hunger cries and that those hunger samples that were correctly identified merely reflect this general bias.

Table 2 presents the responses of Group A to those cry samples in which each mother was evaluating only her own infant. A binomial test indicated that sample type H_3 was correctly identified a significant percentage of times, and that there was a significant percentage of incorrect hunger responses for sample P_3. The conclusion previously provided also summarizes the data where mothers judged only their own infants; i.e., the mothers could not identify the cry-sample types and often thought other samples were hunger cries.

These results support the contention that the acoustic characteristics of the cries of the normal infant appear to carry little perceptual information to the mother with respect to the cry-evoking situation. It might be hypothesized, therefore, that within the normal home situation, the cry generally acts simply to alert the mother, and that any of her suppositions concerning the situation that evoked the crying behavior must be based upon additional environmental cues.

Identification of the Infant Crying

Aldrich, Sung, and Knop (1945) observed significant differences between the cries of individual infants. Illingworth (1955) noted that mothers in four-bedded wards of a maternity hospital claimed they awoke when their own infants cried, but slept through the crying of other infants on the ward. Formby (1967) went on to experimentally test these observations. He attempted to correlate the mother's ability to recognize her own infant's cry with maternal age, parity, method of feeding, and the time interval between delivery and the playback of the recorded cries to the mother. Formby found that the only correlation appeared in relation to this time interval. Prior to 48 hours post-delivery, 12 of 23 mothers tested recognized their own infant's cry. After 48 hours, all 8 mothers tested recognized their own infant's cry.

In this same study, a second group of 10 mothers were asked to record the number of times they were awakened by cries on three successive nights. Formby found a

Table 2. Response percentages of Group A mothers judging only their own infants.

Response Type	H_1	H_3	P_1	P_3	S_1	S_3	Total
			Cry-Types				
Group A							
H	43.8	75.0*	43.8	62.5*	43.8	18.8	47.9*
P	50.0	25.0	31.2	12.5	37.5	43.7	33.3
S	06.2	00.0	25.0	25.0	18.7	37.5	18.8

*Significantly greater than chance at 0.05 level.

significant number of mothers claimed they were awakened on three nights by cries of their own infants. Formby did not specify if or how these responses (second maternal group) were verified.

Murry, Hollien, and Muller (1975) utilized the cry samples from the four male and four female infants described previously to assess the ability of mothers to identify their own infant solely on the basis of crying. The listeners were the mothers of the eight infants who furnished the initial 15-sec of cries evoked by the pain, hunger, and startle stimuli (referred to as P_1, H_1, and S_1 respectively), and the third 15-sec of these same cry samples (P_3, H_3, and S_3). The 48 cry samples were copied and added to the original tape -- a procedure which resulted in a total of 96 cry samples. The listeners were asked to make two (forced choice) decisions after listening to each of the 96 samples: first, was the cry produced by her own infant and second, was the cry produced by a male or female infant.

Of the total of 768 recognition ('yes' or 'no') responses, 699 (91.0% were correct and 69 responses (9.0%) were incorrect. The means for individual mothers ranged from 86.4% to 97.9% and, in all instances, were much higher than the calculated chance level of 60.3% as determined from the normal approximation of the binomial distribution (Hays 1963). The incorrect responses were of two types: some of the incorrect responses (1.2% occurred when the mothers did not recognize their own infant; 60 of the incorrect responses (7.8%) occurred when the mother identified someone else's infant as her own.

In an effort to determine whether these incorrect judgments were systematic in nature, a confusion matrix containing the frequency of incorrect judgments was constructed. The resulting coefficient was r = +0.36, indicating that a slight positive correlation existed between the number of incorrect judgments made by a particular mother and the number of times her infant was mistakenly identified by other mothers. In addition, the correlation coefficient for mutual confusions was also calculated (i.e., whether the number of times mother X identified infant Y as her own infant corresponds with the frequency of Y's confusions with infant X). A positive correlation coefficient of r = +0.44 was found. None of the above correlation coefficients, however, was significant at the 0.05 level.

Table 3. Frequency and percentage of correct sex judgments as a function of cry-xample type. None of the percentages significantly different from chance at the 0.025 level.

| | Cry Types | | | | | | |
	H_1	H_3	P_1	P_3	S_1	S_3	Total
Number of Judgments	101	99	104	100	108	100	612
Number of Correct Judgments	47	44	54	51	56	46	298
Percentage of Correct Judgments	46.5	44.4	51.9	51.0	51.8	46.0	48.7

To estimate the relative influence of the six cry-sample types (H_1, H_3, P_1, P_3, S_1, S_3), the data were grouped according to the frequency of INCORRECT judgments corresponding to each sample type. A two-tail binomial test was utilized and the majority of sample types were not significantly different from chance.

A statistical test based on the normal approximation of the binomial distribution was performed on the sex judgments. This procedure demonstrated that the total percentage of correct sex judgments was not significantly greater than chance. A further breakdown of these data -- according to the percentage of correct responses-- of each individual mother indicated that only one of the eight mothers (listener C) scored significantly higher than chance.

Table 3 reports the frequency and percentages of correct sex judgments as a function of the six cry-sample types. A two-tail binomial test indicated that none of the percentages differed significantly from chance. That is, no particular type of cry sample afforded an advantage over any other with respect to the identification process.

The eight mothers had little difficulty recognizing those cries produced by their own infant. There are two major factors which should be considered in view of these findings. First, the recognition task in this study only involved absolute identification (i.e., whether the infant was, or was not, her own) and mothers based their judgments upon the familiarity of the cry (i.e., the cry was, or was not, familiar). Thus, the methods used in this study tended to maximize the familiar-unfamiliar perceptual dimension.

A second factor to be considered is the relatively long duration (15 sec) of the cry samples presented to the listeners. Hence all (or nearly all) possible temporal and acoustic cues were available to the mothers and assisted them in making their judgments. Accordingly, it is not possible to differentiate among the percepts they may have used in this process.

The results of this study also indicated that the six cry-sample types did not appear to be a differential factor influencing the number of correct recognition responses. Apparently, those cues necessary for successful recognition were equally abundant within each of the sample classes (types).

Listeners were generally unable to auditorily identify an infant's sex. The results of the research on sex judgments may be interpreted in at least two ways: 1) the perceptual characteristics that are utilized in sex judgments of adult voices are not adequate for distinguishing the sex of infants, or, more probably, 2) there is no systematic physical difference between the cries of male and female infants and, therefore, no perceptual differences.

It appears that there are perceptual cues carried in cries which permit the identification of infants by their mothers. However, from early studies, it is not clear as to the type of information carried in infant cries relating to the identification of the infant's gender or the cry evoking stimulus.

ACOUSTIC CHARACTERISTICS OF INFANT CRIES

Cry Fundamental Frequency

Interest in the acoustic parameters of infant vocalizations became evident in 1838 when Gardiner published the first study of infant cries. By means of musical notation, he described the tones of infant cries as lying between the notes A and E on the musical scale. In addition, Gardiner pointed out two components of the cry that correspond to the respiratory cycle. The inspiratory component was observed to be of short duration. The expiratory component was the most pronounced portion of the cry, being longest in duration. Gutzmann and Flatau (1906) recorded the cries of 30 normal neonates and by musical notation located the fundamental frequency at middle A (440 Hz). The musical and phonetic approach to the structure of infant vocalizations gave way to newer methods. Using an acoustical method, Fairbanks (1942) traced the pitch changes of his child's hunger cries from birth (370 Hz) to 4 months (585 Hz) then to 9 months (450 Hz). Since then, the development of electroacoustic devices has made it possible to further study the acoustical structure of infant cry sounds by more sophisticated and noninvasive methods.

As a result of the early work in this area, several terms have evolved for use in describing various acoustic events within the cry. First, the entire cry response to a stimulus is composed of a repetitive series of "cry-cycles." Second, the cry-cycle is defined as having both inspiratory and expiratory components, corresponding to the respiratory phases of inspiration and expiration. The silences as well as the actual vocalizations are included in the cry-cycle. Usually, the inspiratory phase corresponds to the silences, although this phase may contain short duration cries (Truby and Lind 1965). These inspiratory cry utterances have been shown to have a higher pitch than the expiratory cries that precede them.

Acoustic analysis of cry sounds has been carried out primarily on the expiratory phase of the cry-cycle since it comprises most of the actual vocalization. Using pain-elicited cries from 30 normal neonates, Truby and coworkers (1965) categorized three different patterns of expiratory cry. Each of these patterns, 'phonation,' 'dysphonation,' and 'hyperphonation,' was found to be acoustically distinct. Phonation represented primarily glottal excitation with production of periodic laryngeal oscillations. Phonatory cries exhibited a fundamental frequency range of 280 to 786 Hz. Dysphonation was characterized by an alternation of the basic glottal oscillations and accompanied by simultaneous supraglottic turbulence. Acoustically, dysphonation was represented by a spectrum of formant frequencies. Hyperphonation, represented by constrained glottal excitation, showed

fundamental frequences ranging between 1 and 2 kHz.
Both phonation and hyperphonation demonstrated periodic
waveforms with distinguishing fundamental frequencies,
while dysponation proved to be aperiodic. Thus, it was
shown that there exist acoustical correlates of glottal
and supraglottal activity during phonation. It was
also shown that a single cry may contain one or a
combination of the three cry patterns so that no infant
emits a uniform series of cries.

Additional information on expiratory cry fundamental
frequency was provided by Ringel and Kluppel (1964)
who showed that the average expiratory cry of 10
normal, pain-stimulated neonates had a fundamental
frequency of 413.13 Hz. Ostwald and coworkers (Ostwald
and Peltzman 1974) found the fundamental frequency
range for normal neonates to lie between 425 and 600
Hz.

Two longitudinal studies (Fairbanks 1942; Sheppard
and Lane 1968) revealed a consistent increase in cry
fundamental frequency from birth to 4 months of age
followed by a plateau during the subsequent few months.
For the first month of life, the mean fundamental
frequency was 373 Hz within a range of 153 to 888 Hz
(Fairbanks 1942). This was consistent with those data
reported by Ringel and Kluppel (1964). Prescott (1975)
reported that small increases of within utterance f_o
variability were found to exist between the two groups
of different age levels (birth to 10 days and 6 to 9
months). However, Prescott did not demonstrate any
developmental change in the mean fundamental frequency.

Sheppard and Lane (1968) observed that the
fundamental frequency of the male infant's cries was
approximately 30 Hz greater than that obtained for the
female infant's cries during the period studied (birth
to 5 months). However, due to the small sample size (2
subjects), the investigators did not submit these data
to statistical analysis to determine if the fundamental
frequency differences between the sexes was
significant. Although Caldwell and Leeper (1974) did
not examine fundamental frequency, they found no
significant differences between male and female
neonates (0 to 4 days) using the acoustic parameters of
vocalization time, cry latency, and pause time.

Despite the volume of conflicting perceptual data,
there have been only a few studies in which the cry has
been acoustically analyzed with respect to specific cry
evoking stimuli. Wasz-Höckert et al. (1963) attempted
to acoustically distinguish between cries evoked by

birth, pain, hunger, and pleasure using spectrography. The use of cry samples which were felt by the investigators to be "typical" of the four situations raises serious questions about the validity of their results.

Murry, Amundson, and Hollien (1977) systematically analyzed the f_o characteristics of infant cries of four male and four female infants. Since the infants were the same ones who participated in the earlier studies (Muller, Hollien, and Murry 1974; Murry, Hollien, and Muller 1975), they were able to relate the f_o data to their previous perceptual findings.

The first and third 15 seconds of the 24 cry samples were examined by the present investigators in order to determine the amount of vocalization contained in each 15-second sample. The investigators chose the second 15-second segment for acoustic analysis since it generally contained greater vocalization time than the first 15-second segment and since a previous study (Murry et al. 1975) found no difference in the perceptual identification rates of the two segments. Analysis of f_o was carried out by processing the 24 samples on a Honeywell 1508-C visicorder.

Only the periodic information from the visicorder tracing was measured. Table 4 presents the mean cry f_o for the eight infants for each of the three cry conditions. Table 4 indicates that for each of the three cry evoking stimuli, the four male infants produced a higher mean cry f_o than the female infants. The mean cry f_o differences between males and females were 32.7, 25.7, and 41.9 Hz, respectively, for the three cry evoking stimuli. The overall mean difference between males and females was 36.4 Hz. From Table 4, it is apparent that some overlap in mean cry f_o is present-- female subject 6 has a higher mean cry f_o than does male subject 5. Nonetheless, these results clearly indicate that male infants cry at higher f_o levels than do female infants. Table 4 also presents the results of the data as they relate to the cry evoking stimulus. For all subjects, the mean cry f_o for pain evoked stimuli was highest, followed by the mean f_o for hunger. The cries produced in response to startle resulted in the lowest f_o for the group. As can be seen from the table, no one type of stimulus always produced the highest or lowest mean cry f_o for all subjects.

The f_o results provide evidence to support the previous findings of Muller et al. 1974) and Murry et

Table 4. Mean cry f_o for each infant for three conditions of cry-
pain, hunger, and startle.

Subject	Pain X 50	Hunger X 50	Startle X 50
Male 1	403.9	422.2	453.0
Male 3	478.1	492.1	396.2
Male 4	531.6	491.2	493.1
Male 5	415.9	399.9	426.5
Mean ($\bar{x}$)	457.4	451.4	442.2
Female 2	361.1	351.4	386.3
Female 6	453.9	475.3	436.7
Female 7	465.9	441.6	385.4
Female 8	417.7	434.3	392.8
Mean ($\bar{x}$)	424.7	425.7	400.3
Overall ($\bar{x}$)	441.0	438.5	421.3

al. (1975). By analyzing perceptual responses, they found that mothers could not recognize the stimulus which elicited the cry, i.e., pain, hunger, or startle, or the gender of the infant from the cry, even though they could identify their own infant from the voice recordings. Since no significant differences were found for the mean cry f_o for either gender or cry type, it would appear that f_o provides little or no acoustic information attributable to gender or cry type. It can be hypothesized that, in previous research, mothers identified their own infants using cues other than those derived from fundamental frequency.

Table 5 summarizes the available data on cry from infants up to nine months. Where possible, information on the age and gender of the infants is included. While it is not always possible to make direct comparisons since the authors do not indicate gender or age in all cases, there is general agreement among the investigations. These findings hold at least for studies that used cry as the vocal behavior and infants with similar ages.

Of particular interest is the result that the males in the Murry et al. study (1977) were found to have a higher mean cry f_o than did females. Sheppard and Lane (1968) report a similar finding, as do Hollien and Hollien (1976) in their evaluation of SFF data for pre-pubescent children of all ages. Thus, there appears to be a trend indicating that the male cry f_o is higher than the female cry mean f_o for the early ages. The perceptual results of Murry et al. (1975) indicated that listeners could not reliably separate the cries of male and female infants. It may be that the higher f_o values which resulted in a 'pitch cue' tended to confuse the listeners. That is, the listeners may have misinterpreted the f_o differences because they use the pitch cues in the same way they would to discriminate between adults (normally, the male exhibits lower pitch than does the female).

Other Acoustic Parameters of Cry

The uniqueness of an infant's cry was established spectrographically by providing 'characteristic visual-acoustic patterns' for each infant studied (Truby and Lind 1965). The identification of individuality within the spectrograms supports an earlier study by Ringel and Kluppel (1964), in which it was possible to

Table 5. Summary of mean cry f_o data from the present study and previous studies using cry as the vocal behavior.

Investigators	No. of Subjects	Sex	Age	Mean f_o
Gutzmann & Flatau (1906)	17	F	0-5 h	440
	13	M	0-5 h	440
Fairbanks (1942)	1	M	0;4	585
	1	M	0;5	450
Ringel & Kluppel (1964)	6	F	4-40 h	
	4	M	4-40 h	413.1
Sheppard & Lane (1968)	1	F	0;1-0;5	420
	1	M		455
Prescott (1975)	4	–	0;6-0;9	415
	10	–	0;6-0;8	495
Present Study (1977)	4	F	0;3-0;6	416.9
	4	M	0;3-0;6	449.5

distinguish between 10 neonates using the combination of fundamental frequency, SPL, and cry duration.

The duration and intensity of neonatal cries have been studied by Ringel and Kluppel (1964). They showed that the average expiratory cry of 10 normal infants was 1.47 sec in duration and exhibited a sound pressure level (SPL) of 82 dB (measured 12 inches from the mouth). Sheppard and Lane (1968) reported an average duration of cry to be 0.29 sec for 2 normal infants. Caldwell and Leeper (1974) found an average cry duration of 0.65 sec. The disparity between the reported values for cry duration is not understood. The infants studied by Ringel and Kluppel were 4 to 40 hours of age, while infants studied by Caldwell and Leeper were 24 to 72 hours old. One would expect to find some· similarity in the values obtained for duration, since the groups of infants were similar in age. Perhaps the differences in cry duration were due to the use of different methodology. Prescott (1975) observed significant differences in the duration of expiratory cries between the age groups (birth to 10 days and 6 to 9 months) with these differences also existing between individuals of the younger age group. Ostwald, Freedman, and Kurtz (1962) pointed out possible reasons for the variability in the data reported by different investigators for cry duration, pause time, latency, and, perhaps, even f_o. "...differences in weight, size, physical development, as well as the techniques of sampling and recording of particular cries, form the sequence of cries stimulated in each cry response..." are important considerations in evaluating the acoustic data on infant cries. Also, the use of infant subjects of different age levels (different stages of development) by various investigators makes comparisons between reported data difficult.

SUMMARY

The cries of infants provide a verbal communicative link to the parents. Familiarity with the cry sounds of an infant is ncessary to glean information about the infant's emotional state. However, the acoustic information alone is not sufficient to signal the reason for the crying. Thus, the value of the cry as a communicative link is that it alerts the parent to a need of the infant or a change in emotional status.

It is apparent from the research to date that cries do vary somewhat as a result of the situation, the sex of the infant, and the age of the infant. Most of the data from f_o analysis of cries suggest minor variations, the most significant being the trend to higher f_o values in males than in females. Additional acoustic information is now being examined to determine if other parameters distinguish one type of cry behavior from another. This information appears in other chapters of this volume.

ACKNOWLEDGMENTS

The author acknowledges the contributions from The University of Florida, Institute for the Advanced Study of Communication Processes, who provided the support to obtain the original data. The author also acknowledges the contributions of Dr. Harry Hollien, Professor, Institute for the Advanced Study of Communication Processes, Gainesville, Florida; Dr. Eric Muller, University of Wisconsin, Madison; and Dr. Pamela Amundson, University of California, San Diego, who co-authored reports on the perceptual and acoustic characteristics of infant cries.

REFERENCES

Aldrich, C.A., Sung, C., and Knop, C. 1945. The crying of newly born babies: II the individual phase. J. Pediat. 27:89-96.

Borgguist, A. 1906. Crying. Amer. J. Psychol. 2:149-205.

Bosma, J.F., Lind, J., and Truby, M. 1964. Respiratory motion patterns of the newborn infant in cry. In Physical Diagnosis of the Newly Born, ed. J.L. Kay. Columbus: Ross Labs 103-16.

Caldwell, H.S. and Leeper, A., Jr. 1974. Temporal patterns of neonatal vocalization: a normative investigation. Perceptual and Motor Skills 38:911-16.

Eisenson, J., Auer, T., and Irwin, J. 1963. The Psychology of Communication. New York: Appleton-Century-Crofts.

Fairbanks, G. 1942. An acoustical study of the pitch of infant hunger wails. Child Dev. 13:227-32.

Formby, D. 1967. Maternal recognition of infant's cry. Dev. Med. Child. Neurol. 9:293.

Gardiner, W. 1838. The Music of Nature. Boston: Wilkins and Carter.

Gutzmann, H. and Flatau, T.S. 1906. Die stimme des saulings. Archiv. fur Laryngologie und Rhinologie 18:139.

Hays, W.L. 1963. Statistics for Psychologists. New York: Holt, Rhinehart, and Winston, Inc.

Hollien, P.A. and Hollien, H. 1976. Sex differences in SFF for pre-pubescent children. AAPS Newsletter 3:5(A).

Illingworth, R.S. 1955. Crying in infants and children. Biomed J. 1:75-78.

Irwin, O.C. and Chen, H.P. 1941. A reliability study of speech sounds observed in the crying of newborn infants. Child Dev. 12:351-68.

Karelitz, S., Karelitz, R., and Rosenfeld, L.S. 1960. Infants' vocalizations and their significance. In Mental Retardation, ed. P.W. Bowman and H.V. Mautner. Proceedings of the 1st International Medical Conference at Portland, Maine, 1959. New York: Grune and Stratton.

Lenneberg, E.H., and Rebelsky, F.F., and Nichols, I.A. 1965. The vocalizations of infants born to deaf and hearing parents. Human Devel. 8:23-37.

Luchsinger, R., Dubois, C., Vassella, F., Joss, E., Gloor, R., and Weismann, U. 1967. Spektralanalyse des "miauens" bei Cri-du-Chat Syndrome. Folia Phoniat. 19-27-33.

Miller, G.A. 1951. Language and Communication. New York: McGraw-Hill. P. 143.

Muller, E., Hollien, H., and Murry, T. 1974. Perceptual response to infant crying: identification of cry types. J. Child Lang. 1:89-95.

Murry, T., Hollien, H., and Muller, E. 1975. Perceptual responses to infant crying: maternal recognition and sex judgments. J. Child Lang. 2:199-204.

Murry, T., Amundson, P., and Hollien, H. 1977. Acoustical characteristics of infant cries: fundamental frequency. J. Child Lang. 4:321-28.

Murry, T., Gracco, F., and Gracco, C. 1979. Infant vocalization during the first twelve weeks. Paper presented at ASHA Meeting, Atlanta.

Ostwald, P.F., Freedman, D.G., and Kurtz, J.H. 1962. Vocalization of infant twins. Folia Phoniat. 14:37-50.

270

Ostwald, P.F., Phibbs, R. and Fox, S. 1968. Diagnostic use of infant cry. Biol. Neonat. 13:68-82.

Ostwald, P. and Peltzman, P. 1974. The cry of the human infant. Scientific American 230:84-90.

Parmalee, A.H. 1962. Infant crying and neurological diagnosis. J. Pediat. 61:802-3.

Prescott, R. 1975. Infant cry sound: developmental features. J. Acoust. Soc. Am. 57:1186-91.

Ringel, R.L. and Kluppel, D.D. 1964. Neonatal crying -- a normative study. Folia Phoniat. 16:1-9.

Sheppard, W.C. and Lane, H. 1968. Development of the prosodic features of infant vocalizing. J. Speech Hear. Res. 11:94-108.

Sherman, M. 1927. The differentiaton of emotional responses in infants: (I) judgments of emotional responses from motion picture views and from actual observation; (II) the ability of observers to judge emotional characteristics of the crying infants and of the voice of an adult. J. Comp. Psychol. 7:265-84, 335:51.

Truby, H.M. and Lind, J. 1965. Cry sounds of the newborn infant. In Newborn Infant Cry, ed. J. Lind. Acta Paediatr. Scand. Suppl. 163:8-54.

Vuorenkoski, W., Lind, J., Partanen, T.J., Lejeune, J., Lafourcade, J., and Wasz-Höckert, O. 1964. Spectrographic analysis of cries from children with maladie du cri-du-chat. Ann. Paediatr. Fenn. 12:174-80.

Wasz-Höckert, O., Valanne, E., Vuorenkoski, V., Michelsson, K., and Sovijärvi, A. 1963. Analysis of some types of vocalization in the newborn and in early infancy. Ann. Paediatr. Fenn. 9:1FF.

Wasz-Höckert, O., Partanen, T.J., Vuorenkoski, V., Valanne, E., and Michelsson, K. 1964a. The identification of some specific meanings in infant vocalization. Experientia 20:154.

Wasz-Höckert, O., Partanen, T.J., Vuorenkoski, V., Valanne, E., and Michelsson, K. 1964b. Effect of training on ability to identify preverbal vocalizations. Dev. Med. Child Neurol. 6:393-96.

CHAPTER 12

The Reorganization Process
of Babbling

Sei Nakazima

INTRODUCTION

Studies of language acquisition point to the great similarities in language learning for different children and for different languages. The existence of language universals has led linguists to believe that the human brain is "preprogrammed for language learning" (Moskowitz 1978). Language is acquired through stages. It is thought that the mechanisms of language acquisition are rather complex and dynamic. In order to clarify these mechanisms, it is helpful to describe the characteristics of these stages.

When an infant begins to babble, the sounds produced have no particular linguistic significance. The babbling period provides an experimental stage during which the child learns to control his vocal organs and reorganize those sounds into meaningful utterances. This chapter examines and compares the reorganization processes of American and Japanese children as they advance from babbling to language acquistion.

STAGES IN LANGUAGE DEVELOPMENT

Until the age of eight or nine months, infants usually use babbling, not as a means of communication, but, rather, as playing with their phonatory-articulatory organs. From about the age of nine months, infants begin to use their simple, meaningless sounds as a means of evocation and response to voice stimuli. This is the first step of the reorganization process. From about ten months of age, they imitate their parents' or caretakers' speech sounds. This can be identified as the second step of the reorganization process. At the same time, infants develop cognition of the speech sounds they hear. In the third step, at eleven or twelve months of age, they begin to use a few conventional words.

At the beginning of the reorganization process, infants utter very simple, meaningless sounds or repetitive babblings. When they begin to use words, they cannot articulate the phonemes correctly. Even bilabial plosives, which are frequently articulated at the repetitive babbling state, are not consistently produced by infants. Words in various phonatory-articulatory forms are uttered actively and in various situations until approximately seventeen months. For example, an infant may articulate /p/ in /papa/ and also [b], [m], even [t], [k], etc. They use /papa/ not only to refer to their fathers but also to refer to their mothers and other male and female adults. They end this reorganization process around seventeen months of age and begin their phonemicization-symbolization process after that. Both the Japanese and American children in this study demonstrated these basic tendencies of the reorganization process.

A STUDY OF THE REORGANIZATION PROCESS

The speech sounds of six Japanese and four American infants in Japan and one American infant in the United States were studied. The subjects were three female and three male Japanese, two female and two male Americans, who were living in Kyoto, Japan, and one male American, who was living in the U.S.A. Table 1

Table 1. Subjects and recording conditions.

Nationality	Place where S's voices were recorded	Subjects (Sex)	Beginning of recording by taperecorder	One recording per
Japanese	Kyoto, Japan	E.T. (f)	28 days (0 : 0, 28)	1 wk.
		Y.S. (f)	2 mos. (0 : 2)	2 wks.
		Y.N. (f)	1 mo. (0 : 1)	2 wks.
		H.K. (m)	1 mo. (0 : 1)	2 wks.
		T.T. (m)	7 mos. (0 : 7)	2 wks.
		T.Y. (m)	1 mo. (0 : 1)	2 wks.
American	Kyoto, Japan	G.M. (f)	3 mos. (0 : 3)	2 wks.
		F.P. (f)	6 mos. (0 : 6)	2 wks.
		E.D. (m)	7 mos. (0 : 7)	2 wks.
		C.W. (m)	6 mos. (0 : 6)	2 wks.
American	Champaign, Illinois U.S.A.	C.C. (m)	6 mos. (0 : 6)	2 wks.

presents a description of the sex and origin of the subjects. They ranged in age from nine to seventeen months. Tape recorded speech sounds were made of each subject in their home. In addition, one investigator provided descriptions of the babbling situation.

In earlier studies, it was found that infants begin to utter calm, non-crying vocalizations from about one month of age. They begin to change pitch and articulatory forms of non-crying from about two months of age. From month to month afterward, they increase the variety of pitch and articulatory forms, uttering so-called repetitive babblings at about six, seven, or eight months.

Before nine months, as previously mentioned, infants utter sounds not as a means of communication, but, rather, as if they are exploring their phonatory-articulatory mechanisms. At this state, infants' utterances can be considered one kind of what Piaget called "circular reactions"; the repetitive babblings may be classified as "secondary circular reactions" (Piaget 1936). At about nine months, infants begin to coordinate various kinds of schemata concerning speech, as "secondary circular reaction schemata", and to apply them to new situations-- language (Nakazima 1962, 1966).

The turning point in the course of speech development appears to be around nine months of age. Before this time, infants utter sounds not as a means of communication, but as circular reactions. Therefore, this period may be characterized as *the development of phonatory-articulatory-auditory mechanisms at the level of babbling*.

From about nine months, infants develop prelinguistic communication in sounds. They begin to call to familiar persons and to respond to familiar persons' communications by actively uttering simple meaningless sounds, e.g. [ɑ], [a], etc. Shortly after the development of babbling (approximately after nine months), sound production can be characterized as the *reorzanization process of babbling phonatory-articulatory-auditory mechanisms*. Infants begin to reorganize the babbling phonatory-articulatory-auditory mechanisms at the level of language. Until this age, they have developed rather complex phonatory-articulatory mechanisms and have uttered various kinds of sounds at the level of babbling. But they start their reorganization process from the beginning, i.e. simple sounds.

At about ten months of age, infants begin to imitate the speech heard around them. This we identify as the second step of the reorganization process. At the same time, the infant develops cognition of his parents' or caretakers' speech sounds. As Yatabe stated (1949), at the beginning of their infancy, we suppose infants cannot discriminate between external voice stimuli. Parents' speech sounds should be undifferentiated for them. Through the period of babbling, they utter sounds in various phonatory-articulatory forms and hear their own varied sounds. By the end of the babbling state, this kind of experience gradually enables infants to hear external sounds as differentiated stimuli. The differentiation of external sounds as stimuli by phonatory-articulatory-auditory practices at the level of babbling underlies the development of cognition of their parents' speech sounds.

At about eleven or twelve months of age, infants begin to use a few conventional words (Nakazima 1962, 1966). We identify this as the third step of the reorganization process. The reorganization process of babbling phonatory-articulatory-auditory mechanisms continues through several months after one year of age. After this period, from about seventeen or eighteeen months of age, *the phonemicization-symbolization process* develops. Table 2 describes the development of speech from infancy through the babbling and the reorganization stages to the phonemicization-symbolization process.

Tables 3, 4, and 5 describe in detail the phonemic developmental process of evolving /papa/ type utterances. Table 3 presents the analysis by number of syllables. Note that as the age of the infant increases, the number of utterances decreases. There is a larger number of multisyllable productions, while there are fewer overall utterances. The same trend exists for the Japanese and the American infant.

Table 4 presents the frequency of the number of consonants articulated by two of the subjects over a four month period. By one year and three months of age, both infants were including only the [p] in the /papa/ utterances. Bilabial plosives appeared frequently at the repetitive babbling stage. Table 5 shows the percentage of the variety of vowels articulated by the infants. Although no count was available for the American infant at one year, it can be seen that vowel articulation for both infants was at 100% by 13 months of age. The combined information of

Table 2. Development of speech.

Age Year: Month	Development of speech (Nakazima, S.)	Development of sensory-motor intelligence (Piaget, J.)
0: 0	1. The infant cries when he is uncomfortable.	1. The exercise of reflex.
0: 1	2. Development of phonatory-articulatory-auditory mechanisms at the level of babbling. 1) He begins to utter calm sounds when he is comfortable.	2. The first acquired adaptations and the primary circular reactions.
0: 2	2) He changes his phonatory-articulatory forms of these sounds.	
0: 3		
0: 4		3. The secondary circular reactions and the procedures destined to make interesting sights last. The means begins to be differentiated from the end.
0: 5		
0: 6	3) Repetitive babbling.	
0: 7		
0: 8		4. The coordination of the secondary circular reactions schemata. and their application to new situations.
0: 9	3. Reorganization of babbling phonatory-articulatory-auditory mechanisms at the level of language. 1) Development of response and calling to familiar persons in simple sounds.	Objects of the world become objectified and begin to be permanent ones.
0: 10	2) Development of imitation and cognition of his parents' speech sounds.	
0: 11	3) He begins to pick up some of his parents' words and to use them. But he does not use them	
1: 0	as language. In all sorts of situations he utters word sounds	5. The tertiary circular reactions and the discovery of new means
1: 1	and meaningless sounds with various articulatory forms.	through active experimentation.
1: 2	Through these efforts of expression in sounds he begins to notice some kind of symbolic relation-	
1: 3	ship between words and the world and to use words in reference	
1: 4	to what he wants to express.	
1: 5	4. Development of phonemicization-symbolization process.	
1: 6		6. Invention of new means through mental combination.
1: 7		
1: 8		

Tables 4 and 5 implies that the total utterance was articulated correctly for both infants at 15 months. This pattern was essentially the same for all infants in the study.

When one Japanese subject was one year old, her father was in England. She was taught /papa/ (father) while being shown a picture of her father. She was taught /papa/ with a falling intonation. In attempting to imitate her mother, she did not articulate bilabials

Table 3. Development of /papa/, by a Japanese female, E.T., and by an American male, E.D. figure, except average number of /papa/ utterances, shows percentage.

| | Case of E.T., Japanese | | | | Case of E.D., American | | | |
| | Average number of /papa/ utterances | Number of syllables, uttered | | | Average number of /papa/ utterances | Number of syllables, uttered | | |
Age	for thirty minutes	one	two	three and more	for thirty minutes	one	two	three and more
1:0	25	12	66	22				
1:1	15	4	59	37	10	20	80	
1:2	7		42	58	7		56	44
1:3	3		83	17	5		20	80

except in a whisper. One week later, she articulated [p] sound. After that, she uttered /papa/ actively in various articulatory forms for several months, as shown in Table 4.

For the consonant /p/, she articulated not only [p], but also other bilabials [b], [m]. Also, she articulated other plosives [t], [k], [?], and even fricatives like [w], [hw]. For the vowel /a/, she articulated fewer variations than for the consonant /p/, as can be seen in Table 5. Most of the vowel sounds uttered by her were [a] and [ɑ]. Both of them could be grouped as the Japanese vowel /a/. /papa/ is a word of two syllables, but, as shown in Table 3, she uttered one, two, three, and more -- even eight syllable-sounds.

This subject uttered /papa/ not only in various articulatory forms, but also in various situations, as shown in Table 6. At first she pointed to her father's picture and uttered /papa/ sounds, then she uttered these sounds while pointing to a male adult picture on a newspaper, and even at a microphone, at a tooth brush, at a toy dog, etc. She uttered them

Table 4. Frequency and number of consonants articulated by two subjects during a four month period.

| | | Case of E.T., Japanese | | | | | Case of E.D. American | | | | |
Age	[p] Only	includes [b] or [m]	include [t] or [k] or [?]	include [w] or [h]	includes a case of a consonant lacking	[p] only	include [b] or [m]	include [t] or [k] or [?]	include [w] or [h]	include a case of consonant lacking
1:0	25	33	23	13	6					
1:1	60	36			4		10	50	20	20
1:2	75	19			6	28	44			28
1:3	100					100				

Table 5. Frequency and number of vowels articulated by two subjects during a four month period.

	Case of E.T., Japanese			Case of E.D., American		
Age	[a] or [ə]*1)	include [æ]	include [o] or [ü] or [ɯ]	[a] or [ə]**2)	include [æ]	include [o] or [ü] or [ɯ]
1:0	80	16	4			
1:1	100			100		
1:2	100			100		
1:3	100			100		

1) In the Japanese phonemic system, [a] and [ə] are considered to be single vowel /a/.

2) In the (American) English phonemic system, /a/ and /ə/ are considered to be different vowels. To compare the case of a Japanese with that of an American, [a] and [ə] were treated as one item.

spontaneously when she was playing alone and without reference to particular objects. When she was fourteen months old, her father came home. Transfer from the relation of /papa/ with the father's picture to the relation with father himself was easily done. After that, she uttered /papa/ sounds to a male adult other than her father, and even to her mother and to her maid. When she was thirteen months old, /mama/ (mother) was taught to her by her maid. She confused /papa/ and /mama/. She confused /papa/ and /jo:tsjan/ (name of her maid). This kind of confusion among /papa/, /mama/, and /jo:tsjan/ became greater after her father returned home. For example, when she met a parent, she uttered /papa/ or /mama/ or /jo:tsjan/ at random. Then, when she was left alone, she tried to utter another name, and thus she finally reached the correct one. When she was eleven months old, /wanwan/ (bow bow) was taught to her, and at thirteen months of age /njannjan/ (kitty) was taught to her. She confused

Table 6. Percent of time /papa/ was uttered in various situations.

	Case of E.T., Japanese				Case of E.D., American			
		spontaneously uttered				spontaneously uttered		
Age	imitated	correctly used	incorrectly used 1)	uttered when S was alone 2)	imitated	correctly used	incorrectly used 1)	uttered when S was alone 2)
1:0	20	16	36	30				
1:1	6	30	43	21	100			
1:2		22	78			44	28	28
1:3		75	25			60	40	

1) Subjects uttered /papa/ for mother, maid, male adults other than father, etc. in place of father.

2) Subjects uttered /papa/-like sounds without certain relations to any objects when they were playing alone.

/papa/, /wanwan/, and /njannjan/ at this time. For example, she uttered /wanwan/ sounds to her father's picture and mixture sounds of /papa/ and /wanwan/ to a toy dog at thirteen months of age, and mixture sounds to her father at fourteen months.

After these spontaneous and very active trials, when she was seventeen months old, she uttered /papa/ with correct articulation and in a correct situation.

When she began to intentionally imitate her mother's /mamma/ (food) at nine months of age, she responded in repetitive babblings. At eleven months, and even twelve months, when she was hungry, she did not utter /mamma/, but cried or shouted in meaningless sounds. Only after she ate some cookies did she imitate or utter spontaneously /mamma/ sounds. After thirteen months of age, she did not cry, but uttered /mamma/ sounds. When she was thirteen months old, /mama/ (mama) was taught to her. She uttered [mamma]-like sounds in place of [mama]. When she was fourteen months old, /mama/ became differentiated from /mamma/ in articulation. /mamma/ means food in general in Japanese baby-talk. Also, she used /mamma/ for everything to eat or to drink. When she was sixteen months old, /tsja/ (tea) became differentiated from /mamma/; when seventeen months old, /miruku/ (milk) was also differentiated.

When this child was eleven months old, she learned /wanwan/ (bow wow). This too, she uttered in various articulatory forms and in various situations.

During the first several months of the second year, the child tried to imitate her mother's speech sounds actively. It was not as easy for her to articulate bilabials and other plosives, which were articulated frequently by her at the babbling stage.

Tables 3, 4, and 5 compare the case of the Japanese with the case of an American. The male American shows almost the same developmental tendency as the Japanese. When he began to imitate his parents' speech sounds intentionally at nine and ten months of age, he did not articulate bilabials and other plosives. When he was thirteen months old, /papa/ was taught to him. But he did not articulate bilabials. After trials of imitation of /papa/, he uttered it in various articulatory forms and in various situations, although his utterances were not as varied as those of the Japanese infant. He learned /bauwau/ (bow wow) when he was twelve months old. He uttered it in various articulatory forms and in various situations also. He

showed some kind of mixture of /papa/ and /bauwau/.
English /bauwau/ sounds articulated by him cannot be
distinguished from the /wanwan/ sounds articulated by
the Japanese. During the first several months of the
second year, he tried to imitate his parents' speech
sounds actively. It was not easy for him to imitate
either bilabials or plosives correctly. After these
active trials, when he was seventeen months old, he
uttered a few words in nearly correct articulatory
forms and in correct situations.

Let us now examine a few cases of American infants;
two Americans living in Japan (Tables 7 and 8) and an
American living in the U.S.A. (Table 9). Key words used
by infants during the first several months of the
second year are different from case to case, i.e.,
/dada/ (thank you) with a rising intonation by a male,
/mama/ (mother) by a female, /lait/ (light) by a male.
They uttered these words very actively in various
articulatory forms and in various situations. They,
too, tried to imitate their parents' speech sounds. In
these cases also, it was not easy to articulate
bilabials correctly. As for these tendencies, there

Table 7. Speech development of E.D., a male American, in Japan.
M:mother   F:father   S:subject   N: Nakazima

Age	Situations	Speech Sounds*[1]
0 : 9	Responses to M's [dædædæ]:	[t'ejæ:t'eə], [kjækjækjæ æ]
0 : 10	Response to M's [dædædæ]:	[kjædjæ] °°
	Responses to N's [mmamma]:	[p'uba], [baba], [mma m:]
	Response to M's [baba]:	[mæmm̃ammæ]
0:11	Response to M: "Pattycake":	[atæke]
1:0	Response to N's [mmamma]:	[mammam]
	Response to M:"Bow wow wow":	[mambə]
	S pointed at a dog picture and	
	uttered:	[auwə] 1)
1:1	Response to N: "Papa":	[ʔ'aʔ'a:]
	While playing alone, S uttered:	[ʔammaü], [hbamm:], [mmmβwə] 2)
1:2	Response to N's [papa]:	[htjatja]
	Response to N's [mamma]:	[wauwə mamma]
	Looking at a dog picture, S	
	uttered:	[aãwa ba:a]
	Looking at a horse picture, s	
	uttered:	[ba:a wauwə] 1)
	Turning pages, S uttered:	[wauwə wauwə wa]
	Talking to M, S uttered:	[a wa wɪjaʏə] 3)
	Looking at a cow picture, S	
	uttered:	[hauwa] 1)
1:3	Responses to N's [papa]:	[bapa], [waãp'a], [p'ap'a]
	Responses to M: "Shoes":	[çɪ:], [ɪ:], [t'ɪ:]
1:4	Looking at F, S uttered:	[papa]
	Response to M's [papa]:	[p'apa]
	Responses to N's [mama]:	[mamma], [mamɑ]
	Looking at a dog picture, S	
	uttered:	[baüwaü] 1)
	Responses to M: "Miaow"	[mja:], [nja:], [na:]

1) One of the variations of "bow wow."

2) Without relations to any particular objects.

3) Meaningless sounds with conversation like intonation, including
   [wa] sound, a part of "bow wow".

Table 8. Speech development of C.W., a male American, in Japan.
         M:mother   S:subject

Age	Situations	Speech Sounds*
1 : 1	S was fond of giving an object to a familiar person and taking it back, saying /dada/ (thank you). Variations of /dada/:	[djæ], [dedeç], [djo:dja] [djö:ʧʤə], [da:ʤʑə], [ʔɔ̃ʔɔ̃]
1 : 2	Response to M's "Baby":	[eɪ]
1 : 3	Responses to M's "Birdy":	[mə:nɪ], [əbɯ̈]

were no striking differences between American infants in Japan and the American infant in the U.S.A.

Thus, infants utter these few words in various articulatory forms and in various situations. This implies that they are trying to reorganize babbling phonatory-articulatory-auditory mechanisms on the level of language. They practice trials using not only conventionally meaningful words, but also meaningless sounds. A Japanese male infant, at the age of eleven months, after trials of imitation of his mother's [hahaha] (one kind of laughing sound), utters [haha]-like sounds in various articulatory forms and in various situations. He sometimes talked to his parents uttering meaningless sounds, articulated at random.

Okamota (1972) studied babbling and found that when a female infant is about eleven to thirteen months old, she uses a few sounds. At this stage, her comprehension and spontaneous use were not yet integrated; i.e., her mother taught her dogs as /wanwan/ (bow wow) but she uttered /njannjan/ (kitty) spontaneously for dogs.

Murai (1964) found, in an analytic factor study concerning infants' behavior development, that the factor involving the test item "uttering three or four words" has large factor loadings in some intelligence items; the factor involving the test item

Table 9. Speech development of C.C., a male American, in the U.S.A.
         M:mother   S:subject

Age	Situations	Speech Sounds*
1 : 2	S uttered "light" spontaneously or in imitation. Variations of "light":	[laɪtʃ], [laɪ], [aɪtʃ], [aɪ], [haɪtʃ]
1 : 3	S imitated M's "What's that ?":	[hwɪddæn]
	S imitated M's "Please":	[bnɪ:z]

"understanding the mother's verbal orders" has large factor loadings in some mother items.

In early infancy, infants express their own emotions, though undifferentiated, in whole body action accompanying crying. From month to month, from day to day, infants' sensory-motor schemata become gradually differentiated and organized through maturation and practice. As already stated (Nakazima 1962), infants' interest in the external world becomes differentiated through experiences. Based on this kind of differentiation, the external world becomes differentiated as cognizable stimuli. Based on practice and maturation of phonatory-articulatory-auditory mechanisms through the period of babbling, infants' expression in voices become differentiated from bodily emotional expression. Their parents' speech sounds become differentiated from other external stimuli and then become differentiated from each other. From about eleven or twelve months of age, infants pick up a few of their parents' sounds and try to use them as a means of expressing what they want to express. They use not only these learned sounds but also those which are articulated at random.

Some of these examples have been described in this chapter. When the female Japanese was thirteen months old, she used /ija/ frequently. When she had been isolated and wanted to play with someone, she uttered /ija/ (/ija/ means "no"). Therefore, conventionally, when someone wants to deny or refuse anything, he uses /ija/. Nevertheless, she did not use "no" negatively, but positively. In various situations, the infants utter sounds with various articulatory forms. It is thought that during the first several months of the second year, infants, through efforts of expression in sounds, begin to notice symbolic relationships between words and the world, and that they acquire one kind of learning set to use words in reference to what they want to express. Thus, they end their reorganization process of babbling phonatory-articulatory-auditory mechanisms at the level of language and begin their phonemicization-symbolization process.

ACKNOWLEDGMENTS

I would like to express my grateful acknowledgments to Dr. and Mrs. R. Confer, Dr. and Mrs. E. Daug, Prof. and Mrs. S. Kuraishi, Mr. and Mrs. Meyer, Mr. and Mrs.

Prins, Prof. and Mrs. S. Shimizu, Mr. and Mrs. Toyohara, Prof. and Mrs. T. Tsushima, Dr. and Mrs. N. Yanagihara, Dr. and Mrs. Wood, and my wife for their kind cooperation. I appreciate Mr. Y. Takeuchi's cooperation in the use of electronic equipment.

REFERENCES

Moskowitz, B.A. 1978. The acquisition of language. Scientific American.

Maurai, J. 1964. The sounds of infants: their phonemicization and symbolization. Studia Phonologica III: 17-34.

Nakazima, S. 1962. A comparative study of the speech developments of Japanese and American English in childhood (Part One) -- A comparison of the speech developments of voices at the prelinguistic period. Studia Phonologica II:27-46.

Nakazima, S. 1966. A comparative study of the speech developments of Japanese and American English in childhood. (Part Two) -- The acquisition of speech. Studia Phonologica IV:38-55.

Okamoto, N. 1962. Verbalization process in infancy (1)-- Transpositive use of sounds in development of symbolic activity. Psychologias 5:32-40.

Piaget, J. 1936. La Naissance de l'intelligence chez L'Enfant. Delachaux et Niestle. Translated by M. Cook. 1953. The Origin of Intelligence in the Child. Routledge & Kegan Paul.

Yatabe, T. 1949. Language of Children (in Japanese). Kyoto: Hiei-shobo.

CHAPTER 13

Temporal Regularity
in Prespeech

Marsha Zlatin Laufer

In the last decade, researchers studying infant vocalization have been motivated, in part, by curiosity about the sources of systematic phonetic behavior underlying a developing and established phonological system. Whereas it was once thought that the nonmeaningful sounds produced during the first 12 to 18 months of life were discontinuous or unrelated to speech (Jakobson 1941/1968; Nakazima 1972), there is now a growing recognition that these precursor behaviors show regularity (Laufer 1978; Oller 1978; Stark 1978) and a direct relationship with emerging spoken language (Oller et al. 1975; Delack 1975; Murai 1963; also see previous chapter).

Initially, there is a philosophical problem in deciding which aspects of infant vocalization to examine. If we start by imposing and tracing features of a specific language(s), an organization framework is provided. However, there is the risk of biasing our observations and obscuring relevant information. If, on the other hand, the infant is regarded in a quasi-independent manner, the features emerge from the data bank itself. Using primarily the latter procedure to analyze perceptual and acoustic attributes increases the task posed to the investigator, but potentially reduces the bias. The results should reveal (1) features that are ideosyncratic to infant vocalizations, (2) features that show a correspondence with speech, and (3) the nature of change as features undergo alterations associated with a developing vocal tract, a maturing nervous system, increasing auditory control over vocal output, the effect of environmental linguistic input, and the emergence of an interactive communication system.

LONGITUDINAL STUDY

Within this framework, a two-year longitudinal study of four first-born infants was initiated. Two males and two females with normal pre-, para-, and postnatal histories and normal hearing participated. Each child was born within two weeks of the mother's due date and had a birth weight between 5 lbs. and 9 lbs., 6 oz. Prior to the birth of the babies, the parents were selected from a pool of 35 prospective couples and were interviewed extensively. The purposes of the study and data collection and testing procedures were explained in detail. Following the birth of the infants, recordings were started by the parents at home on portable cassette recorders (Sony TC-110A) supplied by the investigator.

The parents sampled early waking and presleep periods, feeding, dressing, bathing, solitary and interactive play. In addition, audio and video recordings were made at two-week intervals in an infant laboratory, which provided a naturalistic playroom setting for observations of the child alone and with his/her parents.[1] Master developmental tapes were prepared for each infant from the original recordings and 443 phonation episodes were selected for preliminary analysis. Cry, discomfort, vegetative, and extremely prolonged sounds as well as phonetic exploratory vocalizations (Zlatin 1975) were not included in this particular sampling. The latter category included such behaviors as squeals, growls, ingressive vocalizations, and shouting. There was a minimum of 100 vocalizations from each infant.

Two trained phoneticians jointly performed a detailed acoustic analysis for each utterance deriving the number of protosyllables, the base structure, and measurements of spectral and temporal features from a combination of the auditory signal and wide- (450 cycle) and narrow-band (45 cycle) spectrograms with amplitude displays (Voiceprint 400 Series). The fundamental frequency data in the form of period-by-period melody plots were also available for a majority of the utterances (Laufer and Horii 1977).

Following the initial survey of the data, segmentation criteria were established and the *protosyllable* was adopted as the basic unit of

---

[1]For further details regarding subject selection and data collection and reduction procedures, see Zlatin (1976) and Laufer and Horii (1977).

analysis. This is operationally defined as a relative peak of sonorance characterized by a rise in fundamental frequency, amplitude, and duration. In its most elementary form, the monoprotosyllable was a definable event with a clear beginning and end. With this unit as a base, attempts were made to systematically segment longer utterances.

The phonetic syllable in linguistic contexts has been believed to be the basic unit for realization of timing patterns (Kozhevnikow and Chistovich 1965). It is associated with a well-defined spectrum in the form of buzz-excited, relatively quasistatic formants. In contrast, the structure for protosyllables (PS), particularly in very early utterances, is typically less adequately resolved. Transitions are often not well-differentiated or absent. Ideosyncratic features, such as a preponderance of subharmonics, noise in the signal associated with incomplete laryngeal valving, striations and amplitude alterations associated with saliva friction and phonatory quality variations, are present. These features are felt to reflect the comparative primitive status of the vocal tract during this period (Laufer 1978; Lieberman 1975; Stark 1978). The protosyllable represents a precursor to the more fully established phonetic syllable. Its characteristics alter in a potentially predictable and systematic manner and reflect both central and peripheral changes that occur in the course of the infant's development.

The base structure for protosyllables was composed of a nucleus of peak acoustic energy in the form of a vocalic (V) or syllabic nasal (N) with an open, steady state resonance or quasiresonance (Oller 1978). The optional components included glottal stops (ʔ), glottal aspirates (h), supraglottal constrictives (C), supraglottal glides (G), and nonsyllabic nasals (N). The distinction between the glottis, as a site of constriction, and the supraglottal area was necessitated by the observation that glottal stops and aspirates constituted the earliest form of vocal tract closure in infant utterances predating the emergence of supraglottal constriction. The former, which appears in protosyllabic forms around the fifth or sixth week of life, are seen and heard in utterances with base structures such as (ʔV, hVh,ʔVh,ʔVʔ) as well as in extended productions with regular alternation (ʔVʔVʔVʔ). Even at this stage, there appear to be constraints on sequences of sounds.

As indicated earlier, a preliminary analysis was conducted to provide the investigator with information about the range of phonetic parameters characterizing the infants' vocalizations during the first six months which could be pursued in more depth. Results of duration measurements for 126 two-protosyllable length utterances, such as (CVCV), indicated that there was a trend toward final PS lengthening; that is, the second of the two protosyllables tended to be longer than the first. For the four infants, $\underline{M}$, $\underline{A}$, $\underline{J}$, and $\underline{G}$, 76%, 70%, 70%, 68%, and 51% of their utterances, respectively, were associated with greater duration of the second of of the two protosyllables. The corresponding $PS_2:PS_1$[2] ratios were 1.79, 1.32, 1.20, and 1.05. Further analysis of the 443 productins revealed that 64 were greater than two protosyllables and, of these, segmentation and duration measurements could be derived for 30. Seventeen of the thirty did show final lengthening. It was decided, however, to pursue the two protosyllable data because the sample size was larger, the utterances were more easily and reliably segmented, and perceptual agreement for the number of protosyllables and constituent structure was high among trained listeners (Zlatin 1976).

Final Syllable Lengthening

The finding of this temporal variant in the utterances of very young infants is of interest in that final syllable or prepausal vowel lengthening characterizes a number of spoken languages, including English (Delattre 1966; Oller 1973; Klatt 1975; Smith 1978). Oller (1973) observed that in production of citation forms, adults exhibit increments of about 100 msec in comparison to nonfinal durations when stress is held constant. The mean ratios of final to nonfinal vowels were between 1.4 and 2.0 with an average ratio of 1.7. The effect appears to be present in word-, phrase-, and utterance-final positions as well as in open and closed syllables. The effect is, however, greater for the latter (Oller 1973; Lindblom 1968). Although final lengthening may serve as a cue marking perceptual boundaries (Haden 1962; Klatt 1976), some

---

[2] The ratios were derived by dividing the duration of the second protosyllable (PS_2) by the duration of the first (PS_1). If PS_2 were longer than PS_1, the ratio was greater than one. If the converse, the ratio was less than one. For example, a ratio of 1.79 indicated that there was a 79% increase in PS_2 duration. See Smith and Oller (1973 for further details.

researchers have suggested production-based explanations. For example, Oller (1979) feels that lengthening may provide additional time for articulatory planning of succeeding constituents and/or allow for examination of constituents that have just been executed. Cooper and Sorensen (1977) have offered the explanation that lengthening may reflect a general slowing down of the mechanism as the end of a constituent is approached.

From a developmental perspective, Smith (1978), in an extensive study of temporal features in the speech of 2- and 4-year-old children and adults found that all three groups showed final syllable vowels that were longer than nonfinal vowels in three consonantal environments. Smith employed nine controlled nonsense words, such as BAB, BAbab, and baBAB which he had subjects imitate. Further, less formal observation of 25 meaningful 2-syllable word productions by an 18-month-old child and another 14-month-old revealed that the children showed increments of about 80% and 32%, respectively, for final unstressed vowels.

In an attempt to address the issue of whether the phenomenon was associated with inherent features of the speech production system or was acquired possibly exceptionally early in the course of phonological development, Oller and Smith (1977) examined the duration characteristics of reduplicated babbling produced by six infants between 8 and 12 months of age. The utterances ranged from two to six syllables in length and consisted of repeated CVCV strings, such as [bababababa]. Using a "non-conservative" measurement criterion where vowel duration included both the voiced portion and the breathy offset, four of the six infants showed the effect with ratios of 1.18, 1.23, 1.24, and 1.08. The extent of lengthening was far less than was shown by adults producing comparable controlled utterances, and the authors cautiously concluded that final vowel lengthening was primarily associated with learning.

The status of explanatory adequacy with respect to this phonetic feature has not been clarified further. At present, there does not appear to be clear unequivocal evidence as to whether final syllable lengthening reflects an inherent physiologically motivated process, a process that is linguistically conditioned, or, as Smith (1978) has proposed, features of each.

288

FINAL PROTOSYLLABLE LENGTHENING IN INFANCY: THE FIRST SIX MONTHS

Stage of Development

The duration of this study spanned the first 24 weeks of life for the infants, a period encompassing the first three stages of vocal development (Zlatin 1974/1975/1976; Oller 1978; Stark 1978). The Phonation Stage (Oller 1978), covering approximately the first four to five weeks, was followed by the introduction of protosyllabic vocalizations in Stage II and early conversations between 7 and 8 weeks. The first protosyllables were characterized principally by glottal modulation with supraglottal constriction coming shortly thereafter. Within Stage II, the infants engaged in protosyllable expansion with an elaboration of various combinations of base structures beginning around 9 to 12 weeks. The Phonetic Exploratory Stage (Zlatin 1975; Laufer 1978) appeared between 15 and 19 weeks and continued beyond six months.

Procedures

The master developmental tape recordings for the four infants and corresponding spectrograms for the first 24 weeks were scrutinized. A total of 446 two-protosyllable length utterances were identified. Of these, 284 (64%) could be segmented and the duration of PS_1 and PS_2 reliably measured. These utterances were characterized by defined spectral changes between protosyllables marked by constrictives and/or silent intervals. The overall average reflects high consistency among the four children whose individual percentages of measurable productions were .67, .69, .63, and .60 of their respective totals. The remaining 162 productions included those where background noise or another person speaking simultaneously interfered with the signal and those which could not be segmented. The presence of intervocalic glides, trills, and saliva friction noise which encroached into the vocalic nuclei accounted for a majority of the latter.

Structurally, the utterances were characterized by a variety of segmental combinations. For the first protosyllable (PS1), the most frequently occurring base structure was (?V) (39%) followed by vocalic, only (27%), (hV) (9%), syllabic nasals (4%), (CV) (4%), and

(?N) (4%). The ordinal position of the first three base structures was maintained by all four children, accounting for 75% of the PS_1 utterances. All other sequences, such as (GV, NV, VC, VN, ?V?, ?Vh, hN, hVN) and (CVN), occurred less than ten times in the corpus. For PS_2, the (CV) sequence accounted for 61% of the utterances followed by (?V) (17%) and (CVh) (5%). All others occurred less frequently, including isolated vocalics, (hV, NV, ?V?, ?Vh, CVC, VC, VN, GV, GVh, ?VC) and (?N).

The total duration for each utterance was determined as well as componential duration of protosyllables, interprotosyllabic silent intervals (ISI), and the duration of segments where possible. Although vocalic quality and stress are important variables in examining syllable length in natural languages (Oller 1973; Lehiste 1970; Oller and Smith 1977; Smith 1978), the reduplicated babbling produced by the 9- to 12-month-old infants studied by Oller and Smith (1977) was not associated with stress contrasts extensively. The infants in the present study were observed at even earlier stages of vocal development and stress variation appeared even less marked. In addition, one component of stress is amplitude or intensity prominence (Lehiste 1970) which requires relatively constant recording conditions, such as mouth-to-microphone distance, for accurate measurement. This criteria could not be achieved, particularly in comparison of one utterance with another, given the variety of sampling sources in the present study.

To date, we have been unable to achieve a consistent correspondence between the open vocalic qualities produced by infants during the first six months, the acoustic spectral variations, and perception. This prohibits analysis, at this time, of specific vocalic types in various contexts that would be more analogous to measurements of inherent or intrinsic vowel duration and contextual effects for adult (Oller 1973) and child data (Smith 1978; Krause 1978; Di Simoni 1974).

In measuring the duration of vocalic nuclei, the steady state portion and adjunct transitions were included. Friction, whether supraglottal or glottal in source, corresponded to the duration of observed turbulence in the spectrographic displays. In the few instances where glides could be readily identified by the nature of the acoustic transition, the halfway point in the transient marked the protosyllable boundary (Klatt 1976). In the case of stops, the duration was marked from the instant of the burst release and a voice onset time measurement derived, if possible.

The highly variable silent intervals between protosyllables were measured but not included in the calculation of duration either for PS_1 or PS_2. For example, an utterance produced by A had the base structure ($?V?V$) and had a total duration of 1216 msec. PS_1 measured 200 msec, PS_2 was 485 msec, and the silent interval was 531 msec. In previous studies where utterances were phonologically bound, the silent intervals, if present, were relatively short and most often corresponded to the period of closure for a following stop. The duration of the interval in this instance would be included in the second syllable (Klatt 1976). Oller (Personal Communication) indicated that when a silent interval was encountered in his data, it was most often ascribed to the first syllable. Silent intervals are important phonetic parameters perceptually signaling the presence of syllable and constituent boundaries (Klatt 1976). Stop gap duration serves as a cue for the voicing charcteristics of the following consonant (Malmberg 1957; Lisker 1957/1969). Since the infants' utterances were not phonologically bound and one could be less sure of the role of the silent intervals, the most appropriate strategy seemed to involve separate measurement and study. The decision to exclude ISIs from calculation of either PS_1 or PS_2 duration was also made because of the desire to compare base structures in instances where they were produced in isolation (e.g. CV) with embedded multiprotosyllabic occurrences, such as (CVCV), (VCV), or ($?VCV$). In isolated productions with a prevocalic stop, the duration of the vocal tract closure obviously cannot be estimated.

The mean data for total duration of two-protosyllable utterances and duration of ISIs are included in Table 1. Interprotosyllabic silent intervals occurred in approximately 50% of the two-protosyllable utterances. Data will be presented demonstrating that the presence or absence of ISIs did not seem to have a marked influence on the derived PS_2:PS_1 ratios.[3] In those instances where an intervocalic stop occurred in the presence of continuous voicing, the PS boundary was

[3]I am grateful to Dr. Kim Oller for suggesting this analysis.

Table 1. Mean data for total duration of two-protosyllable utterances produced by four infants, A, M, J, and G, during the first twenty-four weeks of life and mean data for interprotosyllabic silent intervals (ISI). All data is reported in milliseconds.

	Number of Utterances	Mean Total Duration	S.D.[a] Total Duration	Number of Utterances With ISI[b]	Mean Duration of ISI	S.D.[a] Duration of ISI	Range of ISI
A	54	789	239	35	189	188	10-955
M	49	837	326	29	219	194	40-808
J	85	896	397	44	311	303	30-1301
G	96	652	250	34	187	163	8-466
Total	284	783	327	142	232	231	8-1301

[a]Standard deviation

[b]The corresponding percentages for A,M,J, and G are .65,.59,.52, and .35.

also marked at the instant of the burst release. An overall amplitude drop with associated damping of one or more harmonics above the fundamental typically appeared concurrently with the supraglottal constriction. An intervocalic constrictive was included in the measurement of PS_2, unless a silent interval followed. This decision was made on the basis that open syllables were the most frequently observed in monoprotosyllabic utterances in this data and that they have a higher probability of occurrence both in infant nonmeaningful utterances (Oller et al. 1975) and in world languages (O'Connor and Trim 1953) than do closed syllables.

Two types of durational measurements were made. The first included all constrictives, such as stops, affricates, fricatives, etc., consistent with the view that there may be an inherent temporal organization of the protosyllable paralleling the syllable (Fujimura and Lovins 1977). In addition, during the earliest stages of vocal development, there appears to be less of a distinction between the protosyllable nuclei and margins reflected acoustically by relatively undifferentiated CV ratios. The second measurement procedure was instigated so that the data would be somewhat more consistent with that derived from other investigations of prepausal lengthening (Oller 1973,

Oller and Smith 1977; Smith 1978). The second procedure involved deletion of constrictives in each case where segmentation was possible. Results of the statistical analysis failed to reveal a significant difference between the two forms of measurement.

Two types of measurements were also made by Oller and Smith (1977) in their study of reduplicated babbling. The "conservative" measure deleted the breathy portion of the utterances, which they observed to be frequently associated with the offset or termination of vocalics. The "nonconservative" measure, which was felt to be more representative, included the offset. In the present study, each of the four infants at times exhibited a voiced ingressive following an egressive phase, which was not included in the measurements.

Segmentation of spoken utterances, regardless of whether the source is a young infant, a developing child, or a mature speaker of a language, has been notoriously difficult. The existence of the syllable itself has been debated and the choice for syllable or segment boundaries has been made on the basis of such factors as acoustic definition (Klatt 1976) and distributional analysis (O'Connor and Trim 1953). At this juncture in infant research, Klatt's (1976) expressed aim for adopted convention in reproducible measurement procedures, rather than attempting to achieve necessarily exact correspondence to discrete phonetic events, constituted one guideline for some of the decision making. Our problems in segmentation do not seem to be totally unlike those encountered by a young child learning spoken language.

Results

Consistent with the findings from the preliminary observations, the four children showed final lengthening in this extended analysis of two-protosyllable utterances (Figure 1[4]). A comparison of means, standard deviations, and $PS_2:PS_1$ ratios, presented in Table 2, shows the effects of constrictive inclusion. As expected, deletion of contrictives had more of an effect on the duration of PS_2 than PS_1, with the greatest difference in both instances shown by M. Without constrictives, A, M, J, and G showed final

---

[4]All figures, unless indicated, utilized the measurement data where constrictives had been deleted. This represents the more conservative estimate of the effects of final lengthening.

Figure 1.

MEAN DURATION OF TWO-PROTOSYLLABLE INFANT UTTERANCES

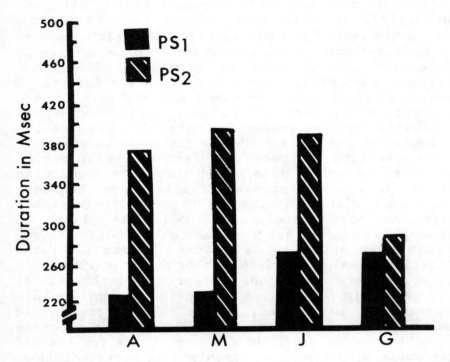

lengthening for 76%,78%,72% and 60% of their two-protosyllable utterances respectively. Measures of variability, derived from a division of the mean by the standard deviation (Oller 1978), revealed PS_2 to be somewhat more stable in duration than PS_1. A series of individual t-tests indicated that the differences between first and second protosyllables were statistically significant (p .001) for three of the four children.

The derived $PS_2:PS_1$ ratios were converted to logarithms using base ten so as not to favor one protosyllable over the other in a distributional analysis. In Figure 2, the final lengthening effect is reflected in the higher proportion of utterances with a positive logarithmic value. Three of the four children for whom the differences were statistically significant showed less variability and more normal distributions than was shown by G. In discussing the temporal features of spoken language, Lehiste (1970)

Table 2. Results of duration analyses for two-protosyllable utterances produced by four infants during the first twenty-four weeks of life. Mean duration (X) and standard deviations (S.D.) are reported in milliseconds. The variability estimates (V.E.) were derived from Mean/S.D.

Subject	N^a	Protosyllable Two			Protosyllable One			Ratio $PS_2:PS_1$	t
		$\overline{X}$	S.D.	V.E.	$\overline{X}$	S.D.	V.E.		
WITH CONSTRICTIVES									
A	54	411	170	2.42	237	112	2.12	1.73	6.31**
M	49	465	232	2.00	247	133	1.86	1.88	5.70**
J	85	433	228	1.90	292	134	2.18	1.48	5.07**
G	96	306	138	2.22	279	158	1.77	1.10	1.28
WITHOUT CONSTRICTIVES									
A	54	376	155	2.43	234	109	2.15	1.61	5.50**
M	49	398	187	2.13	236	119	1.98	1.69	5.13**
J	85	393	205	1.92	279	141	1.98	1.41	4.14**
G	96	294	125	2.35	278	157	1.77	1.06	0.80

[a] Number of Utterances

** $p < .001$

noted that the duration of phonological units within a given range also tend to be normally distributed, although the differences among speakers may be considerable. In this case, the consistency among the children is more striking than are the differences.

As indicated earlier, the presence and variability of interprotosyllabic silent intervals appears to be somewhat ideosyncratic to infant utterances. Since the decision was made to exclude them from protosyllable length determinations, $PS_2:PS_1$ duration ratios were recalculated using ISIs as an independent variable. When silent intervals were present, the mean ratios for A, M, J, and G were 2.12, 2.36, 1.89, and 1.71, respectively. When ISIs were absent, the corresponding mean ratios were 2.86, 2.36, 1.63, and 1.31. Both males, J and G, showed higher ratios when there was a silent interval. M, a female, showed no difference and A exhibited greater lengthening when there was no silent interval. The intent of the present analysis was descriptive only, as it is not clear at this time what the significance of the ISI is in early infant utterances.

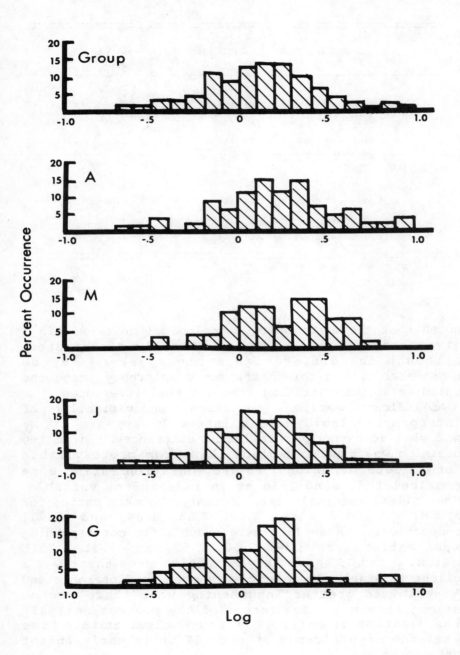

Figure 2.

LOGARITHMS OF PS$_2$:PS$_1$ DURATION RATIOS
TWO-PROTOSYLLABLE INFANT UTTERANCES

Percent Occurrence

Log

Figure 3.

MEAN DURATION OF TWO-PROTOSYLLABLE INFANT UTTERANCES

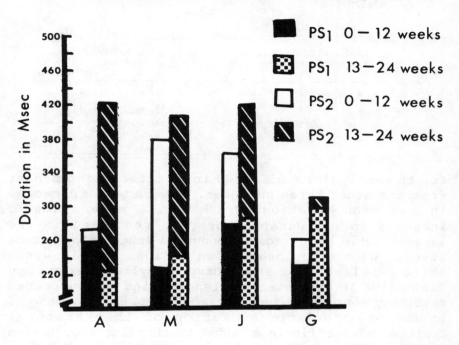

In the course of analysis, weekly mean ratios were derived for each subject. $\underline{A}$ appeared to show a marked change from the first to the second twelve week period. It was decided to examine the whole corpus of data within this frame of reference. The comparison of the first with the second twelve weeks showed that there was, indeed, an increment in the $PS_2:PS_1$ ratio; from 1.28 to 1.54 when measurements from all four children were combined. The change was associated with a slight increase in the mean duration for PS_1 and a more substantial increase for PS_2. Duration also appeared to be more stable in the second period.

The information for each of the children plotted in Figure 3 is contained in Table 3. The increase in the $PS_2:PS_1$ ratio was evidenced by three of the four children, again $\underline{A}$, $\underline{M}$, and $\underline{J}$. $\underline{G}$'s ratio showed a slight decrease.[5] Although she provided the initial incentive

[5]It has recently been brought to my attention that $\underline{G}$, who has rather consistently been at variance with the other three children in a number of the analyses, is left handed. Although it is tempting to want to speculate about a potential role that hemispheric dominance for language might have in determination of phonetic variation, it is certainly premature to do so explicitly at the present time. (Also see Laufer and Horii, 1977).

Table 3. Results of duration analyses for two-protosyllable utterances produced by four infants comparing the first and second twelve weeks of life. Mean duration (X) and standards deviations (S.D.) are reported in milliseconds. The variability estimates (V.E.) were derived from Mean/S.D.

| | 0 - 12 Weeks | | | | | | | 13 - 24 Weeks | | | | | | |
| | Protosyl. One | | | Protosyl. Two | | | Ratio | Protosyl. One | | | Protosyl. Two | | | Ratio |
Subject	$\overline{X}$	S.D.	V.E.	$\overline{X}$	S.D.	V.E.	$PS_2:PS_1$	$\overline{X}$	S.D.	V.E.	$\overline{X}$	S.D.	V.E.	$PS_2:PS_1$
A	260	98	2.65	276	98	2.82	1.06	221	113	1.96	422	155	2.72	1.91
M	229	119	1.92	380	190	2.00	1.66	240	120	2.00	410	188	2.18	1.70
J	280	139	2.01	361	213	1.69	1.29	284	139	2.04	422	194	2.18	1.49
G	236	180	1.31	261	104	2.51	1.10	299	140	2.14	311	132	2.36	1.04

for the analysis, A differed in an interesting manner from the other three children. She showed a decrease in the mean duration of PS_1 and a more dramatic increase in the duration of PS_2, resulting in the largest ratio, or most pronounced lengthening effect at the end of the observation period. The 12 weeks shift parallels the stage of protosyllable expansion. The change in the extent of lengthening and increased stability combine to indicate a developmental component in the prelinguistic evolution of this temporal feature. These findings added to the fact that active experimentation with vocal tract dynamics in the form of phonetic exploratory behavior is about to emerge seems to reflect the infant's growing control over some aspects of his/her own vocal output.

It appears that final syllable or vowel lengthening may have a phonetic precursor manifested in infant vocalizations of limited length during the first six months of life. Before venturing to offer any hypotheses as to the potential source or sources of this regularity, I felt it necessary to conduct at least a preliminary examination of some other temporal aspects of the infants' vocalizations.

Monoprotosyllabic and Multiprotosyllabic Utterances

The duration of monoprotosyllabic utterances, such as (?V, CV, V), was compared with the protosyllable durations from the study of final lengthening. Results showed that the individual mean durations of 462, 471, 438, and 433 msec were greater than those observed from the two-protosyllable utterances (Table 1) for both PS_1

and PS$_2$, although they did tend to be closer to the latter. From his observations of final lengthening in various languages, Oller (1973) has pointed out that monosyllables are, indeed, final syllables, so the close correspondence between the two in the present study is not so surprising.

In the next phase of the analysis, a comparison of each base structure in monoprotosyllabic occurrences was made with the same structure in embedded or multiprotosyllabic contexts. On the average, the duration of nonembedded base structures was 197 msec longer. All four chldren exhibited greater stability of duration in monoprotosyllabic vocalizations. Figure 4 shows combined mean data for three of the structures. The measurements in this figure included constrictives. Further study of specific base structures showed that the duration reduction effect did vary. For example, the differences between embedded and nonembedded vocalics, (V) and (?V) sequences, were greater than for (CV) combinations, which tended to be more variable.

Individual differences among the four children were also demonstrated. Figure 5 depicts the comparisons of

Figure 4.

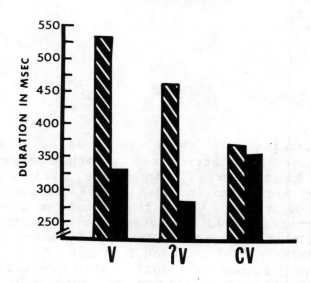

MEAN DURATION OF BASE STRUCTURES

■ nonembedded monosyllabic
■ embedded multisyllabic

Figure 5.

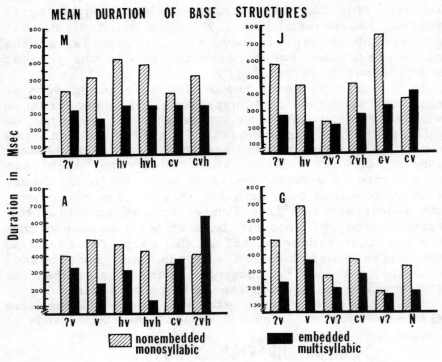

MEAN DURATION OF BASE STRUCTURES

Duration in Msec

M — ?v, v, hv, hvh, cv, cvh

J — ?v, hv, ?v?, ?vh, ɢv, cv

A — ?v, v, hv, hvh, cv, ?vh

G — ?v, v, ?v?, cv, v?, N̩

◫ nonembedded monosyllabic

◼ embedded multisyllabic

all structures for which there was comparative data, i.e., instances of the structures in both nonembedded and embedded contexts. In these histograms, constrictives were also included in the determination of the mean durations. All of the structures analyzed for G were characterized by a greater mean duration of monoprotosyllabic utterances. Ratios of nonembedded: embedded (NE:E) varied between 1.10 for (V?) to 2.04 for (?V). The presence of a postvocalic glottal stop appeared to reduce duration in both contexts considerably in comparison with the duration of other structures.

Six of the base structures produced by M also showed

300

the effect with ratios between 1.18 for (CV) sequences and 1.98 for vocalics. In the analysis of J's data, five of the six base structures showed the effect with NE:E ratios ranging from 1.14 for (?V?) to 2.24 for (GV). Both J and A exhibited a reversal for the (CV) combination with respective ratios of .90 and .92. Four of the six structures produced by A had NE:E ratios greater than 1.00 ranging from 1.24 for (?V) to 3.23 for (hVh).

Open and Closed Protosyllables

The final temporal aspect of the infants' vocalizations to be explored was the duration of open and closed protosyllables. An analysis of monoprotosyllabic utterances revealed that the mean duration of open protosyllables was greater for all four infants than that of closed protosyllables (Table 4). The overall mean was 496 msec (δ = 119 msec) for the former and 384 (δ = 138 msec) for the latter. The data for open protosyllables was derived from base structures such as (?V, hV, CV, GV, NV) and (V). The data for closed protosyllables was derived from base structures, such as (hVh, ?Vh, ?V?, ?VN, CVC, hV?) and (?VC). There were far fewer instances of vocalics followed by a glottal or supraglottal constrictive in productions such as (V?, Vh, VC), possibly corresponding to universal tendencies for syllables to be initiated by a consonant (Fujimura and Lovins 1977) and for languages to be associated with a prominence of open syllables (Bondarko 1969). Infants also continue to exhibit a preference for the open syllable in later

Table 4. Mean duration (X), standard deviation (S.D.), and variability estimates (V.E.) derived from Mean/S.D. of open and closed monoprotosyllabic utterances produced by four infants during the first twenty-four weeks of life. Values are reported in milliseconds.

Subject	Open Monoprotosyllables			Closed Monoprotosyllables		
	$\overline{X}$	S.D.	V.E.	$\overline{X}$	S.D.	V.E.
A	425	105	4.05	412	130	3.17
M	512	199	2.57	328	99	3.31
J	538	236	2.28	393	215	1.83
G	510	140	3.65	419	177	2.37

Figure 6.

MEAN DURATION OF OPEN AND CLOSED TWO-PROTOSYLLABLE INFANT UTTERANCES

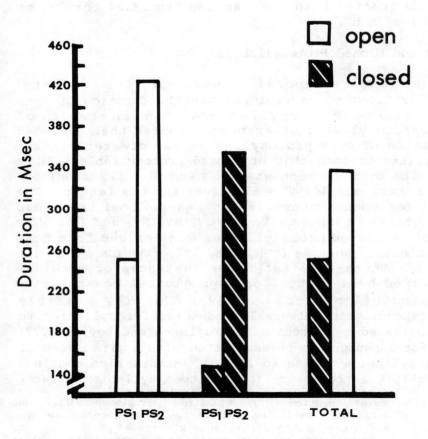

stages of babbling that shows a continuity with phonological characteristics of early words (Oller et al. 1975; Ingram 1976).

The results of the analysis of the two—protosyllable utterances were consistent with the above findings. Figure 6 shows that the mean for open protosyllables was 338 msec compared with a mean of 185 msec for those that were closed. When the data were reorganized to compare open and closed first protosyllables with open and closed second protosyllables, the effects of final lengthening were demonstrated in both contexts. There was, however, a greater difference between PS_1 and PS_2

in the comparison involving closed protosyllables, as was shown by Oller (1973) in his analysis of adult utterances. Oller (1973) and Delattre (1966) found closed syllables to be longer than open syllables in English, German, French, and Spanish; however, there was an interaction with stress. At this stage of development, when infants include a postvocalic constrictive, it tends to be glottal and more often a stop than an aspirate. As shown in G's data, the presence of a terminal glottal stop tends to be associated with shorter protosyllable durations.

DISCUSSION AND CONCLUSIONS

The results of this series of studies focusing on some temporal features of vocalizations indicate that there may be precursors to, and preferences for, phonetic patterns shown in natural languages within the utterances produced by infants as early as the first six months of life. The finding that there was final lengthening in two-protosyllable utterances was the first indication of the potential systematicity of temporal features during this period. Although longer utterances also showed a trend in the same direction, the effect was certainly weaker, and sampling and segmentation problems prohibit any definitive statements.

It is not altogether clear why these results are inconsistent with Oller and Smith's (1977) failure to find lengthening effects greater than 10 to 15% in the reduplicated babbling exhibited by older infants. The number of utterances analyzed for two of their children who failed to exhibit final lengthening was quite limited. In addition to sample size, it is possible that Oller and Smith's procedure of collapsing utterances of varying lengths and comparing final syllable duration with that of all nonfinal syllables as well as differences in measurement procedures contributed. Another factor to consider is that reduplicated babbling consists primarily of open syllables. In the present study and that of Oller (1973), there appeared to be less of a lengthening effect in this context. Reduplicated babbling, as a distinct form of vocalization, may have a rhythmicity and temporal features that are yet to be determined. In an attempt to resolve the discrepancy in findings, research is currently in progress which will continue to follow the four infants $\underline{A}$, $\underline{M}$, $\underline{J}$, and $\underline{G}$ through the second six months of vocal development, a period which encompasses reduplicated babbling.

A comparison of the total duration data with that derived by Smith (1978) for 2-year-old children does show considerable progression toward shorter duration with increasing age and a corresponding reduction in temporal variability. The latter may be associated with increasing neuromuscular control (Smith 1978) and incorporation of these structures into a linguistic context. The mean duration for PS_1 in the present study was greater, particularly for the two males $\underline{J}$ and $\underline{G}$, than stressed initial syllable productions by Smith's ten 2-year-old subjects. However PS_2 means for three of the four infants were consistent with those for unstressed final syllables where the value for PS_2 exceeded 400 msec.

The analysis of base structures, which included vocalics and abutting constrictives in varying contexts, showed that there seems to be a reduction of duration in embedded conditions. This finding points to the possibility of some type of isochrony effect. Developed to describe a linguistic phenomenon, the essence of this principle is that vowels get shorter as word length increases (Fónagy and Magdics 1960; Jones 1948; Lehiste 1970). Oller (1973) has shown, however, that there are variations in isochrony relating to stress and has questioned the validity of the concept itself. When Oller utilized different measuring and syllable ordering procedures, there was a slight tendency for both stressed and unstressed vowels to increase in duration with increasing word length. Oller's analysis involved spoken sentences which may account for some of the differences. Like the linguistic issue regarding isochrony, the presence of this apparent effect in the vocalizatons of young children also needs more attention to further determine consistency and strength as the infant continues through the next series of development stages into the beginnings of meaningful speech.

Regulation of Temporal Features

An important component of all natural langugages is temporal organization. At the macroscopic level, there is rhythmicity and flow (Kent 1976). At the microscopic level, there are distinctive duration characteristics which cue phonemic features and constituent boundaries (Klatt 1976). One may ask if this temporal organization orginates and evolves simultaneously with emerging spoken language or if there is a possibility of an inherent blueprint of sorts that provides a basis and, additionally, sets the stage for the acquisition of relevant language-specific timing features.

The results of the present study and preliminary results of the adjunct analyses point to the fact that the vocalizations displayed by the human infant during the first six months of life reflect greater systematicity than has been previously thought. The behaviors cannot be accounted for, it appears, solely on the basis of peripheral production features of a more or less mechanical nature, as reflected in the motor slowdown hypothesis offered by Klatt (1976) and Smith (1978). Rather, they seem to reflect a type of central programmed regulation. The proposal of such an inherent regulatory device of cortical and possibly subcortical origin has historical precedence although the focus was on purely linguistic behavior. One of the earliest discussions suggesting central regulation over temporal sequences was presented in 1951, by Lashley, in a seminal paper entitled, "The Problem of Serial Order in Behavior." Since then, Lenneberg (1967), Martin (1972), and Kent (1976), among others, have considered the problem in varying contexts.

With respect to infant vocal behavior, an inherent regulatory device has a twofold function. First, it accounts for features that show similarities to and continuity with patterns observed in developing and mature speech. Second, it provides the infant with a neuroanatomical base that, initially, is responsible for directing output features. Early in development, however, it becomes involved in receiving, storing, and elaborating upon both the inherent patterns and those which the infant fortuitously discovers in the course of exploring his/her vocal tract dynamics. The evolving device eventually comes to interact with other systems, as it becomes finely tuned during the language acquisition period, to incorporate and direct the timing of linguistically relevant features at the macroscopic and microscopic levels.

If, as Kent (1976) has proposed, "...syllable units operate at the interface between decisions that are properly linguistic and decisions that are properly neuromotor..." (p. 88), then the neuromotor connective roots of the syllable may lie in the precursor to to that interface-- the protosyllable. The syllable itself has been considered as a unit of neural organization (Fry 1964; Kozhevnikov and Chistovich 1965; Fromkin 1968) and, relevant to the findings of the present investigation, the syllable and disyllable may be the basic structures, or "phonological building blocks", from which words are constructed (Lehiste 1970). The condition that the stronger lengthening effects were found for two-protosyllable utterances is consistent with a continuity theory (Oller et al. 1975). It also would not be surprising that such a central regulator exerts control over relatively limited forms because of its immaturity. The first two years constitute a period of significant growth for the infant with respect to both neuroanatomical and physiological development (Lenneberg 1967) and alterations in the structure and function of the respiratory-phonatory-articulatory system (Stark 1978). It is impossible to say at this time whether or not the proposed device is specific to the regulation of phonetic behavior, as I suppose, or whether the temporal regularities observed reflect a more general underlying mechanism for the control of motor activity, within which vocalization is just on aspect.

We have only just begun to tap the nature of temporal organization of prespeech and early speech behavior. The infant's utterances themselves provide one window to the inner world that regulates them, even though one must admit to translucency and even opacity at times.

ACKNOWLEDGMENTS

This study was supported in part by a grant from the National Institute of Education (NE-G-00-3-0077). I wish to extend appreciation to Dr. Audrey Riker for conduct of the psychological evaluations, to Dr. Carl A. Binnie for conduct of the audiological examinations, to Dr. Raymond G. Daniloff for his extensive cooperative work in the acoustic analyses, and to Dr. Kim Oller for his helpful suggestions.

REFERENCES

Bondarko, L.V. 1969. The syllable structure of speech and distinctive features of phonemes. _Phonetica_ 20:1-40.

Cooper, W.E. and Sorensen, J.M. 1977. Fundamental frequency contours at syntactic boundaries. J. Acoust. Soc. Am. 62:683-92.

Delack, J.B. 1975. Prosodic features of infant speech: the first year of life. Paper presented at the Eighth International Congress of Phonetic Sciences, Leeds, England.

Delattre, P. 1966. A comparison of syllable length conditioning among languages. International Review of Applied Linguistics IV:183-98.

Di Simoni, F.G. 1974. Influence of consonant environment on the duration of vowels in the speech of three-, six- and nine-year-old children. J. Acoust. Soc. Am. 55:362-63.

Fónagy, I. and Magdics, K. 1960. Speed of utterance in phrases of different lengths. Language and Speech 4:179-92.

Fromkin, V.A. 1968. Speculations on performance models. J. Linguistics 4:47-68.

Fry, D.B. 1964. The functions of the syllable. Zeitschrift für Phonetik, Sprachwissenschaft und Kommunikationsforschung 17:215-37.

Fujimura, O. and Lovins, J.B. 1977. Syllables as concatenative phonetic units. Symposium on Segment Organization and the Syllable. University of Colorado, Boulder.

Haden, E.F. 1962. Accent experatoire. Studies in Linguistics 16:23-29.

Ingram, D. 1976. Phonological Disability in Children. New York: Elsevier.

Jakobson, R. 1941/1968. Child Language, Aphasia and Phonological Universals. The Hague: Mouton.

Jones, D. 1948. Chronemes and tonemes. Acta Linguistica 1:1-10.

Kent, R.D. 1976. Models of Speech Production. In Contemporary Issues in Experimental Phonetics, ed. N.J. Lass. New York: Academic Press.

Klatt, D.H. 1975. Vowel lengthening is syntactically determined in a connected discourse. J. Phonetics 3:129-40.

Klatt, D.H. 1976. Linguistic uses of segmental duration in English: Acoustic and perceptual evidence. J. Acoust. Soc. Am. 59:1208-21.

Kozhevnikov, V.A. and Chistovich, L.A. 1965. Speech: Articulation and Perception, Moscow-Leningrad. Translated by Joint Publications Research Service, Washington, D.C. No. JPRS 30.543.

307

Krause, S.E. 1978. Developmental use of vowel duration as a cue to postvocalic consonant voicing: A perception and production study. Ph.D. Dissertation, Northwestern University.

Laufer, M.Z. 1978. Infant voice. In Seventh Symposium Care of the Professional Voice, Part II: Life Span Changes in the Human Voice. New York: The Voice Foundation. pp. 13-22.

Laufer, M.Z. and Horii, Y. 1977. Fundamental frequency characteristics of infant nondistress vocalization during the first twenty-four weeks. J. Child Lang. 4:171-84.

Lehiste, I. 1970. Suprasegmentals. Cambridge: M.I.T. Press.

Lenneberg, E.H. 1967. Biological Foundations of Language. New York: John Wiley and Sons, Inc.

Lieberman, P. 1975. On the Origins of Language. New York: Macmillan.

Lindblom, B. 1968. Temporal organization of syllable production. STL-QPSR 2,3:1-5.

Lisker, L. 1957. Closure duration and the intervocalic voiced-voiceless distinction in English. Language 33:42-49.

Lisker, L. 1969. Stop duration and voicing in English. Haskins Laboratories Status Report on Speech Research SR19/20:27-35.

Malmberg, B. 1957. The phonetic basis for syllable division. Studia Linguistica 9:80-87.

Martin, J.G. 1972. Rhythmic (hierarchial) versus serial structure in speech and other behaivor. Psychol. Rev. 79:487-509.

Murai, J. 1963. The sounds of infants: their phonemicization and symbolization. Studia Phonologica III:17-34.

Nakazima, S. 1972. A comparative study of the speech developments of Japanese and American children (4): the beginning of the phonemicization process. Studia Phonologica IV:1-37.

O'Connor, J.D. and Trim, J.L.M. 1953. Vowel, consonant and syllable -- a phonological definition. Word 9:103-22.

Oller, D.K. 1973. The effect of position-in-utterance on speech segment duration in English. J. Acoust. Soc. Am. 54:1235-47.

Oller, D.K. 1978. The emergence of the sounds of speech in infancy. To appear in Child Phonology: Perception and Production, eds. G. Yeni-Komshian, C. Kavanagh, and C. Ferguson. New York: Academic Press.

Oller, D.K. 1979. Syllable timing in Spanish, English and Finnish. Amsterdam Studies in the Theory and History of Linguistic Science IV, Vol. 9. Amsterdam: John-Benjamins B.V.

Oller, D.K., Wieman, L.A., Doyle, W.J., and Ross, C. 1975. Infant babbling and speech. J. Child Lang. 3:1-11.

Oller, D.K. and Smith, B. 1977. Effect of final-syllable position on vowel duration in infant babbling. J. Acoust. Soc. Am. 62:994-97.

Smith, B.L. 1978. Temporal aspects of English speech production: a developmental perspective. J. Phonetics 6:37-67.

Stark, R.E. 1978. Stages of speech development in the first year of life. To appear in Child Phonology: Perception and Production, eds. G. Yeni-Yomshian, C. Kavanagh, and C. Ferguson. New York: Academic Press.

Zlatin, M.A. 1974. Variations on a theme: [ag$^{\gamma}$ u$^{\vartheta}$]. Paper presented at the Annual Convention of the American Speech and Hearing Association, Las Vegas.

Zlatin, M.A. 1975. Exploratory mapping of the vocal tract and primitive syllabification in infancy. Paper presented at the Annual Convention of the American Speech and Hearing Association, Washington, D.C.

Zlatin, M.A. 1976. Language acquisiton: some acoustic and interactive aspects of infancy. Final Report, National Institute of Education. Project No. 3-4014, Grant No. NE-G-00-3-001. Resume in Resources in Education.

Bibliography

This Bibliography is intended as a supplementary source of references on infant communication. In general, those references appearing at the end of each chapter are not included here.

Abrahamsen, A.A. 1977. Child Language, An Interdisciplinary Guide to Theory and Research. Baltimore: University Park Press.

Allen, G.D. 1976. Development of rhythm in early phonology. Paper presented at the Eighth Annual Child Language Research Forum, Stanford, April 3, 1976.

Antinucci, F. and Parisi, D. 1973. Early language acquisition: a model and some data. In Studies in Child Language Development, eds. C. Ferguson and D. Slobin. New York: Holt, Rinehart, and Winston. pp 607-19.

Bangs, J.L. 1947. A comprehensive historical survey of concepts regarding congenital language disability. Unpublished dissertation, University of Iowa.

Bangs, T.E. 1968. Language and Learning Disorders of the Pre-Academic Child. New York: Appleton-Century Crofts, Inc.

Banikiotes, F.G., Montgomery, A.A., and Banikiotes, P.G. 1972. Male and female auditory reinforcement of infant vocalizations. Develop. Psychol. 6:476-78.

Bar-Adon, A. and Leopold, W., eds. 1971. Child Language A Book of Readings. Engelwood Cliffs: Prentice-Hall., Inc.

Barnard, J.W., Zimbardo, P.G., and Sarason, S.B. 1961. Anxiety and verbal behavior in children. Child Dev. 32:379-92.

Bateman, W.G. 1917. Papers on language development I. The first word. Pedagog. Sem. 24:391-98.

Bates, E. 1976. Language and Context: The Acquisition of Pragmatics. New York: Academic Press.

Bates, E., Benigni, L., Bretherton, I., Camaioni, L., and Volterna, V. 1976. From gesture to first word: on cognitive and social prerequisites. In Origins of Behavior: Communication and Language, eds. M. Lewis and L. Rosenblum. New York: Wiley and Sons.

Bateson, M.C. 1971. Speech Communication: the interpersonal context of infant vocalization. QPR MIT Electronics Lab 100:170-76.

Bayley, N. 1969. Manual for the Bayley Scales of Infant Development. New York: The Psychological Corporation.

Bayley, N. 1970. Development of mental abilities. In Carmichael's Manual of Child Psychology, ed. P. Mussen. New York: John Wiley & Sons. pp 1163-1209.

Beckwith, L. 1971. Relationships between infants' vocalizations and their mother's behaviors. Merrill-Palmer Quart. 17:211-26.

Becky, R.E. 1942. A study of certain factors related to retardation of speech. J. Speech Hear. Dis. 7:223-50.

Bellugi, U. and Brown, R. eds. 1964. The Acquisition of Language Monographs of the Society of Research in Child Development 29.

Belmore, N.F., Port, D.K., Mobley, R.L., and Goodman, V.E. 1973. The development of auditory feedback and monitoring: delayed auditory feedback studies on the vocalizations of children aged six months to nineteen months. J. Speech Hear. Res. 16:709-20.

Bench, J. 1969. Some effects of auditory-frequency stimulation on the crying baby. J. Aud. Res. 9:122-28.

Benda, R. 1967. The significance of babbling to language development: a study of intonation patterns of an eight-month-old child. ERIC Abstract.

Benjamins, D. and Stark, R.E. 1974. Spontaneous crying in neurologically impaired infants. Unpublished paper.

Berko, J. 1958. The child's learning of English morphology. Word 14:150-77.

Bever, T.G., Fodor, J.A., and Weksel, W. 1965. The acquisition of syntax: a critique of contextual generalization. Psychol. Rev. 72:467-82.

Blasdell, R. and Aram, D. 1969. Kinesic, phonetic and prosodic communicative systems of the first-language learner. ERIC Abstract.

Bloom, K. 1977. Patterning of infant vocal behavior. J. Exp. Child Psychol. 23:367-77.

Bloom, L. 1970. Languages Development: Form and Function in Emerging Grammars. Cambridge: The MIT Press.

Bloom, L. 1973. One Word at a Time. The Hague: Mouton & Co.

Bloom, L., ed. 1978. Readings in Language Development. New York: John Wiley and Sons.

Bloom, L., Hood, L., and Lightbrown, P. 1974. Imitation in language development: if, when and why. Cog. Psychol. 6:380-420.

Bloom, L. and Lahey, M. 1978. Language Development and Language Disorders. New York: John Wiley and Sons.

Bogoyavlenskiy, D.N. 1973. The acquisition of Russian inflections. In Studies of Child Language and Development, eds. C.A. Ferguson and D.I. Slobin. New New York: Holt, Rinehart, and Winston, Inc. pp 284-94.

Bohannon, J.N. and Marquis, A.L. 1977. Children's control of adult speech. Child Dev. 48:1002-08.

Bolinger, D.L. 1949. Intonation and analysis. Word 5:248-54.

Bosma, J.F. and Smith, C.C. 1961. Infant cry: a preliminary study. Logos 4:10-18.

Bosma, J.A., Lind, J., and Truby, H.M. 1965. Distortions of upper respiratory and swallow motions in infants having anomalies of the upper pharynx. In Newborn Infant Cry, ed., J. Lind. Acta Paediat. Scand. Suppl. 163.

Bosma, J.F., Lind, J., and Truby, H.M. 1965. Studies of neonatal transition: correlated cineradiographic and visual-acoustic observations. In Newborn Infant Cry, ed. J. Lind. Acta Paediat. Scand. Suppl. 163.

Bowerman, M.F. 1970. Learning to talk: a cross-linguistic study of early syntactic development, with special reference to Finnish. Unpublished doctoral dissertation, Harvard University.

Bowerman, M.F. 1974. Learning the structure of causitive verbs: a study in the relationship of cognitive, semantic and syntactic development. Pap. Rep. Child Lang. Dev. 8:142-78.

Brown, R. and Hanlon, C. 1970. Derivational complexity and the order of acquistion in child speech. In Cognition and the Development of Language, ed. J.R. Hayes. New York: John Wiley and Sons, Inc. Reprinted in Psycholinguistics, ed. R. Brown. New York: The Free Press, 1970.

Bruce, D.J. 1964. An analysis of word sounds by young children. Br. J. Educational Psychol. 34:158-70.

Bullowa, M. 1977. From performative act to performative utterance: an ethological perspective. Sign Lang. Studies 16:193-218.

Bullowa, M. 1977. Linguistics-infant speech from non-verbal communication to language. J. Learn. Disabilities 10:354-55.

Bullowa, M., Jones, L.G., and Duckert, A.R. 1964. The acquisition of a word. Language and Speech 7:107-11.

Burling, R. 1973. Language development of a Garo and English-speaking child. In Studies of Child Language Development, eds. C.A. Ferguson and D.I. Slobin. New York: Holt, Rinehart and Winston, Inc. pp 69-90.

Braine, M.D.S. 1963. The ontogeny of English phrase structures: the first phrase. Language 39:1-13.

Braine, M.D.S. 1971. The acquisition of language in infant and child. In The Learning of Language, ed. C. Reed. New York: Appleton-Century-Crofts.

Bridges, K.M.B. 1932. Emotional development in early infancy. Child Dev. 4:324-41.

Bridges, K.M.B. 1933. A study of social development in early infancy. Child Dev. 5:36-49.

Brown, R. and Fraser, C. 1963. The acquisition of syntax. In Verbal Behavior and Learning, eds. C.N. Cofer and B. Musgrave. New York: McGraw-Hill.

Brown, R. and Bellugi, U. 1964. Three processes in the child's acquisition of syntax. Harvard Educational Review 34:133-51.

Brown, R., Cazden, C., and Bellugi, U. 1969. The child's grammar from I to III. In Second Annual Minnesota Symposium on Child Psychology, ed. John P. Hill. Reprinted in Psycholinguistics, ed. R. Brown. New York: The Free Press, 1970.

Butterfield, E. and Cairns, G. 1974. Whether infants perceive linguistically is uncertain, and if they did, its practical importance would be equivocal. In Language Perspectives -- Acquisiton, Retardation, and Intervention, eds. R. Schiefelbusch and L. Lloyd. Baltimore: University Park Press.

Bzock, K.R. and League, R. 1971/1978. Assessing Language Skills in Infancy. Baltimore: University Park Press.

Cairns, G.F., Jr. 1975. Longitudinal studies of infant vocal production. Paper presented at the American Speech and Hearing Association, Washington, D.C.

Campbell, R. and Wales, R. 1970. The study of language acquisition. In New Horizons in Linguistics, ed. J. Lyons. Harmondsworth: Penguin. pp 242-60.

313

Carlson, P. and Anisfeld, M. 1969. Some observations on the linguistic competence of a two-year old child. Child Dev. 40:569-75.

Carrow, E. 1974. A test for elicited imitations in assessing grammatical structure in children. J. Speech Hear. Dis. 39:437-99.

Carrow, E. 1974. Carrow Elicited Language Inventory. Austin, Texas: Learning Concepts, Inc.

Cazden, C.B. 1965. Environmental assistance to the child's acquisition of grammar. Doctoral dissertation, Harvard University.

Chang, H. and Frehub, S.E. 1977. Auditory processing of relational information by young infants. J. Exp. Child Psychol. 24:324-31.

Chapman, S.K. 1971. The age and order of acquisition of selected morphological structures produced by children age 2 to 4 years of age. Unpublished doctoral dissertation, University of South Carolina.

Chapman, R.L. and Kohn, L.L. 1978. Comprehension strategies in two and three year olds: animate agents or probable events? J. Speech Hear. Res. 21:746-61.

Chen, H.P. 1946. Speech development during the first year of life, a quantitative study. Doctoral dissertation, University of Iowa.

Chukovsky, K. 1968. From Two to Five. Berkeley: University of California Press.

Clark, E.V. 1973. What's in a word? On the child's acquisition of semantics in his first language. In Cognitive Development and the Acquisition of Language, ed. T.E. Moore. New York: Academic Press. pp 65-110.

Clark, E.V. 1973. How children describe time and order. In Studies of Child Language Development, eds. C.A. Ferguson and D.I. Slobin. New York: Holt, Rinehart, and Winston, Inc. pp 585-606.

Clark, H. 1973. Space, time, semantics and the child. In Cognitive Development and the Acquisition of Language, ed. T. Moore. New York: Academic Press. pp 28-64.

Cohen, S.E. and Beckwith, L. 1975. Maternal language input in infancy. Paper presented at the American Psychological Association, August 1975, Chicago.

Cohen, L.B. and Salapetek, P., eds. 1975. Infant Perception. New York: Academic Press.

Cohen, S.E., Beckwith, L., and Parmelee, A.H. 1978. Receptive language development in preterm children as related to care-giver interaction. Pediat. 61:16-20.

Cruse, D.A. 1977. A note on the learning of colour names. J. Child. Lang. 4:305-11.

Cruttenden, A. 1970. A phonetic study of babbling. Br. J. Dis. Comm. 5:110-18.

Cruttenden, A. 1972. Phonological procedures for child language. Br. J. Dis. Comm. 7:30-37.

Cruttenden, A. 1977. The acquisition of personal pronouns and language "simplication." Language and Speech 20:191-97.

Crystal, D. 1970. Prosodic systems and language acquistion. In Prosodic feature analysis, ed. P. Léon. Paris: Didier.

Crystal, D. 1971. Prosodic and paralinguistic correlates of social categories. In Social Anthropology and Language, ed. E. Ardener. ASA Monograph 10. London: Tavistock. pp 185-206.

Cutting, J. and Eimas,P. Phonetic feature analyzers and the processing of speech in infants. In The Role of Speech in Language, eds. J. Kavanaugh and J. Cutting. Cambridge: MIT Press (in press).

Darley, F. 1975. Developmental articulatory problems. Austral. J. Hum. Commun. Dis. 3:41-54.

Darley, F. and Winitz, H. 1961. Age of first word, review of research. J. Speech Hear. Dis. 26:272-90.

Delack, J.B. 1971. Analysis of infant speech sound production and development. Vancouver: University of British Columbia (mimeo).

Delack, J.B. and Fowlow, P.J. 1975. The onotogenesis of differential vocalization: development of prosodic contrastivity during the first year of life. Paper presented at the 3rd. International Child Language Symposium, London.

deVilliers, J.G. and deVilliers, P.A. 1973. A cross-sectional study of the development of grammatical morphemes in child speech. J. Psycholinguistic Res. 2:267-78.

deVilliers, J.G. and deVilliers, P.A. 1978. Semantics and syntax in the first two years: the output of form and function and the form and function of the input. In Communicative and Cognitive Abilities-- Early Behavioral Assessment, eds. F.D. Minifie and L.L. Lloyd. Baltimore: University Park Press. pp 309-348.

Depaulo, B.M. and Bonvillian, J.D. 1978. The effect on language development of the special characteristics of speech addressed to children. J. Psycholinguistic Res. 7:189-211.

DiSimoni, F.G. 1974. Influence of consonant environment on duration of vowels in the speech of three-, six-, and nine-year old children. J. Acoust. Soc. Am. 55:362-63.

Dore, J., Franklin, M.B., Miller, R.T., and Ramer, A.L.H. 1976. Transitional phenomena in early language acquisition. J. Child Lang. 3:1-38.

Doty, D. 1974. Infant speech perception: report on a conference held at the University of Minnesota, June 20-22. Human Dev. 17:74-80.

Drachman, G. 1970. Assumptions about acquisiton. Paper read at Linguistic Society of America Meeting, December 1970.

Eatus, A. 1977. Hemispheric asymmetry in processing dichotically presented speech and nonspeech stimuli by infants. In Language Development and Neurological Theory, eds. J. Segalowitz and F. Gruber. New York: Academic Press. p. 64-73.

Edwards, M.L. 1971. One child's acquisition of English liquids. Papers and reports on child language development. 3:101-09.

Edwards, M.L. 1974. Perception and production in child phonology: the testing of four hypotheses. J. Child Lang. 1:205-19.

Eguchi, S. and Hirsh, I.J. 1969. Development of speech sounds in children. Acta Otolaryngol. Suppl. 257.

Eilers, R. 1975. Infant speech perception: context sensitivity. Paper presented at the American Speech and Hearing Association, November 1975, Washington, D.C.

Eilers, R.E. 1976. On tracing the development of speech perception. Paper presented at the Society for Research in Child Development, March, 1976, New Orleans.

Eilers, R.E. 1977. Perception of voice onset time by Spanish-learning infants. Paper presented at the 94th meeting of the Acoustical Society of America, December, 1977, Miami.

Eilers, R.E. 1978. Discussion summary: development of phonology. In Communicative and Cognitive Abilities -- Early Behavioral Assessment, eds. F.D. Minifie and L.L. Lloyd. Baltimore: University Park Press. pp 299-306.

Eilers, R. and Minifie, F. 1975. Fricative discrimination in early infancy. J. Speech Hear. Res. 18:158-67.

Eilers, R.E. and Oiler, D.K. 1976. The role of speech discrimination in developmental sound substitutons. J. Child Lang. 3:319-329.

Eilers, R.E., Wilson, W.R., and Moore, J.M. 1977. Developmental changes in speech discrimination in infants. J. Speech Hear. Res. 20:766-80.

Eilers, R.E., Wilson, W.R., and Moore, J.M. 1978. Speech discrimination in the language-wise. A study in the perception of voice-onset time. J. Child Lang. in press.

Eimas, P. 1974. Linguistic processing of speech by young infants. In Language Perspectives -- Acquisition, Retardation, and Intervention, eds. R. Schiefelbusch and L. Lloyd. Baltimore: University Park Press. pp 55-73.

Eimas, P. 1975. Auditory and linguistic processing of the cues for place of articulation by infants. Percept. Psychophys. 16:513-21.

Eimas, P. 1974. Auditory and linguistic processing of cues for speech: discrimination of the (r-1) distinction by young infants. Percept. Psychophys. 18:341-47.

Eimas, P. 1975. Developmental studies of speech perception. In Infant Perception, ed. L.B. Cohen and P. Salapetek. New York: Academic Press.

Eimas, P. 1975. Speech perception in early infancy. In Infant Perception: From Sensation to Cognition, Vol. II., eds. L. Cohen and P. Salapatek. New York: Academic Press.

Eisenberg, R.B. 1976. Auditory Competence in Early Life. The Roots of Communicative Behavior. Baltimore: University Park Press.

Elardo, R., Bradley, R., and Caldwell, B.M. 1977. A longitudinal study of the relation of infants' home environments to language development at age three. Child Dev. 48:595-603.

Elbert, M. and McReynolds, L.V. 1978. An experimental analysis of misarticulating childrens' generalizations. J. Speech Hear. Res. 21:136-50.

Engel, W.V. 1973. The development from sound to phoneme in child language. In Studies in Child Language Development, eds. C.A. Ferguson and D.I. Slobin. New York: Holt, Rinehart and Winston.

Ervin-Tripp, S. 1964. Imitation and structural change in children's language. In New Directions in the Study of Language, ed. E. Lenneberg. Cambridge: MIT Press.

Ervin-Tripp, S. 1973. Some strategies for the first two years. In Cognitive Development and the Acquisition of Language, ed. T. Moore. New York: Academic Press. pp 261-86.

Ervin-Tripp, S. and Mitchell-Kernan, C., eds. 1977. Child Discourse. New York: Academic Press.

Ewing, A.W.G. 1930. Aphasia in Children. New York: Oxford University Press.

Fant, G. 1960. <u>Acoustic</u> <u>Theory</u> <u>of</u> <u>Speech</u> <u>Production</u>. The Hague: Mouton.

Fargo, N., Port, D.K., Mobley, R.L., and Goodman, V.E. 1968. The development of auditory feedback monitoring: (IV) delayed auditory feedback studies of the vocalizations of children between six and nineteen months. <u>Annual</u> <u>Report,</u> <u>Neurocomm.</u> <u>Lab.</u> Baltimore: Johns Hopkins University. pp 95-118.

Ferguson, C.A. 1964. Baby talk in six languages. <u>Amer.</u> <u>Anthropol.</u> 66:103-14.

Ferguson, C.A. 1973. Fricatives in child language acquisition. <u>Papers</u> <u>and</u> <u>Reports</u> <u>on</u> <u>Child</u> <u>Language</u> <u>Development</u> 6:61-86.

Ferguson, C.A. 1975. Sound patterns in language acquisition. Georgetown Univ. Round Table Lang. <u>Linguist</u> 1-16.

Ferguson, C.A. 1975. Baby talk as a simplified register. <u>Pap.</u> <u>Rep.</u> <u>Child</u> <u>Lang.</u> <u>Dev.</u> 9:1-27.

Ferguson, C.A. and Slobin, D.I., eds. 1973. <u>Studies</u> <u>of</u> <u>Child</u> <u>Language</u> <u>Development</u>. New York: Holt, Rinehart and Winston, Inc.

Ferguson, C.A., Peizer, D.B., and Weeks, T. 1973. Model and replica phonological grammar of a child's first words. <u>Lingua</u> 31:35-65.

Ferguson, C.A. and Farwell, C.B. 1975. Words and sounds in early language acquisition: English initial consonants in the first fifty words. <u>Language</u> 51:419-39.

Ferguson, C.A. and Garnica, O. 1975. Theories of phonological development. In <u>Fouundations</u> <u>of</u> <u>Language</u> <u>Development</u>, Vol II, eds. E. and E. Lenneberg. New York: Academic Press. pp 153-80.

Ferguson, C.A. 1978. Learning to pronounce: The earliest stages of phonological development in the child. In <u>Communicative</u> <u>and</u> <u>Cognitive</u> <u>Abilities</u> -- <u>Early</u> <u>Behavioral</u> <u>Assessment,</u> eds. F.D. Minifie and L.L. Lloyd. Baltimore: University Park Press. pp 273-97.

Finkelstein, N.W. and Ramey, C.T. 1975. Learning to control the environment in infancy. <u>Child</u> <u>Dev.</u> 48:806-19.

Fisichelli, V.R. and Karelitz, S. 1966. Frequency spectra of the cries of normal infants and those with Down's Syndrome. <u>Psychonom.</u> <u>Sci.</u> 6:195-96.

Fisichelli, V.R. and Karelitz, S. 1969. The effect of stimulus intensity on induced crying activity in the neonate. <u>Psychonom.</u> <u>Sci.</u> 16:327-28.

Fisichelli, V.R., Karelitz, S., and Haber, A. 1969. The course of induced crying activity in the neonate. J. Psych. 73:183-89.

Fitchen, M. 1931. Speech and music development of a one-year-old child. Child Dev. 2:324-26.

Fitzgerald, L.K. 1966. Child Language: an analysis of imitations by Gã children. Department of Anthropology, University of California, Berkeley. Unpublished paper.

Fluharty, N.B. 1974. The design and standardization of a speech and language screening test for use with preschool children. J. Speech Hear. Dis. 39:75-88.

Fodor, J., Garrett, M., and Brill, S. Pi ka pu: The perception of speech sounds by prelinguistic infants. Percept. Psychophys. 18:74-78.

Folger, M.K. and Leonard, L.B. 1978. Language and sensiorimotor development during the early period of referential speech. J. Speech and Hear. Res. 21:519-27.

Fradkina, F.I. 1955. Voznikorenie rechi u rebenka (The emergence of speech in children). Uch. zap. LGPI A.I. Gertseva 12. English abstract in The Genesis of Language, eds. F. Smith and G.A. Miller. Cambridge: MIT Press.

Friedlander, B.Z. 1968. The effect of speaker identity, voice inflection, vocabulary and message redundancy on infants' selection of vocal reinforcement. J. Exp. Child Psychol. 6:443-59.

Friedlander, B.Z. 1970. Receptive language development in infancy. Issues and problems. Merrill Palmer Quart. 16:7-51.

Friedlander, B.Z., Jacobs, C.A., Davis, B.B., and Wetstone, H.S. 1972. Time-sampling analysis of infant's natural language environment in the home. Child Dev. 43:730-40.

Fry, D.B. 1966. The development of the phonological system in the normal and the deaf child. In The Genesis of Language, eds. F. Smith and G.A. Miller. Cambridge: MIT Press. pp 187-206.

Gallagher, T.M. and Craig, H.K. 1978. Structural characteristics of monologues in the speech of normal children: semantic and conversational aspects. J. Speech and Hear. Res. 21:103-17.

Gallagher, R.M. 1977. Revision behaviors in the speech of normal children developing language. J. Speech Hear. Res. 20:303-18.

Garnica, O. 1973. The development of phonemic speech perception. In Cognitive Development and the

<u>Acquisition</u> <u>of</u> <u>Language</u>, ed. T.E. Moore. New York: Academic Press. pp 215-22.

Gilbert, J.H. 1970. Formant concentration positions in the speech of children at two levels of linguistic development. <u>J.</u> <u>Acoust.</u> <u>Soc.</u> <u>Am.</u> 48:1404-06.

Gilbert, J.H. 1970. The learning of speechlike stimuli by children. <u>J.</u> <u>Exp.</u> <u>Child</u> <u>Psychol.</u> 9:1-11.

Gilbert, J. H. 1970. Vowel productions and identification by normal and language delayed children. <u>J.</u> <u>Exp.</u> <u>Child</u> <u>Psychol.</u> 9:12.

Gilbert, J.H. 1973. Acoustical features of children's vowel sounds: development by chronological age versus bone age. <u>Language</u> <u>and</u> <u>Speech</u> 16:218-23.

Gilbert, J.H. 1975. Speech perception in children. In <u>Structure</u> <u>Process</u> <u>in</u> <u>Speech</u> <u>Perception</u>, eds. A. Cohen and S.E. Nootboom. Heidelburg: Springer Verlag. pp 312-38.

Gilbert, J.H. 1977. A voice onset time analysis of apical stop production in 3-year olds. <u>J.</u> <u>Child</u> <u>Lang.</u> 4:103-10.

Gilbert, J.H. and Purves, B.A. 1977. Temporal constraints on consonant clusters in child speech production. <u>J.</u> <u>Child</u> <u>Lang.</u> 4:417-32.

Gilbert, J.H. and Johnson, C.E. 1978. Temporal and sequential constraints on six-year olds' phonological productions: some observations on the 'ambliance' phenomenon. <u>J.</u> <u>Child</u> <u>Lang.</u> 5:101-12.

Greenfield, P.M. and Smith, J. 1976. <u>The</u> <u>Structure</u> <u>of</u> <u>Communication</u> <u>in</u> <u>Early</u> <u>Language</u> <u>Development</u>. New York: Academic Press.

Greenstein, J.J., Greenstein, B.B., McConville, K., and Stellini, L. 1976. <u>Mother-Infant</u> <u>Communication</u> <u>and</u> <u>Language</u> <u>Acquisition</u> <u>in</u> <u>Deaf</u> <u>Infants</u>. New York: Lexington School for the Deaf.

Greer, K.T. 1977. A comparison of language development in true premature infants and small-for-date infants. <u>J.</u> <u>TN</u> <u>Speech</u> <u>Hear.</u> <u>Assoc.</u> 22:54-59.

Gruber, J.S. 1966. Playing with distinctive features in babbling of infants. <u>QPR</u> <u>MIT</u> <u>Electronics</u> <u>Research</u> <u>Lab.</u> 81:181-86.

Gruendel, J.M. 1966. Referential extension in early language development. <u>Child</u> <u>Dev.</u> 48:1567-76.

Guillaume, P. 1973. First stages of sentence formulation in children's speech. In <u>Studies</u> <u>of</u> <u>Child</u> <u>Language</u> <u>Development</u>, eds. C.A. Ferguson and D.I. Slobin. New York: Holt, Rinehart and Winston, Inc. pp 522-40.

Halliday, M.A.K. 1975. Learning How to Mean--
Explorations in the Development of Language. London:
Edward Arnold.

Hammarberg, R. 1974. How reliable is baby linguistics?
Speech, Hearing, Language, Purdue University
Contributed Papers, 3:1-22.

Hart, N.W.M. 1975. A model for language development
based on sample of children's language at various
stages of development -- with practical application.
Austrl. J. Hum. Commun. Dis. 3:61-81.

Haugan, G.M. and McIntire, R.W. 1972. Comparisons of
vocal imitation, tactile stimulation, and food as
reinforcers for infant vocalizations. Develop.
Psychol. 6:201-9.

Hawkins, S. 1973. Temporal coordination of consonants
in the speech of children. J. Phonetics 1:181-217.

Hays, J.R., ed. 1970. Cognition and the Development of
Language. New York: John Wiley & Sons, Inc.

Helstrup, T. 1976. Language acquisition as concept
formation: an experimental approach. Scand. J.
Psychol. 17:297-302.

Highnam, C.L. and Beykirch, H.L. 1976. Normalization
in vowel recognition by children: a developmental
study. Paper presented at the American Speech and
Hearing Association, November, 1976, Houston.

Hovell, M.F., Schumaker, J.B., and Sherman, J.A. 1978.
A comparison of parents' models and expansions in
promoting children's acquisitions of adjectives. J.
Exp. Child Psychol. 25:41-57.

Hubbell, R.D. 1977. On facilitating spontaneous
talking in young children. J. Speech Hear. Dis.
42:216-31.

Hurlock, E.B. 1950. Child Development. New York:
McGraw-Hill.

Illingworth, R.S. 1957. The Normal Child. London:
Churchill.

Ingram, D. 1971. Phonological rules in young children.
Papers and Reports on Child Language Development 3:
31:49.

Ingram, D. 1972. Phonological analysis of a developmentally aphasic child. Institute of Childhood
Aphasia, Stanford University (mimeo).

Ingram, D. 1975. Surface contrast in children's
speech. J. Child Lang. 2:287-92.

Ingram, D. 1976. Phonological Disability in Children.
London: Edward Arnold.

Irwin, O.C. 1941. Research on speech sounds for the
first six months of life. Psychol. Bull. 38:277-85.

Irwin, O.C. 1947. Infant speech: consonant sounds according to place of articulation. J. of Speech Dis. 12:397–401.

Irwin, O. 1951. Infant speech: consonantal position. J. Speech Hear. Dis. 16:159–61.

Irwin, O. 1948. Infant speech: development of vowel sounds. J. Speech Hear. Dis. 13:31–34.

Irwin, O.C. 1952. Speech development in the young child. II Some factors related to the speech development of the infant and young child. J. Speech Dis. 17:269.

Irwin, O.C. 1957 Phonetical description of speech development in childhood. In Manual of Phonetics, ed. L. Kaiser. Amsterdam: North-Holland Pub. Co.

Irwin, O.C. 1960. Language and communication. In Handbook of Research Methods in Child Development, ed. P.H. Mussen. New York: Wiley.

Irwin, O.C. and Weiss, L. 1934a. Differential variations in the activity and crying of the newborn infant under different intensities of light: a comparison of observational with polygraph findings. University of Iowa Studies Child Welfare 9:137–47.

Irwin, O.C. and Weiss, L. 1934b. The effect of clothing on the general and vocal activity of the newborn infant. University of Iowa Studies Child Welfare 9:149–62.

Irwin, O.C. and Curry, T. 1941. Vowel elements in the crying vocalizations of infants under ten days of age. Child Dev. 12:99–109.

Irwin, O.C. and Chen, H.P. 1943. Speech sound elements during the first years of life: a review of the literature. J. Speech Dis. 8:109–21.

Jakobson, R. 1968. Child Language, Aphasia, and Phonological Universals. The Hague: Mouton & Co.

Jensen, P.J., Williams, W.N., and Bzoch, K.R. 1975. Preference of young infants for speech vs. nonspeech stimuli. Paper presented at the American Speech and Hearing Association, November 1975, Washington, D.C.

Jespersen, O. 1922. Language: Its Nature, Development and Origin. New York: Holt.

Jonas, D.F. and Jonas, A.D. 1975. Gender differences in mental function: a clue to the origin of language. Current Anthropology 16:626–30.

Johnston, J.R. and Schery, T.K. 1976. The use of grammatical morphemes by children with communication disorders. In Normal and Deficient Child Language, eds. D.M. Morehead and A.E. Morehead. Baltimore: University Park Press. pp 239–58.

Kagan, J. 1969. On the meaning of behavior: illustrations from the infant. Child Dev. 40:1121-34.

Kaplan, E.L. 1970. Intonation and language acquisition. Papers and Reports on Child Lang. Dev. 1:1-21.

Karlin, I.W. and Strazzulla, M. 1952. Speech and language problems of mentally defective children. J. Speech Hear. Dis. 17:286.

Keat, R.D. 1974. Auditory-motor formant tracking. A study of speech imitation. J. Speech Hear. Res. 17:203-22.

Keat, R.D. 1976. Anatomical and neuromuscular maturation of the speech mechanisms: evidence from acoustic studies. J. Speech Hear. Res. 19:421-47.

Keating, P. and Buhr, R. 1978. Fundamental frequency in the speech of infants and children. J. Acoust. Soc. Am. 63:567-71.

Keitel, H.G., Cohn, R., and Harnish, D. 1960. Diaper rash, self-inflicted excoriations, and crying in full-term newborn infants kept in the prone or supine position. J. Pediat. 51:884-86.

Kewley-Port, D. and Preston, M. 1974. Early apical stop production: a voice onset time analysis. J. Phonetics 2:195:210.

Kimura, D. 1963. Speech lateralization in young children as determined by an auditory test. J. Comp. Physiol. Psychol. 56:899-902.

Kiparsky, P. and Menn, L. 1977. On the acquisition of phonology. In Language Learning and Thought, ed. J. MacNamara. New York: Academic Press.

Kirshenblatt-Gimblett, B. 1976. Speech Play: Research and Resources for the Study of Linguistic Creativity. Philadelphia: University of Pennsylvania Press.

Klima, E.S. and Bellugi, U. 1966. Syntactic regularities in the speech of children. In Psycholinguistic Papers, eds. J. Lyons and R. Wales. Edinburgh: Edinburgh University Prerss.

Kononova, I.M. 1969. Vocal responses in children in the first year of life and their relation to various patterns of behavior. Trans. title from Vopr. Psikhol. 5:119-27.

Korner, A. 1972. State as a variable, as obstacle and as mediator of stimulaton in infant research. MPQ 18:76-94.

Korner, A. 1974. The effect of the infant's state, level of arousal, sex and ontogenetic stage on the caregiver. In The Effect of the Infant on Its Caregiver, eds. M. Lewis and L.A. Rosenblum. New York: Wiley.

Korner, A.F. and Thoman, E.B. 1972. The relative efficacy of contact and vestibular-proprioceptive stimulation in soothing neonates. Child Dev. 43:443-53.

Kornfeld, J.R. 1971. What initial clusters tell us about a child's speech code. QPR MIT Electronics Research Lab. 101:218-21.

Kornfeld, J.R. 1971. Theoretical issues in child phonology. CLS 7:454-468.

Kuhl, P.K. and Miller, J.D. 1975. Speech perception in early infancy: discrimination of speech-sound categories J. Acoust. Soc. Am. 58:556(A).

Kuhl, P.K. 1976. Speech perception in early infancy: the acquisition of speech-sound categories. In Hearing and Davis: Essays Honoring Hallowell Davis, eds. S.K. Hirsh, D.H. Eldredge, I.J. Hirsh, and S.R. Silverman. St. Louis: Washington University Press. pp 265-280.

Kuhl, P.K. 1978. Predisposition for the perception of speech-sound categories: a species-specific phenomenon? In Communicative and Cognitive Abilities -- Early Behavioral Assessment, eds. F.D. Minifie and L.L. Lloyd. Baltimore: University Park Press. pp 229-55.

Lahey, M. and Bloom, L. 1977. Planning a first lexicon: which words to teach first. J. Speech Hear. Dis. 42:340-50.

Langlois, A., Wilder, C., and Baken, R.J. 1974. Prespeech respiratory patterns in the infant. Paper presented at the American Speech and Hearing Association, Washington, D.C.

Lasky, R., Syrdal-Lasky, A., and Klein, D. 1975. VOT discrimination by four- to six-month-old infants from Spanish environments. J. Exp. Child Psychol. 20:215-25.

Leavitt, L., Brown, J., Morse, P., and Graham, F. 1976. Cardiac orienting and auditory discrimination in 6-week infants. Dev. Psychol. 12:514-23.

Lee, L.L. 1966. Developmental sentence types: a method for comparing normal and deviant syntactic development. J. Speech Hear. Dis. 31:311-30.

Lee. L.L. 1970. A screening test for syntax development. J. Speech Hear. Dis. 35:103-112.

Lee, L.L. 1971. Northwestern Syntax Screening Test. Evanston, Ill.: Northwestern University Press.

Lee, L.L. 1974. Developmental Sentence Analysis. Evanston, Ill.: Northwestern University Press.

Lee, L.L. and Ando, K. Language acquisition and language disorder in Japanese. Unpublished paper, Northwestern University.

Lee, L.L. and Canter, S.M. 1971. Developmental sentence scoring: a clinical procedure for estimating syntactic development in children's spontaneous speech. J. Speech Hear. Dis. 36:315:40.

Leeper, H.A. and Leeper, G. 1976. Clinical evaluation of the fundamental frequency of normal children and children with vocal nodules employing a striation counting procedure. Paper presented at the American Speech and Hearing Association, Houston.

Lenneberg, E.H. 1964. Language disorders in childhood. Harvard Educ. Rev. 34:152-77.

Leopold, W.F. 1949. Speech Development of a Bilingual Child, Vol III. Evanston, Ill: Northwestern University.

Leopold, W. 1973. Patterning in children's language learning. In Child Language: a Book of Readings, eds. A. Bar-Adon and W. Leopold. Englewood Cliffs: Prentice-Hall, Inc.

Lewis, M.M. 1936. Infant Speech: A Study of the Beginnings of Language. New York: Harcourt Brace and World, Inc.

Lewis, M. and Rosenblum, L., eds. 1974. The Effect of the Infant on Its Caregiver. New York: Wiley-Interscience.

Lieberman, P., Harris, K.S., and Wolff, P. 1968. Newborn infant cry in relation to nonhuman primate vocalizations. J. Acoust. Soc. Am. 44:365.

Lieberman, P., Crelin, E., and Klatt, D. 1972. Phonetic ability and related anatomy of the newborn and adult human, Neanderthal Man, and the chimpanzee. American Anthropologist 74:287-307.

Liles, R.I., Hoops, H.R., Strauss, M., McClung, J., and Ostrea, E. 1974. A comparative acoustic and perceptual analysis of early crying behavior of congenitally drug-addicted and non-addicted infants. Paper presented at the American Speech and Hearing Association, Las Vegas.

Lind, J. 1971. The infant cry. Proc. Roy. Soc. Med. 64:468-71.

Ling, D. and Ling, A.H. 1974. Communicaton development in the first three years of life. J. Speech Hear. Res. 17:146-59.

Lord, C. 1975. Is talking to baby more than baby talk? A longitudinal study of the modification of linguistic input to young children. Unpublished paper presented at the Society for Research in Child Development, Denver.

Lowell, E.L. and Lowell, M.O. 1978. Interaction of assessment and intervention -- hearing impairment. In Communicative and Cognitive Abilities-- Early Behavioral Assessment. Baltimore: University Park Press. pp 483-501.

Lust, B. 1977. Conjunction reduction in child language. J. Child Lang.. 4:257-87.

Lynch, J. 1978. Evaluation of linguistic disorders in children. In Diagnostic Procedures in Hearing, Language, and Speech, eds. S. Singh and J. Lynch. Baltimore: University Park Press.

Lyons, J. and Wales, R., eds. 1966. Psycholinguistics Papers. Edinburgh: Edinburgh University Press.

Macken, M.A. 1974. Readers, books and articles on child phonology. Linguist. Rep. 16:9-12.

Macken, M.A. 1976. Permitted complexity in phonological development: one child's acquisition of Spanish consonants. Pap. Rep. Child Lang. Dev. 11:28-60.

MacWhinney, B. 1978. The acquisition of morpho-phonology. Monogr. Soc. Res. Child Develop. 43:122.

McCarthy, D. 1929. The vocalizations of infants. Psychol. Bull. 26:625-51.

McCarthy, D. 1930. The language development of the preschool child. Institute of Child Welfare Monographs Series 4. Minneapolis: University of Minnesota Press.

McCurry, W.H. and Irwin, O.C. 1953. Organismic interpretation of infant vocalizations. Child Dev. 23:272.

McGinnis, M. 1963. Aphasic Children: Identification and Education by the Association Method. Washington, D.C.: Alexander Graham Bell Association for the Deaf.

McGlone, R. 1966. Vocal pitch characteristics of children aged one and two years. Speech Monogr. 33:178-81.

McGrath, C.O. and Kuaze, L.H. 1973. Development of phrase structure rules involved in tag questions elicited from children. J. Speech Hear. Res. 16:498-512.

McNeill, D. 1966. The creation of language by children. In Psycholinguistic Papers, eds. J. Lyons and R.J. Wales. Edinburgh: Edinburgh University Press. pp 99-115.

McNeill, D. 1966. Developmental psycholinguistics. In The Genesis of Language: A Psycholinguistic Approach, eds. F. Smith and G.A. Miller. Cambridge: MIT Press.

326

McNeill, D. 1970. The development of language. In *Carmichael's Manual of Child Psychology*, ed. P. Mussen. New York: John Wiley and Sons. pp 1061-1161.

McNeill, D. 1970. The Acquisition of Language: the Study of Developmental Psycholinguistics. New York: Harper and Row, Publishers.

McReynolds, L.V. and Huston, K. 1971. A distinctive feature analysis of children's misarticulations. *J. Speech Hear. Dis.* 36:155-66.

McReynolds, L., Kohn, J., and Williams, G.C. 1975. Articulatory defective children's discrimination of their production errors. *J. Speech Hear. Dis.* 40:327-38.

Mead, M. and Newtown, N. 1967. Cultural patterning of perinatal behavior. In *Child Bearing. Its Social and Psychological Aspects*, eds. S.A. Richardson and A.F. Gutimacher. Baltimore: Williams and Wilkins.

Menn, L. 1971. Phonotactic rules in beginning speech. *Lingua* 26:225-51.

Menyuk, P. 1963. A preliminary evaluation of capacity of children. *J. Verb. Learn. Verb. Behav.* 2:429-39.

Menyuk, P. 1963. Syntactic structures in the language of children. *Child Dev.* 34:407-22.

Menyuk, P. 1964. Comparison of grammar of chldren with functionally deviant and normal speech. *J. Speech Hear. Res.* 7:109-21.

Menyuk, P. 1964. Syntactic rules used by children from preschool through first grade. *Child Dev.* 35:533-46.

Menyuk, P. 1965. Cues used in speech perception and production by children. *QPR MIT Research Laboratory of Electronics* No. 77.

Menyuk, P. 1968. The role of distinctive features in children's acquisition of phonology. *J. Speech Hear. Res.* 11:138-46.

Menyuk, P. 1969. *Sentences Children Use*. Cambridge, MIT Press.

Menyuk, P. 1971. *The Acquisition and Development of Language*. Englewood Cliffs: Prentice Hall.

Menyuk, P. 1972. Clusters as single underlying consonants: evidence from children's production, eds. A. Rigault and R. Charbonneau. *Proc. 7th Int. Cong. Phon. Sci.* The Hague: Mouton. pp 1161-65.

Menyuk, P. and Bernholtz, N. 1969. Prosodic features and children's language production. *QPR MIT Research Laboratory of Electronics* No. 93.

Menyuk, P. and Klatt, D. 1975. Voice onset-time in consonant cluster production by children and adults. *J. Child Lang.* 2:223-31.

Milianti, F.J. and Cullinan, W.J. 1974. Effect of age and word frequency on object recognition and naming in children. J. Speech Hear. Res. 17:373-85.

Miller, C.L. and Morse, P.A. 1976. The "heart" of categorical speech discrimination in young infants. J. Speech Hear. Res. 19:578-89.

Miller, C., Morse, P., and Dorman, M. 1977. Cardiac indices of infant speech perception: orienting and burst discrimination. Quart. J. Exp. Psychol. 29:533-45.

Miller, J. 1974. Phonetic determination of infant speech perception. Unpublished doctoral dissertation, University of Minnesota.

Miller, W.R. 1973. The acquisition of grammatical rules by children. In Studies of Child Language Development, eds. C.A. Ferguson and D.I. Slobin. New York: Holt, Rinehart and Winston, Inc. pp 380-99.

Miller, W. and Ervin, S. 1964. The development of grammar in child language. In The Acquisition of Language, eds. U. Bellugi and R. Brown. Child Develop. Mongr. 29:9-34.

Minifie, F.D., Hixon, T.J., and Williams, F. 1973. Normal Aspects of Speech, Hearing and Language. Englewood Cliffs: Prentice-Hall, Inc.

Minifie, F.D. and Lloyd, L.L., eds. 1978. Communicative and Cognitive Abilities -- Early Behavioral Assessment. Baltimore: University Park Press.

Moerk, E.L. 1977. Pragmatic and Semantic Aspects of Early Language Development. Baltimore: University Park Press.

Moffitt, A.R. 1968. Speech perception by infants. Unpublished doctoral dissertation, University of Minnesota.

Moffitt, A. 1971. Consonant cue perception by twenty- to twenty-four-week old infants. Child Dev. 42:717-31.

Molfese, D.L. and Hess, T.M. 1978. Hemispheric specialization for VOT perception in the preschool child. J. Exp. Child Psychol. 26:71-84.

Moore, M.K. and Meltzoff, A.N. 1978. Object permanence, imitation, and language development in infancy: toward a neo-Piagetian perspective on communicative and cognitive development. In Communicative and Cognitive Abilities -- Early Behavioral Assessment, eds. F.D. Minifie and L.L. Lloyd. Baltimore: University Park Press.

Moore, T.E., ed. 1973. Cognitive Development and the Acquisition of Language. New York: Academic Press.

Moorehead, D.M. and Ingram, D. 1973. The development of base syntax in normal and linguistically deviant children. J. Speech Hear. Res. 16:330-52.

Moorehead, D.M. and Morehead, A.E. 1976. Normal and Deficient Child Language. Baltimore: University Park Press.

Morley, M.E. 1972. The Development and Disorders of Speech in Childhood. Edinburgh: Livingstone.

Morse, P.A. 1972. The discrimination of speech and non-speech stimuli in early infancy. J. Exp. Child Psychol. 14:477-92.

Morse, P. 1974. Infant speech perception. A preliminary model and review of the literature. In Language Perspectives -- Acquisition, Retardation, and Intervention, eds. R. Schiefelbusch and L. Lloyd. Baltimore: University Park Press.

Morse, P. 1976. Speech perception in the human infant and rhesus monkey. Ann. N.Y. Acad. Sci. 280:694-707.

Morse, P.A. 1978. Infant speech perception: origins, processes, and ALPHA Centauri. In Communicative and Cognitive Abilities -- Early Behavioral Assessment, eds. F.D. Minifie and L.L. Lloyd. Baltimore: University Park Press. pp 195-227.

Moskowitz, A. I. 1970. The acquisition of phonology. University of California Language Behavior Research Laboratory, Working Paper 34.

Moskowitz, A.I. 1973. The acquisiton of phonology and syntax: a preliminary study. In Approaches to Natural Language, eds. G. Hintikka, J. Moravcsik, and P. Suppes. Dordrecht, Holland: Reidel Publishing Co. pp 48-84.

Moskowitz, A.I. 1973. The two-year old stage in the acquisition of English phonology. In Studies of Child Language Development, eds. C.A. Ferguson and D.I. Slobin. New York: Holt, Rinehart and Winston. pp 52-68.

Moskowitz, B.A. 1975. The acquisition of fricatives: a study in phonetics and phonology. J. Phonetics 3:141-50.

Mower, O.H. 1952. Speech development in the young child: (1) the autism theory of speech development and some clinical applications. J. Speech Hear. Dis. 17:263-68.

Mueller, K. and Wilson, F. 1978. Listener identification of speaker sex for children from three to nine. Paper presented at the American Speech and Hearing Association, San Francisco.

Muller, E.M. 1971. Some acoustic and temporal characteristics of pain-elicited neonatal cries. M. A. Thesis, University of Florida, March 1971.

Murai, J.I. 1960. Speech development of infants: analysis of speech sounds by sona-graph. Psychologia 3:27-35.

Murai, J. 1961. Speech development in early infancy. Tetsugakukenkyu 474:20-42.

Nakazima, S.A. 1970. A comparative study of the speech development of Japanese and American English in childhood (III): The reorganization process of babbling articulation mechanisms. Studia Phonologica 5:20.

Nakazima, S.A. 1977. A comparative study of the speech development of Japanese and American children (Part 8): Structure and function of one-word sentences. Studia Phonologica 11:35-42.

Nakazima, S., Okamoto, N., Murai, J., Tanaka, M., Okuno, S., Maeda, T., and Shimizu, M. 1962. The phoneme systematization and the verbalization process of voices in childhood. Shinrigan-Hyoron 6:1-48.

Nance, L.S. 1946. Differential diagnosis of aphasia in children. J. Speech Dis. 2:219-23.

Nelson, K. 1973. Structure and strategy in learning to talk. Monogr. Soc. Res. Child Dev. 38, No. 149.

Newfield, M.U. and Schlanger, B.B. 1968. The acquisition of English morphology by normal and educable mentally retarded children. J. Speech Hear. Res. 11:693-706.

Okamura, M. 1966. Acoustical studies on the Japanese vowels in children. The formant constructon and the development process. Jap. J. Otol., Tokyo 69:1198.

Oller, D.K. 1978. Infant vocalizations and the development of speech. J. Allied Health Behav. Sci., in press.

Oller, D.K. 1973a. Simplification in child phonology. Paper presented at the Third Western Conference on Linguistics Meeting, Victoria, B.C.

Oller, D.K. 1973b. Regularities in abnormal child phonology. J. Speech Hear. Dis. 38:36-47.

Oller, D.K. and Warren, I. 1973. Implications of systematic instability in child phonology. Paper presented at the Stanford Child Language Forum, Palo Alto, Ca.

Oller, D.K., Wieman, L.A., Doyle, W., and Ross, C. 1975. Infant babbling and speech. J. Child Lang. 3:1-11.

Olmsted, D.L. 1971. Out of the Mouths of Babes. The Hague: Mouton.

Olney, R.L., and Scholnick, E.K. 1976. Adult judgments of age and linguistic differences in infant vocalization. J. Child Lang. 3.

Osofsky, J.D. and Danzger, B. 1974. Relationships between neonatal characteristics and mother-infant interaction. Dev. Psychol. 10:124-30.

Ostwald, P.F., Slis, I.H., and Willems, L.F. 1967. Synthesis of human infant cries. Eindhoven Inst. of Perception Research, Annual Progress Report 2:109-14.

Parmelee, A.H. 1955. Infant speech development: a report of a study of one child by magnetic tape recordings. J. Pediat. 46:447-50.

Parnell, M.M. and Amerman, J.D. 1978. Maturational influences on perception of co-articulatory effects. J. Speech Hear. Res. 21:682-701.

Parsley, N. and Rabinowitz, M. 1975. Crying in the first year: an operant interpretation of the Bell and Ainsworth (1972) findings. Child Study Jour. 5:83-89.

Petretic, P.A. and Tweney, R.D. 1977. Does comprehension precede production? The development of children's responses to telegraphic sentences of varying grammatical adequacy. J. Child Lang. 4:201-09.

Pierce, J. 1974. A study of 750 Portland, Oregon children during the first year. Stanford University Pap. Rep. Child Lang. Dev. 8:19-25.

Pike, E.G. 1944. Controlled infant intonation. Lang. Learning 2:21-24.

Popova, M.I. 1973. Grammatical elements of language in the speech of preschool children. In Studies of Child Language Development, eds. C.A. Ferguson and D.I. Slobin. New York: Holt, Rinehart and Winston, Inc. pp 269-80.

Porter, J.H. 1977. A cross-sectional study of morpheme acquisition in first language learners. Lang. Learn. 27:47-61.

Prather, E.M., Hedrick, D.L., and Kern, C.A. 1975. Articulation development in children aged two to four years. J. Speech Hear. Dis. 40:179-91.

Priestly, T. 1975. One 'idiosyncratic strategy' in the acquisition of phonology. Paper presented at the International Symposium on Child Language, September 1975, London.

Prutting, C.A. and Rees, N. 1977. Pragmatics of language: applications to the assessment and remediation of communication behaviors. Short course presented at the American Speech and Hearing Association.

Raffler-Engel, W. von. 1970. The relationship of intonation to first vowel articulation in infants. Paper presented to the Prague Symposium on Intonology.

Ramer, A.L.H. 1976. The function of imitation in child language. J. Speech Hear. Res. 19:700-17.

Ramsey, C.T. and L. Ourth. 1971. Delayed reinforcement and vocalization rates in infants. Child Dev. 42:291-97.

Rebelsky, F. and C. Hanks. 1971. Fathers' verbal interaction with infants in the first three months of life. Child Dev. 42:63-68.

Rebelsky, F., Starr, R.H., and Luria, Z. 1967. Language development: the first four years. In Infancy and Early Childhood, ed. Y. Brackbill. New York: Free Press.

Rees, N. 1972. The role of babbling in the child's acquisition of language. Br. J. Dis. Comm. 7:17-23.

Rees, N.S. 1975. Imitation and language development: issues and clinical implications. J. Speech Hear. Dis. 40:339-50.

Reiber, M. 1965. The effect of music on the activity level of children. Psychon. Sci. 3:325-26.

Rheingold, H.L., Gerwirtz, J.L., and Ross, H.W. 1959. Social conditioning of vocalizations in the infant. J. Comp. Physiol. Psychol. 52:68-73.

Ringwall, E.A., Reece, H.W., and Markel, N.M. 1965. A distinctive feature analysis of prelinguistic infant vocalization. In The Development of Language Functions, ed. K.F. Riegel. Ann Arbor: Center for Human Growth and Development, Report 8.

Roe, K. 1975. Amount of infant vocalization as a function of age: some cognitive implications. Child Dev. 46:936-41.

Roeper, T. 1971. A child's mental structrues: theoretical issues in language acquisition with evidence from German. Doctoral dissertation, Harvard University.

Roth, P. and Morse, P. 1975. An investigation of infant VOT discrimination using the cardiac OR. Research Status Report I, pp 207-18. Infant Development Laboratory, University of Wisconsin.

Routh, D.K. 1969. Conditioning of vocal response differentiation in infants. Develop. Psychol. 1:219-26.

Rūke-Dravina, V. 1973. The process of acquisition of apical /r/ and uvular /R/ in speech of children. In Studies of Child Language Development, eds. C.A.

Ferguson and D.I. Slobin. New York: Holt, Rinehart, and Winston, Inc.

Ruja, H. 1948. The relation between neonate crying and length of labor. J. Genet. Psychol. 73:53-55.

Sachs, J. and Johnson, M.L. 1972. Language development in a hearing child of deaf parents. Unpublished paper presented to the International Symposium of First Language Acquisition, Florence, Italy.

Saltz, E. and Dunin-Markiewicz, A. 1978. Development of natural language concepts, IV. The relationship between semantic organization and learning. J. Exp. Child Psychol. 25:442-58.

Salus, P.H. and Salus, M.W. 1973. Rule-ordering in child phonology. Paper presented at the Stanford Child Language Forum, Palo Alto, Ca.

Salus, P.H. and Salus, M.W. 1974. Developmental neurophysiology and phonological acquisition order. Language 50:151-60.

Sander, E.K. 1972. When are speech sounds learned? J. Speech Hear. Dis. 37:55-63.

Schachter, F.F., Shore, E., Hodapp, R., Chalfin, S., and Bundy, C. 1978. Do girls talk earlier? Mean length of utterance in toddlers. Develop. Psychol. 14:388-92.

Schlesinger, I.M. 1971. Production of utterances and language acquisition. In The Ontogenesis of Grammar: A Theoretical Symposium. ed. D.I. Slobin. New York: Academic Press. pp 63-101.

Scollon, R. 1976. Conversation with a One Year Old. Honolulu: The University Press of Hawaii.

Shatz, M. and Gelman, R. 1973. The development of communciation skills: modifications in the speech of young children as a function of listener. Monogr. Soc. Res. Child Dev. 38:1-38.

Sheppard, W.C. 1969. Operant control of infant vocal and motor behavior. J. Exp. Child Psychol. 7:36-51.

Sheridan, M.D. 1964. Disorders of communication in young children. Monthly Bulletin of the Ministry of Health and the Public Health Laboratory Services 23:20.

Shipley, E.F., Smith, C.S., and Gleitman, L.R. 1969. A study of the acquisition of language. Language 45:322-42.

Shohara, H.H. 1935. The genesis of articulatory movements of speech. Quart. J. Speech 21:343.

Shvachkin, N.K. 1948. Razvitie fonematiceskogo vosprijatija reci v rannem vozraste (The development of phonemic speech perception in early childhood). Izy. Akad, Pedagog. Nauk. RSFST 13:101-32.

Shvachkin, N.K. 1973. The development of phonemic speech perception in early childhood. In Studies of Child Language Development, eds. C.A. Ferguson and D.I. Slobin. New York: Holt, Rinehart, and Winston, Inc. pp 91-127.

Shvachkin, N. 1973. The development of phonemic speech perception in early childhood. In Studies in Child Language Development, eds. C.A. Ferguson and D.I. Slobin. New York: Holt, Rinehart and Winston.

Siegel, L. and Sameroff, A. 1971. Monitoring system for infant movement, vocalization, and nurse interaction. Behav. Res. Meth. Instr. 3:305-06.

Silvestri, S. and Silvestri, R. 1977. A developmental analysis of the acquisition of compound words. Lang. Speech Hear. Serv. Sch. 8:217-21.

Simon, C.T. 1957. The development of speech. In Handbook of Speech Pathology, ed. L.E. Travis. New York: Appleton-Century-Crofts.

Simon, D. 1974. Some measurements of the speech of children. Speech and Hearing Work in Progress. University College, London, Department of Phonetics and Linguistics.

Simon, C. and Fourcin, A.J. 1978. Cross-language study of speech-pattern learning. J. Acoust. Soc. Am. 63:925-35.

Sinclair, H. 1974. On pre-speech. In Papers and Reports on Child Language Development 8. Stanford Committee on Linguistics. Stanford University.

Smith, N. 1973. The Acquisition of Phonology: A Case Study. London: C.U.P.

Smitherman, C. 1969. The vocal behavior of infants as related to the nursing procedure of rocking. Nursing Res. 18:256-58.

Snow, C. 1972. Mother's speech to children learning language. Child Dev. 43:549-65.

Spitz, R.A. and Cobliner, W.G. 1965. The First Year of Life. New York: International Universities Press.

Spring, O.R. and Dale, P.S. 1977. Discrimination of linguistic stress in early infancy. J. Speech Hear. Res. 20:224-32.

Stampe, D. 1969. The acquisition of phonetic representation. Papers from the Fifth Regional Meeting of the Chicago Linguistic Society, 443-51.

Stampe, D. 1972. A dissertation on natural phonology. Doctoral dissertation, University of Chicago.

Stark, R.E. 1978. Features of infant sounds: the emergence of cooing. Child Lang. 5:379-98.

Stark, R.E., Rose, S.N., and Benson, P.J. 1974. Classification of infant vocalization behavior. Paper presented at the American Speech and Hearing Association, Las Vegas.

Stark, R.E., Rose, S.N., and Benson, P.J. 1978. Classification of infant vocalization. Br. J. Dis. Comm. 13:41-47.

Stern, D.N. 1974. Mother and infant at play: the dyadic interaction involving facial, vocal and gaze behaviors. In The Effect of the Infant on Its Caregiver, eds. M. Lewis and L.A. Rosenblum. New York: Wiley-Interscience.

Stern, D.N., Jaffe, J., Bebbe, B., and Bennett, S.L. 1975. Vocalizing in unison and in alteration: two modes of communications within the mother-infant dyad. In Developmental Psycholinguistics and Communication Disorders, eds. D. Aaronson and R.W. Ricker. New York: The New York Academy of Sciences.

Strain, B.A. and Vietze, P.M. 1975. Early dialogues: the structure of reciprocal infant-mother vocalization. Paper presented at the biennial meeting of the Society for Research in Child Development, April 1975, Denver.

Strain, B.A., Vietze, P., and Dokecki, P.R. 1975. Interpersonal proximity and vocal behavior in the mother-child dyad. Paper presented at the Animal Behavior Society and Human Ethology Meetings, May 1975, Wilmington, North Carolina.

Streeter, L. 1976. Language perception of 2-month-old infants shows effects of both innate mechanisms and experience. Nature 259:39-41.

Stubbs, E.M. 1934. The effect of the factors of duration, intensity, and pitch of sound stimuli on the responses of newborn infants. Iowa Stud. Child Welf. 9, No. 4.

Sugarman, S. 1973. A sequence for communcation development in the pre-language child. Hampshire College Honors Thesis.

Sugarman-Bell, S. 1978. Some organizational aspects of preverbal communication. In The Social Context of Language, ed. I. Markova. London: Wiley.

Swoboda, P., Kass, J., Morse, P., and Leavitt, L. 1978. Memory factors in vowel discrimination of normal and at-risk infants. Child Dev. 49(2):332-39.

Swoboda, P., Morse, P., and Leavitt, L. 1976. Continuous vowel discrimination in normal and at-risk infants. Child Dev. 47:459-65.

Swope, S., Anderson, D.C., Berry, R.C. and Kennedy, A.J. Acoustic parameters of infant cries: a longitudinal study.

Templin, M.C. 1957. Certain Language Skills in Children. Minneapolis: University Press.

Thoman, E., Leiderman, P., and Olson, J. 1972. Neonate-mother interaction during breastfeeding. Develop. Psychol. 6:110-18.

Till, J. 1976. Infants' discrimination of speech and non-speech stimuli. Unpublished doctoral dissertation, University of Iowa.

Tingley, B.M. and Allen, G.D. 1975. Development of speech timing control in children. Child Dev. 46:186-94.

Todd, G.A. and Palmer, B. 1968. Social reinforcement of infant babbling. Child Dev. 39:591-96.

Tomlinson-Keasey, C. 1972. Conditioning of infant vocalizations in the home environment. J. Genetic Psychol. 120:75-82.

Tonkova-Yampol'skaya, R.V. 1973. Development of speech intonation in infants during the first two years of life. In Studies of Child Language Development, ed. C.A. Ferguson and D.I. Slobin. New York: Holt, Rinehart and Winston.

Trehub, S. 1973. Auditory-linguistic sensitivity in infants. Unpublished doctoral dissertation, University of Iowa.

Trehub, S. 1973. Infants' sensitivity to vowel and tonal contrasts. Develop. Psychol. 9:81-96.

Trehub, S. 1975. The problem of state in infant speech discrimination studies. Develop. Psychol. 11:116.

Trehub, S. 1976. Infants' discrimination of two-syllable stimuli: the role of temporal factors. Paper presented at the American Speech and Hearing Association, November 1976, Houston.

Trehub, S. 1976. The discrimination of foreign speech contracts by infants and adults. Child Dev. 44:466-72.

Trehub, S. and Chang, H.W. 1977. Speech as reinforcing stimulation for infants. Develop. Psychol. 13:170-71.

Truby, H.M. 1960. Some aspects of acoustical and cine-radiographic analysis of newborn infant and adult phonation and associated vocal tract activity. J. Acoust. Soc. Am. 32:1518.

Truby, H.M. 1962. A technique for visual-acoustic analysis of the sounds of infant cry. J. Acoust. Soc. Am. 34.

Tyack, D. and Ingram, D. 1977. Children's production and comprehension of questions. J. Child Lang. 4:211-24.

Underwood, B.J. and Schultz, R.W. 1960. Meaningfulness and Verbal Learning. Philadelphia: Lippencott.

Uzgiris, I.C. and Hunt, J. MCV. 1975. Assessment in Infancy: Ordinal Scales of Psychological Development. Urbana, Illinois: University of Illinois Press.

Valanne, E.H. Vuorenkoski, V., Partanen, T.J., Lind, J. and Wasz-Höckert, O. 1967. The ability of human mothers to identify the hunger cry signals of their own newborn infants during the lying-in period. Experientia 23:768.

Velten, H.V. 1943. The growth of phonemic and lexical patterns in infant language. Lg. 19:281-92.

Vihman, M. 1976. From pre-speech to speech: on early phonology. Paper presented at the 8th Child Language Research Forum, April 1976, Stanford University.

von Raffler Engle, W. 1973. The development from sound to phoneme in child language. In Studies of Child Language Development, eds. C.A. Ferguson and D.I. Slobin. New York: Holt, Rinehart and Winston. pp 9-12.

Vuorenkoski, V., Wasz-Höckert, O., Koivisto, E., and Lind, J. 1969. The effect of cry stimulus on the temperature of the lactating breast of primapara: a thermographic study. Experientia 25:1286-87.

Washington, D.S. and Naremore, R.C. 1978. Children's use of spatial prepositions in two- and three-dimensional tasks. J. Speech Hear. Res. 21:151-65.

Wasz-Höckert, O., Lind, J., Vuorenkoski, V., Partanen, T.J., and Valanne, E. 1967. The spectrographic and auditive identification of the cry of the normal newborn and young infant. Dev. Med. Child Neurol. 9.

Waterson, N. 1971. Child phonology: a prosodic view. J. Linguist. 7:179-211.

Weeks, T.E. 1971. Speech registers in young children. Child Dev.. 42:119-31.

Weiman, L.A. 1976. Stress patterns of early child language. J. Child Lang. 3:

Weinberg, B. and Zlatin, M.A. 1970. Speaking fundamental frequency charcteristics of five- and six-year old children with mongolism. J. Speech Hears. Res. 13:418-25.

Weiner, F. and Bernthal, J. 1976. Acquisition of phonetic features in children two to six years old. In Distinctive Features: Theory and Validation, ed. S. Singh. Baltimore: University Park Press. pp 178-204.

Weir, R.W. 1962. _Language in the Crib_. The Hague: Mouton.

Weir, R. 1966. Some questiions on the child's learning of phonology. In _The Genesis of Language_, eds. F. Smith and G.A. Miller. Cambridge: MIT Press. pp 153-68.

Weisberg, P. 1963. Social and nonsocial conditioning of infant vocalizations. _Child Dev._ 34:377-88.

Whitaker, H.A. 1973. Comments on the innateness of language. In _Some New Directions in Linguistics_, ed. R.W. Shuy, Washington, D.C.: Georgetown University Press.

Wilson, W.R. 1978. Behavioral assessment of auditory function in infants. In _Communicative and Cognitive Abilities -- Early Behavioral Assessment_, eds. F.D. Minifie and L.L. Lloyd. Baltimore: University Park Press. pp 37-60.

Winitz, H. 1961. Repetitions in the vocalizations and speech of children in the first two years of life. _J. Speech Hear. Dis. Monogr._ Suppl. No. 7, 55-62.

Winitz, H. and Irwin, O.C. 1958. Infant speech: consistency with age. _J. Speech Hear. Res._ 1:245-49.

Winitz, H. and Irwin, O.C. 1958. Syllabic and phonetic structure of infants' early words. _J. Speech Hear. Res._ 1:250.

Wolff, P.H. 1959. Observations on newborn infants. _Psychosom. Med._ 21:110-18.

Zakharova, A. V. 1973. Acquisition of forms of grammatical case by preschool children. In _Studies of Child Language Development_, eds. C.A. Ferguson and D.I. Slobin. New York: Holt, Rinehart, and Winston. pp. 281-83.

Zelazo, P.R., Kagan, J., and Hartman, R. 1975. Excitement and boredom as determinants of vocalization in infants. _J. Genetic Psychol._ 126:107-17.

Zeskind, S. and Stern, K. 1975. Acoustic analysis of the cry response. Symposium on the Influences on the Behavior of the Newborn. Meeting of the Southeastern Psychological Association, Atlanta.

Zlatin, M.A. and Koenigsknecht, R.A. 1976. Development of the voicing contrast: a comparison of voice onset time in stop perception and production. _J. Speech Hear. Res._ 19:421-47.

Index